Cultural Dialectic

Twentieth-Century American Jewish Writers

Daniel Walden
General Editor

Vol. 10

PETER LANG
New York • Washington, D.C./Baltimore • Bern
Frankfurt am Main • Berlin • Brussels • Vienna • Oxford

Jane Statlander

Cultural Dialectic

Ludwig Lewisohn and Cynthia Ozick

PETER LANG
New York • Washington, D.C./Baltimore • Bern
Frankfurt am Main • Berlin • Brussels • Vienna • Oxford

Library of Congress Cataloging-in-Publication Data

Statlander, Jane.
Cultural dialectic: Ludwig Lewisohn and Cynthia Ozick / by Jane Statlander.
p. cm. — (Twentieth-century American Jewish writers; v. 10)
Includes bibliographical references.
1. Lewisohn, Ludwig, 1882–1955—Criticism and interpretation. 2. Ozick,
Cynthia—Criticism and interpretation. 3. American fiction—Jewish authors—
History and criticism.4. American fiction—20th century—History and criticism.
5. Jewish fiction—History and criticism. 6. Jews in literature. I. Title. II. Series.
PS3523.E96 Z88   813'.52—dc21   2002072946
ISBN 0-8204-5849-X
ISSN 0897-7844

Die Deutsche Bibliothek-CIP-Einheitsaufnahme

Statlander, Jane:
Cultural dialectic: Ludwig Lewisohn and Cynthia Ozick / Jane Statlander.
–New York; Washington, D.C./Baltimore; Bern;
Frankfurt am Main; Berlin; Brussels; Vienna; Oxford: Lang.
(Twentieth-century American Jewish writers; Vol. 10)
ISBN 0-8204-5849-X

The paper in this book meets the guidelines for permanence and durability
of the Committee on Production Guidelines for Book Longevity
of the Council of Library Resources.

Printed in the United States of America

Table of Contents

Preface and Acknowledgments

It took a decade of researching, writing and seemingly endless revising to produce a study that would not just rehash the well-worn arguments about a Jewish versus a Goyish Ludwig Lewisohn and Cynthia Ozick. I had always intuited that such a duality of warring worlds was itself unJewish. This conception, or misconception, was used to measure the authors by, instead of the reverse — to let the authors and their writing emerge out of a neutral ground. I prefer a contrasting mode of investigation. Jewish dialectic, *pilpul*, with its hermeneutical and philosophical line of reasoning, argumentation and analysis, has been used down through the ages to study Tannaic oral law. *Pilpul*, synonymous with language and its use, can itself cross the borders into Gentilism if it wanders into too ardent and creative demonstrations of intellectual agility and brilliance. The linguistic enterprise has no cultural, ethnic, religious or national boundaries.

Two individuals have greatly helped me give birth to this present study. I would like to express my deep gratitude to Drs. Michael Lee and Jennifer McDonnell of the University of New England, Australia, for their dedication to reading and re-reading this manuscript.

Equally important is my debt to a giant on the American literary landscape, Daniel Walden, whose overt and tacit encouragement made this project possible. As well, it is a pleasure to acknowledge Dr. Murray Roston of Bar Ilan University, Israel, for the moral support and help he gave amid the great distress I encountered in trying to get this project off the ground. I also owe thanks to Dr. Harold Fisch, also of Bar Ilan, for focusing my attention on Ludwig Lewisohn.

Foreword

The goal of this book is to lay bare a slippery conundrum of culturism: cultural dialectic and its manifestations in five works each of Ludwig Lewisohn and Cynthia Ozick.

My intention here is not to add yet another voice to the ongoing dispute between a Gentile Lewisohn and Ozick versus a Jewish Lewisohn and Ozick. Rather than describing a duality of Hebraic versus Gentile, this book employs a philosophically Jewish dialectical approach, *pilpul*, which describes a complementary webbing of consciousness and centerlessness. The central objective is to define and analyze the elusive concept of cultural dialectic as it ambiguously manifests itself in Lewison's *Up Stream*, *Holy Land: A Story*, *The Case of Mr. Crump*, *The Island Within*, *Trumpet of Jubilee*; and Ozick's "The Pagan Rabbi", "Envy; or, Yiddish in America", "Levitation", "The Shawl", "Rosa", and *The Cannibal Galaxy*.

Taken separately, the terms "cultural" and "dialectic" each open onto a vast panorama of varying and sometimes competing significances. Culture signifies a totality of social, national, personal, ethnic, artistic, intellectual and linguistic elements. Dialectic is not Western philosophical dualism of irreconcilable opposites, but rather the Judaic non-polarizing dialectic, *pilpul*.

Chapter One
Background and Overview

Defining Terms

The title of this study, "Cultural Dialectic in Ludwig Lewisohn and Cynthia Ozick," at once evokes a slippery rubric of uncertainty and equivocation. By itself, the term "dialectic" would lead to too narrow an application and understanding of the scope and relevance of this undertaking. Yoked with the word "cultural", the sense of "dialectic" intended here broadens and deepens into a clearer picture of specifically what cultural dialectic can be understood to signify in itself; and more generally, how it can be expanded to describe and analyze the work of the writers under examination. Nevertheless there remains the nagging perception that cultural dialectic is too easily characterized by, and lends itself too willingly to, a pervasive sense of ambiguity which resists all maneuvers to explain or contain it in a neatly tied package. It would appear, therefore, that the central, paradoxical task at hand is to analyze, describe and state, in the clearest way possible, the impossibility of being absolutely clear about the exact meaning of "cultural dialectic". This is precisely because the term, best characterized by the word "ambiguity", is by definition the very essence of uncertainty and elusiveness.

As well, the nature of language itself is a contributing factor to this instability of meaning. For whatever is meant by the term, meaning is inextricably linked to the cultural, perceptual, and total world view of any community of "speakers" (writers) and "listeners" (readers); and to the personal micro-perspectives of each listener/reader. Writing viewed as language processing, and the significance rendered/renderable from it, is therefore a complex interplay of a multitude of cultural, perceptual, personal, societal and subliminal factors which are as inseparable, or as difficult to decipher, as they are unmistakably, glaringly present.

In this vein, Hayden White describes the juncture of "narrative discourse" and the representation of historical realities. The narration of "real events," he explains, cannot be realized through "form" that is neutrally discursive. Instead, every narrational undertaking involves "ontological and epistemic "decisions that clearly contain "ideological" and "political" agendas. In this way, representing historical occurrences and describing the manner in which they occur in essence necessitates that history be rendered by way of myth. Thus historical narratives have more in common with dream states of consciousness than with either conscious thinking or classical conceptions based on a notion that it is indeed possible to unearth historical facts in the stories told and then duplicate them in narrational form. In this classical mode, past literary narration was employed to merely embellish the true story. As well, not only were clear distinctions made between truth and fiction, but it was thought possible to easily discern facts from creative invention.

White, on the other hand, puts forth a theory by which the line between what is real and fictionally derived discourse is dissolved due to the differing ontologies of their true or imagined referents. Instead factors of commonality are stressed

> as semiological apparatuses that produce meanings by the systematic substitution of signifieds (conceptual contents) for the extra-discursive entities that serve as their referents. In these semiological theories of discourse, narrative is revealed to be a particularly effective system of discursive meaning production by which individuals can be taught to live a distinctly "imaginary relation to their real conditions of existence," that is to say, an unreal but meaningful relation to the social formations in which they are indentured to live out their lives and realize their destinies as social subjects.[1]

For the purposes of this study, the most significant aspect of White's thought is in its application to the concept of cultural dialectic in that it points to the fundamental reality that every human entity, as both a personal and social subject, is comprised of a paradoxical bundle; an intricate mesh of socially, environmentally, subjectively generated "semiological apparatuses". Narrative discourse, therefore, allows us to view the text or story—that is, the narration of writers involved in the process of story-telling—

> for its universality as a cultural fact and for the interest that dominant social groups have not only in controlling what will pass for the authoritative myths of a given cultural formation but also in assuring the belief that social reality itself can be both lived and realistically comprehended as a story. Myths and the ideologies based on them presuppose the adequacy of stories to the representation of the reality whose meaning they purport to reveal. (*Content* x)

In this way, culture, society, and any and all societal monoliths of authoritorial designations over what and how knowledge is known and communicated as an epistemological endeavour, intersect in the semiotic production of narrative accounts forced from the writer's perceptions of social and personal realities, filtered through and by what this study designates as cultural dialectic. In line with White's premise, Ozick, describing Leon Edel's biography of Henry James, echoes his conception of the narration of history as imaginative storytelling: "Leon Edel's ingenious and beautiful biography of Henry James, which is as much the possession of Edel's imagination as it is of the exhilaratingly reported facts of James's life."[2]

The concept of "culture", as Raymond Williams explains, "is one of the two or three most complicated words in the English language."[3] Apart from a historically intricate development through a few languages of European origin, the central reason for its lack of simplicity is that "it has now come to be used for important concepts in several distinct intellectual disciplines and in several distinct and incompatible systems of thought." (*Keywords* 76–77) Generally, in its original sense as husbandry activity, the term was used as "a noun of process; the tending of something." (77) From Germany, Williams continues, the eighteenth century saw the important appearance of a new sense of the word, to mean not just the rough equivalent of civilization as it had been understood—"cultivation and good breeding" in the world of human endeavour and people, but a somewhat more broadened sense of the word to signify high intellectual, aesthetic, social and artistic achievement. Nineteenth-century Romantic/Germanic applications of the word came to signify a distinction "between 'human' and 'material' development." (79) As well, the term resonated with the sense of "folk-culture." The twentieth century witnessed the development of the word as an anthropological and sociological concept. There are, therefore, Williams summarizes, three general areas of use for the word "culture": the generalized "process of intellectual, spiritual and aesthetic achievement"; the sense of it " as a particular way of life whether of a people, a period or a group"; and finally a most general meaning as "the works and practices of intellectual, especially artistic activity." (80)

The intended usage of the word as it is meant here is a combination of all three applications. In this way the term can be used to describe a process that addresses Cynthia Ozick and Ludwig Lewisohn on a personal, ethnic, national, artistic, intellectual, social and linguistic level—in short, the total environmental and personal dynamics at play in their lives and work; and the extreme intricacy of artistic production that such a complexity can generate.

Williams' concept of culture is a complex hybrid of its scientific sense combined with how literary criticism would apply the term. As contemporary uses of the word delineate it, the term "culture" can be seen as a protest against the bourgeois middle class, and also as a statement of anticapitalist sentiments. The emergence of the Romantic movement was in many ways characterized by antimaterialism, anticapitalism and anti-industrialism. Furthermore, Williams calls for a sociology of culture that views the term in the largest sense possible. As such, his definition can sometimes present a disoriented, confused, directionless picture. Nevertheless, Williams seeks to define a sociology of culture "as a convergence, and as a problem of convergence."[4] It

> is in fact an attempt to rework, from a particular set of interests, those general social and sociological ideas within which it has been possible to see communication, language and art as marginal and peripheral, or as at best secondary and derived social processes. A modern sociology of culture, whether in its internal studies or in its interventions in a more general sociology, is concerned above all to enquire, actively and openly, into these received and presumed relations, and into other possible and demonstrable relations. As such it is not only reworking its own field, but putting new questions and new evidence into the general work of the social sciences. (*Sociology* 10)

Williams grants that it is very difficult to define "culture". He attempts to describe it as an idea of convergence created from its anthropological and sociological concepts as both a distinct "whole way of life", as a "signifying system" inherent in "all forms of social activity", as applied to "artistic and intellectual activities", and the many "signifying practices" of the word from "journalism, fashion and advertising—which now constitute this complex and necessarily extended field." (13) Williams transforms a simple notion of culture as economic determination and Marxist doctrine into a richly meshed understanding of culture as the inherent interaction between writers and writing, and the specific interrelations between the former and real contexts. This is to say that writers at work at storytelling must necessarily have an interactive relationship to the various sociological and cultural factors in and around them. Thus all societal, which is to say, environmental or cultural experiences and effects, in complex interaction with writers on a subjective and personal level, shape how we are to understand writers and their writing. In formulating his theories, Williams has had to undermine and refute the duality inherent in Western metaphysical, Christian and Marxist philosophies, of which with regard to the latter his work is a direct offshoot. This is to say, he had somehow to subvert and change the duality of determinism *versus* free will so basic to the aforementioned philosophies. Williams wrests the idea of determinism from both the realm of blind Fate as well as the romantic notion that the human spirit is totally free to create its own being, existence, sociology and cultural influences. In describing the concept of superstructure, Williams does not view it as "the imitation or the reproduction of the reality of the base in the superstructure in a more or less direct way."[5] Neither does his paradigm consist of

> the notion of "homologous structures" where there may be no direct or easily apparent similarity, and certainly nothing like reflection or reproduction, between the superstructural process and the reality of the base, but in which there is an essential homology or correspondence of structures, which can be discovered by analysis. ("Base" 379)

Williams argues that the base consists of the true sociological, cultural life of humanity which is "of a process and not a state." (380) Thus there is a dynamic, indeterminate, highly flexible connection between the societal and culture-permeated base and human endeavour. Even more so, borrowing from Lukacs, Williams adds the sense of a "social... totality of social practices... opposed to this layered notion of base and a consequent superstructure." (381) This "totality" includes "the central, effective and dominant system of meanings and values, which are not merely abstract but which are organized and lived." (383) Williams cuts deeper by distinguishing between "residual and emergent forms". By residual he means that the base by which

> experiences, meanings and values, which cannot be verified or cannot be expressed in terms of the dominant culture, are nevertheless lived and practiced on the basis of the residue—cultural as well as social—of some previous social formation. (384)

The emergent form describes the continual creation of "new meanings and values, new practices, new significances and experiences." (385) Williams' concept of the interaction between people and their society describes a complex, ambiguous, ever-shifting process of social and cultural replacement, displacement, change and formation which well defines and circumscribes the concept of cultural dialectic as this study understands and employs it.

In combination with the term "cultural", this study speaks of "dialectic" instead of "duality" or "dichotomy". Unlike the concept of dialectic employed here, the Western philosophical basis of the term "duality/dichotomy" rests on the premise of a fundamental division of the world into two totally separate and mutually exclusive realms of matter and mind, physical and spiritual, body and soul. Victor Strandberg's study of Cynthia Ozick's art [6] exemplifies a complex ambush to which readers of Ozick's (or Lewisohn's) work can fall prey. The book title would presume to represent several closely connected suppositions. The first rests on the assertions that Ozick's intellectual (does this include the perceptual or aesthetic?) reactions to the world are, or could somehow be, Gentile, Pan, "Greek". Do a Jewish-American writer's conflicted or ambiguous responses to the Gentile world that surrounds her/him—be it intellectual, aesthetic, emotional—define that writer's mind as "Greek"? As well, Strandberg ignores a basic conflict within Judaism itself: that of the mystical and rational streams, that is, *Hasidim* and *Mitnagdim*. Finally, by dualistically structuring his argument, Strandberg cannot help but discover a dichotomous writer in Cynthia Ozick.

In contrast, this study moves beyond Strandberg's dualistic reading closer to Williams' paradigm, to argue rather for a basic cultural dialectic that reveals and confronts a much more complex tapestry of contrasting and/or complementary (rather than co-annihilating) forces. The essential difference, then, between the concept of duality and that of dialectic is in the impossibility of a state of commingling in the former, as opposed to the paradoxical cohabitation, the state of perpetual shifting of unlike aspects and forces which continually create still newer combinations of cultural dialectic with the latter. Judaism's own cultural dialectic of rationalistic and mystical points of view which, as well, are co-mingled rather than existing as pure realms, weave into the complicated and rich tapestry of Lewisohn's and Ozick's lives and art, to further confound any rendering of these writers' lives or work in absolutely pure terms. Of Gershom

Sholem's massive efforts to translate, explain and elucidate *Kabbalah* (Jewish Mysticism) in general, Ozick asserts:

> Scholem cut through disdain and rejection to begin, single-handedly, his life's task of reconstructing the story of Jewish mysticism.
> Kabbalah—grounded in a belief in divine disclosure and the irrepressible hope of redemption—was historically both an inward movement and an outward one.[7]

Ozick's attitude toward this German-Jewish intellectual giant and Lewisohn's contemporary, who signified, like Lewisohn, the renaissance of interest in Judaism in general, was written after visiting the scholar in Jerusalem.

To return to cultural dialectic, the term "dialectic" has been chosen to represent what is deemed a more exact description of the type of conflict that underlies Ozick's and Lewisohn's work. Williams outlines the history of this term. The fourteenth-century sense of the word, from the Latin *logic* and the Greek *dialecktike*, defines it as "the art of discussion and debate, and then by derivation, the investigation of truth by discussion." (*Keywords* 91) In the medieval period it meant "the art of formal reasoning". By the seventeenth century, the term became more generally applied to signify argumentation. With German Idealism, the concept was extended to include not just disputation as related to the examination of a matter, but also to "contradictions in reality". (92) Kantian dialectic will not be discussed here, since the term as Kant employed it does not fall into an easily characterizable sense of how "dialectic" is applied in this investigation.[8]

The dialectic of George William Friedrich Hegel (1770–1831) is the very essence of conflict. His Romantic philosophy[9] was formulated as an attack on Kantian metaphysics. Hegel's dialectic declares that for every assertion there is another equally "correct" one, since all assertions are made not from an ultimately supreme and eternal pinnacle of truth, but from a specific and relative point of view. In this way, there are diverse and competing truths that incessantly fall and dissolve one into the other, forming yet another truth. Thus thinking progresses in the direction of the truth by negating whatever came before. Each statement is simultaneously replaced by an opposing assertion, which is then itself replaced. The thinking that contemplates this process also progresses until it is "collected" into a final cosmic triadic whole of three essences: Idea—

Nature—Spirit. Hegel's dialectic is a characteristically romantic notion of the incessant, mystical fusion of polar opposites which unceasingly create new polarities. This dialectical triadic system—a kind of agnostic notion of the Father, Son and Holy Spirit—is a type of dialectical enterprise in itself: the antithesis of Kant's "thesis".

Friedrich Engels (1820–1895) and Karl Marx (1818–1883) transformed the German Romantic Ideal sense of a spiritual dialectic into a Materialist philosophy of competing social classes in the economic sphere, in which the exploitative capitalist would be ultimately replaced by a proletarian worker. This concept of "replacement" not found in Hegel's thought would occur through revolution which would physically destroy the capitalist bourgeois class. Viewed as a totality, Romantic philosophy as well was at the substance and heart of the ongoing battle between Mind/Matter, Spirit/Body that underlies Western philosophical rhetoric, that is, language itself, as A.N. Whitehead insists. Thus, in fundamental ways this dichotomy generated a duality of its own: a difficult-to-concretize ideal theoretical frame, juxtaposed with the impossible-to-discount reality of matter.

The very essence of this duality, as Whitehead asserts, is derived from Plato, on whose ideas "European philosophy is founded."[10] As he asserts, this set the mood of negativity and failure into the frame of Western philosophy. As W.T. Jones explains: "Plato doomed himself [through duality] to disappointment. Hence his thought is tinged with sadness. In [a] theory that... creates an inseparable chasm between the idea and the actual, there is an inevitable pessimism arising from foreordained failure."[11] In classical Hellenistic culture the dual (dualistic) realms of nature and spirit played havoc with humankind through the assortment of gods under the whimsical rule of Zeus. These gods were as characteristically capricious as nature, and as equally blind to the suffering of humanity. Thus the philosophical speculations of the great Western metaphysical tradition, beginning with pre-Socratic philosophy, attempted in absolute terms to distinguish and grasp the difference between matter and spirit. In short, the basis of philosophy's dualistic inquiries were focused on discerning and explaining the world of spirit, which Zeus's pantheon represented, *versus* the struggle to grasp nature and the natural world. With both the realm of spirit (the gods) and matter (nature), an all-pervading sense of arbitrariness permeated everything connected to these two realms. At the same time, and through the force of dualistic logic, morality stood somewhere unintegrably outside of both nature and the spirit that Zeus's gods represented. This nature-spirit duality is at the heart of Ozick's concept of Pan and the pitilessness of Hellenistic philosophy which the Nazis extended into their horrifying twentieth-century application. For Lewisohn, as for Ozick, Hellenism is the basis both of degeneracy and aesthetic artistic exaltation of beauty.

The gods meted out punishment, not for infractions of some moral code, but for annoying them. These gods were capricious, petty, egotistical, lustful and unscrupulous, and the object of homage that was not for their inherent moral goodness, but simply because worshipers believed they were mightier. Beyond them, stronger and blinder even than these gods, faceless Fate/Nature engulfed all in a rage and fury without feeling, pity, sentiment, piety, morality or even purpose. Nature was also deaf and blind to human or supernatural influence or will.

It is with the philosophical investigations of Jacques Derrida that a Western philosophy predicated on Hellenistic cultural attitudes, beliefs and thought, receives its first insider's attempt to reconstruct its dualism of mind and body into something totally alien to the nature of the dualistic enterprise. That challenge, which always existed in and through Judaic philosophy, became the essence of Derrida's unique philosophical perspective.

This contemporary French philosopher, in his deconstructive analysis of Western philosophy from Martin Heidegger backward to Plato, most closely resembles the essence of Hebraic thought which is roughly synonymous with Midrashic hermeneutics. This has earned for him, as Geoffrey H. Hartman and Sanford Budick coined it, the title of "Reb Derrida", Rabbi Derrida.[12]

Derrida's epistemological critique of Western (and indirectly, Christian) philosophy describes how the West comprehends and communicates knowledge. He strips the West down to its most fundamental cluster of previously unassailable bodily parts: the notion of a self-evident, inalienable authority on concepts like "truth" or "beauty". As he expresses it, higher levels of authority such as "aletheia, transcendentality, consciousness or conscience, God, man" are all presumed self-evidently true and right.[13]

As such, authority at any level has always been believed to exist at exactly the "center" in "the structurality of structure". (Derrida 231) Contradictorily, this "center" is removed, singular, structureless, at the same time that it constitutes the selfsame component inside a structure that is the structure. Like the Western God-concept of an immovable Mover, the "center" is the place from which and on which all structural and hierarchical systems emanate or base themselves. This structuring gives the structure "a center or [refers] it to a point of presence, a fixed origin." Thus "center" also means "origin" and is deemed to be without "play" since it is the sign's order. As an antidote for such an idolatry of presence, Derrida stresses the inherent interdependence of significations and values, minus a conceptualized system, in which each and every aspect of that system mutably affects the other, and maintains or aborts the system's inner stability. Derrida's deconstructive mode thus deconstructs a Heideggerian metaphysics that places "time" in position as the central authority, and attempts to demonstrate that all "meaning" or value is centerless and authority-less—an unstable designation. Derrida's concept of a non-static, fluid and centerless center resembles Williams' ideas of a non-static, ever-changing environment in which culture and society become a type of placeless place, filled with individuals whose relation to that placeless non-place is constantly in flux. The closed hierarchical system of a godlike value, concept or expression governing the lower level in Derrida's schema is replaced by the unstable value, idea, or meaning which changes, or is changed by, the instability of all the parts in a paradoxically centerless, placeless place and a beingless "Being", *Hashem*, meaning "the Name", the Spirit or spirit of Torah. In the same way, Judaism's conception of God, *Hashem*, is without physical presence, reference point, site of origin, location or even name; addressed as "the Name" because, paradoxically, there is no name or descriptive terminology with which to locate His/Its beingness. *Hashem*, of no place, is every place; the centerless everything, everywhere; the authority without authority to determine without determining which acts each human being will perform in a choice-filled universe. Also designated as *Yahweh*, "the Name" is itself a non-name consisting of a tetragrammaton composed of the Hebrew letters *yud, heh, vav, heh*; and is the most commonly used biblical designation for God. This "name" is probably associated with the statement in *Exodus* 3:14: "*eyeh asher eyeh*", "I am that I am",[14] which itself is a virtual linguistic creation.[15]

Like the designation *Yahweh*, Derrida's sense of "meaning" with centerless meaning(lessness) is the inconceivable, the all-permeating, ever-changing high play of language without dogma; free, undesignatable, indefinable—an open, dialectical, ever-changing, ever-shifting phenomenon. Finally, Derrida excommunicates the duality at the heart of Western thinking, describing a human-centered universe which turns all into a creation of linguistic play; a Midrashic dialectic of unbridled excursions in art, creation, open language. Derrida's metaphysics strikes exactly at the locus point of Lewisohn's and Ozick's personal, aesthetic and philosophical concerns. As Jews, intellectuals, writers and creators at work in the wider Gentile world, they both confront/ed some essential Jewishness on the stage of secular, that is, occidental endeavors and interests. With each, the interaction of various ethnic, racial, cultural, nationalistic, linguistic, aesthetic, philosophical, personal, Western, Oriental and various other concerns describe a highly intricate pattern of cultural dialectic in which elements and forces do not vie to destroy one another but coexist in vibrant, dynamic, if not ambivalent, textual richness.

In the same way, Hebrew thought as objectified in Scripture posits a paradoxical unity of the physical and spiritual, body and mind. Instead of the Greek *Deus ex Machina* that arbitrarily resolves conflict, the Hebrew *Yahweh* is a faceless/centerless, merciful, omnipotent, omniscient Force that rules the world of Its creation. Created *ex nihilo,* through the force of God's will in a Big-Bang entry into existence, nature and all it contains followed in the volition of God's creative desire. In this way, nature is the effect, manifestation and testimony of God's power and magnificence, instead of God's equal competitor and parallel Reality of the Material[16] itself.

Since in the Hebraic cosmology nature and soul, body and spirit, the physical and mental exist not in opposition, that is in duality, but in some complementary union of contrasting forces, Hebrew dialectic (*pilpul*), as opposed to a Western dialectic of conflicting opposites, weaves all forces into a deep, intense web of contrasting influences and aspects, paradoxically held in some sort of aesthetic whole or unity through the richness and interlinking of their varied parts. The Oral Law and the written law that is Torah, as traditionalist rabbinic authority dictates, comprises the totality of what is called Hebrew Scripture. As it is stated, the proof for the necessity of Oral Law as an inseparable part of the Written one is in God's instructions to Moses as found in *Deuteronomy* 31:19, to instruct the Israelites in Torah by "putting it in their mouths". Biblical authority asserts that without the Oral Law no one would know how God's commandments should be executed, because exact specifics are not known from the written text. It is Oral Law which, by its need for discussion and debate, created *pilpul*, Hebrew dialectic. This dialectic is characterized by the same general sense of "argumentation" or line of reasoning as employed in Western philosophical thought. Oral Law is basically legalistic discussion on points of Torah, such as lawyers would have on the multi-faceted legalities involved with one person being accidently kicked by a horse belonging to another. Every point implied or stated in the Written Law (Torah) is argued out in the Oral Law and its own written texts, the *Talmud*. The Oral Law was recorded in written form when it was feared that it could be lost, forgotten and misunderstood. The Oral Law is constantly being added to, changed, debated and challenged by consequent generations of rabbinical scholars.

This *pilpul* is then given a reinterpreted form in *Halacha*. The term *Halacha* means "walking/going" from the Hebrew verb *lelechet*, to go, and relates to all legalistic matters. On the other side of *Halacha* is *Aggadah*, the nonlegalistic lighter side of Torah. Basically, *Aggadah* is story-telling: an elaboration and development of written, oral and interpretative Law to serve as a form of moral instruction. Thus in literary terms, Torah is the Text/text, *Talmud* the record of scholarly debate on the Text, *Halacha* the interpretation of this debate/dialectic, and *Aggadah* the collection of spin-off stories created to incorporate all of the previous. As well, there is a general hermeneutical tool in use called *Midrash*, a subgroup of *Aggadah*. The word *Midrash*, from the Hebrew verb *lidrosh*, meaning to inquire/require, serves to discover the subsurface meanings and significance in the literal Torah text.

Midrash itself consists of didactic instruction, folklore, speculations on God, legends, stories, history, adulations of Israel, dream interpretation, praises and other types of informal discussion. *Midrash* is the dialectical and hermeneutical rendering, explaining, understanding, discussing, analyzing and investigating of the text/Text; be it the Torah itself, commentaries on Torah, or commentaries on commentaries of Torah. *Midrash* sets out to discover meaning—itself unstable, changing, mutating through the intricacies of *pilpul*—imbedded in the written text. All of this, it can be safely said, is part of, if not the foundation, of the cultural baggage, the linguistic parameters, the cosmological realms of Ludwig Lewisohn and Cynthia Ozick.

In contrast to *Midrash*, Christian interpretative tools use homily, another mode from Greek exegesis, to illuminate the literal meaning of the Scriptural text. As previously discussed, Hebrew textual analysis has an intricate and complex hermeneutical system for rendering (unstable) meaning that can be endlessly undermined, changed, controverted and annihilated, through a subtle hair wisp of intellectual or artistic performance, even by the creator himself. Hebrew textual analysis uses the text as a hermeneutic totality, to discuss not just what a specific term, phrase, sentence or word "means", but also the significance of the sounds, shapes, vocal patterns, *te'amin* (musical notations), *tagin* (other visual additions), the patterns of sound, repetition, or nonexistence of any of the above; plus other general patterns, psychological and ontological realities, the nomenclature of God, astrology, numerology, a vast dialectic of cultural and semiotic possibilities. As Joseph Dan stresses:

> It should be emphasized that these methods are in themselves not mystical, and any message, even the mundane or humorous, can be and was reached in these ways. This kind of midrashic treatment is completely neutral on possible meaning and was used in the Middle Ages and modern times (relying on sources originating from the Ancient period) by every Jewish preacher and exegete, each according to his own preferences and tastes. Pietists, philosophers, traditionalists and mystics shared the same midrashic tradition.
> The possibility of using the totality of the text is created by the nature of the original Hebrew language of the Jewish scriptures. This is in marked contrast to the fact that Christians in the Middle Ages and modern times have usually had to use a translated [in most cases a twice-translated] text.[17]

In the larger picture, dialectic is created through and by the pagan/ Christian and Hebrew text/Text, the hermeneutical means to render meaning from them, the meanings rendered from them, the designated authority/authorities on that meaning, and even the writer/owner of the text/Text.

The "conflict" delineated in *Greek Mind/Jewish Soul* that Strandberg believes he is describing in Ozick's art is not part of the closure of Western duality but rests elsewhere, in the Oriental frame of Judaic thought and consciousness. The struggle Lewisohn's and Ozick's texts undergo consists of wedding consciousness to conscience in a paradox of the "open" text that defies the simplicity of dualistic solutions. For this reason, any attempt to reach definitive nondynamic explanations for the life and work of Lewisohn and Ozick is doomed from the start. To call Ozick or Lewisohn "Jewish writers" shortchanges the depth and breadth of their aesthetic, artistic, philosophical and cosmological endeavors. Conversely, to describe their art as Western, Gentile, Greek, Pagan falls short from another direction. That they are/were writers and creators cannot be denied, and it is probably through the convoluted conundrum of language that a reader can only begin to grasp the complexity of the art that represents these writers' creative output. When the subject of language is breached, as it must be, we are led back to the dialectic exegesis of Midrashic concern, which of necessity uncovers a fundamentally Hebraic core to their work. Moreover (as will be discussed), given the Puritan, which is to say the Tanach-based, nature of American literature and culture, Lewisohn and Ozick of necessity are Hebrew-Scripturally rooted, both through their own personal Judaic roots and through America in whose culture they are also rooted. We are again reminded that this circular intermeshing of cultural dialectic can offer no simple answers or solutions.

An interchange between Cynthia Ozick and John Updike is a representative example which demonstrates the differences between Hebraic and Western dialectics, and also the Christian's (typologized) conceptions of Jewish thought, thinking and being. In an essay, Cynthia Ozick offers a retort to John Updike's description of Jewishness as "'in part a religious condition but.... a Jew, like Jehovah, simply is in some realm beyond argument.'"[18] Ozick takes Updike to task for his Christianized conceptions of Judaism and the history of its thought and texts. As she declares:

> Since the entire rabbinic tradition is [dialectical] argument (as opposed to [Christian] credo), and since, consequently, nearly all varieties of Jewish intellectuality, including the Bechian secular-modern, are heirs to a mode of discourse wherein nothing is "beyond argument", it is hard to guess what Updike is imagining here. Having brilliantly assimilated the major texts of Protestant theology, he strangely does not assume (after millennia of Jewish texts) equal or greater (because more weightily cumulative) nuance and complexity in Jewish self-definition; what emerges for him is the naive, faintly mistrustful, vaguely poetic, puzzlement implicit in the phrase "A Jew, like Jehovah, simply is." This formulation, even if it does just manage to escape meaninglessness, slides nevertheless into the exotically intergalactic. "Jehovah" is a foreign word to the Jewish ear; so is "faith" in its Protestant sense. ("Bech" 122)

Christian consciousness such as that Updike describes is forged and conceived in duality, and cannot help but bear witness to a cosmology of polemical spheres in which its primary adversarial competitor is Jewish being (or non-being). Ozick here replays the two-thousand-year-old war waged on Judaism by Christianity. Ozick also inferentially calls to mind the Pauline church's fundamental goal of supplanting the Text and identity of Judaism, and the Jew himself. Updike's benign rendering of Jewishness belies the efforts that his earliest Christian forebears undertook to erase Jewishness from memory. As James H. Charlesworth,

Eugene J. Fisher and other scholars in Comparative Religion explain, and as Ozick's retort to Updike implies, the supplantation of Christianity for Judaism is a fundamental tenet of Christian philosophy:

> However, Christianity could never regard Judaism as just another religion. The Roman Catholic church insisted that its roots were sunk deep in the history of Israel, that the events recounted in the New Testament were the fulfillment of the promises made in the Hebrew Bible (now called the Old Testament), that its founder was the Messiah and son of David expected by Jewish tradition, that it was the heir of God's covenant with Israel—in short, that it was the "true Israel" (*verus Israel*). (*Religion* 158)

Ozick's answer to Updike underscores a painful rift between Christian and Hebrew thought and attitude. The former, viewing itself as a "completion" or improvement of the latter, misreads or remains ignorant of the discourse and conceptual basis of Hebraism itself. Implied throughout Ozick's rejoinder is the fundamental typology of self-other that Updike's Protestant perspective seeks to foist on Jewish identity. Thus, through Updike's creation (his Jewish character, Bech), this Protestant author reveals more about Christianity's notions of what Jewishness is, or its recreation of Jewishness, what Ozick calls "the exotically intergalactic", than what Jewishness in fact is. Ozick also distinguishes here between *pilpul*, Hebrew dialectic, that is, argument in a wholly open frame and whose outcome ends in surprise, *versus* the anchored, prescriptive, rhetorical "analysis" of a line of argument whose conclusion is already foreordained. In visual terms, Hebraic thought is a webbing out that begins from some designated but not authoritative point of "a beginning", travelling on whatever roads to unknown destinations and conclusions; limited or sparked by the qualitative level, brilliance or pedestrianism, depth or shallowness, of the linguistic, intellectual and perceptual abilities of the polemicist. Christian thinking, as Ozick implies, is a hierarchically structured frame in which, through "credo", the conclusions are either already preordained or the variables for argumentation are limited.

Judaism is thus a paradoxical mix of Talmudic insistence on mapping out the ubiquitous and intricately complicated intermeshing of personal responsibility within a societal frame and the very denial of closure and meaning of the text and the word. In many ways, Hebrew thought and its philosophy negate ultimate truths—save for that of the Creator and Torah—and all attempts to imprison the thinking process and the language it employs to express its content: the sense of God that negates presence, that defies all conceptual categories of physicality; whose "center" is without center or place. This sense both reflects and underscores the openness of Hebraic hermeneutics.

In relation to Ozick and Lewisohn and their work, and in spite of biographical information that would locate Lewisohn's introduction to *Midrash* at a chronologically later time in his life, a dialectic of dialectics is ever present, in that both are/were from their birth homes Jewish with Hebraic/Yiddish colorations of mindset, thinking and reflection; a linguistic basis in Hebraic scripture and its Commentaries in *Mishnah, Talmud, Halacha, Aggadah* and *Midrash*; a Hebrew-Yiddish cosmological frame for interacting with experiences, ideas, feelings: a philosophically Jewish approach to meaning, language and the world in the fullest sense of scope and depth. In this sense, every Jew is a born Midrashist, a storyteller.

However, both writers write in the European language of English. Thus their thinking processes, feelings, cosmology and how they experience the world become modified by another philological linguistic frame that is inherently alien to their "natural", environmental and personal inclinations. In this way, what is created is a cosmological mixture of Western and Hebraic frames, which are themselves endlessly spinning off and evolving into other frames and manifestations; dialectics circumscribed by ambiguity and meaning that relentlessly self-destruct and transform into the uncircumscribable and undecipherable. Moreover, through this quagmire of ambiguity Ozick and Lewisohn, along with their creations, remain both a part of and a stranger to the cultural, linguistic, anthropological and social frames that both are and are not theirs; in which they are viewed as both foreign and belonging. This phenomenon is further intensified in Lewisohn, due to the imposition of his earlier hermeneutic cultural-linguistic base on a later English/American one.

Furthermore, this study, which desires to demonstrate the complex texturing of dialectic in the lives and work of two Jewish-American writers, is also constrained by the language in which the study is communicated (English), and by the world view in which the English language is rooted and expressed. The scope and extent of the sense of ambiguity generated by dialectic results in a highly complicated mix of language, a vortex of conflicted linguistic enterprise where messages, signs, their impact and meaning can be described as ambiguous at best, and indecipherable at its other extreme.

The term "dialectic" most closely approximates and describes the nearly uncombinable mix of Hebraic cultural/linguistic consciousness and cosmology with a European/Gentile/Christian frame. This Judaic/non-Judaic polemic perhaps poses the greatest challenge to the paradoxical balance to the cultural dialectic itself. How then to render in a clear way the fundamental idea of ambiguity, the nature of which subverts the very clarity on which a discussion of Lewisohn's and Ozick's work should rest?

The early (Catholic) Church was easily able to develop its dogma because it relied on an unambiguous, closed textual frame. In Hebraic hermeneutics, on the other hand, it is very difficult to create dogma from the "obscurities" that appear and disappear in biblical texts. The totality of semiotic messages in the Hebrew text, combined with the biblical text in its original multidimensional, multi-signifying Hebrew language base, produces an irreparable gap between Judaic and Christian exegesis. Thus there is a complex, ambiguity-filled, rich dialectic beneath every line of Scriptural verse where, as stated earlier, ambiguity subverts the traditional notions of dialectic. Every word can be argued from many directions and be valid, since there are no ultimate proofs for any interpretation. As Joseph Dan puts it, "every verse can be and was interpreted in fully legitimate ways to support conflicting arguments. An opponent's way of interpreting a scriptural verse would rarely, if ever, be considered as falsifying the text." (Dan 129)

Midrash, as already described, is textual commentary in story form. It employs dialectic as logical analysis through argumentation. As exemplified in "The Pagan Rabbi", hermeneutics sometimes gives way to outlandish interpretations in which the dialectical process of argumentation creates or discovers logically beautiful aesthetic patterns that could negate the very God-based moral principles the process originally set out to analyze and interpret. Thus the imagination and the moral self must set boundaries in order to participate in investigating scripturally based *Midrash*, or storytelling, and in the hermeneutical process of analyzing the supra/subtexts comprising the specific Midrashic text.

Historically, through the negative influence of Pauline Christianity (as contrasted with Judaic "Christianity", or a Hebrew Joshua rather than a Greek Jesus), Hebraism itself has been denigrated for its complicated, dense system of legality. This density is explored through *pilpul*, the Hebrew dialectical process steeped in the search for meaning through interpretation, which until fairly recently had always been ignored or remained undiscovered by theological as well as aesthetic and literary investigations. Now, however, *Midrash* is deemed to be a significant and rich area of research for contemporary literary inquiry. It is precisely in this context that the term "dialectic" is used, to mean not just logical analysis and argumentation, but also the hermeneutics of literary and textual investigation.

In a special way great writers, such as Henry James for Cynthia Ozick or Matthew Arnold for Lewisohn, were/are admired for their combined aesthetic sensibilities and humanness. Arnold's influence on Lewisohn was very strong at an early critical stage in the latter's intellectual development. In the same way, Henry James affected Ozick's aesthetic and literary sensibilities. Ozick referred to James as "the large-hearted Henry James".[19] For her, "James was a genius" who "invented an almost metaphysical art." ("Justice" 23) Equally as important, "James was an uncanny moralist" who "scarcely ever failed." (23) Ozick also read and digested, albeit in varying degrees of intensity, Matthew Arnold's work and the spirit of his being. Matthew Arnold, who was appreciated by both Lewisohn and Ozick for his high aesthetic and moral sense, vociferously condemned middle-class English and American societies for what he perceived as their Hebraic roots. Ozick writes on Arnold:

> When Matthew Arnold said that he would not like to have been born a Jew... he did not mean that he disliked anyone who denied the divinity of Jesus, or even that he disapproved of the denial itself. His objection was pragmatically related to an idea about civilization. He pitied the inassimilable: he thought it "better" to be in the "mainstream"; he wanted to be civilized by which he meant belonging to the locally prevailing mythos—to the West as Christendom.[20]

Through Ozick's pen, the picture that emerges of Arnold was a portrait of a great gentleman and aesthete who, by default rather than hatred, valued mainstream (Gentile-Christian) culture over everything. For him, Hebraic thinking was the sole reason for the existence of "provincialism" both in England and America. As he asserts: "From Maine to Florida, and back again, all America Hebraises."[21] Arnold's broadside attack on Puritanism, combined with Lewisohn's growing dissatisfaction with a Puritanical America, could not help but intensify the latter's repugnance toward America's Puritan-based culture. Lewisohn later transformed his anti-Puritanism into a moral and aesthetic aversion to establishment Christianity—as opposed to the real Jewish message of Joshua/Jesus. As well, Ozick as writer has generated her own manifestations of Puritan-baiting, as in her portrayal of Jane, the narrator's puritanical wife in "The Pagan Rabbi", who studiously avoids sex and is portrayed as having the stereotypical qualities of Puritan values. In this cultural context, Puritanism becomes equated with Pan, while sexuality is shown as one of the qualities that is the very essence of the Mosaic spirit. Arnold's call, *vis a vis* "culture, beauty and intelligence," (Arnold 72) is an appeal for a type of Platonic Greek form of "perfection" consisting of "sweetness and light." (54) In contradistinction is the absence of this in middle-class America and England, which elevated "doing" over "thinking" and "salvation" over "perfection".

Arnold's cosmology is divided into another two-levelled tier, that of the Hellenic elevation of mind over body *versus* the Hebrew elevation of "right action" over beauty, thought and reason. As he describes it: "The governing idea of Hellenism is spontaneity of consciousness; that of Hebraism, strictness of conscience." (132) However, as Geoffrey H. Hartman and Sanford Budick maintain, Arnold believed that for all of its fine attributes, Hebraism cannot and does not "speak to intellectual, aesthetic or artistic pursuits and endeavours." (*Midrash* ix) In relation to Arnold and writers in general, Hartman and Budick assert that "what Hebraism is, however, has rarely been recognized." (ix) Arnold's dichotomy between Hellenistic "consciousness" and Hebraic "conscience" failed to address the profound complexities inherent in Hebrew thought and philosophy. Structuring it, as he was forced to do, on the very rhetoric of Western philosophy, Arnold, as Hartman and Budick observe, could not avoid the pitfalls of dualistic thinking. Arnold

> did not or could not see that Hebraism had already achieved, through the presiding genius of midrash, an extensive and deep spontaneity, as well as an extraordinary web of consciousness, not easily matched in the western tradition. Nor did he envisage the possibility of a partnership of conscience and consciousness—in one full functional criticism—which did not forthwith collapse dialectically into a univocal resolution. (ix–x)

Thus Jewish *Midrash* is characterized by, and exemplifies, what contemporary critical theory calls the "open" text in its spontaneity and webbing of consciousness, as opposed to the closed, authorial one which is dualistic, canonistic and monolithic in its rigidly applied typological conceptions. In the "open" text, there is neither writer nor reader, critic nor artist, but literary or scriptural "life" perceivable in "the shuttle space between the interpreter and the text", (xi) creating a paradoxical ambiguity of textual signification. This textual interpretation "does not paralyze itself". (xi) In its stead can be discovered an interpretative enterprise merged into the energy of the text itself. Thus it yields a seemingly infinite line of other texts, pre-texts, intertexts, pulled off "in a spirit of high serious play." (xi) All of this results in a slippery "effacement of self", (xi) which neither makes authorial claims on the text, nor professes to ultimately know what it means.

In *Midrash* the joy of the creator, who remains faceless and subordinated to the Text of texts, gives way to an inscrutable mythos of non-private genius. In a splendid paradox of the most authorial, but also the most open of texts, Torah's commentators achieve an impenetrable combination of the sacred with a faceless, individualistically distinct talent, while at the same time acknowledging a moral universe held in balance by the Creator of creators. In many ways, *Midrash* brings us full circle to that mix of interpretation and artistic activity. What is of interest in the present context is the way in which *Midrash* and Hebrew thought in general can be seen as an inherent part of the Jewish-American writers who are the subject of this study. As Hartman and Budick declare: "What now seems particularly interesting is the unclassifiability and waywardness of Midrash, its ability to function without apparent boundaries." (xiii) These non-boundaries, this study suggests, include not just those between the text and reader, but between the created text and writer, the reader and the text.

In significant ways, Pauline Christianity and Hebraism have been locked for two millennia in a death-and-life-struggle for dominance over the text/Text, the word/Word. Like John Updike, Matthew Arnold, even in his overtly civilized and refined rhetorical manner and style, betrays a complexity of fundamentally errant assumptions regarding Judaism and Christianity. Like Updike, Arnold firstly confuses the historically Judaic Joshua with the fabricated, Hellenistic Pauline Jesus. Likewise Ozick criticizes Updike for reverting to Origen, Ambrose and hundreds of years of doctrinaire Christianity, "and in such ancient terms to define his Jew." ("Bech" 124) The central focus of Ozick's argument is that Updike has falsified what is already "false" by lending American Jews "the Grace of his imagination", instead of reaching beyond "to something like historical presence." (124) Arnold, as well, relies on the typological underpinnings inherent in Pauline Christianity that transformed the Hebraic concept of

Joshua, son of Miriam and Joseph, into the version of Saul/Paul of Tarsus. Arnold's linkage of Jew to Christian is the code (form of typology) in which Judaism reads as Christianity; that is, the Judaism of Pauline Christianity's usurpation. This is the reason for Arnold's dichotomous chapter title, "Hebraism and Hellenism", which he expresses as follows:

> As one passes and repasses from Hellenism to Hebraism, from Plato to St. Paul, one feels inclined to rub one's eyes and ask oneself whether man is indeed a gentle and simple being, showing the traces of a noble and divine nature; or an unhappy chained captive, laboring with groanings that cannot be uttered to free himself from the body of this death. (Arnold 136)

Arnold's rhetoric reveals the typology imbedded in the Christian word, text and pretext, and also the inherent negativity of Western thought which Jones describes. This typology presumes the suppression, disappearance and waylaid placelessness of Jewish identity, thought and Word/Book, dating from the time of the Pauline Church's inception. How else can Arnold's equation of "Hebraism" with "St. Paul" be understood?

Further on, Arnold assigns a rather benign and naive characterization *vis a vis* the relationship between Judaism and Christianity: "As it is justly said of Christianity which *followed* [italics added] Judaism and which set forth this side with a much deeper effectiveness and a much wider influence..." (138) Arnold fails to mention the bloodstained history of Judaism and Christianity, or to offer any insights into either Judaism or Jewish identity itself. If Christianity had a deeper effect and wider influence, then Judaism can be understood to have been somehow ineffective and of marginal influence.

From the Hebraic perspective, there is Leo Baeck (1873–1956), a German Reform rabbinical authority, learned in comparative religion, renowned as a secular scholar and head of German Jewry from 1933 into the Nazi era. In 1942, passing up chances to escape from Germany, he was sent to the Theresienstadt concentration camp. For the purposes of this study, Baeck's importance rests on the work he initiated as early as 1905, when he began his radical revision of Christianity and Christology. (*Religion* 95)[22] Both Ozick and Lewisohn were/are greatly enamored with Leo Baeck, the man who selflessly led his persecuted German-Jewish community at the most difficult time in modern German history. Lewisohn was already a professor at Brandeis University where, on October 30, 1955, he attended a ceremony in which Jacques Maritain, Paul Tillich and Leo Baeck were honored. As Melnick describes:

Baeck's emphasis that day on what a half century earlier he had identified as *The Essence of Judaism*—its conception of God and those moral command-ments which flowed from it, "eternal and unchanging" despite "ceremonial forms [that] are transient and modifiable"—could only have confirmed for Ludwig the worthiness of the challenge he had given his people. Baeck as the leader of German Jewry in its darkest years, had seen mankind at its worst and knew of the need to oppose the idolatrous nihilism against which Ludwig had repeatedly lifted his voice.[23]

Ozick's own connection with Baeck's work, which began at an earlier more impressionable age than with Lewisohn, will be discussed at greater length in the Ozick Introduction.

Baeck's writing and thought is reflected, directly and indirectly, in the work and thought of Ludwig Lewisohn and Cynthia Ozick. Relatedly, one of the philosophical and theological underpinnings of this study of cultural dialectic in the work and lives of Lewisohn and Ozick rests on the uneasy relationship between Judaism and Christianity. This two-thousand-year-long connection has been a cultural dialectical process in itself: conflicts, hostilities and the pernicious conceptual frame of the Church's perception of its Judaic roots. Competing authority over the Word of God and formulations of anti-Jewish doctrine, in order to sub-stantiate and wield the Church's preeminence over the older and therefore more legitimate faith, have stressed the adversarial nature of that relation-ship. Christianity from its Gentile inception and embodiment in the Church itself, that is to say the Church from Paul onward, has had to travel a bumpy and even paradoxical road of cultural dialectic in order to wrest power and authority from its Hebraic origins. Of necessity, it had to admire, respect and attempt to incorporate Judaism's tenets, while simul-taneously instituting its own necessary legislation and plan to undermine Judaism's dominance and influence.

Paul's Hellenistic cultural frame, Hellenism itself, has been generally vilified for both its pagan qualities and attractiveness to assimilating He-brews. Indeed, for writers like Ozick and Lewisohn, Hellenic culture's emphasis on amorality, pitilessness and beauty were all the necessary ingredients for the twentieth-century Nazi extermination of Jews. Ozick's assault on Allen Ginsberg is an example of her many attacks on Helle-nism. Ginsberg, she says, "recapitulates the Hellenization of Jewish Christianity."[24] In relation to the deification of a man: "When man is turned into a piece of god he is freed from any covenant with God." ("Yiddish" 163) Finally, she equates Ginsberg with the synonymity of aestheticism, paganism, America and Christianity in saying that the "Jew feels alien to the aesthetic paganism of a churched America." (162)

The history of the conflict between Hebraic and Hellenic cultures began in the Macabbean Age of Jewish history (200–150 B.C.E.), when the Greek Antiochus threatened to supplant Hebrew culture with a Greek one. His· goal was to bring Greek culture to the Judean Jewish masses and thereby create a political foothold in which to expand his empire. In time, the Jewish rank and file almost completely adopted Greek culture, and its religious observances began replacing Judaism. As Solomon Grayzel describes:

> Now that the Hellenizers had full control of Judea's government, they began to build gymnasiums within Jerusalem in which the young people were encouraged to spend a great deal of time. The young priests neglected their duties in the Temple in order to engage in sports. Greek styles in dress, Greek names, the Greek language became stylish in Jerusalem. And, worst of all, the Hellenized life brought with it looseness in religious observance as well as the characteristically Greek looseness of morals.[25]

Thus throughout the Holy Land, the majority of Jews spoke not just Hebrew and Aramaic but also Greek. As Gideon Bohak reveals:

> The impact of Hellenism on Hebrew can be gauged from the vocabulary in rabbinic literature; numerous Greek words entered the Hebrew language (and many are still commonly used in modern Hebrew) as did many concepts, legends and theories, whose Hellenistic origin is indisputable. At the same time the rabbis opposed too close an acquaintance with, and study of Greek culture, which they saw as pagan and idolatrous, by definition the antithesis of Judaism. The upper classes, however, adapted a through-going Hellenistic style of life which was often assimilationist. (*Religion* 316)

Through the Greek cultural influences on and of Paul, the newly established Church began a process of Hellenization of the originally Hebraic content and signification of Joshua/Jesus's message, even changing the Hebraic form of the name, Joshua, to the Greek form, Jesus. This transference continued simultaneously with the final disappearance of Judeo-Greek culture in the Diaspora. Interestingly and significantly, the only traces of Judeo-Greek culture that remained "were preserved", albeit in a transformed form as Bohak relates, "by the Christian church." (316) Ludwig Lewisohn and Cynthia Ozick picked up the thread of this Greek-Hebraic clash, for example in Lewisohn's successive reanalyzes of the figure of Jesus from a god-head to a fervently religious Judean Hebrew involved with Torah law. Lewisohn finally exposes what he sees as the essentially Hebraic, if not perhaps misguided Judaic, essence of Jesus's teachings. The Christian Church, as opposed to those real Christians who follow the true Jewish message of the Hebraic Jesus, is an alien, anti-Jewish, Hellenistic, pagan force that wrongly seeks/sought to convert and subvert Jesus's Jewish message and signification into a Gentile, pagan frame. Thus both Ozick and Lewisohn linked Gentile-Christian culture with Hellenism, including its basis in pagan Greek culture and ideas.

The following is a more specific examination of typology in the historical and theological frame of the Judaic-Christian polemic, from its beginnings in the early Church to its later manifestations in Puritanism and early-American culture and rhetoric. This polemic figures prominently in the larger portion of Ozick's and Lewisohn's artistic, social, personal, linguistic, societal and cultural concerns; and helps create the frame, if not the base, of Ozick's and Lewisohn's complex cultural dialectic.

Israel's history itself, as tradition describes it, has been a continuous repetition of one theme: God tests and Israel perseveres, succeeds, or fails the test. One of the greatest tests in its long history has been Christianity. Through the mouth of Moses, God describes the intense suffering His people will undergo at the hands of a "no-people" because Israel has been "perverse and crooked." To punish the Israelites, God says in *Deuteronomy*, "I will hide my face from them, I will see what their end will be.... They have moved me to jealousy with a no-god,... I will move them to jealousy with a no-people. I will provoke them to anger with a vile nation." (32:1, 20-22) Almost from its inception, the Church tested Israel's ability to withstand hostility, such as with the creation of Paul's Church, the Crusades and the Inquisition. Moreover, the Church ensured that Jews would lead intolerably miserable lives wherein their very existence on earth would bear witness and prove their erroneous rejection of Jesus as the Savior.

The story of Jesus's life, from his birth to crucifixion, is described in *Matthew*, beginning with the "genealogy of Jesus Christ, son of David, son of Abraham", to Joseph and his immaculately conceived son, Jesus. (1:1)[26] Also born, as stated, was one of the greatest polemics of the last two thousand years. The very first, small group of believers in Jesus as the Messiah was tolerated, since this group's believers continued to observe Jewish ritual and to respect and follow the Law. However, when

Saul/Paul began talking of the "divinity" of Jesus, saying that faith was sufficient without Law, and that circumcision of the heart was enough, this group was deemed heretical. Continuing to call their belief and practice the "Hebrew" faith gave the pagans the chance to now be called Israelites. What began to be called "Christianity" was seen as being far easier to digest, as described by Solomon Grayzel, than Judaism's "strange and mysterious customs" and commandments, especially the unexplainable, pain-filled act of circumcision. (Grayzel 141) Christianity asked only faith in God and Jesus. (148–150) In his youth, Lewisohn embraced Christianity and its belief in the messiahship of Jesus with great fervency and earnestness of being. It seemed that he had been totally emerged in the faith of the Christian message.

The believers in the divinity and messiahship of Jesus were now the true Hebrews, who were convinced that all the covenant promises described in Hebrew Scripture were directed at them. If the Church had accepted the Hebrew rite of circumcision, it would also have had to agree tacitly that the old covenant of the historical Israelite nation was fully operative. As Jeremy Silver and Bernard Martin state, this "would have weakened the Church's claim that a new covenant, confirmed in the blood of Christ, superseded the old covenant, confirmed with a drop of the blood of each male child."[27] The sign of the drop of phallic blood in the Hebrew ritual had been typologized into the sign of Jesus' blood in the new covenant. Thus the old form, embodied in and changed by the new one, could be said to have not been eliminated or refuted, but just transformed into a newer one. It was possible to exchange the "old" sign of the blood of the Israelite for the new sign of the blood of the pagan-Gentile through the Messiahship of Jesus. Both Ozick and Lewisohn finally held the worship of a man-god as a contemptible and idolatrous notion. They also blasted the concept of "inward" signs as a wholesale inversion of Hebraic ethics that necessitates "outward", active signs. Circumcision, thus stated, became an "inward" sign.

From the early Middle Ages, the church's by-then officially instituted anti-Hebrew policy was based on a substitution of itself in the place of the Israelite nation. Ozick's characterization of Lucy in "Levitation" as having been in love with the idea of the "Ancient Hebrew" parallels John Updike's own typological perceptions of Jews as Christians in disguise. As Ozick intones in relation to her polemic against John Updike's characterization of the Jew:

But seen from the perspective of the Jewish vision... [Updike's] Jewish Bech
has no reality at all, especially not to himself: he is a false Jew, a poured-out
becher, one who has departed from Jewish presence. For Updike to falsify the
false—i.e. to lend the Jew in America the Grace of his imagination—would
have been to get... to something like historical presence, and a living Bech.
But that, I suppose, would have required him to do what Vatican II fought
against doing: forgive the Jew for having been real to himself all those centuries, and even now. And for that he would have had to renounce the darker
part of the Christian imagination and confound his own theology.
("Bech" 124)

This substitution was implemented through a pattern of "foreshadow-
ing" events from the past, projecting their meanings and images on
figures and events of the present, to give prophetic significance to things
of the future. Augustine had used the figures and events of Hebrew
Scripture, projected onto the birth, life and death of Jesus, to state that
Jesus had fulfilled the messianic prophecies of Hebrew Scripture. As Jeremy Cohen states, "His new covenant of grace had abrogated Mosaic
Law, and... his church had replaced the synagogue as the community of
God's 'chosen'."[28] It was thus Augustine who established the Hebrew-
Christian typology that became the tradition for supplantation of "New"
for "Old." (Cohen 20)

Cohen further states that Augustine's thinking was "innovative". He
answered pagan criticism by affirming "the perfect concordance of Old
and New Testaments", but the "old" one in God's "plan of redemption
was primarily prefigurative". (13) In this way, many Hebrew Scriptural
ideas had "lost their validity after Jesus's crucifixion." (13) Augustine
also stated that, although the Jews did not now deserve to survive, God
spared them for the benefit of the Church, so that in preserving the "old
Testament", they will be witness to the correctness and historical validity
of Christian prophecy, to heed it, and then at the End of Days, to convert
to Christianity. The Jews, in Augustine's characterization, are blind to the
truth of which their own biblical tradition gives proof. In an ironic twist
and reversal of Augustinian philosophy *vis a vis* the Jews, Lewisohn in
the characterization of Mrs. Morrison in *Holy Land* renders her in a state
of threatened blindness as if to symbolically demonstrate her own (Christian) blindness to the Jewishness of Jesus and the Christian faith. Mrs.
Morrison also represents the embodiment of the writer's deconstruction
of Christianity's own penchant for blinding its followers to the truths of
Judaism. Significantly, it is the *Holy Land* narrator and the Zionist

hospital's good Jewish doctor who transform Mrs. Morrison's brush with sightlessness into the ability to see (but only on the grossest level of reality). She remains incapable of insight into the truth on a higher spiritual and perceptual plane.

Just as the Church was to have replaced the Old Book and its people, and the Protestant Reformation sought to become the authentic voice of the (Jewish) Christian message, so finally did Calvinist Puritanism view itself as the truest form of new Israelites returning from exile, through a long sojourn in a wilderness, to finally reach their "Promised Land", America. By the seventeenth century, the Christian tradition, as previously stated, had a well-laid groundwork through which the Puritans of the New England Colony could perceive themselves as God's chosen, at the forefront of the soon-to-come final stage of world redemption. The Puritans saw themselves as the Israelites, and both were "types" of Jesus. "Typology," Sacvan Bercovitch states, "became a staple of Protestant writers," merging the Old and New, with the Promise of the Old Testament totally fulfilled in the New.[29] Typology was concerned with *litera-historia*. Early Puritan figures like John Winthrop and Cotton Mather (the latter wrote a biography of Winthrop) were, through hermeneutics, both "beyond time" and also located in time and place. Winthrop was both Americanus and Nehemiah: both "here" in the now, and "there" in the past of the great biblical patriarchs and prophets. Nehemiah was a "correlative" type of Christ figure, Bercovitch states, which makes deeper the perception of him as a foretype "'of the ancient story'." (*Puritan* 36) For Mather, Winthrop was governor of Israel. Jerusalem, Babylon, Israel, and now America, were focal points in the great plan of redemption. Winthrop embodied and overlapped, in his time of being, all the historicity of a biblical past to the future, as the present messiah of the new Israel. Mather's "Nehemias Americanus" declares that a history of redemption is moving forward. The Puritan's theocratic type was the Hebrew who "stands not with but behind the Puritan." The restored Jerusalem, together with Nehemiah, form the background "for the greater New World Jerusalem". (55–56)

The Puritan's errand into the wilderness of America, in the final days, would end when redemption came. The world's end would come, as Perry Miller describes, first with illumination, then an explosion, and finally the world would be engulfed in fire. This destruction would then be followed by glory, peace and perfection. Until then, the Puritan com-

munity had a mission identical to that of the old Israel: to be a moral light
for the world. Nevertheless, with the ambiguity in the word "errand", the
Puritans, as God's children, began to be "in grave doubt about which had
been the original errand."[30]

It was this moral imperative that shaped the American idea which, as
Milton R. Konvitz asserts, is the basis of the Israel idea.[31] Like Israel,
America—through the New England Puritans' conviction that they were
the true Israel—claimed a special character for itself. From the early Puritan era to the twentieth century, as Konvitz states, America, like Israel,
has also been on a "quest for the teleological explanation for [its] moral
significance." (Konvitz 17) There is thus a teleological questing that is
"typed" from Israel to America. (17) Similarly and in ironic reversal,
Ozick's character, Jane, in "The Pagan Rabbi", representing the eternal
Shiksah, Puritanism and Gentile America, becomes displaced by Sheindel
and her Yiddish, European, Holocaust-survivor Jewishness. Thus
Sheindel, and all she personifies, is the true/truer/truest embodiment of
the Old-New Jerusalem/Israel, which paradoxically is to say, America.

The idea of a promise or covenantal contract made between a god
and a people is unique to Israelite history. Israel's prophets (most importantly, Hosea, Jeremiah and Ezekiel) describe the relationship of God and
His people as husband and wife, which is itself a covenant of marriage.
In *Exodus*, God warns Israel not to run after other gods: "For I, the Lord
your God, am a jealous God." (34:14) The meaning of "betrayal" and
"jealousy" have a sexual significance. Ozick's and Lewisohn's (Jewish)
aversion to the deification of the human being, Jesus, and thereby shun-
ning the Christian establishment, is rooted in a sense of betrayal: of one's
personal history, the Jewish people and its unique monogamous relationship with the God of Abraham, Isaac and Jacob. The root of the Hebrew
verb for betrayal is *zanah aharay*, literally, "to whore after." The word
"covenant", or in Hebrew *brit*, is defined by Steven Katz as "a general
obligation between two parties confirmed either by an oath, a solemn
meal, a sacrifice, or by some other dramatic act."[32] In executing such a
covenant, there is not only the ceremonial ritual, but also a visual manifestation of the agreement. As Katz explains:

> The Sabbath, the rainbow, and circumcision are each a "sign" of a great cov-
> enant established by God at a critical stage in the history of mankind; the
> Sabbath is the sign of creation; the rainbow is a sign of the renewal of man-
> kind after the Flood; and circumcision of the beginning of the Jewish people
> and the Hebrew nation. (Katz 156)

The covenantal idea has a juridical meaning. "The Law" in Scripture, and in its later commentary in *Halacha* (Law), was physically, spiritually, emotionally, mentally and legally binding. In the same way, in Ozick's short story, "The Shawl", set in a Holocaust Death Camp, the character Rosa desperately attempts to keep her baby Madga alive by binding her with/in the fence of the shawl (the Law). The warnings of the prophets or of God were usually decreed via the form of a (written) lawsuit. God institutes a suit against the Israelite nation, with heaven, earth or mountains as witness. The Ten Commandments can thus be seen as factual, juridical proof of the Covenant. When Moses descended with tablets in hand, this document, sworn and signed, expressed, as Katz asserts, "the validity of the given relationship." (160) As he descended, Moses' rage at seeing the Golden Calf and the behavior of the Israelites was understandable; this people had made a sworn promise to God. "Thus the worship of the golden calf," Katz adds, "which signifies the breaking of the covenant, is followed by the breaking of the tablets by Moses, the mediator of the covenant." (160)

Because the Land was God's (since He created everything) and therefore holy, its purity had to be constantly guarded. The shedding of innocent blood, idolatry, licentiousness or defilement of God's law could all cause heavenly retribution. Indeed, Scripture gives reasons, as Silver and Martin state, "that the land might actually, on God's orders, vomit out Israel." (Silver 56) The Land's lushness, richness and plenitude do not exist separate from God's will. The Land's fertility and greenness are "not intrinsic to the Land. It is God who places fertility here. The Land remains green only so long as God wills it." (56) Thus the natural world has no will or life separate from God. God was not identified through and by the Land; the Land served to prove God's wisdom, power, loyalty and covenanted promise.

The Calvinistic Puritan, state Perry Miller and Thomas H. Johnson, "thought the Bible was the revealed word of God, the word of God from one end to the other, a complete body of laws, an absolute code in everything it touched upon."[33] The colonial Puritan John Winthrop had wanted to build a society focused on one mission, whose achievement would be the greatest reward and wealth. He warned the Puritan colonists to go forth and possess the land without becoming its possession. In the entire history of the world, here was a human enterprise, as Miller describes, "so dedicated to a holy cause." (*Errand* 6) These were not just a covenant people, Miller explains, but the covenant people with a "doctrine of the national covenant" that could allow God's chosen, the Puritans, as John Cotton and others said, to ferret the social conscience of this new place more than is expected of other nations.[34] The Covenant for the Puritans, Miller adds, was "the master idea of the age."(*New England* 21) The colonial civil covenant was thus not just deduced from the Covenant of Grace of the Christian Bible, but from "the Old Testament." Jacob wrestles alone with Jehovah, but Israel makes its bond with God seen in something "visible—a church, a nation… As a people they are chosen because by public act they have chosen God." This is a conscious act of dedicating the nation to a "'communal decision'", as Miller explains using John Cotton's words. (21) Lewisohn raged against an America that did not keep its covenant on a number of levels. Firstly, it did not keep it with him. As he states in *Up Stream* and elsewhere, he gave all of himself; worshipped as hard and zealously as any American-born Christian; cultivated the same attitudes, beliefs, mindset; but all to no avail. His cultural, racial, ethnic alienness still set him apart from the truer Americans. Secondly, in his view, America was not true to its own Enlightenment Liberal values and democratic cultural attitudes.

Perry Miller first describes the effect and connection of typology in and on American literary history in his 1948 Introduction to Jonathan Edwards' "Images or Shadows of Divine Things." "Typing" itself figured most prominently in late sixteenth and seventeenth-century English literature, and then (what was in the process of becoming) American literature. In any case, it was nearly synonymous with Puritan thought, beginning, as we have seen, with Calvin. It was so much a part of the colonial theocratic polity that Gurdon Saltanstall, in a sermon given for the Boston General Assembly in 1697, could say: "'These Figurative Terms… are obvious; and need not much to be said for their Explication.'"[35] Bercovitch in the "Introduction" to his book says that the "study of typology in colonial America has come of age and… has proved beyond any doubt an invaluable addition to our knowledge of the period." (*Typology* 3) Thus, all of those early colonial thinkers who helped formulate "the New England Way" believed that only through "the Types" can the truth of Christ be understood. They all shared the Reformation's conviction that the thing signified by the Scriptural words is literally the same as the type, and so Bercovitch, quoting John Norton, describes, "'as the New Testament giveth light unto the Old, so the Old Testament giveth light unto the New. Tis the same Christ and the same Gospel which the Saints in the Old Testament belong unto believers living under the New Testament... not only David, but also... us.'"[36]

The study of Puritan literature, Thomas M. Davis states, is impossible without realizing the centrality of typology in "Puritan texts"; and by extension, he includes American literature as a whole.[37] Puritanism's use of typology reaches back, as Bercovitch also notes, to the Reformation; and so, as Davis asserts, it was not just a preoccupation of the seventeenth century. Indeed, its origin extends back to the first Christian Church that needed to validate its existence to a hostile environment. Davis draws a very clear line from Puritanism to Hebrew Scripture in saying: "Thanks to Perry Miller and Sacvan Bercovitch, we are aware that typology was part of the cypher in which American Puritans encoded their aspirations for the new nation." (Davis 26)

The Church's "New" versus "Old" typology can also be viewed metalinguistically. In appropriating the "signs" of Israel's Covenant, it could be said to have used the evasive, ambiguous, paradoxical language that we call "literature" as a sober, unambiguous meta-language. The Church's semiotic undertaking of attaching new meanings to old signs can be seen as a vigorous effort to reassign signification. In this way it had a body of "readers" in mind, specifically the pagans of Rome who were wavering between choosing the "Old" sign or the "New". As Jonathan Culler asserts, "The real subject is the implications of thinking about signs."[38] Thus typology can be viewed as a semiotic enterprise:

> Reflection on signs and meaning is, of course, nothing new. Philosophers and students of language have of necessity always discussed signs in one way or another, and the advent of semiotics has helped to reveal, for example, that what had previously been sneered at as medieval scholasticism was in many respects a subtle and highly developed theory of signs... [which brings] together the linguistic and non-linguistic. (Culler 21–22)

In this discussion, the writing of American philosopher Charles Sanders Pierce and Swiss linguist Ferdinand de Saussure is especially prominent. It could be said that the Church capitalised on what semiotics describes as indeterminate meaning by identifying the effect that the significance of meaning, things and occurrences have for a participant or observer in those acts. (21) In this way, the Church made what Paul Korshin describes as predictions that connected Hebrew Scriptures and Christian gospel with a search for "signs, shadows, figures of something past or yet to come." (*Typologies* 4) The Israelite "sign" of the ritual bath (*mikveh*), for example, became the newly embodied sign of the baptismal bath. The subject of the Christian textual message is not as much "submerging a believer in water" as it is the language used to express it. In replacing the "Old" for a "New" system of belief, to quote Culler, Paul challenged us to "order their multifarious forms" and to see "them as manifestations of a 'language' whose fundamental units and oppositions he must identify." (Culler 29)

Paul's language of both filial identification with, and vilification of, the Hebrews served a double purpose and represented a complex message. Thus the myths which the language of Christian texts and commentary generated became endlessly re-created and reproduced in culture and thought through these millennia. The figure of the Jew became imbedded with the promise of conversion, since it is only he who does not realize what the signification of the "new work" really means. Paul's language attempted to overturn the "old" language of Hebrew identity, signified most importantly by circumcision. Paul's *Romans* can be seen as a metalinguistic strategy to capture Jewish identity. In the words of Michael Ragussis, the "Christian word is an ambiguous sign of a 'battle of the Books', part of a battle of mastery over the figure of the Jew."[39] Ragussis traces the origin of "figurative conversion" of the Jew to the beginning of Christianity itself, in the first through the fourth centuries during the Christian-Hebrew war for dominance. To show proof of its validity, Christianity had to demonstrate that it had "inherited, and thereby replaced, Judaism's role as the interpreter of those sacred texts that had been until now the source of Jewish authority in the pagan world." (Ragussis 137)

The Church initiated a rereading of the Hebrew Bible, Ragussis asserts, "with two goals in mind: first, to authorize the legitimacy—even the historic primacy... of Christianity;... second, to undermine Jewish authority through construction of a fictitious figure, 'the Jew'." (137) By doing this, the Hebrew Bible itself was used to defame the Jews; the *Adversus Judaeos* literature of this time insisted that this Hebrew Bible "proved" that the Israelites were not capable of being the owners of God's word, because they misread, mistranslated, and mutilated it.

What ensued was the fight for who was really God's chosen people, and what in fact constituted, or should be able to represent, Jewish identity. As Ragussis continues: "The full transfer of power from one community to another, which in this case meant the full absorption of

Judaism into Christianity, was represented in the act of naming, by which the church designated itself as the New Israel." (137) Ragussis speaks of the "authorial act" through which the word "Jew" or "Christian" is "relocated" for the explicit purpose of rewriting their identities. This, he states, is a revision of history and "is a constantly repeated act, embedded within a variety of discourses, always a sign of ideological struggle, but a sign under cover." (139)

The new American Puritan church rewrote the Hebrew biblical text as well. It believed that the Puritans, especially the most righteous of them, were sent by God, like Ezekiel, to warn the wicked; because, as in Ezekiel: "they turned not from wickedness... [and] will die in iniquity." They must say to the house of Israel, "Thus the Lord God says: 'Repent, turn yourselves from your idols, and turn away your faces from all your abominations... And my people Israel will bear the punishment of their iniquity.'" (*Ezekiel* 2, 3:14)

John Winthrop echoed the words of Jeremiah in describing his fallen, sinful "Israel", in Miller's words, who misbehaving could "expect immediate manifestations of divine wrath". (*Errand* 6) The content of the Puritan clergymen's church sermons consisted of litanies of sins which the backsliding Puritan people had committed. The structure, built on models in the Jewish Bible, became a literary model, the jeremiad. The jeremiad, as Miller describes, "with its ritualistic incantation" (8) and sense of moral urging, became the basis of American rhetoric and prose which is the central stylistic form in American literature, and through which Jewish-American writers explore the complexities of the Israel-America dilemma. Sacvan Bercovitch states that the jeremiad "has played a major role in fashioning the myth of America."[40]

This form, taken from the original Hebrew biblical texts, came down through the European churches and was converted in its meaning and structure by the colonial Puritans. By the eighteenth century, the jeremiad had become a ritualized form connecting critical assessments of society with exhortations to mend the spirit, the public face and the private sense of self; to make changes in American society with its underlying undercurrents of meanings, symbolic designations and thematic reoccurrences that the society now manifested. All of this serves to make the cultural dialectic in Ozick's and Lewisohn's work even more complex, since the "Jewishness" of these Jewish writers mixes with the "Jewishness" imbedded in American culture's rhetoric and language. As Ozick states: "The novel at its height in the last century was Judaizing in that it could not have been written without the Jewish Bible; in America especially, Hawthorne and Melville and Whitman are Biblically indebted." ("Yiddish" 167)

In this way, the myth became "the fact" that is America. "Myth," Bercovitch states, "may clothe history as fiction, but it persuades in proportion to its capacity to help people act in history. Ultimately, its effectiveness derives from its functional relationship to facts." (*Jeremiad* xi) As Bercovitch describes, the jeremiad's rhetorical form and the myths it encompassed, in becoming the basis for the American literary structure, ultimately wedded morality to secularism. (3) This jeremiad that the Puritans also called the "political sermon" because of the theocratic underpinnings of Puritan society, was used to convey the "dual nature of their calling", Bercovitch continues, "as practical and as spiritual guides," and to suggest that this "church-state teleology was wedded to politics, and politics to the progress of the kingdom of God." (xiv) This is to say that ingrained in what we call "the American myth" is the idea of chosenness and covenantal promise. Thus this jeremiad form became, in the twentieth century, what Bercovitch terms a "state-of-the-covenant address". (4) Its underlying message was the sense of mission that had to be accomplished, that which the chosen people turned their backs on; or in twentieth-century literature, to ask not only what exactly the Mission was, but what was the identity of the doer of that Mission. This stylistic mode copied from Hebrew Scriptures became, from both Ozick's and Lewisohn's Hebraic and American cultural milieu, a doubling of both an American and a Hebraic/Jewish attitude of mind, linguistic orientation and part and parcel of the complex cultural dialectic in their respective works.

The American myth and mind, with its polemics of sacredness and secularism, was and is accompanied by, as Miller and then Bercovitch affirm, a sense of ambiguity. It is this sense of ambiguity of both personal identity and language in this Jewish-American polemic that Jewish-American writers either outspokenly, tacitly or covertly affirmed; or else vociferously denied. In any event, it was the intermesh which they could not avoid confronting on some level. The biblical rhetorical modes, structure, the general complex and richly ambiguous hermeneutical nature of Hebrew Scriptures and its rabbinical interpretative tradition; plus the nature of Ozick's and Lewisohn's complicated cultural, linguistic, ethnic, social, aesthetic, nationalistic, intellectual, personal frames; to which is added a country, America, which Arnold accurately identified as both abundantly Hebraic and Christianly Gentile; work together to create multi-leveled, deep, obscure, indeterminate and cryptically uninterpretable messages.

What Miller "meant by ambiguity," Bercovitch explains, "was opposition". (10) The "mission", what Miller called "the errand", was either for the individual or for another; the jeremiad is either to "discourage or encourage", to threaten or give hope. The Puritans had felt that theirs was a failed errand. Thus, as Miller and Bercovitch explain, they created their own mission, writing "allegory and chronicle in the framework of the work of redemption." (14) This sense of mission, as Miller, Bercovitch and this writer all contend, has "the ambiguity of the FIGURA" (14) woven into the very fabric of the American character. It combines the allegorical, historical chronicle with the prophetic. Failure, in this sense, was the concomitant quality of success. The jeremiads expressed not just what was, but also what should be—the dream and the reality. "When Miller emphasized," Bercovitch recalls, "the affirmative 'psychology' of the Puritan sermons, he interpreted the sermons themselves as certain psychologists interpret wish-fulfillment dreams." (17) What was important, he continues, was not that all should end happily, but to uncover "the conflicts that prompted the need for fantasy in the first place." (17) What became the most real was the emotional turbulence of the self-nation, private-public, damned-saved, sacred-secular polemic. Thus in the duplicity of "Jewish" as twice-over American, or American as twofold "Hebrew", the work of Ozick and Lewisohn as so-called Jewish-American writers can be seen in terms of a need to exhort and explain the who, what, where, and how of the America-as-Israel FIGURA. The writing of their "book" becomes/became a chronicle of a secular morality-bound faith in process. In significant ways, both Lewisohn's and Ozick's respective works demonstrate this emotional conflict of personal and impersonal voices; those messages of self and the art emanating from that private place of being and of social/moral responsibilities; raw secularism mixed with abundant sallies launched in the name of morality and redemption against backsliding Americans, American Jews, world Jewry, Gentiles, and Jewish and Gentile intellectuals within a highly intricate, unframed frame of *Midrash* and a long history of Hebraic hermeneutic interpretative modes. For whatever their art represents or means, it is nothing if not the very substance and essence of ambiguity. True, both Ozick and Lewisohn can be said to be vehemently opposed to the vacant moral posturing of the Puritan ethic. Ozick's characterization of Jane in

"The Pagan Rabbi", and Lewisohn's numerous textual and essayistic allusions, such as in *Up Stream*, underscore these writers' jeremiac scorn for the Puritan-American value system. Nonetheless, their very scorn betrays affinities, even gross flirtations with, Puritan-American and Gentile culture in general. The net result is ambiguity, equivocation, meaningful meaninglessness and meaningless meaning. In Cynthia Ozick's "The Pagan Rabbi", Rabbi Kornfeld loses his selfhood in this trap of all meanings and no meanings. As a Talmudic scholar, he is both able to glean meaning but also so able to lose himself in it because of its unframable fluidity. Lewisohn's texts, such as *Up Stream*, *The Case of Mr. Crump* and *The Trumpet of Jubilee*, are also the very essence of linguistic subterfuge where language and meaning are as elusive as they are ambiguous.

Historically and biblically, the act of covenant-making involved the giving of one's "word": orally, but more importantly, in writing. "Getting it in writing" became the historical, juridical, and testimonial proof of God's promise. Covenantal Law, in the form of the Ten Commandments, was not just given/written by God, it was also taken/read by the covenanted community who bore witness to that document. Within the continuum of Israelite literature and history, the work of America's Jewish writers can be seen as an attempt to "tell the story", to bear witness, to get into written form, as a matter of historical fact or fiction (since it is their own personal "fact"), the "Word", written to a community of readers. Each of their respective creative enterprises is a "sign" bearing witness to God's covenant.

The act of telling the story itself has a moral signification in defining, through the narrative construct, the moral responsibilities and morality— or a lack thereof—of the characters as well. "Jewish existence," states Alan L. Berger, "is fundamentally rooted in the notion of covenant."[41] The covenant is the foundation of the Jewish proclamation of redemption, and it announces a special relationship between God and the Israelites, based on two assumptions: the people's witness, and Divine protection. God's love for His chosen people was both inscrutable and freely given. Covenantal existence provides a means for interpreting the dialectical relationship between historical events and religious response. "To put the matter directly, covenant meant a sanctification of history." (Berger 1) As well, that history has to be forever scrutinised. This constant anxious scrutiny of history always leads to ambiguous conclusions. Covenantal existence seeks to express the dialectic between redemption and the discomforting counter-evidence of history. Thus decoding history becomes, and is, the central covenantal activity for American-Jewish writers. This expression has a moral base in the Covenant, but it is an equally secular enterprise. Thus Jewish-American writers, specifically Ozick and Lewisohn, reflect the larger cosmology of Judaic (biblical) hermeneutics. Telling the story as a form of bearing witness to the lives of others is a responsibility, an incumbent debt, as Victoria Aarons states, including both narrative construct and the "action" that dramatizes it. That is, a community of "listeners or readers" is established in the works themselves, wherein the characters and the writers-as-characters in the fiction they create become active participants or witnesses to the stories of others in the fictive community, stories that mirror their own. This imagined history and fictive discovery of the facts of one's past help define the ambiguous self of the present.[42] A duality of voices is thereby created: the character-narrator's struggle to morally define and articulate experience of the past and present which point to a redeeming future, and the writer's implicit and often ironic judgment of that character and him/ herself as character. The Jewish-American writers' storytelling has been not just an attempt to form the writer's individual identity, but a manifestation of "bearing witness". (Aarons 5) It is used as a means of perpetuating and refashioning the identity of a communal heritage. Through this restructuring process, what results is a kind of tradition of discontinuity wherein identity, itself linked to a past, is uncovered by the writer—either as discovered fact or as an imaginative invention itself.

Ozick's and Lewisohn's call is, as Ozick expresses it, for "the recovery of Covenant [that] can be attained only in the living-out of the living Covenant; never among the shamanistic toys of literature."[43] In this is voiced the Midrashic sense of a literature/text, not in the narrow service of an author and his/her text, but the complex interrelation created by a literature that is itself a secular/moral Midrashic commentary on Torah. This "literature" is like the *pilpul* dialectic (not duality) of exploration carried by the imagination into the unknown, even frightening, outer limits of thinking, while hopefully still remaining anchored in the conscience. The only duality that can possibly be termed as such in Lewisohn or Ozick consists of the externalized (not personal), historical battle between Christian and Jewish identity for dominance over the text/ Text.

However paradoxical the form of the dialectic they employ in this war, it nevertheless, as this study asserts, serves both to shore up and to undermine, to clarify and to cloud, the cultural dialectic that their work and lives represent. The term "culture/cultural" is used here to describe and underscore a tangle of what can be broadly equated with the social, educational, religious, economic, artistic—in a word, anthropological—connections between human beings and their environments: the anthropological baggage that each member of the human race contains within him/her, the encoded messages inculcated by the environment and heredity into each and every human entity. In asking why Jews continue to live in America, Ozick's answer is:

> Not only do we flatter Gentiles, we crave the flattery of Gentiles. Often in America we receive it. We have produced a religious philosopher who can define himself as Jew only by means of the pressure of Christian philosophers—he cannot figure out how to be Jewish without the rivalry of polemics, because polemics produce concern and attention, attention flatters. Our indifferent disaffected de-Judaized novelists are finally given the ultimate flattery of mimicry: a celebrated Gentile novelist writes a novel about an indifferent disaffected de-Judaized Jewish novelist.... Jews who yearn faintly after Judaism come to Martin Buber only by way of Christian theologians. ("Yiddish" 171)

For Cynthia Ozick, this cultural dialectic is comprised of her relationship to her Russian shtetl ancestry; (Eastern) Europeanism; her poetic/artistic/aesthetic nature; her Manhattan birth and life there; the Yiddish language and its culture; America; the metropolitanism of East-Coast America; her female gender; a traditional Jewish upbringing; her birth in America/New York just a year before the Great Depression of 1929; being Jewish in America and born early enough to "experience" the Holocaust from its beginning stages to its end; a post-Holocaust world; American-New York anti-Semitism; her orientation to rationally based (as opposed to Chassidic), non-mystically oriented Judaism; her birth in America and native language of English; loyalty and love for Israel; her personal feelings of affinity for and comfort in America; a happy, peaceful childhood growing up in a secure and loving home; and a penetratingly intelligent, highly sensitive and artistic nature.

Ludwig Lewisohn's cultural dialectic is even more complicated. Its components can be listed as: his German birth and ancestry; his early life as a Berliner; the timing of his birth at the height of the *Haskalah*, the Jewish Enlightenment and the general Enlightenment in the Europe of that time; an emotionally unstable father; the consanguinity of his mother and father (first cousins); the financial failures of his father; their inherently uneradicated Jewish/Yiddish roots; their intense pleasure and satisfaction with High German culture (music, literature, philosophy, theatre, the German language); the American South; his artistic/aesthetic/ poetic sensibilities; a penetrating intelligence; the Holocaust; a post-Holocaust world; a highly painful marriage to Mary Crocker, a Gentile grandmother and mother of four nearly twenty years his senior; anti-Semitism; frustration and rejection by the academic world; artistic frustration in the publishing world; desire for personal expression and freedom; his religious connection to Judaism, Methodism, Catholicism and Christianity in general; his Europeanism; his patriotic Americanism; and his revived Jewish identity.

These factors in Ozick and Lewisohn create a dense mesh of ambiguity, contradiction, richness, complexity, and paradox that defy the simplistic logic of a culturally dichotomous characterization, or a historically linear description of a "before and after" (that is, a time "before" they were totally devoted to a Jewish identity as opposed to the time "after" when they discovered the true path). Ozick's and Lewisohn's complex cultural orientations mix with the Hebraically dialectical mode they use as the most natural course of expression for them. Thus, this study finds its point of reference in the societal, nationalistic, religious, linguistic, historical, anthropological and aesthetic dimensions of reality *vis a vis* the two writers under investigation.

When we turn to the history of the Jews in America, we can see it as very much a part of the picture of European-Jewish immigration to America. The various waves of immigration, and the circumstances under which the act of emigrating from the various European points of origin accrued, strongly colored the experience of the immigrant or immigrant family in the new American homeland; a new promised land.

Jewish Eastern-European immigration to America from Eastern Europe, Poland, Rumania, Hungary, Czechoslovakia, Russia, Ukraine, Bulgaria and the Slavic countries, began in the 1880s with the mass immigration of two million Jewish people. The dual revolutions that occurred in the American colonies and France profoundly affected Jews and the world in general. The characteristics of freedom and democratic ideals sharply contrasted with the Jews' ghetto and shtetl life. The rise of anti-Semitism also spurned nationalistic yearnings. As Solomon Grayzel states:

> The modern period has been characterized, furthermore, by a heartbreaking yearning among the Jews for a sense of being at home. During the nineteenth

> century the Jew became a full citizen of his native land, especially in Western Europe and America. But it became clear, when the nineteenth century was two-thirds over, that the advances of the Jews were being spurned and their cooperation rejected by a substantial number of the very people and classes from whom they had expected understanding. A new theory of anti-Jewishness was invented and given a high-sounding name—antisemitism. This was a terrific blow to the Jews who were just beginning to feel at home in the land of their birth. (Grayzel 488)

This new wave of hatred was instrumental in the creation of modern Zionism and its yearning for a Jewish home in Palestine, the Jews' historical biblical homeland.

Ozick's own parents emigrated from northwestern Russia. They arrived in America some time before Ozick's birth in New York in 1928. They emigrated to escape the disastrous rule of Alexander III, who had ascended to power after the assassination of his father by revolutionaries in 1881. The relatively benign rule of the father was replaced by a new terror-filled reign which immediately witnessed a flood of pogroms and spilled Jewish blood. There had been emigration of less than 10,000 in a span of fifty years from 1820 to 1870; the 1870s experienced emigration in excess of 40,000. Thus, during the rule of Alexander II (1855–1881), and his infamous son, Alexander III (extending to the decade before the turn of century), all hopes of the Jews for acceptance and improvement in their lives had disappeared.

The Lewisohn family's emigration to the United States in 1890 occurred not because life in Germany had proved intolerable for them or for Jews in general, but because Ludwig's father had brought the family very close to financial ruin through poor judgment and ill-managed family business investments and assets. The family of Ludwig's mother, Minna Eloesser, had emigrated in 1872 from East Prussia to Berlin when Minna was twelve. Minna had also felt restricted by the generally oppressive life of East Prussian Jewry, the lack of opportunities for females and the great emphasis put on worship and piety. The legal enactments of 1872 in the German social fabric elevated the Jews from outcast to partner. The Jews assimilated in varying degrees, and when they didn't, they changed traditional worship to some more neutral display of Jewishness, or beyond to baptism. Ludwig was born exactly ten years after the formal German emancipation of the Jews. Indeed, for the Lewisohns, as proud and culture-enjoying Berliners, immigration in 1890 to America's Southern shores was indeed a step down.

Cynthia Ozick's early life was strongly affected by her Russian family's upbringing in the Russian Pale. For them, after a long period of shtetl life punctuated by pogroms, life in America, with whatever problems it presented to Jews or immigrant Jews, was a dream come true. In spite of the economic hardships of the Great Depression and post-Depression years, life in New York City afforded every cultural possibility: it was a lively and dynamic environment.

The German immigrants of Lewisohn's time would have found it easier than the East European Jews to melt into American culture. The former were more familiar with an Enlightenment-based cultural environment. In certain ways more sophisticated than the East European Jews, the German Jews were more able to transfer their sense of freedom and liberalism from Germany to America. As traditionalists maintain/maintained, and indeed both Lewisohn and Ozick repeatedly insisted, this liberalism could/would/will lead to their downfall and gradual disappearance as they became more and more absorbed into the mainstream culture. The Russian Jews (mostly Poles who had been absorbed into the Russian state), like the Jews of the other Eastern European countries in the nineteenth century, found life in America both more difficult and easier compared to the German Jews. It was more difficult for the Russian (Polish) Jews of the Pale because they had no expectations that their life under the Czar would or could improve. As well, there was not even a defined base of cultural life or a literature in Russia of that time. As Grayzel asserts:

> Some kind of culture could be found only among extremely few of the Polish and Russian upper classes who had received their training in Western Europe. There was thus nothing in the environment to stimulate the Jews to emulate the non-Jewish population, as was the case in Germany. This resulted in throwing the East European Jews back upon their own cultural resources. Fortunately, the Jewish population of Eastern Europe was large and it possessed a tradition of learning. The masses of the [East European] Jews were not lonely and lost as were the comparatively small number of German Jews; consequently the desire [of the] East European Jews to be adopted by the Christians as equals was confined to a very few. (Grayzel 515–516)

Ozick's background *via a vis* that of Lewisohn, therefore, would explain the stronger attachment/adherence she has had to Judaism for all of her life. Jews of the Russian Pale were in the grasp of a strongly infectious piety. The German Jews, on the other hand, were in the grip of the

(Gentile) Enlightenment. The latter, as Irving Howe describes it, "by contrast, had worked out for themselves a reconciliation between their Judaism, which they saw strictly as a religion, and the styles of Western thought."[44] In opposition to Ozick's background, this specifically German phenomenon could help explain Lewisohn's ambiguous attitudes towards his Jewish ancestry, and the greater complexity of dialectic created by his serial raptures with several forms of Christian belief systems. In the same vein, Ozick describes another form of cultural dialectic:

> that on occasion history can reverse itself, that on occasion the majority will be jealous after the minority, that now an Esau will wish to live in Jacob's tent.
>
> The usual proposition—Jacob putting on goatskins to impersonate Esau—has often and often flowered in history; frequently enough in the mask of fiction. Cultural impersonation is an ancient risk, and remains interesting. ("Esau" 133)

In its totality, therefore, the cultural dialectics at work in Cynthia Ozick and Ludwig Lewisohn's life and works, in their most specific and most universal senses, underscore the nature of a particularly Hebraic consciousness in the paradoxical blend of a human-centered play-filled world, combined with the super-conscious expressions of a prescriptively circumscribed existence. As well, through the non-simplistic cultural dialectic intermesh of a Hebraic America and an American (Gentile) Hebraicness, Ozick and Lewisohn, embracing both secular and messianic modes in their lives and writing, could spin (and were spun into) a complex and enigmatic mix of Gentile-midrashic ambiguity. Interestingly, therefore, within this complex cultural dialectical context, Jewishness itself becomes the cultural basis for a principally Gentile culture, America, in which Hebrew Scripture is the stylistic and structural foundation of its language and all of its linguistic endeavours. The incorporation, mimicry of the signification, style and structure of biblical rhetorical and linguistic modes in the form of the jeremiad from Jeremiah's prophetic language; the unadorned, simple and compressed style of biblical language itself; the Hebrew Scriptural message of moral necessity, mission and chosenness combined within an equally secular frame; all point to Ozick's and Lewisohn's literary output which is itself a vast ambiguity of cultural dialectic. Within this dialectic, what is Judaic cannot be separated from what is not. Thus all American writers, Jewish or Gentile, to some degree and in some way partake in, and are colored by, Hebrew

Scriptural language, its meaning and its philosophy. This is the basis of what Milton R. Konvitz argues, as well as Perry Miller, Sacvan Bercovitch and Sam B. Girgus and scores of other scholars. Addressing American Jewry, Girgus, in his significantly entitled book, asserts:

> The history of Jews in America is to a considerable extent the history of an idea. It is the story of how Jewish history was transformed by the idea of America and how, in turn, Jewish writers, intellectuals, artists, and public figures helped to sustain and modernize this idea.[45]

Jewish-American writers, or American writers who are also Jews, thus carry a heavily weighted bundle of complicated cultural baggage. For in this vein, they are both doubly Jewish and also twice-over American; they can claim a special, even preeminent, place in the history of American letters. Thus Jews who are in equal measure vociferously and undeniably Jewish, and who claim cultural allegiance to America and all she represents, can in all truth claim, as Lewisohn and Ozick have done, that they see no contradiction in identifying both as Jews and Americans. Even more so, they can occupy a special place in American culture in the naturally Hebraic nature of their (Jewish) American voices. Ozick sums up what amounts to an (ambiguous) explanation of the complicated nature, as manifested in Ozick's and Lewisohn's life and work, of cultural dialectic:

> Gentile Readers, should this essay invite any, may or may not be surprised at this self-portrait of a third generation American Jew (though the first to have been native born) perfectly at home [in America] and yet perfectly insecure, perfectly acculturated and yet perfectly marginal. I am myself sometimes taken aback by these contradictions, but what I do *not* feel uneasy about is the thesis of American pluralism, which, I think, calls for a mood vividly different from that of Saint Paul in the ancient world. Paul's tactical "Be all things to all men" cannot apply; my own striving is to be one thing all the time, and to everyone, to speak in the same voice to every interlocutor, Gentile or Jew; not to have one attitude or subject matter (or imagining or storytelling) for one kind of friend and another for another kind. ("Yiddish" 152)

Ozick's ambiguous message here as both a Jew and an American, a citizen of a Christian as well as a Judaized America, perfectly fits the concept of cultural dialectic that is the subject of this study of Cynthia Ozick and Ludwig Lewisohn.

Notes

1   Hayden White, *The Content of Form: Narrative Discourse and Historical Representation* (Baltimore: The Johns Hopkins University Press, 1987) x.
2   Cynthia Ozick, "The Lesson of the Master", *Art & Ardor* (New York: Alfred A. Knopf, 1983) 295.
3   Raymond Williams, *Keywords* (Glasgow: William Collins, 1976) 76.
4   Raymond Williams, *The Sociology of Culture* (Chicago: University of Chicago Press, 1981) 9.
5   Raymond Williams, "Base and Superstructure in Marxist Cultural Theory", *Contemporary Literary Criticism: Literary and Cultural Studies*, ed. Robert Con Davis and Ronald Schleifer (New York: Longman, 1989) 379.
6   Victor Strandberg, *Greek Mind/Jewish Soul: The Conflicted Art of Cynthia Ozick* (Madison: University of Wisconsin Press, 1994).
7   Cynthia Ozick, "The Magisterial Reach of Gershom Sholem", *Art & Ardor* 140.
8   See Emanuel Kant, *Critique of Pure Reason*, Trans. N. Kemp (London: Smith Macmillan, 1924) 604–610.
9   G.W.F. Hegel, *The Phenomenology of Mind*, Trans. J.B. Baillie (London: Allen and Unwin, 1949) 123–127.
10   A.N. Whitehead, *The Adventure of Ideas* (New York: Mentor, 1964) 229.
11   W.T. Jones, *The Classical Mind, Vol 1: The History of Western Philosophy* (New York: Harcourt Brace and Jovanovich, 1980) 191–192.
12   Geoffrey H. Hartman and Sanford Budick, *Midrash and Literature* (New Haven: Yale University Press, 1986) xi.
13   Jacques Derrida, "Structure, Sign and Play in the Discourse of the Human Sciences", *Contemporary Literary Criticism* 232.
14   Passages quoted from the Jewish Bible, in this instance and hereafter, are taken from the Hebrew Masoretic Text, which exists in one version only. All translations to English are by Jane Statlander.
15   *The Oxford Dictionary of the Jewish Religion*, ed. R. J. Zvi Werblowsky and Geoffrey Wigoder (New York: Oxford University, 1997) 277–278.
16   These words are capitalized in order to emphasize that they are competing forces considered equal to God, the word for whom is also capitalized.
17   Joseph Dan, "Midrash and the Dawn of Kabbalah", *Midrash and Literature* 128.
18   Cynthia Ozick, Footnote to "Bech Passing", *Art & Ardor* 122.
19   Cynthia Ozick, "Justice (Again) to Edith Wharton", *Art & Ardor* 18.
20   Cynthia Ozick, "Esau as Jacob", *Art & Ardor* 134.
21   Matthew Arnold, *Culture and Anarchy* (Cambridge: Cambridge University Press, 1960) 20.

22   See also Walter Kaufman's introductory remarks to Leo Baeck's *Judaism and Christianity* (New York: Leo Baeck Institute, 1958).

23   Ralph Melnick, *The Life and Work of Ludwig Lewisohn, Vol I, II* (Detroit: Wayne State University Press, 1998) II: 521–522. Melnick cites "Four to Receive Degrees, Chapels to Be Dedicated," *Justice* 21 (October 1955), 1, 23; and "Three Faiths in Harmony", *Life* 21 (November 1955) 113.

24   Cynthia Ozick, "Toward a New Yiddish", *Art & Ardor* 162.

25   Solomon Grayzel, *A History of the Jews* (New York: Mentor, 1968) 63–64.

26   *The Authorized Version of the Holy Bible of 1611* (Third Millennium Publications: Gary, SD, 1998).

27   Jeremy Silver and Bernard Martin, *A History of Judaism, Vol. I* (New York: Basic Books, 1974) 23.

28   Jeremy Cohen. *The Friars and the Jews: The Evolution of Medieval Anti-Judaism* (Cornell: Cornell University Press, 1982) 19.

29   Sacvan Bercovitch, *The Puritan Origins of the American Self* (New Haven: Yale University Press, 1975) 36–37.

30   Perry Miller, *Errand in the Wilderness* (Cambridge: The Belknap Press of Harvard University, 1956) 3.

31   Milton R. Konvitz, *Judaism and the American Idea* (Ithaca: Cornell University Press, 1978) 17.

32   Steven Katz, *Jewish Ideas and Concepts* (New York: Schocken Books, 1977) 156.

33   Perry Miller and Thomas H. Johnson, *The Puritans: A Sourcebook of Their Writings* (New York: Harper and Row, 1938) 43.

34   Perry Miller, *The New England Mind: New Colony to Province* (Boston: Beacon Press, 1953) 24.

35   Gurdon Saltenstall, The Boston General Assembly, 1677. Saltenstall's opening Assembly statement is reproduced in Sacvan Bercovitch, *Typology in Early American Literature* (Boston: The University of Massachusetts Press, 1972) 3.

36   John Norton, "The Evangelical Worshiper", *Three Choices and Profitable Sermons*, Cambridge, 1664) 33. Reproduced by Sacvan Bercovitch, *Typology* 5.

37   Thomas M. Davis, "The Traditions of Puritan Typology", ed. Paul Korshin, *Typologies in England: 1650–1820* (Princeton: Princeton University Press, 1982) 11.

38   Jonathan Culler, *The Pursuit of Signs: Semiotics, Literature, Deconstruction* (Ithaca: Cornell University Press, 1981) 21.

39   Michael Ragussis, "Representation, Conversion and Literary Form: Harrington and the Novel of Jewish Identity", *Critical Inquiry* 16/1 (Autumn 1989) 115. See also Michael Ragussis, *Figures of Conversion: "The Jewish Question" and "English National Identity"* (London: Duke University Press, 1995).

40   Sacvan Bercovitch, *The American Jeremiad* (Madison: University of Wisconsin Press, 1978) xi.

41   Alan L. Berger, *Crisis and Covenant: The Holocaust in American Jewish Fiction* (New York: State University of New York Press, 1985) 1.

42   Victoria Aarons, *A Measure of Memory: Storytelling and Identity in American Jewish Fiction* (Athens: University of Georgia Press, 1996) 1–3.

43   Cynthia Ozick, "Literature as Idol: Harold Bloom", *Art & Ardor* 199.

44   Irving Howe, *World of Our Fathers* (New York: Simon and Schuster, 1976) 497.

45   Sam B. Girgus, *The New Covenant: Jewish Writers and the American Idea* (Chapel Hill: The University of North Carolina Press, 1984) 3.

Chapter Two
Ludwig Lewisohn

Introduction and Background

Ludwig Lewisohn's life and work raise an important and fundamental question about the nature of truth and fancy; the difficult-to-locate boundary between the historical record and fictive "reality"; the line between art and fact. At this intersection is revealed the basic paradox, the ambiguity of historicity and art.

Moreover, the very quintessence of cultural dialectic resides at the heart of this discontinuous, complex mesh; this riddle of the essence of art and nature. Hayden White, in his essay on history and its relationship to the literary endeavor,46 speaks of the "historical account" or the "transformation of the [historical] chronicle into story". (*Metahistory* 5) He questions the very status/nature of the telling or re-telling of history in which "the historian may take it as his task to reinvoke, in a lyrical or poetic manner, the 'spirit' of a past age", (4) the facts of which are now no longer in existence and are unverifiable. Instead, he asks us to consider that "the difference between 'history' and 'fiction' resides in the fact that the historian 'finds' his stories whereas the fiction writer 'invents' his." (6) Nevertheless, the historian, in putting these stories in narrational form, must arrange the events in the story in a way that can be comprehended with a "beginning, middle, and end", (7) exactly as the fiction writer does.

However, this is not to say, as White's concept goes, that literature is false and science, or the recitation of history, true. In this way, stories are created from real-life details and facts, and are also chronicles. (7) Thus in order to render facts into a coherent and understandable form, the storyteller, as well as the historian, must use an imaginative operational mode called "emplotment" (7) through which raw factual data are transformed into narrational stories.

In the Prologue to *Up Stream*, a book that is an "autobiographical" work, Lewisohn asserts:

The world is full of stories, and many of the stories are true. But they are not true enough. An artistic pattern comes between the teller of the tale and his reality.... [Every serious novelist and thinker] has had an anterior vision into which he lets his facts and even his emotions melt. And this anterior vision— of a fable in the one case, of a logical structure in the other—is nothing but a mask. For both the novelist and the philosopher is [sic] only an autobiographer in disguise. Each writes a confession; each is a lyricist at bottom. I too could easily have written a novel or a treatise. I have chosen to drop the mask.[47]

In the indistinct realm of cultural dialectic, the dropping of one mask can reveal yet another, or even multiple masks, disguising other faces. Much has been written, for example, about Lewisohn's "return" to his Jewish roots. This simplistic viewpoint, however, masks a highly complex, indecipherable mesh of diverse and seemingly unrelated components, influences, multiple forces, competing identities and realities.

Five of Lewisohn's works will be dealt with in this study: *Up Stream* (1922), *Holy Land* (1925), *The Case of Mr. Crump* (1926), *The Island Within* (1928) and *Trumpet of Jubilee* (1937). These works will be viewed in light of the time periods in which they were written. This is to say, the study divides Lewisohn's life (1882–1955) and work into three time frames: 1882–1904; 1904–1922; 1922–1955. These divisions are not clear-cut, and the years at the "end" of the earlier ones represent new directions in his life and work that describe an ongoing, and therefore ultimately boundary-less, process.

In other words, the time from his birth in 1882 to his death in 1955 does not reveal a linear, horizontal progression from assimilation to full-blown Jewishness, but rather a net of life-events, creative output and experiences that more closely resemble the nature of *pilpul*, Jewish dialectical argumentation: spirals of consciousness and their manifested creative output, simultaneously emerging and disappearing, on various levels and from varying directions. Although Lewisohn's psychic move from repressed or suppressed Jew, masked with a Christian face, to conscious Jew cannot be denied, what is probably closer to the truth is that Lewisohn's open revelation of his Jewish identity did not preclude the ongoing inclusion in some way, on some level, of everything he felt himself to represent, to "be" before that point. His "coming out" to reveal his Jewishness did not change but merely complicated the dialectic that had been gaining momentum like a massive, rolling snowball from his birth to his death. For example, if Lewisohn as Jew rejected the divinity of the

Jesus he prayed to in his youth, he nevertheless retained the perception of Jesus as part of the ongoing, if perhaps troubling, story of Judaism.

Lewisohn's deconstruction of Christianity also includes a detailed analysis of Christology. He begins his analysis with a retrospective look at the early years of his process of assimilation, when he, as he describes in *Mid-Channel*,[48] "read the Gospels with ready-made reverence and belief." His acceptance of Jesus as his personal savior, he states, never became "complete". (*Mid-Channel* 288) He never dreamed of realizing that "the Gospel narratives" were composed at a much later date than the rest of the Christian Bible, or "of doubting" their "newness and uniqueness or the transcendent quality of their ethical and spiritual revelation." (288) He then quickly realized "that one must probably reject Trinitarian Christianity on scientific grounds." (288) He continues: "I was never so lost as not to honor the instinctive aversion to Christianity of Jews on account of the sufferings and persecution of our people." (288) Calling the Gospels "a pure fiction", he asserts that "Jewish history and Jewish literature... establish the substance of the Gospel narratives within an order of intellectual and religious development, in which they assume a completely different aspect." (288)

He then analyses his "attitude to Jesus", explaining that it went through "three phases". Firstly, he experienced a "liberal Christian" phase, in which he embraced Christianity with the open innocence of an impressionable child. The next phase "was the liberal Jewish" one: "Let bygones be bygones, and let us accept Jesus among the great teachers." (288) Now, however, after some seven years of study of Biblical texts and commentaries, "I know that the Jesus represented in the Gospels was a notable spiritual personality, a mast of human speech at its simplest and highest, but as a teacher neither original nor important." (288–289) Jesus' "positive ethics" are those of the Jewish oral tradition as it existed in some form from the days of Hillel (1 B.C.E.) and his school. Hillel was an early rabbinic authority and Pharisaic leader, Sanhedrin member and Palestinian Jewry spokesperson, and liaison with Roman officials. (*Religion* 323) The controversial sayings attributed to Jesus rest upon his large margin of ignorance of the great tradition of his people. Instead of informing himself better, "he substituted... an uninquiring anger that neither loves one's enemy nor turns the other cheek." (289) We "know Jesus only through the Gospels which are late and distinctly anti-Jewish and controversial." (*Mid-Channel* 289)

Although it is the Gospels' Jesus that the world worships, it is this very Jesus, this Jew, who never "deeply touched the world." (289) The thing that "has moved men... founded empires and destroyed them again, is the christ myth with its great metaphysical drama of original sin and ...vicarious atonement... heaven and salvation." (289) One fact glares out at us: "Jesus was an observant Jew." (289) In fact, the oldest Gospel, *Mark*, takes Jesus' "Jewishness most profoundly for granted (12:29): 'First of all commandments is, "Hear, O Israel, the Lord our God is one Lord."' What have the Trinitarians done with that saying? Jesus declared the Unity of God. The Sh'ma Israel of the ages was on his lips." (290)

Of Jesus' Last Supper, typologized from the first Passover Seder, Lewisohn says:

> Were it not for the furious anti-Jewishness of the militant early Church from which the Gospels sprang, we might have had record of his using some legend or ritual, some *Haggadah shel Pesach* [instructive Passover stories] where-with to celebrate the feast of his people.... He came to die, and on his lips was that cry from the twenty-second *Psalm*: "*Eli, Eli, Lama sabachatani* [My God, my God, why did you forsake me?]".[49] (290)

The church, Lewisohn reminds us, followed Jesus in time, not vice versa. "This Jew died at the hands of the Romans a conscious martyr among the martyrs of Israel." Any hostility of Jesus, Lewisohn continues, to any parts of his forefathers' beliefs was due to ignorance of the oral tradition. (292) Lewisohn ascribed Jesus' hostility toward the scribes and Pharisees, the biblical scholars of the time, to the gaps in Jesus' knowledge of

> the teachings of the tradition well; and partly it may have been that the young idealist from Galilee, the villager, resented the learned and subtle people of cities and councils. But it may also have been that he had had unfortunate personal encounters with hypocritical individuals that prejudiced him so bitterly. (293)

In summing up, Lewisohn adds that Jesus' sermonizing

> falls cleanly and immediately into two parts: the far greater part which re-states with an incomparable spiritual sweetness and poetic persuasiveness the traditional ethics which Jesus, the Jew, received from his Jewish predecessors and which is therefore true but not new; the smaller part which, expressing his ascetic condemnation of human life, his moral pessimism, his assumption of a mystical and supra-human authority, the Jew rejects at once with every

instinct of his heart and mind as both impossible practically and philosophically absurd. (296–297)

Lewisohn's christological analysis has all the markings of ambiguity: Jesus is both of, and not of, Hebraicism; both of, and not of, Christianity. He shows emotional sympathy, but also intellectual scorn, for this simple but charismatic Jewish personality, Jesus.

The sole offspring of Jacques and Minna (Eloesser) Lewisohn, Ludwig was born in Berlin, Germany on May 30, 1882, to Jewish free-thinking first cousins. His parents, like most German Jewry, were greatly influenced by eighteenth century Enlightenment rationalism, and by Moses Mendelssohn (1729–1796), the German-Jewish emancipation advocate, philosopher, secular and biblical scholar, whose thought profoundly influenced German Jews. (*Religion* 454–455)

Liberal thought can create boundaries that are difficult to locate or define. When these boundaries are connected to culture and personal identity, what often emerges is a picture which defies simplification or reduction to monotonic categories. The impact of the life and thought of Mendelssohn on the lives of German Jewry cannot be overestimated. He began as a brilliant young Talmudic student who become a self-taught scholar, not just in Judaic learning but in Western philosophy and ancient and contemporary languages as well. Like other German Jews of that time, he was profoundly influenced by Enlightenment liberalism. Never denying his identity as a Jew, Mendelssohn began to reflect on the status and position of Jews, and tried to offer some solution to the dilemma of German Jews who desired to remain connected to their heritage but who also wished to be a part of the larger cultural environment around them. This was exactly the issue that Mendelssohn addressed. He tried to re-dress the mental walls that Jews, so long excluded from Gentile culture, had built as a complement to the actual ghetto that had always been imposed on them. He began by translating the *Tanach*[50] into German, and a biblical commentary in Hebrew written with the perspective and cultural milieu of the then-contemporary German Jews. As well, he persuaded wealthy German-Jewish friends to establish a Jewish day school with a dual, German-Hebrew, curriculum. Mendelssohn was severely criticized by the majority of German Jews of that time. His ideas were viewed as too outlandish. Nevertheless, deeply drawn to the liberalism of the Enlightenment, he believed, perhaps naively, that Jews could be liberal and also maintain traditional beliefs. True to the liberal influence, he

insisted that individual consciousness was supreme. He neglected, however, to foresee that the liberalism of one Jewish generation—especially
this first one—could bring annihilation of Jews and their tradition in the
generations to follow, since they would not have (as he had) a strong
foundation in Talmudic and biblical learning.

Ironically, while Mendelssohn was breaking down barriers on the
Jewish side, the Christians continued their ages-old exclusion and slander
of the Jews on the other. As Solomon Grayzel explains: "In Prussia itself
not even Mendelssohn could obtain the right to live as a free man. Again
and again the king refused to grant this fighter for German culture the
right to consider himself a permanent resident of Berlin." (Grayzel 471)
In many ways, Mendelssohn's life and thought were both a reflection of,
and a model for, German Jewry in the century and a half that preceded
the Holocaust.

The first time frame, from Lewisohn's birth on May 30, 1882, until
1904, can be represented by five value-culture systems: German, Jewish,
American, Southern, Christian. All five co-mingled into a hard-to-define,
indistinguishable mixture, illuminating a rich cultural dialectic in which
each dialectical shift became more complicatedly composed of still
newer, more complicated combinations.

Much has been said of Lewisohn's linear journey from assimilation
to return. For example, Adolph Gillis in his 1933 study asserts that the
Lewisohns "were Jews not by conviction but by sole accident of birth…
[and] were to all appearances as Christian and German as their neighbors."[51] Gillis' statement, in retrospect, seems rather myopic and
ill-founded. He appears to base his assertions on Lewisohn's own assessment and perception of his life in Berlin and South Carolina. As well,
Gillis would appear to be so close to Lewisohn's cultural milieu that he
seems to have forgotten—if indeed his assertion is valid at all—that it is
nearly impossible for one's cultural, native, and ethnic origins to leave
virtually no traces. The Lewisohn physiognomy would have been enough
to mark the family as Jewish. Thus to the Christians around them, be it in
Berlin or South Carolina, they were always, unmistakably "Jewish". Nevertheless, the Lewisohn family's identification with Judaism was, if not
overtly strong, in truth never broken. As Ralph Melnick in his recent
biography of Lewisohn remarks about Ludwig's mother, who bitterly
fought with her first cousin/husband on this point, the identification, if
not actual observance in some way of Jewish tradition, was not a nego-
tiable point. Even the gut aversion of Ludwig's father to such

observances could have been a display of the battle he was fighting within himself . As Melnick describes:

> When Minna died, she took with her Ludwig's last visible connection with the Jewish world from which she had drawn much of her own strength during the long years of isolation and disappointment. German and French culture had been her means of outward expression, but her spiritual life had been rooted in the ethos of her Jewish ancestors and to a timeless place, separated from both the America to which she had given her son and the Berlin in which she had spent her own adolescence and early married life. She was Ludwig's tie to this older world, to the religious claims of her people, which seemed to violate, in an increasingly positive way, the overbearing rationality of the academic and literary communities to which he aspired. (Melnick I: 174)

The young Lewisohn's life in Berlin was a seemingly contradictory tapestry of Gentile-German and Jewish ways, attitudes, consciousness and thinking. As the author expresses it in *Up Stream*: "In truth, all the members of my family seemed to feel that they were Germans first and Jews afterwards." (*Up Stream* 17)

With Lewisohn born just a decade after the German civil legislation that gave Jews full social and civil rights equal to Gentile citizens, this period exactly corresponded to a highly impressionable age in this, and any, child's life. Young Ludwig and his family savored their culturally sophisticated Berlin life as fully free citizens. As well, with the large migration of Jews from the small outlying towns to the big cities that occurred as a result of the new optimism and freedom, many Jews came to Berlin and the other large cities to enjoy their new status. Thus with greater numbers of Jews in the cities, plus the liberalization of civil laws, Jews could also enjoy the familiarity of social life with other Jews who were also enjoying their new freedoms. In this environment, as Melnick explains, "acculturation became widespread" (Melnick 1: 23) in one way or another.

Lewisohn's description of his paternal grandfather in *Up Stream* highlights the cultural paradoxes at play in his family in particular, and the all-pervasive influence that the general tenor of the Enlightenment had on German-Jews in general:

> My people were Jews of unmixed blood and descent who had evidently lived for generations in the North and North East of Germany. I have before me now a picture of my grandfather taken in the sixties. Despite the fact that he performed rabbinical functions to scattered congregations in East Prussia, I

observe that in contravention of the Law, his face is clean-shaven and that he has no ear-locks; he is clad in the Western European fashion of his day.... He had much rabbinical learning, but a whimsical contempt for the ritual law; his familiar friends were the Protestant Pastor and the schoolmaster of the village. (*Up Stream* 15)

Lewisohn's mother, Minna, as he describes in *Up Stream*, was born in East Prussia of which Poland was also a part. At age twelve, along with her brothers and widowed mother, she migrated in 1872 to Berlin when her father, the rabbi, died. Minna was greatly dissatisfied with the twelve years of her life spent in the East European town from which she came. As Lewisohn puts it: "Her girlhood was not happy. The social environment was cruelly rigid; one breathed according to law. She wanted to enter a seminary for teachers; she also begged to be allowed to learn book-keeping." (22) Even in Berlin she continued to be "intensely troubled, rebellious against the forces that held her." (22) She was considered "unconventional and shrank more and more within herself." (22)

The only understanding and sympathetic ear she received was from Ludwig's future father, Jacques, her first cousin. They felt very compatible with each other. They had the same tastes in literature, music and drama. As well, Jacques was said to be poised to inherit a lot of money from his foster parents. As Ludwig observes, his mother "thought, quite rightly, that money means liberty in the higher and finer as well as in the coarser and more obvious sense." (23) They were married in 1881 and Ludwig was born a year later, within a mere decade of the emancipation of the Jews in German society. Ludwig was thus born into life in a fully liberated country whose Jewish population felt great optimism for the future, and to parents who could afford him a comfortable life-style which, as Melnick says, "came to resemble that of most non-Jewish, progressive, middle-class Berliners whose world they, like so many other Jews of their social group hoped to join." (Melnick I: 25) Lewisohn describes his mother in *Up Stream* as sincerely Jewish, but nevertheless "a spiritual child of the German folk... the very soul of her homeland." (*Up Stream* 21) This attitude from his mother, coupled with the extreme secularity and progressive mindset of his father—besides the general enlightenment environment around them—created in the little boy both a disdain for the cultural backwardness of Oriental Jewish belief and a desire to meld into the larger, highly sophisticated High German, Berlin cultural milieu.

In *Up Stream*, Lewisohn describes the two distinct cultural strands of his early childhood in Berlin. One is represented by the scene of the Lewisohn home on Christmas Eve. The young boy excitedly waits for the first glimpse of the Christmas tree and the toys prepared there for him: "And my mother takes me by the hand and leads me to the table and I feel as though I were myself walking straight into a fairy tale." (18)

Juxtaposed with this vividly recollected image is the one of Ludwig being taken to the large and majestic synagogue on Yom Kippur, the holiest day of the year in the Jewish calendar, to "see" his maternal grandmother who, as Lewisohn describes it, attended services there as was her "custom, in pious remembrance of her husband." (18) Of these two images, Lewisohn, as he writes in *Up Stream*, experienced the Christian one as "native and familiar to the heart of the child that I was." (19) Regarding the second, he perceived the Jewish scene as "a little weird and terrifying and alien." (19)

When Jacques, Ludwig's emotionally unstable father, lost all of his small inherited fortune in reckless and ill-advised business ventures, Minna suggested that they emigrate to St. Matthew's, South Carolina, America, to join her brother Siegfried and his family, who had been living there for many years. In 1890, when Ludwig was eight years old, the family left Germany bound for America's shores. Slowly, the joy of the thought that this emigration would snap Jacques out of his constant depression, changed to shock then horror. As Melnick expresses it: "Wonder became terror as parents and child looked with rapidly growing apprehension upon the unpolished, rural world that was replacing the lost civility of Berlin." (Melnick I: 27)

Embarking first in Hoboken, New Jersey, the family finally arrived by boat at the Charleston, South Carolina harbor, then to St. Matthew's.[52] Lewisohn recalls, "I very distinctly shared my parents' sense of the wildness, savagery and roughness of the scene, their horrified perception of its contrast to anything they had ever known or seen." (*Up Stream* 37) Their very first meeting with Uncle Siegfried did not improve their initially negative perception of life in America or the South:

> At ten o'clock we reached Saint Mark's and trudged out of the car. A man with heavy moustaches and clad in a red sweater lifted me from the platform. From my previous experience of life I judged him to be a porter or a cabby. To my disgust and amazement he called me by name and kissed me on the mouth. It was my uncle. (37)

This ostensibly remembered scene by Lewisohn of his first encounter with Siegfried, as Melnick asserts, clashes with the account given by Siegfried's daughter, and also serves to underscore the culture shock suffered by shifting from a genteel Berlin life to America's South:

> The recollections of Siegfried's daughter Cora provide an important basis upon which to judge the accuracy of her cousin Ludwig's memory, and the depth of his trauma. Though the years undoubtedly affected her ability to recall the past, as they had his, the extent of their perceptual differences is most telling. The gruff, sweater-clad uncle who became Ludwig's earliest memory of St. Matthew's was, according to Cora, "a very educated gentleman, graduate of two colleges... [who] to his last day never wore a sweater." Siegfried, in fact, had been greatly upset by reading in *Up Stream* what he considered a grossly inaccurate description of his first encounter with his nephew. (Melnick I: 33)

As well, as Lewisohn recalls his aunt in *Up Stream*, she, "though a woman of some kindly qualities, was a Jewess of the Eastern tradition, narrow-minded, given over to the clattering ritual of ...'meaty' and 'milky'—and very ignorant." (*Up Stream* 41) The author also remembers her "scolding her little girls in a mixture of Yiddish and English." (41) However, again contradictory statements by Cora describe her mother, Siegfried's wife, in an entirely different light:

> But the very ignorant Aunt Fannie of Ludwig's memory little resembled the woman Cora remembered as her mother—a native Charlestonian, graduate of its well-respected Memminger High School (for young ladies), with an excellent command of English, a little knowledge of German (acquired from her husband), and not the slightest familiarity with a single word of Yiddish, the language Ludwig recalled her using on numerous occasions to scold her children. (Melnick I: 33)

Interestingly, Cora also vividly recalled her "Uncle Jack" as a very angry man who resented "Judaism and that my mother kept up the Tradition, lighting Friday night candles, Passover, High Holidays, etc. He thought himself above everybody, and my mother was nothing compared to his intelligence." (33) Perhaps this was a way of emotionally distancing himself from these too-openly Jewish relatives. Nevertheless, Jacque's personality, as described by Melnick and Lewisohn, did not lend itself to building warm relationships.

Minna, on the other hand, was greatly loved by Fannie and the rest of the family. The Eloessers could easily see "how greatly the continuous tension between Jacques and Minna had disturbed Ludwig, who witnessed their many bitter quarrels over the issue of religion." (33) Minna's answer to the conflict of belief systems and cultures was to attempt to strike a balance. She consented to allow Ludwig to take part in church activity after "asserting her right to maintain some minimal level of Jewish observance within her home." (34) Also, probably because her own English language skills were so inadequate, she believed that Ludwig would quickly acquire a good level of English by attending the Christian full-time schools.

Though they maintained contact with their relatives, they chose not to socialize with the other Jews or even the German-Americans. Ludwig's parents sought out what they perceived as the best social elements: "Hence, without a shadow of disloyalty to their German training, they desired to be at one with such of their English-speaking countrymen as shared their tastes in art and... literature and... their outlook on life." (*Up Stream* 58)

Here in this South Carolina town, the Lewisohns, in Ludwig's own description of the event, began their fall from high culture to a much lower one. Their repugnance toward what they viewed (at least from Ludwig's perceptions) as the Eloessers' cultural backwardness was accompanied by an equal aversion to the former laborers and shopkeepers of the Gentile-German world they left behind, who the Lewisohns viewed as equally lacking in culture. If they didn't associate with any of these groups in Berlin, so their logic went, why should they now? Like the Eloessers, the other Jews were tradition-oriented, and fully respected and accepted by the Gentile community because of it. As Lewisohn relates in *Up Stream*, it was the Lewisohns whom Christians of the town did not trust, especially Jacques, because of his agnostic or atheistic attitudes. Only "one Jew" was regarded with "suspicion by the severer among his Gentile neighbors. The reason was strange and carried great significance: he did not perform the external rites of the Jewish faith." (42–43)

Generally speaking, the Lewisohns were not able to find their social or cultural niche. Acceptance of the Jews of the town was impossible for them. Even in 1916, in the Introduction to Georg Hirschfeld's *The Mothers*, the author could speak of this type of Jew in terms of "archaic Orientalism" which was the very antithesis of High Culture, sophistication and "the finest artistic sensitiveness and power."[53]

Nevertheless, by degrees the family became more and more socially isolated, while Ludwig apparently grew more and more fervently

Christian, which he, and no doubt his parents, believed would gain him entry and acceptance into the best of schools. As Ludwig describes his mother, she constantly stood holding a German-English dictionary. Minna taught Ludwig so well that he was accepted to the High School of Charleston at the age of eleven years. He desperately wanted to belong, to find his place. Upon entering the school, he became a baptized Methodist. As he declares in *Up Stream*: "I accepted Jesus as my personal Savior, and cultivated, with vivid faith, the habit of prayer in which I persisted for many years." (*Up Stream* 50–51) By age 10, as Lewisohn asserts, "my emotional assimilation into the social group of which I was a physical member was complete." (51) At the same time, while beginning to withdraw from the Jewish children in his village, he continued to nurture his "old life" of reading German Teutonic tales. (51) In his initial year there, he was also "taunted with being a foreigner and a Jew." (65)

The high school gave him a strong basis in the classics, cultivated in him an inherently keen aesthetic sense and brought him to identify himself as a writer. From this high school, as well, Lewisohn met what he perceived to be the very essence and embodiment of "the peculiar ideal of the Christian gentleman. [This high school principal] had both sweetness and strength, profound piety and wide charity." (66) This kind of Christian became the model for Lewisohn's "good" Christian type and helped bring greater complexity to the dialectic at work in his life.

If the principal became the epitome for him of a positive form of Christianity, his Latin teacher, Della Torre, was in Lewisohn's eyes the combined, exact equivalent of Germanic high Culture and breeding, plus the aesthetic sensibilities of the artist-writer. Lewisohn expresses great admiration for Della Torre's immense influence in his life: his balanced and healthy personality; religiously devout but still able to enjoy life; art-loving but free of professional jealousy; and perhaps most importantly, the appreciation of literature he awakened in Lewisohn.

From this point on, only literature in the English language would occupy the young teenager's thoughts, energies and time. Abandoning all German literature of his past, even the German language, Lewisohn became an ardent Anglophile and literary aesthete. Most importantly, these teachers inspired Lewisohn to become a teacher of the English language and its literature; but, most essentially, a writer. The author describes the awareness of himself as a writer and aesthete:

It was in the third year of High School. He was teaching us to scan Virgil. We were repeating a passage in unison. Suddenly he swung on his heel and pointed his finger straight at me: "That is the only boy who has a natural ear for verse!" he cried. A keen, strange quiver went through me. I realized the meaning suddenly of the constant scribbling which I had been impelled to during the preceding months. I had a gift for literature! I knew it now; I never doubted it again. My fate had found me. (68)

Having ostensibly abandoned his Jewishness and all Teutonic connections, embraced America, the South, and with it Christianity, as his own, and now, secure in his identity as a writer and aesthete in/of the English tongue, he felt confident enough to say: "It is clear then that, at the age of fifteen, I was an American, a Southerner and a Christian. My home, it may be urged, was foreign in spirit." (77) He believed that the process of becoming a full American was "complete". (77) He, nevertheless, could say that his American self was not identical to his friends at the schools he attended by its

touch of self-consciousness and... militancy. It was at this time that, in my thoughts and emotions, I came upon a distinct and involuntary hostility to everything either Jewish or German. I seemed to have a premonition that, in some subtle way, these elements in my life and fate might come between me and the one thing in the world I cared for supremely—the poetry of the English tongue. (77)

In truth, literature and writing became the matrix of the complex dialectic in his life and work. It was the one common denominator and focal point of reference for all strands of cultural dialectic operating in his life and work. As well, it was probably his writing talent that helped him gain entry to genteel Southern society. In 1897, after four years in the High School of Charleston, Ludwig graduated at age fifteen. He soon after began undergraduate studies at the College of Charleston. It was his luck that his beloved teacher, Thomas Della Torre, was also transferred to there from the high school. Lewisohn does not identify him by name in *Up Stream*. Della Torre should not be confused with the real-life Harris, Ferris, Lewisohn's teacher and literary mentor. But in spite of all Lewisohn had done to "advance" himself in high Southern society, Harris[54] "never, I think, quite forgave me for being what I am." (83) His mother, Minna, always "had a perception, unreasonable but very real, of the ultimate truth.... And often my mother would hint at a touch of disloyalty in him to me." (83) In fact, the writer could admit that "in the best and deepest hours we spent together there was in him a shadow of withdrawal from me—a shadow of watchfulness, of guardedness.... A shadow, but it was there." (83)

Nevertheless, Lewisohn gave the whole of his being, thoughts, feelings and motivation over to total immersion in his beloved teacher's perspective. Lewisohn also absorbed Harris' disdain for American culture and zeal for everything that England stood for. "His attitude to the intellectual and artistic life of America," Lewisohn explains in *Up Stream*, "was a little detached, a little patronising, a little amused." (84) The only thing worth taking seriously "in American life to him was its continuing of those English social traditions within our older commonwealths of which he was the product." (84) Harris was the typical Southerner, Anglo-American and Virginian aristocrat. In contrast, Thomas Della Torre, Lewisohn's Latin instructor, was of Italian descent, with a burning, energetic nature and high aesthetic sense. (Melnick I: 44)

During this period of his life, Lewisohn enjoyed the friendship of a number of wealthy and influential members of Charleston society. Nearly every one of them was a "Pan-Angle" of unmixed blood—except for one: "But he, a wealthy Jewish physician who had turned Methodist in his boyhood, avoided all questionable subjects, prayed at love feasts in church and, though he surreptitiously distributed alms among the poor Jews of the city, achieved a complete conformity of demeanor." (*Up Stream* 87)

What is striking here is the re-reflection onto Lewisohn's own perception of himself and other Jews who became Christians but always remained Jews. By turning Methodist, the physician should have been considered a Methodist; but, like Lewisohn's reference to his basic identity as a "Jewish physician", the doctor nevertheless always remained a Jew. Strangely, Lewisohn tells us that he continued to attend "the Methodist church, taught Sunday School and was a leader in the [church's] Epworth League." The reason for continuing this connection, the author states, was "partly through the influence and friendship of the physician" and also because he found a lot of "unreserved human friendliness among these people. And I needed this." (88) Nevertheless at those critical points in his life when friendship could have made all the difference, Lewisohn ultimately "came [to] a point at which I felt excluded.... As tribesmen their resistance to me was tacit but final." (88–89) It was for this reason that, although Lewisohn "was the most prominent student on the [college] campus", he was not admitted to a Greek college fraternity. "I did not know then," he observes, "that the fraternities do not admit Jews." (89) At age eighteen, he was having an all-too-painful lesson in the conflicting polarities of cultural and ethnic identities.

Also by this age, Lewisohn had all but replaced his fervor in religion with the same intensity in literature and writing. As he says in *Up Stream*, "the world began to clear for me." (89) He began to analyze and perceive the talk and actions of the Gentile society around him with great clarity and objectivity. He began to feel more and more isolated from the society around him, as his intellectual and aesthetic perceptions became more in focus. He began to move from a Christian to a secular, naturalistic point of view. Reading Huxley, Darwin, Draper and Lecky, and discovering a new cosmology of the universe, he concluded: "This picture of the universe was so overwhelmingly and evidently nearer the truth than that represented by Christian doctrine that all my emotional forts collapsed at once." (91)

Studying at Charleston College for an undergraduate and graduate degree at the same time, he chose Matthew Arnold as the subject of his Masters thesis. He was profoundly influenced by this English writer and thinker, who like Lewisohn, had moved from being an ardent Christian to a humanist and naturalist. Fully throwing himself into the ethical pessimism of Jonathan Swift, Samuel Johnson and Matthew Arnold, Lewisohn, especially under Arnold's influence, fell into an ever-growing scepticism. Arnold's inherent genteelism, elegance of manner, soul and thought were offset by a Jeremiacally judgemental attitude toward the middle-class and what he considered vulgarly poor taste. Arnold's polemics were reserved for American and English Puritanism. His frill-free austerity, elite sense of nobility and courage in the face of his dead faith were all extremely relevant to Lewisohn's life as well. Thus it was logical for Lewisohn to choose Matthew Arnold for his Master of Arts thesis. As Gillis tells us, Lewisohn quoted Arnold's lines from "Empedocles on Aetna": "Once read thy own breast aright,/ And thou hast done thy [sic., with] fears;/ Man gets no other light,/ Search he a thousand years./ Sink, in thyself! There ask what ails thee, at that shrine." (Gillis 7) From now on Lewisohn, like Arnold, would believe only in himself.

Arnold's *Culture and Anarchy* is an analysis of English and American societies, specifically those elements in both cultures that have a bearing on his great cosmological duality of Hebraism and Hellenism. While apparently sympathetic to Jews, a deeper inspection reveals a perception of Christianity's role as first the replacement, then superseder, and finally transformer of Hebraicism into a distinctly different and, as Arnold implies, superior belief system. This is evident in the following assertion:

> But the intense and convinced energy with which the Hebrew, both of the Old and of the New Testament, threw himself upon his ideal of righteousness, and which inspired the incomparable definition of the great Christian virtue, faith—"*the substance of things hoped for, the evidence of things not seen*"— this energy of devotion to its ideal has belonged to Hebraism alone. (Arnold 38)

The Hebrew, synonymous with the Jewish people of the past, present and future, as known and accepted from Hebrew Scripture, has been transformed into a newer, perfected model: the believer in Jesus as the savior of the Jewish people and the world. In parallel, Lewisohn read himself as a disguised Jew parading as an American, Southern, Christian. Having unmasked the guise of his once-Christian face, he cannot be sure of what in truth is revealed as his public or private face/s. Arnold, on the other hand, needs no mask. In the complex dialectic that is his life and work, Lewisohn is perpetually the man of his Gentile tribe, even in rebellion against that tribe. A demasked Lewisohn reveals the Jew under the surface—or at least the Jewish physiognomy that was impossible to hide. There are other masks being demasked and masked again. This constitutes the very early stage in Lewisohn's complex intellectual development and the multi-cultural evolutionary process of the complicated dialectic operating in his life and work. In terms of Arnold, Lewisohn seems to have separated Matthew Arnold the human being from Arnold the intellectual. Lewisohn continued to admire Arnold as the kind, magnanimous human being he was. Even in 1950, years after Lewisohn began his re-reading and re-analysis of all that he had read in his youth, he still continued to admire the great human qualities that Arnold represented. On one of his rare vacations, as Melnick documents, the author carefully chose his reading material:

> There was certainly enough else to keep him going in the interim, enough to exercise his mind and emotions. On his table for reading that summer were Reinhold Niebuhr's *Human Character and Destiny* ("Can't follow him to

ultimate conclusions but infinitely prefer him to the beastly pagans"), Brander Matthews's own copy of Matthew Arnold's letters ("discarded by Columbia Library; next discarded by Brandeis Library"), and the Buddha's discourses. (Melnick II: 393)

Lewisohn's choice of reading matter reveals a complex intellectual, cultural, emotional, dialectical mesh, and a mental inquisitiveness with a superimposed and interwoven Jewish consciousness. On this reading material Melnick comments:

> The latter [Buddha's discourses] in particular, struck him, "despite their pessimism, their yearning for the *reant*, for nothingness, [as] a triumph of the human spirit of the first order," especially in Karl Eugene Neumann's exquisite translation, an "unimaginably great achievement." Yet he couldn't help thinking that here again was "another terrifying instance of the losses which assimilation inflected [sic, inflicted] on the Jewish people." Why hadn't Neumann devoted such brilliance to Jewish text instead? (393)

This complexity included Lewisohn's attitude about German and everything connected to German culture. At the same time that he was translating and re-reading Goethe and keeping up his contact with the German friends he acquired along the way. As Melnick notes, Lewisohn was enable to feel completely satisfied with German culture but was also unable to separate himself from his German past. The same was true for Arnold and the other writers he had grown to love. "Listening to a recording of Mahler's songs, he was struck by this inner conflict." (393–394) Lewisohn was feeling greatly wounded by the hurt that "Western culture" had inflicted in his life and in those of other Jews. So much of its culture broke "'down into filth, ordure and utter bestiality.'" (394) Of American and English culture in particular, he bitterly reveals, "'I studied Old English and Gothic and middle English and Middle High German and did not dream of the one thing needful to such a being as I am in such a world as the present.'" (394) Now, in mid-life, Lewisohn would have to make up for the time he had given over to secular study. He was ready to plunge himself into Hebraic learning. In this early stage, Arnold's philosophical scepticism and naturalistic point of view would be a stepping-stone to Sigmund Freud and others.

Arnold's concept of "culture" is a "march towards perfection". (Arnold 48) Puritanism-Hebraism, as found in England and America, marches to a different drummer. In its need to isolate, it stunts and enfeebles its adherents. It is the very absence of culture. Hellenism, on the other hand, is "the two noblest of things, sweetness and light." (54) Thus Hellenism, in its two noble qualities, becomes "one law" with the essence of poetry. Anything else is "provincialism". (14) "English Philistinism" can be found in "the Puritan and Hebraising middle-class, [whose] Hebraising keeps it from culture and totality." (20) As for America, "it is notorious that the people of the United States issues from this class, and reproduces its tendencies, its narrow conception of man's spiritual range.... From Maine to Florida, and back again, all America Hebraises." (20) Arnold also helped carry Lewisohn's thinking to where he could more objectively perceive the America he wanted so much to accept and to have accept him.

Lewisohn's thesis was accepted in fulfillment of his Masters of Arts requirements. It was soon afterward taken for publication, in three installments;[55] Part I, "His Poetry", analyses those essential components in Arnold's philosophical point of view that influenced his poetry. Lewisohn begins by describing "Arnold's view of nature", which he asserts "is the view of modern science. Nature is calm, restful, cruel, but just." ("Study" I: 443) Lewisohn also makes note of "Arnold's despair" (443) which he says was "the despair of the intellect which saw the ancient faith of a world passing away, and found nothing to replace it." (444) In another observation, Lewisohn reveals as much of himself as he does of Arnold:

> Now, there was undoubtedly in Arnold's nature a certain conflict between emotions drawing him toward the beliefs and ideals of his youth, and his intellect, which caused him to discard those ideals; but it is just this conflict which many of us experience, and the final victory of intellect, of truth, over sentiment, which tends to make Arnold's poetry an intellectual and moral tonic. (447)

Another statement that shows significant parallels in Lewisohn's life focusing on Arnold's poetry and prose:

> Arnold's poetry contains, however, not only religious views, but contains, also, in the main, the ideas on man and on human life to promulgate which he abandoned verse for prose. These ideas burn through his poetry, and, though he delivered them in prose with the air not of a prophet but of a man of the world, he left the nobler region of literature only because he felt an inner necessity to preach in the Philistine wilderness. (448)

Like Lewisohn, "Arnold," he says, "is prepared to accept with joy and calm any issue, to accept the truth; whatever that may be." (450)

Part II of the study, entitled "Formative Influences: The Influence of Goethe", analyses the profound effect that Goethe had on Arnold's life. Lewisohn also describes Goethe as one of the three most influential writers in his own life. He shows the direct correlation between Arnold's conception of provincialism and that of Goethe. ("Study" II: 148) From Heine, Lewisohn observes, Arnold took "Hebraism and Hellenism, the two great spiritual forces." (156) Finally, in Part III, Lewisohn sums up the four sins of the Puritan middle classes:

> that is to say, against the great bulk of the English and American people as Arnold saw them. The charges are that the middle class has narrowed itself by concentration upon a crude religion; it is inaccessible to ideas; it fixes faith upon material well-being; it has no care that its light be not darkness. ("Study" III: 315)

Arnold, Lewisohn concludes, was a "reformer" who "preached culture, the cultivation of the intellect, the suppression of passion and prejudice. He preached reason and justice." (319)

Lewisohn was on his way to reaching the goals he had set for himself: becoming a published writer in the English language and a teacher. He next undertook a much more difficult essay, "Southern Literature from the Beginning Until the Civil War", which was printed in serial form in the Sunday editions of the *Charleston News Courier* from July 5 to September 20, 1903, under the title, "Books We Have Made". As Gillis remarks, the "We" in the title is noteworthy (Gillis 8) for its self-inclusion into the annals of Southerners, which is to say, those who belong. Another noteworthy fact is that this was an extraordinary task for someone so young, and shows proof of the well-balanced existence of two outstanding qualities: a thorough and careful sense of scholarship, and a very vibrant, imaginative creativity. At the end of this long essay on literature of the South, Lewisohn offers one explanation for the dearth of literary activity in the South:

> Since the close of the great war, South Carolina has produced but little literature. For over a decade the State lay prostrate under the intolerable tyranny of a barbarous and inferior race [Northern occupation].... The higher things are yet to come. They will come. (9)

A teaching job was all Lewisohn needed. Feeling so thoroughly Southern, his writing accepted by his fellow South Carolinians, a respectable means to earn a living, and to give his parents the emotional lift they so needed, was all that was lacking. It was never to be, however, in South Carolina. Lewisohn describes in *Up Stream* how, after the acclaim and honor given him by the acceptance for publication of his long essay on Arnold, other to-be-published articles on the horizon, and his brilliant success at Charleston College,

> "a board of Episcopal clergymen elected me to the chair of English in a local academy. But the aged clergyman to whom the school really belonged arose from a bed of illness and removed the trustees he had himself appointed for electing a person distasteful to him. He used this expression quite openly in a letter to the Courier." (*Up Stream* 100)

This event, at age nineteen, greatly shook his self-confidence. It now seemed to him that no matter what he accomplished in his life, irrespective of the admiration others had for his intellectual capabilities, his writing ability, his perseverance, his (or so it seemed) seamless ability to meld into the society around him, he nevertheless at the end found himself rejected, outside. No matter what he did or said, he was still the German immigrant, the little Jew whose physical characteristics and strange name were, as he remarked, "Jewish." (103)

It was 1902. Lewisohn was just twenty years old when he made a grave decision to pick up anchor and move to Manhattan to begin his doctoral studies at Columbia University. For certain, a move out of the provincial South would greatly increase his prospects for the future. At Columbia, Professor Trent, a liberal-minded, kindly man, admired Lewisohn's talents and helped him. Trent saw in this doctoral studies student great imagination and sensitivity—perhaps to an excessive degree. He gave Lewisohn Crevecoeur's *Letters from an American Farmer* to edit. The payment of fifty dollars that Lewisohn received meant little compared to the literary acclaim he received from just having his name appear on the title page with Professor Trent's. Soon, Lewisohn realistically believed, he could justifiably ask for a position at Columbia University, or barring that, a strong recommendation for a position somewhere else. Somehow, though, he was beginning feel an uneasy sensation. He was certainly a Southern Gentile gentleman—faultlessly so. He had, like a sponge, absorbed every Southern quality, mannerism, voice inflection, attitude, and point of view to a flawless degree. Ultimately, however, somewhere deep inside he had his nagging doubts about it. He was not Anglo-Saxon by birth. What's more, his name and facial characteristics were uncharacteristically non-Anglo-Saxon. As Gillis expresses it, he looked foreign, even Semitic, with the strong-lensed eyeglasses that only magnified the "intense semitic darkness" of his face. (Gillis 12)

The final and profoundly crushing blow to Lewisohn's hopes, as he describes it in *Up Stream*, came in 1904, when in the spring, the students scrambled for jobs. Twenty-two-year-old Ludwig wrote to the Head of Columbia University's English Department, Carpenter,[56] about jobs. It is then that Ludwig's Jewishness was pointed out, isolated as the reason for his potential failure to obtain a teaching position. He was told that his "Jewish birth" was the debilitating factor in being able to get a job. (*Up Stream* 121–122)

Lewisohn would never recover from this profound shock and jolt of reality. He would be forced now to really lower the mask of his masquerade as a Gentile, Southern Anglo-Saxon, and to look with a cool and detached eye at the real Ludwig Lewisohn. All the cultural threads within the dialectic of his life—Jewish, American, German, Southern, Christian—either buried or now destroyed, were left hanging in a pile of confusion. Seeing himself as

> an outcast.... A sentence arose in my mind which I have remembered and used ever since. So long as there is discrimination, there is exile. And for the first time in my life my heart turned with grief and remorse to the thought of my [Jewish] brethren in exile all over the world. (123)

As well, of one thing he was absolutely certain. He desperately wanted to be an acclaimed writer in the English tongue because his proven talent warranted such a status. From this first period of his life Lewisohn produced one type of work: literary criticism. At age twenty-two, he was ready, in his personal and professional life, to embark on a sorting-out time of transition from an impossible-to-reconcile dialectic of repressed/suppressed and fully self-created identities, that he now saw were personally and realistically impossible to maintain as a totality. Exactly how to sort all of this out, Lewisohn was in a great quandary:

> I didn't know how to go on living a reasonable and reasonably harmonious inner life. I could take no refuge in the spirit and traditions of my own

people. I knew little of them. My psychical life was Aryan through and
through.... I didn't know what to do with my life or with myself. (125)

The second period of his life, from 1904–1922, was, as stated, a time
of difficult self-adjustment, turbulence, transition and change. Lewisohn
abandoned his fervent Germanicism while still remaining tied to, as he
perceived it, German culture's extraordinary achievements. He had already experienced grave disappointment with what he viewed as
America's hypocrisy, her lack of sophistication, repressiveness, and
Arnoldian absence of cultural intellectuality and aesthetic sense. He had
developed a severe scorn for Southern values, especially those toward
women, who were viewed as either pure madonnas or sluts and whores,
and were not believed to have physically sexual feelings or thoughts; and
toward sexuality in general. He discarded all of the Puritanical values his
Southern upbringing had engendered in him. Finally, he rejected the
Christianity that had rejected him During this period he became a Socialist, a naturalist, a Freudian, a Nietzschean. He now embraced the life,
work and philosophy of Matthew Arnold as well, more as a belief system
in itself than as an interesting and worthy focus of his intellectual efforts
(as was the case with Arnold in the first period of his own life).

In this second time frame, Lewisohn produced seven types of writing:
a novel of personal unfulfillment, *The Broken Snare*, 1908; autobiography, *Up Stream*, 1922; translations from German works; drama, *A
Night in Alexandria: A Dramatic Poem in One Act*, 1909; literary essays
on German literature, *German Style: An Introduction to the Study of
German Prose*, 1910, *The Spirit of Modern German Literature*, 1916;
literary essays on English and American literature, *The Modern Drama:
An Essay in Interpretation*, 1915, *A Modern Book on Criticism*, 1919,
The Drama and the Stage, 1922; and European literary essays, *The Poets
of Modern France*, 1918. The list also includes many Introductions to
works of others, especially German writers, and other essays on culture,
society and literature.

Lewisohn's identification with, and love for, English literature and
culture—aside from any connection it did or could have to a Gentile or a
Christian cosmological point of view—became the point of intersection
between his moral decision to drop all masks and his profound desire to
be a writer in the English tongue, to join the ranks of its great literary
figures. His meeting and marrying in 1906 the Gentile, Mary Arnold
Child Crocker, mother, grandmother and nearly 20 years his senior,

seemed to symbolize that intersection point. How could he hate Americans or the English when their literary and cultural heritage was steeped in some of the greatest writers of the English language who ever lived? He announces in *Up Stream* that he cannot be bitter or flippant. He is slowly analyzing all the events, people, thoughts and feelings of his life. He can't say he hates Gentiles, or his English wife Mary. He "can never speak as an enemy of the Anglo-Saxon race." (126) However, that race's "duality of conscience" will "destroy civilization through disasters yet unheard of," (126) as Lewisohn also seems to be describing at the end of *Trumpet of Jubilee*.

Not able to sever his connections to his American and English ties, to his great and lasting love for the literary culture it produced, and also unable to accept this people who refused to see him as a native son, Lewisohn came closer to the role of Jeremiac writer who excoriates an erring people, or as the writer who brings redemption to the world through his art. His art was also, at least apparently, a search for truth about the world and himself. As he says in *Up Stream*:

> My youth had been passed amid so much falseness that my mastery of fact was quite inadequate for the practice of a real moral freedom. I had no way at all of seeing things as they really are, no power of measuring the origin and direction of the forces that rule men and the world.... The young creators of new values come to grief so often not because their values are wrong, nor because their rebellion is not of the very breath of the world's better life. They come to grief because they have no mastery of fact, because they carry with them the false old interpretations and conventional idealizations of man, and nature, and human life.... Nevertheless the world now opened itself to me in a new guise. I had been accustomed, as I had been taught, to approve and to disapprove. Now for the first time I watched life honestly and lost myself in it and became part of it with my soul and my sympathies, detached only in the citadel of the analytic and recording, ever more of the judging mind. (115)

As he attempted to understand the world around him and himself, he was also growing into a more accomplished writer. For this he needed to have a keen, totally objective eye and a mind uncluttered by culturally oppressive baggage. By delving into himself and beginning to make sense of the things around him, he was forced to grow as a writer. They went hand in hand. Nevertheless, although Lewisohn said he wanted to find truth, he found only disillusionment and lies—some of them still his own lies. The writing of *Up Stream,* he insists, was an attempt to get to the bottom of truth: about himself and the world.

Up Stream

The earliest years of Ludwig Lewisohn's life, as with those of Cynthia Ozick, already evinced the faint signs of the writer-in-the-making in cameo with a moral universe: the eye/heart of the young artist perceiving, experiencing and adjusting the world into varying degrees of righteousness; justice or its lack; the prophet-in-process with a yet unformed, virgin voice. In all the stages of creative progression, it is, however, difficult to discern if the art is in the service of morality, or *vice versa,* that ethical considerations breathlessly follow behind the amoral quirkiness of the artistic imagination. In all of it, the "word" both reflects and undermines the "Word" (of the God of Moses, Abraham and Isaac). The "book" simultaneously mirrors, parodies and insults the "Book", the *Torah* given to Moses at Mt. Sinai by God. The carefully carved "word" or "book" is so beautified, so canonized, as to be the object of abject worship, both reflecting and in competition with the Book and the Word.

Truth and fabrication, justice and inequitableness, the twists and turns in the process of forming the perfectly rendered word, the web of ambiguous and conflicting messages, a dialectic at once cultural, religious, personal and linguistic, all hang in the balance. As Sacvan Bercovitch states it succinctly: "Language has the capacity to break free of social restrictions and through its own dynamics to undermine the power structures it seems to reflect."[57]

Like literary history, literary "historical" texts and narratives are inscribed in aesthetic judgment and therefore inherent in the process of interpretation; aesthetic structures shape the way we understand history, so that tropes and narrative devices may be said to use historians to enforce certain views of the past. (*Reconstructing* viii)

In this way, the service paid by history to aesthetics—and not the reverse—calls into question the very nature of historical description as a rendering of truth or fact. Rather, at the heart of the narration and narrative process is the idea of conflict and dialectic as an end-product in itself that forms its base. Thus, in place of historical factuality, there is "discontinuity and disruption." (viii) Textual dislocation, displacement, is the result of the art process. Lewisohn describes it as "an artistic pattern [that] comes between the teller of the tale and his reality." (*Up Stream* 9) Lewisohn's *Up Stream* very much reflects this complexity of directions and worlds: the dialectical progression/development of a sensitive young child into the full-blown artist.

Erroneously labeled by Lewisohn readers an "autobiography", the book, significantly subtitled *An American Chronicle*, could well serve the opposite function. Not necessarily historically based, a chronicle is in fact a minute narrative account, the story of the (perceived) life of a quasi-epic character performing in his/her own life story. Thus, truth and reality combine· in a dialectical conundrum of which language is its crux. As with Ozick, Lewisohn begins his story with a prologue statement which both reveals—explains—and conceals; demasks and masks; exposes and hides, makes distinct both truth and falsehood. Intentionality is not at issue; for it is the nature of language as an open-ended, centerless enterprise which leads the writer wherever it may, on which responsibility or blame can be pinned. This is what Lewisohn calls "an artistic pattern". (9)

Lewisohn pronounces that he will tell the total "truth" by dropping the "mask" (9), but the reader is hard-put to discover when and where the mask has been dropped and who the real Ludwig Lewisohn is. As Werner Sollars comments in his study,[58] in a sub-section entitled, "The 'Real' Ludwig Lewisohn: American Identities of a German-Jewish Immigrant to the South":

> In his autobiography [*Up Stream*] Ludwig Lewisohn presents us with a dazzling variety of identity choices. He attributes some of his character traits to his German background, others to his tenuous Jewishness, and still others to his Southern upbringing. Far from soberly describing the confluence within himself of these different elements, he is strongly evaluative and curiously Roycean in accounting for the process [of his assimilation into American life]. (Sollars 452)

Textual dislocation and displacement is therefore the result of the art process. Lewisohn describes this process and the writer in it as having "an anterior vision into which he lets his facts and even his emotions melt." The writer is "a lyricist at bottom." (*Up Stream* 9) *Up Stream* is thus a testimony to a variety of competing realities that the author attempts to decode through the linguistic process of telling the story of his life.

Significantly, there are even a number of versions of the life story, *Up Stream*, with conflicting stories within each version. The first Boni and Liveright edition (1922), in part was written while still under the heavy influence of his first wife Mary; already disillusioned with their marriage, and in spite of his prefatory exhortations against dishonesty, it is replete with complimentary portrayals of her. Even by 1921, the author had already lost all interest in her as a woman, a wife and an inspiration for his writing. The love-struck starry-eyed romanticized passages of the first edition had been eliminated and replaced with realistic appraisals of Mary's true personality and descriptions of the wicked, black shadow she had cast in his life. In the 1922 edition we find:

> But we, under one umbrella, recked little of the world. The weather cleared and brightened as October came. We lingered on Riverside Drive and heard the rustle of the leaves under our feet and waited until the sun set in a bronze haze over the palisades. We sat on a bench under the bare poplars with all the stars of heaven for our own. We were, of course, aware of the necessary briefness of this period, but we dwelt with all our might in the days and hours—numbered days and hours—that were given us. The windfalls grew fewer and fewer, the weather colder and colder. With a brave and lovely brightness in her eyes Mary took me to the boat. For the present we were defeated and I had to seek refuge at home. (131)

However, in the 1924 German version of *Up Stream, Gegen Den Strom: Eine Amerikanishe Chronik*, a page devoted exclusively to *"Meiner Geliebten Frau Thelma"* ("My Beloved Lady Thelma")[59], including also a bar from a musical score (Thelma was a singer), makes it amply clear that Lewisohn had a new romantic direction in his life.[60] Strangely enough, the German version's *"Vorwort"* (Prologue), contains an earnestly stated intention to tell the whole truth and uncover all lies: *"Ich Zog nes vor, dir Maske fallen zu lassen.* [I have chosen to drop the mask.]" (*Gegen* 11) However, it is a virtually word-by-word translation of the original English language edition. As Ralph Melnick explains:

> Written while he was still living with Mary, the first edition of *Up Stream* had been laudatory and filled with references to "we". Both the praise of Mary and her inclusion in positive ways had now been removed. A German edition (*Gegen den Strom: Eine Amerikanishce Chronik*) published in late 1924, though dedicated to *"Meiner Gleibten Frau, Thelma,"* had allowed the original text to stand. June 1926 had marked the first time he had reread the book, and as he explained in the new introduction to this second edition, "I can view it objectively now, because I dwell in another moral world. I have proceeded on from *Up Stream* to the necessary continuation and expansion of it in *Israel*—a spiritual and intellectual rather than a literary process—and I have emerged from that old moral world of pain and sordidness into which an overwhelming accident of life plunged me, into one of unhoped-for peace and beauty." His aim was to set right that "small number of passages," now "changed or expunged," wherein he had deliberately falsified "one element in

my life... and one character." Where veracity and frankness had otherwise ruled, he had let "a mistaken kindliness and shame" over "the all but unbelievable physical and moral facts" of his misguided and faltering marriage set the tone in these "passages". He owed himself, his readers, and Thelma, "the light and inspiration of my new and other life," the chance to draw a truer portrait of this sordid chapter. (Melnick I: 418, *Up Stream* x–xii)

Besides the various versions of Lewisohn's life story, there are also the truths of the various accounts of the author's life in German culture. One of these describes the grandeur of the life of the small child in the Berlin of the late 1880s, in which there existed "an air of homely and familiar comfort." (*Up Stream* 11) In this first chapter entitled "A Far Childhood", the writer recalls the existence of himself as a six-year-old cocooned in the secure and protective life created by parents who were both Jewish by birth (or affliction) and patriotically, culturally German: "I remember being driven for hours through the black-draped city on that icy day in 1888 on which the old emperor's body lay in state in the cathedral." (11)

The apparent serenity recalled by the small child is shot through, however, with conflicting messages set within conflicting worlds. There are, for example, as earlier quoted, the descriptions of the mixed worlds of German and Jewish life, with Lewisohn remarking about the "unmixed blood" of his family and also describing his grandfather who, although a rabbi, had both "a whimsical contempt" for Jewish law and "a Protestant pastor" as a good friend. (15)

Lewisohn's family was both thoroughly Jewish and also contemptuous of it. Only one of Lewisohn's relatives, an uncle, "had married", as Lewisohn relates in *Up Stream*, "a Gentile woman, and for years the marriage was a stormy one." (17) Like a foreboding of his own hellish first marriage to Mary Crocker, his account of this uncle could carry the message of the potential tragedy inherent in marrying out of one's cultural affiliation. Nevertheless, as Lewisohn asserts, his family felt more Germanic than Jewish:

They were not disloyal to their race nor did they seek to hide it. Although they spoke unexceptional High German they used many Hebrew expressions both among themselves and before their Gentile friends. But they had assimilated, in a deep sense, Aryan ways of thought and feeling. Their books, their music, their political interests were all German. I remember but one phrase disparaging to their Christian countrymen. It was a curious one: "What can one expect? The Gentile has no heart!" (17–18)

The German language skills of Ludwig's parents, although common, did not bar them from feeling "Aryan". In truth, they were between two worlds: a Jewish and a German one. This Jewish-Gentile ambiguity is repeated once more:

> Two scenes stand before me which symbolize the character of the social group from which I sprang. This is one: I am sitting in a half-darkened room and my heart beats and my cheeks burn. It is Christmas Eve. I look out through the dark pane and across the street. Ah, there, behind an uncurtained window, a tree with candles. Quickly I turn my eyes away. I do not want to taste the glory until it is truly mine. And at last, at last, a bell rings. The folding doors open and there—in the drawing room—stands my own tree in its glimmering splendor and around it the gifts from my parents and my grandmother and my uncles and aunts—charming German toys and books of fairy tales and marchpane from Konigsberg. (18)

This story of the experience of Christmas by a Jewish boy reveals the depth to which the child Ludwig, like his parents, assimilated Aryan-Christian ways of thinking and feeling. The Christian story enthralled the little boy, as well as the Christmas scene of the lit tree and exciting presents.

> And the other scene: It was my grandmother's custom, in pious remembrance of her husband, to visit the temple on the chief Jewish holidays—New Year and the Day of Atonement. And once, on the day of the great white fast, I was taken there to see her. The temple was large and rather splendid; the great seven-branched candelabra were of shining silver. The rabbi, the cantor and the large congregation of men were all clad in their gleaming shrouds and their white, silken praying shawls and had white caps on their heads. I can still see one venerable old man who read his Hebrew book through a large magnifying glass. The whiteness of the penitential scene was wonderful and solemn. Then the first star came out and the great day was over and in the vestibule I saw my grandmother being reverently saluted by her sons who wished her a happy holiday. Two scenes. But the first was native and familiar to the heart of the child that I was: the second a little weird and terrifying and alien. (18–19)

Lewisohn's childhood estrangement or isolation from his Jewish heritage was, for all appearances, nearly complete.

The author also recalls his mother. Her ideology in life was based on German values. Ludwig's parents wanted only a "liberal education" for him which their society believed "was the necessary foundation of right and noble living." (27) Herself a writer, albeit a frustrated one, Ludwig's mother who, like the father, is not referred to by name in *Up Stream*, is portrayed as the intellectual and artistic taskperson of his formative years, and remains, throughout, the poetic spirit behind the boy's mastery, after they emigrated to America, of learning and language acquisition: "I do not know how I learned English. My memory which is so clear on things quite trivial fails me at this crucial point. My mother characteristically desired to engage a teacher for me." (44)

There is another version of Ludwig's German cultural foreignness in matters of perception and language, in not just an American town but a small Southern town, where the author remembers himself in 1890, the year the family emigrated to the United States, as an eight-year-old boy

> in my little German velvet suit and cap seated aloft on sacks of cottonseed in the postmaster's shop and explaining, in some sort of English, the peculiarities of German life to a crowd of tall, rough tobacco-spitting but evidently tenderhearted yokels. Tenderhearted! For they asked the quaint little German boy to come again and again and never teased him but were, in what must have been their amusement, unfailingly gentle and considerate. (45)

The scene is of the young writer-in-the-making groping for the language that could express his thoughts; enthralling even an uncultured group of low-class Southern Americans with a story of his remembered Berlin. Lewisohn's memory is cemented to and riveted in language, this young artist's vehicle with which to decode the world. Even here and then, he is the sagaciously precocious or ageless height of subtle, penetrating discrimination and refinement; the very depth of acute perspicacity; the natural storyteller holding his listeners spellbound with his tales; so delighting in him, they ask, as if maneuvering his fate, to come back and tell them more stories.

Even after the process of Americanization has begun in earnest, the narrator, looking back on that ten-year-old writer-in-the-making, observes: "My old [German] life, however, was not dead. I read Homer and my German legends with the same imaginative naivete as before." (51) The fledgling writer continues to find his German tales fascinating even though

> I did absorb unconsciously, of course, a very large set of moral and social conventions that are basic to the life of the average American. I stress the word absorb. There can be no question of reflection or conviction on the part of the child. But at the age of ten my emotional assimilation into the social group of which I was a physical member was complete. (51)

Interestingly, in writing this, the adult Lewisohn of the early 1920s leaves this description of his Americanization ambiguously hanging. In the dialectic of cultural assimilation, what was being assimilated? Who, at this time, did Lewisohn become? What was his identity? With the outbreak of the First World War in 1914, and the warring animosity between America and Germany, Lewisohn, now a university professor at a Midwestern university, speaks of the American libel against Germany:

> Then it will be written down how huge populations devoid of gallantry or mercy, aching themselves through their emissaries to dabble in the blood of any at their feet... took up the cry of "Hun" and poisoned the minds of young people and little children in three continents not against the fierce competitions that end in hate and blood, but against the soul of the German people. It will be written down in the history books. But to the man and woman on the street historic truth is pragmatic. Truth is what prevails. That is one reason why I think this Christian-capitalistic civilization will be overturned. At its core festers a cancerous lie. It feeds on spiritual tissue. (199)

Lewisohn's polemically outspoken condemnation of America causes him to leave his long-sought-for university post. Yet, the 1922 version of *Up Stream* ends with an idyllic scene of a Lewisohn cast as "the philosopher," who

> driven by a noble urge, seeks to make rational his universe by assigning to creative values a permanent validity. I share that speculative hope.... Yes, beauty is immortal and of immortal goodness.... He [the philosopher] sits in an armchair by the window, a volume of Plato or Goethe on his knees. (245)

This German Romantic scene, with its spotlight on classic/German culturism, sets the writer-thinker aside from the rest of humanity. As creator, artist, message-bearer, prophet, Lewisohn feels justified in casting himself in the role of the truth-sayer, perhaps misunderstood by the society around him. Lewisohn describes two major areas of reality: one "public", the other "private". (9) These, he says, never intersect. In choosing "to drop the mask", he declares himself to be the one real, honest voice on the American literary scene:

> It is not a simple thing to do. One likes to be decorous. The folds of this mantle of civilization we wear in public, and often enough, in private, are graceful and accustomed. They give a dignity to the figure that the mind may lack. But if no one will ever speak out for fear of wounding his own susceptibilities or those of others, this hush of cowardly considerateness and moral

stealth in which so much of our life is passed will either throttle us some day or sting us into raw and mad revolt. (9–10)

Lewisohn's allusion here to public and private realms of experience discloses, as previously discussed, certain paradoxes and truths fundamental to American literary discourse, and uncovers, as with Ozick, a need to understand the meaning of the American experience *vis a vis* the reality of other conflicting truths, what Bercovitch calls "the rhetoric of American identity." (*Puritan* ix) This concept of identity, which for Lewisohn adds yet another self to his inner world, rests, as Bercovitch points out, at the intersection of "the interaction of language, myth and society." (ix) Thus truth and personal history are also built on mythical perceptions of people, place and time and cultural influences set in a context of the linguistic rendering of that reality. This would define, it would seem, those characteristics inherent in the American Romance Tradition. This, however, is not the subject of this study.

Lewisohn makes allusion to 1920s America which, he asserts, maintains "a desire to avoid singularity." (*Up Stream* 9) On the other hand, he declares himself ready to tell "each other the quite naked [that is, private] and, if need be, the devastating truth." (9) His call is no less than that of the prophet-bard Jeremiacally excoriating (his) Americans for their sinful infractions of morality and aesthetic taste: "In every other country men have spoken out in prose or verse and have recorded their experience and their vision and their judgment on this civilization in which we are ensnared. But no one has spoken out in America." (10)

Lewisohn's stated intention is to bring the private world of real beliefs, hopes, dreams, reality, that is, the artistic vision, however unsophisticated, that burns in each and every human heart, onto the center stage of public discourse. This polemic of public-private is the subject of Philip Fisher's essay, "Appearing and Disappearing in Public: Social Space in Late-Nineteenth Century Literature and Culture". In it, Fisher describes American culture as a duality of public-private, in which the news media, an idea and/or a movement were brought to public attention through "the personal appearance of a charismatic lecturer on a platform before a crowd." (*Reconstructing* 156) This effected a type of "theatricalization" of events or happenings:

> The platform from which moral or political emotion sensationalized ideas, just as the newspaper did events or the department store did merchandise, had also made possible the appearance of an author before the no-longer invisible

audience. Now the public might have him "in person" while he would enjoy the visceral attention and emotion that his words might, ordinarily in private, evoke. (157)

Fisher describes this "space of performance", that was itself the subject matter of the most well-known American paintings by Thomas Eakins, done in the late nineteenth and early twentieth century, in which is depicted "the performance of a skilled master before an audience." (157) One such painting, entitled "The Gross Clinic", shows a most private professional act, the performance of a surgical manoeuvre by a surgeon who is viewed as a nobly celebrated hero figure, in a wholly private act that is made public to the spectators sitting in the operating theatre. As Fisher asserts:

> Eakins brings surgery into public view by means of this painting in the same way that the novelists of Realism and Naturalism or the journalistic muckrakers would bring into the light of public scrutiny the normally invisible and often deliberately concealed affairs of political and economic life. (158)

However, obtaining and attracting an attentive audience could not be managed by simply making viewable that which had been imperceptible. Needed was the most visible state of stage-setting. It is not the surgery itself in Eakins' painting that is the subject, but the very performing of the act of surgery as in a dramatic theatre, on a stage set lit with spotlights illuminating the star performer, any supporting actors/actresses, a breathless audience, and the melodrama of stage props such as scalpels and a bloody, supine, anaesthetized human body.

As in *Holy Land*, throughout *Up Stream* we see the multicultured author steadily gaining voice and the ability to perform in a variety of scenes and on a number of stages of life. In his German scenes, he is the gallant, supercilious master of *kulture* and intellectuality, performing in front of a cast of culturally inferior Americans (whom he, nevertheless, is desperately trying at the same time to woo or imitate). The next cultural influence in the complex dialectical mix of the author's life is America; that is to say, America as a place and membership for those, like the Lewisohns, with feelings of inferiority and disenfranchisement from being Jewish, and thus doubly foreign, in parallel to their nearly innate sense of German superiority. After a nearly mythical voyage over "a primaeval, chaotic, brutal sea", (*Up Stream* 34) it was a kind of birth

experience for the Lewisohns to finally set foot on American soil. As
Lewisohn recounts in *Up Stream*:

> Our land-fall was still gray but quiet. Afar lay a dim, hook-like shore. The
> voyage had liberated my father's mind from terror and madness. He was so
> strengthened and cheered that even my mother smiled. To come to land at all
> seemed, after our tremendous experience, almost like coming home. (34–35)

Their initial sense of America, upon disembarking:

> the pier at Hoboken was rough and wild, a place of hoarse cries and brute
> haste and infernal confusion. A kindly German-American fellow passenger
> helped us; saw to it that our luggage was not unduly searched and put us in a
> rumbling hack on our way to an hotel. (35)

They decide that it is culturally necessary to cross the river into Manhattan "and see a city so great and famous as New York." (35) However,
what the author chooses to write of his remembrance about it is its
"grime and rattle". (35) They are in the grip of "a curious timidity". (35)
Significantly and symbolically, they "did not go uptown nor into the
financial section, drifted somehow into a lake of mud shaken by trucks
and drays on Canal Street and retreated to Hoboken." (35)

This first experience of northern East Coast American life is overwhelming. Led around by a father whose poor judgement caused them
the financial ruin that brought about their emigration in the first place,
and a mother who simply sought any alternative to bring cheer, calm and
peacefulness into her husband's life and moods, they, as their fate would
have it, drift into the muck of the "bottom" (they choose not to go
uptown), and to the most ethnically Jewish part of Manhattan (Canal
Street), where they might have found the cultural support to pull themselves up and succeed. With no other direction in sight, they return to
Hoboken, defeated already. Later on in his life, Ludwig would have a
much different perception about Manhattan: as a refuge from the narrowness he would finally perceive in Southern life.

As newly arrived immigrants to America's shores, their next blunder
is to take the wrong mode of transportation to South Carolina: "Being ill-
advised we took ship again and spent nearly fifty hours on a coastwise
voyage South." (35) Entering the South Carolinian bay and Queenshaven
Harbor, the young Ludwig finds it to be

one of the most beautiful in the world. In its fold lies the old city with its gardens and verandahs and its few slender spires. Golden-green islands extend its curves. The coloring of sea and sky, in whatever mood, is of so infinite and delicate a variety as though the glow and splendor of all the jewels in the world had been melted there. And over city and bay lies a rich quietude that steals upon the heart through the liquid softness of that untroubled air.... For that city and bay came to mean my boyhood and youth, high passion and aspiration, and later a grief that darkened my life. (35–36)

America is a blank slate for the Lewisohns to write a new life story on; and Southern America a wilderness filled with what looks to them like animal-like people toiling in a place outside the boundaries of civilization. Boarding a train from Queenshaven to the town of St. Mark's, where Minna's brother and his family lives and are awaiting their arrival,

I recall vividly the long, shabby, crowded car and its peculiar reek of peanuts, stale whiskey and chewing-tobacco. Half of the passengers were burly Negroes who gabbled and laughed weirdly. The white men wore broad-rimmed wool-hats, whittled and spat and talked in drawling tones. I very distinctly shared my parents' sense of the wildness, savagery and roughness of the scene, their horrified perception of its contrast to anything they had ever known or seen. (36–37)

The unspoken remembrances of an elegant and refined Berlin are juxtaposed here and elsewhere against the savage, rough, still (culturally) uncivilized wilds of the American North and South. By far the greatest trauma for the newly-arrived Lewisohns in this new land is in meeting Minna's brother, Ludwig's uncle, who arrived some years before and is already at home in this Southern American town of St. Mark's, South Carolina. Ludwig, thinking him to be a "porter" or cab driver, registers his observations of this uncle with "disgust and amazement". (37) He cannot believe that this uncivilized-looking man is part of his cultured Berlin family.

Lewisohn's shift from German to American Southern culture happens quickly. It is, however, not without its dialectically ambiguous grey areas of perception:

Soon I was merged into it [St. Mark's] and felt quite at home. No, not quite. During at least a year, at lengthening intervals of course, I felt a sharp nostalgia for the land of my birth and its life. Suddenly, at the edge of the forest, a sense of grief would overcome me.... And I would weep bitterly. (38–39)

The Lewisohns have left Berlin, Germany, not because of political or religious oppression, but due to the economic calamity Jacques, Ludwig's father, brought on the family. His plunge into a deep moodiness and profound depression made emigration to America the only viable option. The family has been accustomed to the active cultural life of Berlin—classical music, theatre, intellectually alert friends—and to the type of Jewish friends who were of a high intellectual and cultural level. Thus, in young Ludwig's perception, the uncle's life-style is a profound shock to them:

> My uncle and aunt received us into their queer little house which was huddled, as though for protection, against the shop. The walls of the house were of the rudest; the wind blew through knot-holes in the timber. My father and mother were bitterly disappointed. (41)

The physical scene is enough of a blow to them, but it isn't all their horrified perceiving eyes encounter. Instead of looking forward to a life with cultured friends who are Jewish but not uncouthly so (which is to say that these cultured Jews left behind all *Oriental* traces of an uncivilized ghetto life-style), the Lewisohns find themselves surrounded with primitive Jews in their very own family, who disgustingly separate meat from milk and observe Jewish holidays. (41)

Lewisohn's uncomplimentary remembrance of his aunt is based on several significant cultural characteristics. Firstly, the little boy perceived her as being overwhelmingly Jewish without any mix of American, that is, Gentile influences. Secondly, the author bitterly juxtaposes the animal sounds of the geese he hears squawking "loudly in the muddy yard" with the primitive Yiddish and English vocal utterances of his aunt. Yiddish is not only the language of identity of East-European Jews but, as a mixture of German and Hebrew, it could appear to those on the level of Berlin culture to which the Lewisohns subscribed to be a gross debasement of the pure and utterly refined language they considered German to be. It is assumed that the aunt's English could not be at a high level as well.

The mother, father and son, as the narrator relates, cannot believe the decline in their life-style that has just begun. "My mother sat down on the springless bed, a picture of desolation. The sudden plunge unnerved her. All through the voyage we had lived on our accustomed plane of civilized comfort. Only here did the descent begin." (41–42) Compared to the Berlin they knew, America is an unsophisticated, rough and raw wilderness; a cultural wasteland. It transformed Minna's own brother, Siegfried! How would Minna educate her son Ludwig in the high cultural level of the Berlin they left?

Minna, like Ludwig having very strong ties to Germany, nevertheless knows that she has to pursue an aggressive process of Americanization with the most culturally elevated of St. Mark's citizens. Thus, although she strongly identifies with Judaism and its people, she has to do what she believes is best for her son. Jacques cares little (as he expresses it) for his Jewish background. Her rigorous assimilation of her son into American and Southern cultures begins. As Melnick characterizes the result: "Ludwig thus came to suffer the confusion of an eight-year-old child asked to live in three worlds at once. Competing truths in one so young led to an undying skepticism that destroyed any possibility of intellectual or emotional certainty in his early life." (Melnick I: 32)

The Eloessers, Minna's family, have always been culturally, even religiously, affiliated Jews. As stated earlier, the family has had generations of rabbis among its descendents. (*Up Stream* 32) However, in order to succeed, Minna's son Ludwig has to associate with and learn from the most educated among the townspeople. His uncle, aunt and cousins, in the perception of the author's parents, are not part of this educated and cultural elite. They are too identifiably Jewish for Minna, Jacques or even Ludwig. As Melnick observes:

> For Ludwig, it was a devastating time. The inner turmoil he experienced further deepened the insecurity known by all émigré children, and forever colored his perception and memory of the people and events of this time. Though *Up Stream* was to have been an indictment of the puritanical America against which he was struggling, Ludwig, even in his fortieth year, was unable to overcome his bitter memories of Siegfried and his family. Of the forces at war within him as a child, his Jewish identity, so foreign to this new land, became the most difficult to assimilate. As practicing Jews, the Eloessers remained an unconscious symbol of all that had caused his earliest experience of discomfort and profound sadness. (Melnick I: 32–33)

The vivid and painful account of the Lewisohns' first meeting with the Eloesser family is not necessarily consistent with the facts surrounding that encounter or with the recollection of Cora, Ludwig's cousin, the daughter of Siegfried, as earlier discussed. Also Lewisohn's accounts of both his uncle, aunt and cousins are in sharp contrast, as stated, to Melnick's description of the same event.

In Cora's recollections, her parents could clearly see how deeply the ongoing arguments that Ludwig's parents had over the issue of Judaism so severely affected Ludwig, "who witnessed their many bitter quarrels over the issue of religion. There was little they could do, however, aside from offering Minna words of comfort, for Jacques was unapproachable." (33) Ludwig's multicultural attachments and influences were creating a complex if not confusing cultural dialectical mix.

Minna tries to find a compromise between attaining for her son the American Dream (which necessarily involves some degree of immersion on Gentile society), and their Jewish heritage, in spite of Jacques' apparent disgust for it. As Melnick asserts, Minna didn't want Ludwig to lose any part of his multiple cultural attachments: "She attempted a compromise between these conflicting desires, only consenting to church-related activities for Ludwig after asserting her right to maintain some minimal level of Jewish observance within her home." (34)

As Ludwig recalls, the degree of his father's stubborn resistance to Jewish practices is shown in the mini-story the author tells about the small group of Jewish families in their village, and Jacques' relation to them and their life-style:

> Of these there were about ten families, all recent immigrants, and so alien in speech and race and faith. Most of them, moreover, were quite prosperous. Yet between them and these Southern villagers the relations were hearty and pleasant and consolidated by mutual kindness and tolerance. Only one Jew, and that was my father, was looked upon with some suspicion by the severer among his Gentile neighbors. The reason was curious and significant; he did not perform the external rites of the Jewish faith and, upon entering a fraternal life insurance order, he smiled and hesitated when asked to affirm categorically his belief in a personal God. (*Up Stream* 42–43)

Ludwig's affiliation to Christianity and Gentile culture becomes stronger and stronger. The Lewisohns feel closer to people like the landlord and his family, members of the Methodist Church. As the author asserts: "But culturally we really felt closer to the better sort of Americans in the community, and so there began in those early days that alienation from my own race which has been the source to me of some good but of more evil." (44)

It is suggested by their landlord's wife that Ludwig attend the Methodist Church Sunday School classes to "improve" his language skills. He, therefore, also begins attending its church services. "I cannot tell,

Lewisohn recalls, "by what swift stages I entered the faith and spirit of the place." (50) By ten years of age, the author remembers his "emotional assimilation... complete." (51) At the same time, Ludwig disassociates himself "from my cousins and... the other Jewish children in the village." (51) In parallel, the young Lewisohn is also fervently absorbing his first introduction to English literature: Addison, Byron, Swift. Moreover, his mother continues to train her son in the English language through its literature.

Another business bankruptcy in St. Mark's brings the family to Queenshaven, where the Lewisohns can find no social group to belong to. The upper crust, "old Southern slave-holding aristocracy" will not accept this German-Jewish family. The poorer Catholics or Presbyterians are not educated enough for the Lewisohns. Those seeking upward mobility "were not going to impede their progress by... acquaintance [with] a little family of German Jews." (58) Lewisohn thus wonders why his family didn't become part of either "a German-American" or "a Jewish" group. (58) The result of Ludwig's parents' bad judgment "was utter friendlessness." (59) The Lewisohns are caught in a cultural trap of their own making.

Nevertheless, by 1897 Lewisohn, feels himself nearly totally at home in the American South. As he writes:

> It is clear then that, at the age of fifteen, I was an American, a Southerner and a Christian. My home, it may be urged, was foreign in spirit. But that was·true to a very much slighter extent than may be supposed. For my father and mother were both bookish people and all the books they read were English.... My Americanization was, nevertheless, complete. It differed, to be quite scrupulous, from the Americanism of my comrades at school and college, but it differed by a touch of self-consciousness and a touch of militancy. It was at this time that, in my thoughts and emotions, I came upon a distinct and involuntary hostility to everything either Jewish or German. I seemed to have a premonition that, in some subtle way, these elements in my life and fate might come between me and the one thing in the world I cared for supremely—the poetry of the English tongue. (77)

As sure as Lewisohn feels that he is fully integrated in this American, Southern, Gentile culture, he also feels a sense of disquiet about some impending doom looming ahead.

Ludwig is primarily drawn to the ritual aesthetics of Methodist and Catholic worship. He is deeply attracted to, as he asserts, "the poetry and beauty... the deep human need voiced by the Church.... [This] alone reached my mind and emotions." (50) By degrees, however, the aesthetics that so absorbed his interest with the church change direction. It is then that he becomes equally as engrossed in the aesthetics of writing and literature, becoming so overwhelmed by their power that, as he admits, "I went neither to Sunday School nor to church." (62)

With his unnamed high school Latin teacher, Lewisohn believes that he has found the most perfect prototype of gentlemanly qualities: Christianly virtuous , aristocratic, noble blood line and the purest sense of aesthetic refinement. His influence on the author, as described earlier, had a profound effect on Lewisohn, both personally and professionally. He becomes not only Lewisohn's ideal male figure, but also the most important figure—outside of his mother's influence—in the author's aesthetic and artistic development:

> It was in the third year of High School. He was teaching us to scan Virgil. We were repeating a passage in unison. Suddenly he swung on his heel and pointed his finger straight at me: "That is the only boy who has a natural ear for verse!" he cried. A keen, strange quiver went through me. I realized the meaning suddenly of that constant scribbling which I had been impelled to during the preceding months. I had a gift for literature! I knew it now; I never doubted it again. My fate had found me. (68)

This Latin teacher, who as stated, Melnick identifies as Thomas Della Torre, is the embodiment of all that to Ludwig seems true and good in the world: the moral, genteel man with the spirit of the aesthetc. Under his wings and tutelage, Lewisohn knew: "Some day, somehow, I would be a poet." (69) The teacher, Harris/Ferris, shows Lewisohn how to make a writer of himself. He is the budding young writer's most critical and heartless aesthetic judge. Lewisohn "recognized in him... a singularly subtle and exquisitely tempered, literary intelligence." (82) However, it is his mother who sees the real person under the ideal that Lewisohn perceives his to be.

> My mother, with a woman's sensitiveness, had a perception, unreasonable but very real, of the ultimate truth. At home I spoke of Ferris daily during my four years at college. He and his influence filled my life. And often my mother would hint at a touch of disloyalty in him to me. I always defended him hotly, and indeed her reasons were invariably quite wrong. But the sting of the situation was that I knew her to be in the right. In the best and deepest hours we spent together there was in him a shadow of withdrawal from me— a shadow of watchfulness, of guardedness.... A shadow, but it was there. (83)

The mix of Gentilism, Christianism, Americanism, Judaism, Europeanism and aestheticism, up to this time held tightly controlled, compressed, compartmentalized by the young boy growing up into the young man, is in danger of disintegrating, dissolving into the greater truths of his being, represented, as Lewisohn himself describes in *Up Stream*, by his mother's keen ethnic judgment about the potential Gentile enemies outside. Nevertheless, the acute artistic perceptiveness which as already noted, Ferris represents, leaves the aspiring writer ostensibly undaunted. From him, as described, Lewisohn also begins to acquire in the aesthetic realm certain anti-American attitudes:

> My true life was given over to the absorption of Ferris' teaching, of his intimate, unspoken, but ever richly implied point of view. That point of view I can sum up in but one word, and that word is—England. His attitude to the intellectual and artistic life of America was a little detached, a little patronizing, a little amused. The serious thing in American life to him was its continuing of those English social traditions within our older commonwealths of which he was the product. But the home of his soul and of his imagination was by some Surrey land or Kentish field or Westmoreland lake. To me, whose love of English poetry had been so largely an aesthetic rapture, he communicated those other and richer associations which soon blended in my inner life, as they had done in his, into a spiritual loyalty to England that was all the deeper because we were forbidden the more obvious loyalties granted to her children and her citizens. (84)

Lewisohn thus also acquires another cultural affinity, England: a mix of a people, country, poetry, aesthetics, and language, all of which he adopts as his own. For several reasons, this is a significant step in the dialectical progression of his life. Firstly, it extricates him from a childishly blind allegiance to all things not just American, but also Southern. Secondly, relieved of these emotional dependencies on the South and America, Lewisohn begins to view them objectively, even too critically. His reading, for example, of Matthew Arnold served to help him calcify what becomes a very extreme anti-American point of view. Thirdly, by developing an attitude and frame of mind that eventually totally rejects all aspects of American culture, the author is in a freer state of being to reconnect with his own Hebraic culture; in fact, he can return to those other cultural influences of Germany, Europeanism, and the Jewishness and aesthetics he absorbed from his mother. However, Lewisohn can still describe how, by the year 1898 or 1899—at age 16 or 17:

I was a Pan-Angle of the purest type, so was Ferris, so were my classmates—
lads of English and Anglicized French Huguenot descent—so were the half
dozen cultivated lawyers and business men and journalists in the community
who, about this time, began to take an interest in me and my work. (87)

With continuing blindness to the Hebraic aspects of his own physiognomy and certain other hard-to-describe-clues that mark him as foreign
and Jewish, Lewisohn significantly describes one other person who does
not fit into this pure Pan-Angle type. After listing those who do belong to
this group, the author adds that there is another one: "a wealthy Jewish
physician" who became a Methodist early in his life. He now does not
discuss the issue, although he gives charity to "poor Jews". (87)

This description is strange for several reasons. One reason is that
Lewisohn blindly includes himself in the Pan-Anglo group, but not the
"Jewish" physician. Another is that his description of this physician is
very telling: the author, otherwise so exact and pedantic with every
nuance of meaning and turn of phrase, describes him as a "Jewish physician who had turned Methodist." By not saying "a physician, born
Jewish, who became a Methodist", Lewisohn's choice of words would
signify that the physician, born a Jew, would always remain a Jew, even
while "turning", that is, pretending to be a Methodist. Furthermore, as he
would a little later in life be so unfailingly accurate in appraising the
demeanor, attitude and behavior of others, Lewisohn fails to see that the
story he tells of the "Jewish physician" is his own story. Moreover, how
is it that Lewisohn, another Jew, is privy to the personal, even secret,
experience of this physician? How does the author know these facts
about the physician? Is it because, being Jewish himself, he was told this
by the other Jew? Why doesn't this self-described mask-dropper,
Lewisohn, tell us the real story of this revelation? Having avoided "all
questionable subjects", how does Lewisohn know of these "facts"? Is the
story true?

We know that Lewisohn's story of himself as the "purest type of Pan-
Angle" is a false one. A little later on, the author asserts:

I still, during these years, attended the Methodist church, taught Sunday
School and was a leader in the Epworth League. I did this partly because, up
to my junior year, my Christian faith, though cooler, was still unshaken,
partly through the influence and friendship of the physician whom I have mentioned. (88)

Absurdly, two Jews who spend their lives pretending to be other than what they are, that is, another factual representation of true identity, can only trust and confide their "truths" in the secure frame of their shared heritage, and with each other. Stranger still, finding comfort in one another because of this common background, they use their relationship—or so Lewisohn relates—to fortify their beliefs in the "Christian faith". If the physician feels Jewish enough to give charity to poor Jews, why doesn't the author perceive this fact and relate it to the truthful story of his own life? Does the author tell the story of the physician in order to put the reader to sleep, to confuse, to create a web of ambiguity which masks rather than demasks truth and reality? Thus, all of Lewisohn's stories are called into question in this conundrum of jumbled cultural dialectic. Perhaps the only truth lies in the mysterious maze of language; in the process of artistic expression. Lewisohn does tell the reader:

> The relations between my classmates and myself were very cordial; several of them often visited me as I did them. Yet there always came a point at which I felt excluded. They themselves belonged to a definite social group. They neither drew me into this group nor did they have the good sense or good feeling to be silent before me concerning these more intimate affairs. I do not think their exclusion of me was at all a matter of reason or determination; it was quite instinctive. (88)

By age nineteen, and in his last year of college, the author can finally say:

> As tribesmen their resistance to me was tacit but final.... But of the fundamental fact there could be no doubt. It was terribly confirmed to me by an incident in my senior year. I was the most prominent student on the campus. My classmates called themselves my friends—voluntarily and without my seeking. And these very friends gathered to form the first chapter of a Greek letter fraternity at our college and—left me out. I did not know then that the fraternities do not admit Jews. (88–89)

The one truth emerging for him is the slowly but steadily evolving reality that the ability to do true art depends on telling the truth, or all of the truths, to oneself. At this same time, age eighteen to nineteen, as the author describes:

> For in my eighteenth year the world began to clear for me. Until then my passion for literature had been so exclusive that neither my reasoning power

nor my power of observation had developed. These were now somewhat suddenly awakened and were the source of constant, sharp revelations. (89)

What has been called his "return" to Judaism was for Lewisohn then
just the growth into a mature artistic voice. Through art and the writing
process he isolated, perceived, and tried to braid within himself the multi-
cultural forces of which he was the product. Redefining his
self-perception as a Jew came, in part, to serve his artistic vision, the ability to make an art that is true, authentic. Going into emotional and
intellectual exile helped him find his voice, his artistic direction. Leaving
his parents' home and the South to attend Columbia University in Manhattan, Lewisohn, although dissatisfied with his professors, finds the
intellectual, emotional freedom to help form his aesthetic and artistic
voice and vision:

> I read them with joy, with a sense of liberation, with a feeling that no other
> books in the world had ever given me. I struggled against that feeling; I
> seemed to myself almost disloyal to the modern English masters, to the very
> speech that I loved and which I hoped to write notably some day. But a con-
> viction came upon me after some months with irresistible force. All or nearly
> all English books since Fielding were literature. This was life. All or nearly
> all the English literature by which our generation lives is, in substance, rig-
> idly bounded within certain intellectual and ethical categories. This was
> freedom.... And in English fiction, in 1904, all the people really held the
> same elevated sentiments, sentiments which were mostly false and unneces-
> sary, and of course couldn't and didn't live up to them. (112)

The author finds the teachers to help clear his life of falsehood and master the factual representation of reality:

> My youth had been passed amid so much falseness that my mastery of fact
> was quite inadequate for the practice of real moral freedom. I had no way at
> all of seeing things as they really are, no power of measuring the origin and
> direction of the forces that rule men and the world. (115)

In short, Lewisohn became a writer. Now, at age twenty-two, all he needs
are more shocks to the Jewish part of his cultural dialectic.

In dire need of a fellowship as well, to begin and finance his Columbia University doctoral studies, he goes to an interview with the English
Department Head, Professor Brewer:

Among the group of students to which I belonged it was taken for granted that... I would undoubtedly be chosen. I record this, heaven knows, not from motives of vanity but as part of the subtler purpose of this story. The faculty elected my friend G--. I went, with a heavy heart, to interview Professor Brewer, not to push my claims to anything, but because I was at my wits' end.... Brewer leaned back in his chair, pipe in hand, with a cool and kindly smile. "It seemed to us," he stuttered, "that the university hadn't had its full influence on you..." The truth is, I think, that Brewer, excessively mediocre as he was, had a very keen tribal instinct of the self-protective sort and felt me—what I was hardly yet consciously—the implacable foe of the New England dominance over our national life. I wasn't unaware of his hostility, but I had no way of provoking a franker explanation. (119–120)

The writer's "story" emphasizes how, by degrees, the budding artist becomes the full-blown writer through the painful process of self-identification. Becoming a "Jew" by signification and designation will open Lewisohn totally to the world of the artistic enterprise. The final blow comes the following spring:

I couldn't face Brewer's cool and careless smile. I wrote him a letter—a letter which in its very earnestness and passionate veracity must have struck like a discord upon the careful arrangements of his safe and proper nature.... His answer lies before me now and I copy that astonishingly smooth and chilly document verbatim: "It is very sensible of you to look so carefully into your plans at this juncture, because I do not at all believe in the wisdom of your scheme. A recent experience has shown me how terribly hard it is for a man of Jewish birth to get a good position. I had always suspected that it was a matter worth considering, but I had not known how widespread and strong it was. While we shall be glad to do anything we can for you, therefore, I cannot help feeling that the chances are going to be greatly against you." (122)

Lewisohn's story, here described through a "letter", that is, writing as the enterprise of art and language, is set against the "letter" of Professor Brewer in a frame of warring tribalism: Judaism versus Christianity; one letter/Book attempts to vanquish the other. Brewer's chillingly clear and concise rhetoric establishes Lewisohn as a dislocated nonperson and himself as a "located" individual of power. Ludwig is put into a paralysis of impotence. His self-worth and the potency of his word, his writing, his "letter", has been overpowered by the enemy. Ludwig's word/letter has been rendered powerless:

I sat in my boardinghouse room playing with this letter. I seemed to have no feeling at all for the moment... A numbness held my soul and mutely I watched life, like a dream pageant, float by me.... I went into a bakery and, catching sight of myself in a mirror, noted with dull objectivity my dark hair, my melancholy eyes, my unmistakably Semitic nose.... An outcast.... for the first time in my life my heart turned with grief and remorse to the thought of my [Jewish] brethren in exile all over the world. (122–123)

The Jewish segment of his various and varied culturalisms is suddenly thrown into stark relief. Summoning Freud, Lewisohn calls himself to task for having lied in his secret heart about the realities around him all the years he was growing up. The searching beam of his growing writer's detached and objective observational skills now turns on its owner. Lewisohn recalls how he failed to heed the warnings of his instincts:

The subconscious self has a tough instinct of self-preservation. It thrusts from the field of vision, as Freud has shown, the painful and the hostile things of life.... At one blow now all these delusions were swept away and the facts stood out in the sharp light of my dismay. (123)

On one level, the writer knows that anti-Semitic attitudes and beliefs are real and not just fictionally conjured-up stories: he has experienced the emotionally isolating effects of anti-Jewish sentiment and knows them to be real. However, knowing little or nothing of his own Hebraic heritage, he can find no counsel, refuge or comfort in the Judaism that he is naturally grouped with. He can't claim allegiance to any one cultural frame:

I didn't know how to go on living a reasonably harmonious inner life. I could take no refuge in the spirit and traditions of my own people. I knew little of them. My psychical life was Aryan through and through. Slowly, in the course of the years, I have discovered traits in me which I sometimes call Jewish. But that interpretation is open to grave doubt. I can, in reality, find no difference between my own inner life of thought and impulse and that of my very close friends whether American or German. So that the picture of a young man disappointed because he can't get the kind of a job he wants, doesn't exhaust, barely indeed touches the dilemma. I didn't know what to do with my life or with myself. (125)

Lewisohn again makes his message ambiguous. The reader is hard put to understand exactly what the author's words signify. In his avowed and solemn oath to tell the whole truth by dropping the mask, Ludwig can still end the chapter entitled, "The American Discovers Exile", on a highly unclear note. Admitting to a "strange" Anglo-American "dualism" in himself, and desponding of "the Brewers" of the academic "world", he can say of himself at age twenty-two:

> I do not wish to speak bitterly or flippantly. I am approaching the analysis of thoughts and events beside which my personal fate is less than nothing. And I need but think of my Queenshaven youth or of some passage of Milton or Arnold, or of those tried friendships that are so large a part of the unalterable good of life, or of the bright hair and gray English eyes of my own wife, to know that I can never speak as an enemy of the Anglo-Saxon race. But unless that race abandons its duality of conscience, unless it learns to honor and practice a stricter spiritual veracity, it will either destroy civilization through disasters yet unheard-of, or sink into a memory and into the shadow of a name. (126)

In spite of all his self-awareness and perceptions of mind, at age twenty-four in 1906, Lewisohn marries Mary and sets out on his course of being a writer. With the help of Theodore Drieser, his first book is published. Although it receives much positive critical acclaim, the conservative forces in American society are hostile:

> The Presbyterian editor of the Queenshaven Courier, a friend of mine—(I thought)—arose in his wrath and his terror for the young person and abused my book in terms that were literally foulmouthed.... An old college friend from Queenshaven asked me, months later, what my wife thought of the book. (143–144)

Drowning in self-pity, and theatrically at arms against the commotion and hand-wringing his first book creates by having been perceived as a morally subversive novel, the author, ascribing human characteristics to the book, cries:

> How could my poor little book brave such an array of forces? It didn't sell. It didn't sell at all. I wrote another without one touch of the sensuous beauty of the first—a bare, plain, austere transcript from life, holding within itself, because it is the very core of reality, a massive moral implication. This book, of which I am still proud in retrospect, was published too. And Anthony Comstock, that human symbol of the basic lies of our social structure, confiscated the copies and caused the plates to be destroyed. I was beaten, broken, breadless. I was a scholar and forbidden to teach, an artist and forbidden to write. (145)

Lewisohn believes that he is a total "failure" because he tells the whole truth, uncovers reality and is thus punished for it by the reading public. By age twenty-eight, he still believes in the invincibility of his skill at telling the entire truth, uncovering lies. His writing, he feels, is true, whereas that of others is "false to the shallow core of them and dishonorable." (149) It is, however, still possible for this truth-uncovering writer to write, for example, that "Mary... and I had each other." (150) The portrayal of his relationship with his wife Mary is too rosy, optimistic and upbeat to be believable from a sensitive and perceptive writer whose allegiances by this time to Southern, American and Gentile value systems begin to crumble. His wholesale emotional embrace of Mary and the cultural baggage she brings with her somewhat seems to ring on a false note.

By 1917, at the age of thirty-five, Lewisohn finds both his Jewish and artistic voice. Still skewered by the multi-culturism of his complex identifications and the patchwork of his life, in the final chapter of *Up Stream* Lewisohn can assert:

> Americanization means, of course, assimilation. But that is an empty concept, a mere cry of rage or tyranny, until the question is answered which would never be asked were the answer [not] ripe: Assimilation to what? To what homogeneous culture, to what folkways... to what common instincts concerning love and beauty, to what imaginative passions, to what roads of thought? We have none such that can unite us. (235)

Lewisohn claims, paradoxically, a greater belonging to America than those members of the Anglo-Saxon tribe, by virtue of his absorption in, and of, "the linguistic and literary tradition of the English race." (236) As a writer with mastery of the English language he feels in the right to assert:

> What Anglo-American has a deeper sense for the order and eloquence and beauty of his own tongue than I? But when, in old days, I desired to translate my Americanism in that high and fine sense into action, I was told that I was not wanted. Yet I was to be Americanized. I am even now to be assimilated. Suppose I intend rather to assimilate America, to mitigate Puritan barbarism by the influence of my spirit and the example of my life? (237)

When critic Stuart Sherman makes a declaration that Lewisohn perverts "the national genius", the writer's retort is: "But suppose I am the national genius." (237) Lewisohn's cry is a call to redemption through the word, the story. The Jewish soul/voice cannot help but bring truth and veracity from its depths, to lead humankind to universal peace and return to God. Through *Torah*, the Word/Book of God given to humanity, artistic truth which is synonymous with the word of God, can the world be saved. This notion/belief is depicted in the description in *Up Stream* of the old Russian Jew who reads *Torah* and *Aggadah* in Hebrew, and is as well fully abreast of all world news and politically active. He drinks a little brandy and smokes "Russian cigarettes"; he also reads "Hamlet and Faust in Yiddish translations". He is, in short, the perfect Jew: intellectual, really Jewish, knowledgeable in Hebrew Scriptures, has a good heart and is "wise". (237–238)

This, for Lewisohn, is the best combination of all dialectic: the prophetic, (which is to say, Jewish) consciousness, at one with the Word of God but also sensitive to and expressive of the sense of beauty in the world. The artist-writer is the redeemer, the savior of souls; the standard-setter and describer of truth, falsehood, aesthetic taste, great literature, justice, beauty, goodness—in short, the road to salvation. "But the critical spirit which is also the creative spirit has arisen among us and it has arisen, naturally and inevitably, in the form of a protest and a rebellion against the life and the ethos which is also described here." (247) *Up Stream*'s final call is to see life for what it is. Lewisohn ends this dialectical message with an equally dialectical and enigmatic statement:

> All that I have written is true. It is true of America. It is true, in other degrees, of mankind. But I have written of America for the simple reason that I am an American and I have spoken strongly for the equally simple reason that the measure of one's love and need is also the measure of one's disappointment and indignation. (247)

Perhaps the enigma lies in the dialectic of the individual who is at home everywhere; at rest with all humanity; leading humankind to salvation with the story:

> A few of the books of our new writers are read by many for the story, as a matter of fashion, often quite unreflectively. But most of them are read by a handful of people only. This handful means little among our overwhelming numbers and we who love this new literature and are sustained by it are often deceived in regard to its significance as either a symptom or a sanative. Shall I now say, in order to end agreeably: It is always darkest before dawn? No;

for that kind of professional optimism is precisely one of our national vices. The hour is dark. But that shall not prevent us from working and striving for a better one that may come hereafter. (247–248)

Lewisohn, through his Jewishness (and Americanism), and the moral rights that tribal affiliation gives him entitlement to, will work to bring about the Messianic age through the spirit and power of the story.

Background Discussion I

Lewisohn had spent nearly the entire Second Period at work on *Up Stream*. The world, his world, with all of the complexity of the streams of cultural dialectic flowing through it, into it, combining, recombining, would begin to come into focus. His fated encounter and marriage to Crocker would contribute the painful crucible for forging his complex identity and making sense of the universe.

At age twenty-two, he felt that he might be finding his way: immersion in English literature and writing, a free attitude toward sex, and an open, non-judgmental humanness. Unfortunately, he would too late discover that he had misread what he believed was Crocker's open attitude to sexuality. She was, as he would learn, out to use her sexuality as her only weapon or asset in a world that left little else for women to protect and defend themselves. It is impossible to ever know the full dynamics of that marriage and who was to blame, if any one person could be blamed. Lewisohn, highly sexual by nature, naive, vulnerable, confused, emotionally tied to his mother, still immature, chronologically young in years, and also very kindly, was a prime target to be trapped by an aging, married mother of four, motivated by financial woes. However, Lewisohn's depiction of her in his "autobiographical" work *Up Stream* greatly conflicted with the real events transpiring in his life.

In truth, the "novel", *The Case of Mr Crump,* which he had been writing for many years, is more autobiographical than *Up Stream.* For example, in *Up Stream* he states:

But I met Mary that year.... Bread came somehow.... We had each other. I recall September days full of a soft, grey drizzle.... But we, under one umbrella, recked little of the world.... We sat on a bench under the bare poplars with all the stars of heaven for our own.... With a brave and lovely brightness in her eyes, Mary took me to the boat. (131)

Lewisohn had exiled himself in Paris because of his bitter divorce proceedings with Mary Crocker. After finishing *The Case of Mr Crump*, as Melnick describes, Lewisohn observed:

> "With the composition of *The Case of Mr Crump* I had for the present re-
> leased and made objective the experiences and observations of American life
> that beat against my consciousness." He had "wrought experience into art,"
> transforming his own story into a psychological novel of epic proportions.
> "The novel is in my opinion developing on autobiographical lines.... Autobio-
> graphical it must be, in that deep impressions can only be born out of deep
> experiences." (Melnick I: 414, from *Mid-Channel*, 168–169)

Thus the Second Period of Lewisohn's life and work, from 1904–1922, began with the wake-up call and shock of his rejection because of his Jewishness by the academic establishment and ended with the publication of *Up Stream*. In this transitional time, he demonstrated explosive, vociferous reactions to everything he had believed in throughout the First Period. This now was a time, not of the "return" marked by the Third Period, but of elimination, reaction, rebellion, hatred, "anti-isms" of everything that American and Christian culture, attitudes and ideas represented. Or rather, Lewisohn, through the writer's eye and hand, seemed to want to remake or reform America into the kind of place that could be mutually accepting of both. This period would also bear witness to the bitter conflict Lewisohn had at Ohio State University in 1917. Due to the author's German loyalties, and the entry of America into a World War with Germany, he was forced out of his teaching post there. During this period, first his mother dies, on October 12, 1912, then his father March 1, 1920. As Melnick describes:

> The unhappy memories of a marginal life, and a sense of helplessness before
> the emotional and cultural forces driving him from Mary, shattered Ludwig's
> last hopes for himself and society once Jacques died. Forces that could not so
> easily be overcome raised serious and fundamental questions in his mind,
> questions that neither he nor his friends and associates had raised in the past,
> questions of how one lived "from within outward,".... His unique past and the
> troubled present that had given rise to these thoughts had forced him now to
> seek his own counsel, and to look for new ideas within a vastly different cul-
> tural heritage from that of his colleagues or his wife—"For my friends... were

identified not only by landscapes and speech but, in spite of their radicalism, by fundamental instincts with the American fold and its ways".... Some new direction was needed if he was to set a different course for the years that remained. New questions had to be asked, and a new set of answers, bearing some meaning beyond the illusory importance of the moment, had to be found. (262–263)

Up Stream was the summation of his thoughts about this need of making a transition, of finding a new way. Begun as a protest of American culture, the book ended, albeit somewhat mutedly, as a statement of his renewed identity as a Jew. As Melnick recounts:

He could not mask it [its Jewish intent] effectively enough to assuage Spingarn's [his publisher's] fears that the Jewishness of his protest would damage the book's marketability or endanger the chance for other Jews to seek acceptance within the gentile community. Ludwig had already masked the Jewishness of his vision as much as he could without destroying the intent of his work. There was no possibility of changing it further merely to suit someone else. "I couldn't rewrite without reliving." He was determined to be honest and to be accurate. (297)

Ludwig Lewisohn was now separated from the English expatriate, America-residing Mary Crocker Lewisohn, himself an expatriate living in Europe with a young woman: the half-Jewish Thelma Spear, nine years his junior, who was aspiring to become an opera singer. Lewisohn had met her while he was still living with Mary Crocker. As Mclnick, citing *The Case of Mr. Crump,* asserts: "Ludwig wrote in *Crump* of his first meeting the 'dainty, shapely little figure with a mass of deep golden hair,' and of how he had been immediately struck by her.... Her 'breath of earnestness and of devotion' had reached out to him." (314)

Of interest here also is the reliance that Melnick places on the factuality of Lewisohn's retelling of the details of his life with Mary Crocker and the beginning of his life with Thelma Spear, as well as other autobiographical events. Ludwig had had an affair in the summer of 1920, three years before his first encounter with Thelma. As Melnick tells us, this first affair caused him to understand that he greatly needed a woman like Thelma:

He spoke again of this earlier affair in *Crump*, and of the meaning it had held for him as he grew more assertive in his search for "an immediate and liberating act," likening this relationship, in its attack upon convention, to that of a white Southern man's open love for a black woman—a social metaphor that he undoubtedly found particularly pleasing to draw. (315)

In a quotation from *Crump* Melnick adds: "[She] was the type of woman over whom a man might go to pieces. He didn't care. Better to be destroyed by a beautiful adventuress if she was one, than to decay with [Mary]." (315–316)

Lewisohn, perhaps also unconsciously, saw in Thelma's half-Jewish/half-Christian being the symbol of the combined identities of a good, or at least neutralized, form of Gentilism with the gradual inclusion of Jewish beinghood in his life; she seemed to represent the complexities of Lewisohn's own dialectic of self and identity. In his life as an expatriate living in Europe with Thelma and writing to T.B. Wells of *Harper's*, he was experiencing, as Melnick reports Lewisohn saying, "'I am having a sort of creative rebirth.'" (395)

He was just finishing the manuscript, *Holy Land*, the writing of which he had to interrupt to attend, "for an entire week", (395) the Zionist World Congress being held in the same city in which they were living, Vienna. Melnick views this first short story by Lewisohn as "an allegory of the recent transition in his life." (393) As he asserts: "The references... [in *Holy Land*] are clear." (393) Melnick sees in the husband and wife characters, Mr. and Mrs. Lew Morrison, the representations of a former Ludwig Lewisohn self. The "Mrs.", was the person of Mary: a little silly, shallow, past the shadow of her youth, messy, a Methodist, "who grew increasingly disturbed by the Jewishness of her surroundings" in the Holy Land. Summing up, Melnick observes: "In 'Holy Land,' Ludwig had said his final good-bye to the world of his assimilating youth and to the woman [Mary] with whom he so clearly identified it. Never again would either appear so benign." (393)

Holy Land combines the many elements in the perplexing cultural intermix of Lewisohn's life and work into a terse mirror of the dialectic so fundamental to that life and writing. Besides the feeling of belonging, Lewisohn had been searching for that special knowledge, that ages-old wisdom; deep intelligence coated with Culture; for that special sensitivity to humanness and human frailty; awareness in a much deeper way; a sense of sexuality untainted by shame; laws created for human beings with all their shortcomings, not those created for perfect celestial beings devoid of reality. In short, through the successive levels, first Matthew Arnold, then Sigmund Freud, and finally Martin Buber and Chassidism,

Lewisohn apparently found himself. However, why, on a deeper, more complex level, were these new-found realizations of such great import to him?

Through earnest self-searching, and the hostile aversion to his being that he found around him, he now openly acknowledged his Jewishness. However, it was not solely because he was born a Jew, nor that he suffered for it, that he began flamboyantly to display his new-found identity. Rather, Jewishness for him—as it is also with Ozick—was synonymous with (it can be argued that it, in fact, *is*) the Book/book; the Word/word: in short, the literary enterprise, writing, the communication of the word. Succinctly put, being a full and self-accepting Jew made him a better writer. The writer as the keeper of the word/Word, or book/Book, has the divine obligation to bring the word/book (as Word/Book) to all of humanity. Gabriel in *Trumpet of Jubilee* searches for, and finds, the ultimate significance of life. "Jewish meaning" is the same as "universal meaning".[61] This is the greatest form of artistic expression: Gabriel as prophet, poet and Jew. Gabriel begins to record his "verses" in a strangely exciting mixture of Hebrew and English. As Ozick would do years later, Gabriel muses over whether the meaning he created though his Hebrew-English verses would "create a form for itself through him in the English language?" Like Gabriel, Lewisohn's ideal would seem to be that very mixture of dialectical culturality cemented in and through art, which would appear to be the very synonym of Jewishness. The following quotation from *Up Stream* perfectly illustrates this:

> I knew an old Jew from the south of Russia. He wore a long beard, and you could see where his earlocks had been. He had a habit of hiding his hands in his sleeves. He read Torah and the legends of his people in the sacred tongue. He read Hamlet and Faust in Yiddish translations. He read not only the political news but also the well-conducted literary columns in the Yiddish papers, and cast a thoughtful vote. He sat in his cafe on Second Avenue [Manhattan] and discussed many notable matters and drank tea and occasionally a thimblefull of brandy and smoked Russian cigarettes. He was a wise man and a charitable one and died poor. His son became Americanized. He knows neither Hebrew nor Yiddish. His English is less foreign than his father's was, but far more vulgar and corrupt. (*Up Stream* 237–238)

This is a picture of the very quintessence of a true, or truer, Renaissance man who resolves all culturally dialectical strands into the perfection of cultural savvy, attainment, performance: European, steeped in the tradition of his people without having to be overtly demonstrative of it (or realizing that, in tune with the Enlightenment, one can be fully Jewish but also fully steeped in modernity). He reads *Torah* in Hebrew, as a book, and furthermore because it is the Book, and he both knows and lives Jewish history. This already distinguishes him as a literate, astute learner/reader. As well, reading Hamlet and Faust in Yiddish translation serves, as in Ozick's stories, to dissolve, transform, alchemize some of the greatest cultural achievements of the two most sophisticated and elevated cultures, England and Germany, into a dialectic of diverse complexity. Here is where Jewish consciousness from the very soul of the Jewish people, that is, Yiddish, *Mamalushen*, becomes an indecipherable part of Western secularism, which in turn is magically (re)transformed into a form of Jewishness. This "old Jew", fully in the past, is also in the history-making present. He is a totally up-to-date reader (in Yiddish) on politics, current events, the world, and contemporary literary happenings reflected through Jewish awareness/perception; he is also a participating member of the American country in which he lives. An aesthete, he has his favorite cafe for sophisticates in one of the most Jewish areas of the world—the lower East Side of Manhattan. Too Jewish himself to worry about the then-contemporary period in American history when the consumption of alcohol was illegal (the Prohibition), he drinks enough to show that he cares not at all for the law, but not enough of it to cross the cultural frame of his Jewishness into Gentileness. Cigarette-smoking and alcohol-sipping frame this portrait of him as one of the cultural elite. As a full Jewish being, where his Jewishness is the key to his sophistication and humanity in the world, he displays both wisdom and charity. The proof of this old Jew's savvy is that he could ubiquitously understand everything in the world by being totally himself. The paradox is that his son, who knows English better, is more American than his "old Jew" father, has lost his essential Jewishness and can only know the world through an incomplete, fractured, imperfect prism of vulgarity and corruption.

Lewisohn had found the key; he now understood what had gone wrong in his life and in the life of other "enlightened" Jews before him. Like the tale of the "old Jew", he dissolved America into Israel, purified its culture in the exalted fire of *Torah*, blended Europeanism into Manhattan and the larger American culture. In short, he dialectically assimilated, not his Jewish self into the greater Gentile American world, but America into his newly-discovered Jewishness. This "old Jew" was leisurely sitting—like almost all of Ozick's characters—not in a sidewalk cafe in Europe or Tel Aviv, but in Manhattan, America. Regarding this, Lewisohn asserts in *Up Stream*:

> The doctrine of assimilation [by Jews into American culture] driven home by public pressure and official mandate, will create a race of unconscious spiritual helots. We shall become utterly barbarous and desolate. The friend of the Republic, the lover of those values which alone make life endurable, must bid the ...Jew... preserve his cultural tradition and beware of the encroachments of Neo-Puritan barbarism—beware of becoming merely another dweller on an endless Main Street; he must plead with him to remain spiritually himself until he melts naturally and gradually into a richer life, a broader liberty, a more radiant artistic and intellectual culture than his own. (240)

If anything, this quotation, it would seem, boldly highlights Lewisohn's outright call for an assimilating/assimilation mix of all dialectical elements through a mirror and base of Jewishness.

Through 1924 and 1925, still technically part of *The Nation* staff, Lewisohn wrote articles from Jerusalem and Palestine. A footnote at the bottom of one 1924 article states: "Mr. Lewisohn will send letters from Palestine through the winter."[62] His absorption and immersion in *Torah*, Buber and Chassidic thought are clearly obvious in this 1924 essay. For Lewisohn, this is, as the title expresses, his return to Jerusalem, albeit temporarily, and to his Jewishness. Describing the boat's passengers on the vessel taking the author, fellow-Jews and others to the Holy Land, Lewisohn writes:

> There is an elderly cloak-and-suit manufacturer who lives in the Bronx [who] has slipped away from his assimilated family to get a glimpse of Israel. [There is also] a group of... bearded Jews.... Their phylactery boxes project from their foreheads, they are draped in their great, graying praying shawls. They rock back and forth and chant the words their fathers chanted centuries before England had a name. They, at least, are not going east. They never left the Mediterranean world.... To them dream and reality were never divided. They are going from Jerusalem to Jerusalem. ("Return" 724)

The word "Israel" is an outright encoded statement about Hebrew Scriptural Israel, the birthright of the Jewish people given by God. The newer past of assimilatory Jews into an ever other-assimilating America, in the person of the "elderly cloak-and-suit manufacturer" who lives in Jewish New York City, returns to his ancient past—but, like the journeying protagonist in *Holy Land*, he is there just temporarily. This image is juxtaposed with those fully real Jews, the Orthodox, who never left the spirit of the land of Israel. Lewisohn underscores the cultural preeminence of *Torah* and Hebrew identity over anything else by elevating—through the right of historical seniority—the (Hebrew) words and their enculturated language over the language and culture of England. Unlike Lewisohn, who is a son of Palestine, but nevertheless a visitor there, these Orthodox Jews, through their more total cultural anti-assimilation, and therefore personal identity homogenization, have always been one with Israel/Palestine. The voyage they are taking is merely geographical, not a spiritual, emotional journey of selfhood.

In Israel, Lewisohn says, one can find his/her soul. However, "the tourists and merchants", he excoriatingly chides, "bring eyes and minds and leave their souls at home." (724) The most "complicated... case" is with the "Jewish pioneers, the *chaluzim* whose songs are heard from the steerage at twilight." (724) These returning Jews have a twofold struggle. They have left a place that was not completely uncomfortable for them. They had material and physical comforts—they were even "successful" in their lives. But their spirits were wanting. They have lost themselves:

> They are putting off a spiritual garment that chafed and ached. But it had been long worn and its very imperfections were familiar. A garment— a world.... If their adventure is to be a triumph, their souls must melt into a new earth and a new heaven...the beginning of the end of a journey home. (724)

Such earnest pep talks, however, directed at backsliding Jewish brethren, may not have assuaged Lewisohn's own personal conflicted cultural dialectic between living in America or Palestine (Israel). The historical fact is that the author did not make Palestine his home. When all was said and done, he still hung his hat in an American abode. It is true that his fervent and exhausting lobbying efforts for the establishment of a Jewish state, out of necessity on American soil, probably precluded a life in any other geographic location of the world. As Melnick notes, Lewisohn was constantly torn by the conflicts generated by his American and Israel cultural affinities. The establishment of the Jewish state of Israel created a moral dilemma for American Jewry. With the *Torah* homeland now in existence, how should Jewish life in America be constructed or perceived? As Melnick describes,[63] Lewisohn

> objected to the use of American cultural attributes as any basis for reconstituting Jewish life. "It is a sorry spectacle to see *this* civilization or, rather, this

foul relapse into Godless barbarism in which we live made the *criterion* of faith and practice. This world, this America, are worth helping to save, not worth imitating. That is what I find so supremely shocking." (Melnick II: 387)

Lewisohn's shock and dismay can also have been directed at himself. It is an agonizing conundrum: American Jews, Lewisohn concludes (and Ozick agonizes as well), cannot create or maintain a true Jewish value system and life in a Gentile country, even the United States of America. Therefore:

Why not, as an alternative, push for massive immigration of American Jews to Israel, if the prospects for a Jewish renewal in America were so bleak that its most vocal advocates could offer only a program characterized by "theological thinness"? Such a solution was, of course, being advocated by the Zionists in Jerusalem. "Fascinating and moving," Ludwig said of their proposals, "but quite out of contact with American reality.... It is unrealistic to expect this peripheral, emotionally half-dejudaized people, bedeviled and bewildered by the liberalistic slogans of 40 years ago, to know and feel and execute their ultimately necessary destiny [of immigration to Israel]." (388)

The story, *Holy Land*, finds the narrator, possibly a thinly disguised Lewisohn, caught in this dilemma of cultural dialectic. Here he is seen transculturally at home in all places with all people; a proud pilgrim to his ancestral historical homeland, but a visitor nevertheless.

Holy Land: A Story

The title sets the stage for the duplicity inherent in this story's message/s. The chosen words, "Holy Land", are counterpoised with "A Story". The conspicuous absence of any article, especially "the" with "Holy Land", set against the subtitled words, "A Story", which with the indefinite article "a", effects a perplexing message.

The "land" referred to is that which is designated by God for Abraham, Isaac, Jacob and the Israelite nation through all future generations. As the *Torah* states: "And to your seed after you I will give the land." (*Genesis* 35:12–13) God gave "the Holy Land", in Hebrew *eretz ha kodesh* or *adamat ha kodesh,* to his holy people, the Israelites. The article "the", *ha,* signifies particular singularity. Why, therefore, does

Lewisohn, with the writer's acute sensitivity to every visual sign on the page (or its absence), omit the word "the" at the beginning of the story's title?

One answer for this is offered by the story's pre-title and title page inscriptions. Just preceding the title page is: "There be A wyshe I have for thee/ This Chrystmasse-tyde:/ May joye and alle gladde thynges/ The seasonne brynges/ Gette to thee and abyde." On the title page is written: "Printed for Harper & Brothers Publishers on old Murray Hill for distribution among their friends at this Christmas Season."[64] The message of these two inscriptions is clear: the story's publication in 1926 was directed toward a Christian readership. Financial considerations notwithstanding, the story's message, beginning with the title, is ambiguous enough to be perceived as a Christian message, a non-Christian message, both a Jewish and Christian message, or a Jewish message. This publication of *Holy Land* was preceded by another, the first appearance of the story in print, minus the Christmas inscription and also without the article "the".[65]

The question is, therefore, why is the article missing from its historically rightful place? Biographical information and the simultaneously published *Up Stream* point to a change in cultural direction, from a generally Christian perspective to a Judaic one, with Lewisohn's Jewish identity and affiliation coming to the foreground of his life. As well, in the German and revised English editions of *Up Stream*, it is already possible to discern his Judaic affinities, messianic-prophetic fervor, insistence on truth-telling and desire to fully understand himself. Nonetheless, the reader is left with an obscure, equivocal, ultimately impenetrable message: To what/which/whose "Holy Land" does the title make reference, and to what/which/whose "Holy Land" does Lewisohn subscribe? The second question must be asked, since his work can be considered highly biographical.

Written with a first-person narrator, the story on its most literal level traces and describes, from the perceptual viewpoint of the narrator/author Lewisohn, the travel experiences and espousal relationship of Mr. and Mrs. Lew Morrison from Albion, Wisconsin, U.S.A.; the relationship of the narrator/author Lewisohn with Mrs. Lew Morrison, who is variously referred to as "Mrs. Morrison or "the wife", with Mr. Lew Morrison, usually referred to as "Lew"; and with the two as a unit.

The story begins on a ship, the *Venetia*, on a voyage from some unclear location to an equally unspecified end destination. The ship appears to be moving, similar to the language the author uses to describe the story as a whole, to a paradoxically centerless locus; a place or places both with and without geographical focus; a place or places simultaneously physically identifiable and allusively metaphorical, even transcendent; co-instantaneously personal, national-cultural and universal. The vessel is somewhere in "the middle" between the European waters of the Atlantic Ocean and the Mediterranean Sea. Thus there are some known, or nearly-known, facts. The ship has probably set sail from some European port, and its next, or first, point of disembarkation is Alexandria, Egypt. Nevertheless, the ship, like the narrator/author, is ambiguously between worlds— "in", but also transversing them.

The *Venetia* is a kind of Tower of Babel that only a wise writer-as-prophet can heal, organize, understand, render "readable", interpret its cacophony of messages aboard. Although the story can be said to begin on the first page of its printed text, the story/stories themselves began at varying time frames before the initial physical page. When the story "begins", a blond-haired man sitting near the narrator is telling "stories" which began before the text itself opens. There are many stories, big and small, that have preceded the story *Holy Land*. Significantly, the story "ends" in the physical place "Palestine". Thus the story's ultimate destination is "the Holy Land" of Israel, the land of God's promise. Or is it?

The narrator is an acutely perceptive Joshua, a clandestine Jeremiah, or perhaps the/a messiah who comes to save the Morrisons from disaster and perhaps the reputation of the Jewish people/nation/name that could be destroyed by Gentiles unsympathetic to all things Jewish. This messiah sits perceiving and judging the aesthetic defects, or attributes, of this microcosm of humanity: God's world of people in miniature. He is enjoying the sophisticated table-talk of his happenstance dinner companion: "The blond man across the table from me, the man with a cheery, knowing squint, gossiped in a mixture of languages about Egyptian politics.... I listened carefully to the blond man." (*Holy Land* 1)

There are a number of coded message imbedded in this little scene. The words, "the blond man", are repeated twice within five lines, and his savvy is re-reflected in the narrator's attentive absorption in the former's observations about Egypt's political "stories". This blond, Aryan male, of perhaps German origin, is the self-composed, well-informed, alert digester of the world around him; conversant in an unnamed number and variety of languages; the very same kind of social, intellectual, linguistic and, most importantly, culturally ubiquitous frame that Lewisohn would have appeared to value in himself and others.

The narrator then becomes aware of language consisting of "haphazard, half-articulate sounds farther to my right" that have "a winning, teasing familiarity." (1) He realizes that it's "a woman's voice" (1) speaking American English. The narrator is so generally exhilarated by the sounds of language around him that one might conclude that the meaning is of less import: all linguistic enterprise appears to excite the narrator/writer. These female vocal sounds, the narrator observes, "stole upon me." (1) They are the resonances of America, articulations of a once-loved/still-loved past. Stealing into him in this way, the narrator registers his surprise at the pleasant effect these modulations have upon him. The talk/speech of the "blond man" is thus juxtaposed with that of the woman. He speaks of "Egyptian politics"; she of the chicken they are eating at the meal table: "I don't think much of this chicken, do you, Lew?" (2)

The narrator absorbs this clash of cultural options: the blond man's European cosmopolitanism versus the woman's naive, childish, ignorant, artless, rudimentary patter; in short, American small-talk. As Lewisohn dryly observes in *Up Stream* about average American university students:

> There is not a vicious face [among them].... Dull faces, vacant faces. Not one that expresses any corruption of heart and mind. I look about me again and watch for one face that betrays a troubled soul, a yearning of the mind, the touch of any flame. There is none... all are incurably trivial. (*Up Stream* 155)

In giving his full attention to this American couple, he begins to observe each of them carefully. He makes a quick sketch of the wife for the reader as a typical American female: "She was frankly middle-aged, tall, thin, wistful—wistful yet positive. She sucked her teeth in a comfortable self-satisfied way at the memory of the real chicken to which she was accustomed at home." (*Holy Land* 2)

The reader is given here the message of Mrs. Morrison's "real" chicken from her real world of America, and the contentment she has at being at home in herself, her country and belief system. Revealing the secret of her relatively advanced age, the narrator both incriminates and sentimentalizes this American female and the culture from which she comes. Similarly, the husband, with a name that bears a strong resemblance to that of the author, Lew Morrison, "large, comfortable, fleshy, turned to her a kindly, crinkled, shrewd face." (2) Both of them are Lewisohn's pure American types, evincing that combination of money, cunning, alertness, casualness, innocence, generosity, greyness, middleness and forbearance that marks the profile of the American Abroad. Where some might fling themselves into thought of a historical past, Mrs. Morrison's memory extends no farther than that of "the real chicken" of her homeland. Nevertheless, Lew's kindliness (perhaps more like pragmatism) is, like his wife's, colored by a decidedly chauvinistic attitude: "'We've had worse 'n this.' 'I'd like to know where!' 'Oh, at a lot o' these places.'" (2)

For Lewisohn's American prototype, what's foreign is foreign; no distinctions are made between things outside of the Morrisons' cultural sphere. The words "these places" designate an absence of any particularity, a simplistic "us/them" frame of reference. As for the narrator, in a description of the interaction between himself and Lew Morrison, the former is the very perfection of omniscience itself: "His vivid, unimaginative grey eyes met mine. He saw that I understood and grinned a grin of male fellowship. He almost winked as he said to her, but obviously for me to overhear: 'The drinks are a whole lot better.'" (2–3)

The gastronomical fare is not so bad after all. The reader is made party to those qualities that in fact contribute to the overall positive effect Lew has on the narrator and, it seems, the narrator on Lew. Mr. Morrison's unimaginativeness, posited against (we can assume) the narrator/writer's creative inventiveness, is overshadowed by the sense of masculine camaraderie shared by their mutual bad-boy mischievousness: they both flaunt an unwillingness to accept the Puritan/American standards of morality and behavior that Prohibition dictated. This law, which forbade the manufacture, transportation, sale and possession of alcoholic beverages, was in effect throughout the U.S. between the years 1920 and 1933. In the neutral territory of their floating mini-world, where alcoholic drinking and smoking are culturally acceptable and/or out of the realm of any one cultural frame, they are free of what Lewisohn had on many occasions described as the perversity of American life. Here in this "no place" they can leisurely indulge themselves.

As well, the couple appears self-consciously to perform for the narrator: "She followed his glance and, also for my benefit, gurgled in her genuine though so belated girlishness: 'Why, Lew Morrison, I'm surprised at you!'" (3)

Leaving his dinner table, the narrator strolls out of the dining room:

A few minutes later I came upon them on deck. She was resting on her deck chair, eager even in her reclining position; Morrison was standing by the railing, generously moistening the end of a handsome American cigar. He nodded and said: "I *thought* you were an American!" (3)

The passage is loaded with innuendo. Is the narrator/Lewisohn an American? What is Mrs. Morrison so eager about in her reclining position? The quotation has an unmistakably sexual message. Do the narrator's obviously masculine attributes excite her? Is he a dream vision of a pure, virile, American type? The narrator, it would appear, is caught in a threesome of competition and desire. Lew, the great guy that he is, not only drinks alcohol and smokes cigars, he is a beacon in the sexless, colorless world of American cultural life—albeit out of that country's borders. Mrs. Morrison appears unable to choose between such overwhelming examples of American male potency. As Lew moistens the tip of his "handsome American cigar", the phallic innuendos become impossible to ignore.

The mask has been dropped—or has it? The narrator, a thinly masked Lewisohn, has been caught out, discovered. Pretending to be something else (?), he is revealed to be exactly what through all of his childhood he prayed to be accepted as: an American in every way. Why is Lew so absolutely convinced (shrewd man that he is) that the narrator is an American? Is it the narrator's perfect English; physiognomy (even though presumably Semitic); intellectual brilliance masquerading as empty-mindedness; mental yearning; flamelessness of heart, mind or soul; triviality; lack of keenness; low-browness; ascetic status quo; stupidity; "averageness"? These are the characteristics that in *Up Stream* Lewisohn assigns to the type known as "American". (*Up Stream* 156–157) Oddly, Lew Morrison becomes the yardstick, the measure, the prototype of all proper and improper attitudes; the height of discernment. The narrator appears to measure himself through Lew's perception:

In a moment, under his dryly humorous, tolerant glance she was telling me about them; about herself. She spurted. It wasn't the tourist season. American had evidently been few. Since she could speak only English and that, as she said, maybe "not so good", she was famished for communication. (*Holy Land* 3–4)

The lover's sofa becomes the psychiatrist's couch. Mrs. Morrison, feeling somehow lost, wants to talk, to communicate; to undergo the Freudian "talking cure". Through language, the universe and all its living things can be saved; God's world can be healed. The narrator, as prophet/ artist/writer, can cure Mrs. Morrison's dis-ease, unease. The writer, with the divine fire reflected in him (and her) can redeem humanity, usher in the messianic age.

The Morrisons are, to be sure, good, perhaps even culturally-minded people. Mrs. Morrison tells the narrator: "Oh, yes, we've been all over Europe. London and Paris and Venice. Did you see the churchyard where Gray wrote his elegy? Didn't you just love it? London was crowded. Oh, wasn't it *just*? But the Exposition was dandy!" (4) No matter what their shortcomings, the Morrisons' appreciation for literature make them totally redeemable in the narrator/author/Lewisohn's value system.

The narrator's lighthearted derision mixed with nostalgic affection turns decidedly positive in the next scene: "She leaned forward; she tucked a wisp of straight brownish hair back under her Leghorn traveling hat. The wistfulness in her face was more marked now than the positiveness, than the communicativeness." (4–5) Mrs. Morrison is ready to tell a story; a story of a story of the "Battle of the Stories"—Christianity versus Judaism:

> "I always felt like I wanted to see the places where our Lord lived. We're not so terribly religious." There was a queer little apology in her voice. She meant, of course, that they weren't bigoted and rancorous. But I knew that from the way she had teased her husband about drinking. "I've always thought—" She stopped. She was articulate enough in her way. But any speech beyond the special formulas of her environment found her shy. (5)

The Morrisons have the profile for salvation: a love of literature, with not-so-bad communicative skills themselves; and a deliciously wonderful sense of rebelliousness toward the worst in American culture. Unfortunately, they are not multicultural and able to communicate well in any national framework. The narrator, on the other hand, is a cultural chameleon; drop him anywhere and he is indistinguishable from the others around him. As well, his English communication skills and sympathetic ear give momentum to Mrs. Morrison's confessional mood. He is the psychiatric midwife of a very special talking-cure revelation process; the artistic director of the unmasking scene that follows:

I sat down on an unoccupied chair beside her. She looked away from me. "It's like this. We're Congregationalists. But my father—he's been dead for years and years—he was a Methodist minister. I want to tell you he was a saint if ever there was one." (5–6)

Like the narrator/author/Lewisohn, Mrs. Morrison is a religious crossover who also wants to piece together the historical-belief background of her life. She wants to return to her roots, to peel away the fake and reveal the truth of it all. Mrs. Morrison's reflections of her past evoke sweet memories of the narrator/author's own childhood experiences with the Methodist Church and Christians who were a saintly combination of kindliness, piety, compassion and tolerance. Lew doesn't seem to mind the relative intimacy of the narrator with his wife. For the narrator, in this couple's company he has the best of both the male and female worlds: the tenderness of the mother-female figure combined with the camaraderie of an even-tempered father-male figure. Oedipally speaking, this is a perfect set of parents and/or stage set for the narrator-author to exhibit his humane sensibilities, his stunning intellectual and communicative virtuosity.

Mrs. Morrison's allusions to a hymn re-reflect Lewisohn's *Up Stream* descriptions of the effect that church music had on his early conversion to Christianity. (*Up Stream* 50) As well, her allusion to "the places where our Lord lived" brings the ages-old dialectic of Christianity and Judaism to the fore; it bares its very nerve line. This story serves up a long list of contrasts: cunning-creative/spiritual; unimaginative/inspired; impotent/virile; narrow-minded Puritan/indulger in physical pleasures; foreign European/American; out-of-place/possessing identity and place; ignorant, naive/knowledgeable, sophisticated; uneducated/educated; uncultured/cultured; bad Christians/good Christians; good Jews/bad Jews; backward/civilized; conventional/unconventional; blond (Aryan)/dark (foreign, Jewish, exotic); and Christian/Jewish.

Lew decides to reveal the truth about why they've taken this trip to Palestine:

"Tell you a secret about the wife. The ladies got up some sort of a club in Albion a couple o' years ago. She's quite a leader in it. Well, they read papers there about… about authors, say, or the trips they've been on. So the wife sort of figured out that if we took this trip she'd certainly have an original subject!" He laughed a merry but subterranean kind of a laugh—an inward

chuckle. She was accustomed to his teasing. Her protest was a formula:
"Why, Lew Morrison, how can you say that!" (*Holy Land* 7–8)

After Lew's story, the truth still remains ambiguous. It's just a story
after all. Lew reveals nothing of the real reason that they've made this
trip to the Middle East. On the other hand, the narrator realizes that Mrs.
Morrison's story is more in line with the truth as to why they have come
to the Holy Land. At the same time, the feelings of goodwill, back-home
familiarity and the narrator's impressive coupling of sensitivity and mas-
culinity, as viewed through the narrator's perspective (for, after all, that's
what the reader has to go by), have quickly cemented a certain kind of
fondness of one for another in this trio. Lew has other stories about why
they are on their way to Palestine:

> "We had a pretty good year up our way. I'm in the contracting business 'n'
> connected with the First National of Albion. The farmers had money—all of
> 'em, seems like. Well, I'd just as soon've gone to Florida or to the Coast.
> But she"—he nodded toward his wife—"wanted to take this trip. It's been
> kind of a dream she's had. Just like she told you. Well, I'm having a good
> time, all right. They got some mighty fine Scotch down in the smoking room
> and they don't hardly charge you nothing for it." He winked at me. "Shall we
> have a drink?" (8–9)

Going their separate ways after the ship docks in Alexandria, the narrator thinks he has caught sight of "a slightly bewildered face" (9) of
Mrs. Morrison. Perceptible reality can fool one into thinking that something is real when it isn't; or perhaps one's perception can point us to the
truth. The narrator can only say: "But I wasn't sure." (9) Losing sight of
the Morrisons, they also pass into the world of the forgotten for the narrator, who "was hurrying through to make my connection for Palestine at
Kantara." (9–10)

The Gentile-Christian Morrisons and the Jewish (?) narrator, at this
point would appear to have the same end destination: Palestine. On the
other hand, in a story that simultaneously demasks/unmasks/masks,
nothing is sure; most especially the real destination of both the narrator
and the Morrisons. Even less certain is the nature and identity of the destination itself: which or what is this "Holy Land" to which they are
traveling? The narrator appears unflappably certain of his final point of
destination. In contrast, they are perceived by him as being confused,

hesitant, not sure where, how or even why they are going. When Mrs. Morrison finally catches sight of the narrator after a separation of twelve days, they appear totally relieved, reassured:

> Mrs. Morrison saw me at once and fluttered happily, as though in sudden sight of refuge, in my direction.
> "Well, did you ever!" she exclaimed. Her husband, following closely, grasped my hand with unexpected cordiality. They scarcely waited for my invitation to sit at my table, they were so obviously relieved to find me. (10–11)

Could it be that the narrator/writer or narration/story is the end destination point in their search for the Holy Land: is he their redeemer? Is art/writing the true messiah, as book/Book and Jewish word? Can writing save the world, redeem nations? It would appear that the narrator/writer/Lewisohn, whose home is in various locations, is at home with everyone, exactly as befits a universal Redeemer—but with a twist: He is the prophet of the book/Book.

As well, the narrator/Lewisohn/writer is a wonder of intermixture. In the very-American Morrisons' perception, as viewed through the narrator's eyes (that is, the story), the narrator, so obviously American, is also extremely self-composed and well-acquainted with the European and Middle Eastern landscapes (what isn't he acquainted with?). He seems as much at home in Jerusalem as he was on the ship or in New York. One finally wonders what his "place" is and where he fits exactly. When he sees them,

> they strolled hesitantly into the dining room of the Allenby Hotel in Jerusalem. There were only half a dozen people in the rather bare room: a long-faced bronzed old Egyptian merchant and his young European wife, a couple of blond, chirpy Englishmen, a well-groomed American Zionist. (10)

The narrator is at home with all of them and each sees him as one of theirs. As on the ship, most cultural areas of the world are represented in the hotel dining room: European, English, Arabian, Jewish-American, and a Zionist as well. The code words "American Zionist" represent Israel/Palestine as the God-bequeathed homeland of the Jewish people, the Israelite nation, the fated connection between America and Israel, and the clear idea, perhaps, that one can be a zealous Zionist and also an American. Thus Lew and Mrs. Morrison, as Christian Americans, in the cultural dialectic of *Holy Land*, are posited against the American Zionist.

The latter is one of a small number of American Jews to support the (re)establishment of the Jewish State of Israel, a minuscule sampling from the entire Jewish-American spectrum of social and religious affiliations in the years before the Holocaust. In a pre-Hitler world, this stand (voiced as well by Lewisohn) seemed farfetched and irritatingly aggressive. More accurately, the number of American Jews who supported the (re)establishment of the State of Israel was minuscule at the time of the publication of Lewisohn's *Israel* in 1925. However, the number of supporters grew in direct proportion to the constantly unfolding horrific news of the Holocaust in progress.

In parallel, the Morrisons have become noticeably unhappy. Their chance meeting with the narrator gives them the much-needed oxygen to follow through with their goal to visit the sites connected to Jesus. In complaining about their guide, there is an indirect compliment paid to the narrator, whose omniscience and cosmopolitanism have greatly impressed them. Their Cook Tour guide's English was too fast to be intelligible. The discerning and cultured narrator/writer, perceiver of all truths, whose cultural savvy (read as dialectic) and highly articulate communication of the English language (read as American and English), appears destined to lead them through this Holy Land, whose ownership and rightful place still remain mysteriously unknown.

The first signs of an answer to this soon appear:

> I asked them what their impression of the Holy City was. Morrison said "Oh, I guess it's all right." His wife looked at me a little wanly. "It's wonderful, wonderful!" I looked at her closely. She seemed unaccountably more faded than before. "The light is terrible," she said. I advised smoked glasses. They already had them. There was something pathetic about her, something at once eager and frustrated. "Suppose we take a walk this afternoon," I suggested. With a quite uncharacteristic gesture she put her hand over mine. "Oh, that would be dandy!" That word "dandy" seemed, in this place, of an innocent weirdness; it seemed of a strange, remote childlikeness. My eye happened to fall on the face of the Egyptian merchant. It had suddenly a pharaonic cruelty and agelessness. (11–12)

The narrator/writer/Lewisohn is now in an ambiguous balance *vis a vis* the Christian pilgrims in search of the Holy Land. An American, he is also a son of the Israelite nation; or is he? He is also struck by the remembrance of the harsh affliction of the Israelite nation at the hands of the Egyptians, glimpsed in the physiognomy of the merchant. To where, to whom does the narrator belong?

Lew's answer to the narrator's question about the Holy City is shrouded in noncommittal ambiguity. The way a person experiences Jerusalem is the litmus test of his/her connectedness to the Jewish people. Mrs. Morrison is noticeably unhappy that her (typologized) Holy Land is not what she remembers it to be from her preacher-father's stories. The narrator/psychiatrist/writer/savior examines Mrs. Morrison's very soul, the inners of her mind. He realizes that the couple is clearly disappointed. He now holds more interest for them than their lifelong conception of a savior named Jesus who, as their Christian story goes, was born and died in this selfsame Holy Land.

It is clear that the Morrisons are visionless, incapable of true messianic spiritual insight: Mrs. Morrison is blinded by the power of Jerusalem's (holy) light. She complains about the Jerusalem "light" which filters from and to Heaven, God's Holiness made manifest in the physical place, Jerusalem. The light of Jerusalem is in reality blinding against the most heavenly blue of skies. Even with "smoked glasses" (that is, sunglasses), they are only irritated by this light. Mrs. Morrison, in fact, has been fading in the shock of the light and the magnitude of its strength. They were unprepared for the real thing. The narrator quickly takes charge of this disarranged, hopelessly displaced, Christian-American couple.

Mrs. Morrison's unexpectedly intimate, more than friendly, covering of the narrator's hand with hers, says it all. She thus signals her complete trust in him; designates him as the messiah to lead her through all the wonders and splendors his body, mind, soul and heart can afford her. The sexual facet of their relationship (albeit fantasized), becomes manifest. Mrs. Morrison fits the profile of a certain Christian type of female that Lewisohn was drawn to since his childhood. In *Up Stream* Lewisohn describes scenes that demonstrate this type as a mixture of religious fervor and sensuality. (*Up Stream* 90) For example, it goes with Mrs. Morrison's desire for "our Lord" and rapture over the hand of salvation offered by the narrator combine to form a kind of spiritual eroticism or erotic spiritualism. From another direction, the same is found in the narrator who becomes the man-savior sensuously moved by the innocence of the Christian female palpitating for spiritual direction, Jesus the man and "Lord", and the masculine messiah figure who will lead her to a heavenly state of ecstacy, as in the narrator's description: "A faint, beautiful emotion came into her eyes." (*Holy Land* 6) Thus, through sensual, sexual fantasy, the chemistry of assertive virility and female suppleness, the narrator/writer/Lewisohn as Israelite in disguise, can vanquish the Christian part of the Jewish-Gentile dialectic.

The narrator deals with another area of the dialectic in a similar way: shifting back and forth from a Jewish/Christian to a Jewish/Arab one. Both are explored in a complex and subtle weave of unmasked/masked stories of vanquisher and vanquished, in which the narrator-as-writer-as-messiah vanquishes the world through the word/Word, the story/Story, and heavenly linguistic enterprise. In the second, the Arab is seen in cameo through a number of characteristics, including the pharaonically cruel face of the Egyptian merchant. For Israelites, this immediately conjures up the infamous Pharaoh from the story of Passover (believed to be Ramses II) who was punished with ten plagues for his hardness of heart and for his savage 200-year oppression of the nation of Israel. The first reference to the Arab is when the narrator tries to maintain sight of the Morrisons in Alexandria, but loses "sight of them in the turbulent Arab crowd." (9) In 1925, the year this story was written, Zionism was still a nonthreatening dream; and Arab-Jewish relations had not deteriorated to the point of the year 1947, when the United Nations partitioned Palestine into Jewish-Arab states and the Arabs immediately declared war on the Jews. Thus, the narrator's/Lewisohn's clear distaste for Arabs is not as much religious as cultural. For those who, like the narrator, are of a Western, Anglo-Saxon, Germanic cultural background, Middle Eastern Arab culture can be a shock:

> We entered at the Jaffa Gate. Mrs. Morrison and I walked on ahead. Morrison followed. I guided her down the steps of the uneven, crooked little street. I kept her from being jostled. She seemed frightened. I told her that the Arabs meant nothing by bumping into her. They simply had no sense of orderliness. (13)

As the narrator/writer/messiah/doctor/guide leads them through what was to be the Promised Land, Mrs. Morrison and Lew are both the epitome of amazement and awe for the former's depth of wisdom and omniscience, and full of a growing disappointment for these sites connected to the stories of Jesus. Mrs. Morrison wants to view the real places of Jesus' deeds brought to life for her through the narrative of her now-dead preacher-father:

> "Well, I want to tell you, my father just told his people about Jesus. You just felt's if you could see Nazareth and Galilee and all the places that our Saviour

was in, you know. And somehow"—she straightened up and brightened up
into her more conventional self—"I've always said that early impressions last
longest. Don't you think so yourself? My, but it's a grand day!" (6–7)

The stories Mrs. Morrison heard as a child now seem somehow truer
than the real life places where her feet are now treading. Her father was a
very convincing storyteller, and thus had the makings of a redeemer, like
the narrator. The narrator, as messianic guide, in effect is reshaping the
Morrisons' perception of what it means to be a Christian and Jew; he is
leading them through a new (old) reading of Christianity, and therefore of
Judaism from its very origin: detypologizing the mythologized stories that
form the Christian's perception of both Judaism and Christianity. Why
would the church (through her father's words) mask the Jesus of the
larger story—the birth and death of Joshua/Jesus? Why would her
father's stories about Jesus feel somehow alien to the places the narrator
is telling her that Jesus inhabited? What emerges is a contrast of Jesuses:
one Jewish, the other Gentile. Mrs. Morrison is confused. Who is the real
Jesus, and who is the charming, seemingly omniscient male travelling
companion guiding them through what was supposed to be The Holy
Land (of her father's stories)?

The full disappointing truth comes through to the Morrisons when
they enter—as the bigger story goes—the pathway of Jesus's last walk:

> The Via Dolorosa was fairly empty and still. It was no feast day. It lay for-
> lorn between the blind walls in its alternation of fierce light and sharp, black
> shadows. A few filthy Arab children, waiting for stray tourists, cried for
> alms. Mrs. Morrison stumbled over the smooth cobblestones. "This is where
> our Lord..." She panted a bit. I nodded. "Did you imagine it differently?" I
> asked. "Oh, I don't know." She tried to sound cheerful. (14)

The narrator's description can be read metaphorically as well. This
part of the Jesus story, the account of his last walk to the crucifixion, is a
mixture of truth and fiction in its varying "light" and darkness. So stir-
ring a story is set "forlorn" and "blind" between metaphoric fictiveness
and narrational reality. Mrs. Morrison goes the way of her own Via
Dolorosa, carrying the cross of the growing disappointment within her.
The scene becomes a snapshot of the political and cultural complexity
that Jerusalem/Israel represents; and the hard reality a Christian must face
to realize that Jesus/Joshua was and is a genetically alien being for them.
He was of this place of intermixed Semitic cultures. His being and

cultural heritage point toward a people not theirs. His very existence becomes a painful realization, and they must try to untangle its intricacies. Can it be true that their Lord is of the very same people their 2000-year-old story has vilified?

> She glanced shyly into the greasy, open shops, nervously dodged the large wooden platter of a cake-vender, stared at the magnificently severe faces of two old Galician Jews. I pointed out to her a window in an immemorial arch that spanned the alley. "Look, here you have a symbol of the ancient East. There is something fantastic and humble and arrogant, something mean and yet elevated about this arch, this window." She said nothing. From behind came Morrison's first remark, "I guess they don't try to clean up much around here." (13–14)

The Morrisons are becoming more and more crushed with disillusion, but they try to maintain a civil demeanor. Walking the path of their own personal self-discovery and the suffering it is causing them, they see no one and nothing resembling the Jesus of their remembered stories; they see just the physiognomy of Semitic faces: "filthy" Arabs, and the magnificent, severely drawn "faces of two old Galician Jews". Even more disappointing bafflement greets them:

> We knocked at the gate of the French convent built over the house of Pontius Pilate. In the cool little church a French nun with an expressionless face explained in accurate but uneloquent English something of the associations of the spot. In the cool gloom behind the altar, amid a flat smell of faded flowers, she showed us the ruined facade of the Roman Governor's house.
> The nun disappeared the moment her toneless voice had done its duty and we were back in the fierce glow of the light. The Morrisons stood beside me. He was grave and noncommittal. Her eyes wandered. "I suppose it's the way you're brought up," she said thoughtfully. There was a genuine gentleness in her tone. "I know, I know we mustn't judge. My father always said so. But do you feel just at home in Catholic churches?" (14–16)

The author Lewisohn, as he relates to the reader in *Up Stream* and as Melnick describes, was the trans-culturalist, transplanted as a child from a German culture to an American one, and he held the acquisition and production of language in any form in high esteem. At the height of his father's feelings of impotence, the elder Lewisohn had trouble pronouncing words, producing language. As the author relates in *Up Stream*: "My father held his hand to his mouth; one of his delusions was that his tongue was slightly paralyzed." (*Up Stream* 31) As well, throughout *Up*

Stream is conveyed the sense that the acculturation of language—be it the German or English the young Ludwig learned through his mother's strict but thorough teaching methods—was of utmost importance. As Melnick relates, Lewisohn "later recalled that his life truly began after [his maternal grandmother] had taught him the [German] alphabet." (Melnick I: 25) In the narrator's/writer's/redeemer's understanding of sins, the nun's "uneloquent English" sends her immediately to hell. She is of the fallen, bringing forth sin from the vulgar carnality of her throat and vocal cords; a moral outcast, unredeemable. To know language is to know God.

The Jerusalem (visionary) light continues to blind the Morrisons; in their response, the Morrisons remain blind to its holiness. It is becoming ever clearer to which Holy Land the story title refers. Alone, on "business" in "the north", the narrator describes the scene: "I saw Haifa, glittering through the night from the heights of Carmel, and Safed upon its holy hill. Through the thronging hills I drove over the lofty roads to Tiberias." (*Holy Land* 17) Unlike the Morrisons, the narrator/writer/savior is able to know holiness when he sees it. The narrator is at home here. He sees just godliness and light around him.

So omniscient is he that, even being in the North, he finds out that

> Mrs. Morrison's left eyelid had become slightly inflamed. She had seen so many Arabs horribly blind from trachoma that a sort of panic had seized both her and her husband and he had asked whether there was such a thing as a decent doctor in this damned hole. (17)

Like the unknowledgeable, naive, sightless Christian Americans, the Morrisons, the spiritually sightless Arabs are also rendered blind by the light of the Holy Land, and the promise of it by God to His people, the Israelites. Lew is beginning to show the strains of their lack of attunement to the place.

From here on, the story would appear to point in one clear direction: to the holiness of a redeemed Palestine-into-Israel as the promised homeland of the Jewish people. The word "Zionist" which first appears on the first page of the text is the code for this Palestine as the Jewish homeland.

> The Jewish hotel keeper had, of course, taken the Morrisons to the clinic at the Zionist Medical Service where an English-speaking oculist had reassured them. They had been enormously relieved and grateful. Mr. Morrison had wrung the doctor's hand. A fee being refused, he had sworn that he would

send a check to Zionist headquarters. Mrs. Morrison had remarked, almost with tears of joy, that some of her *best* friends in Albion were Jews—lovely people, fine citizens. They had then driven off at once. (17–18)

In this relatively brief story, the words "Jew", "Jewish", "Zionist" appear ten times in the text, interlacing the parts of the subtexts into a subliminal but present-directed message: this land where they are now standing is of and for the Jewish people. At the story's conclusion, the narrator finally names it with the article "the" intact: "But this is the Holy Land." (23) The formula is by now more than clear: the combination of Jewishness, Zionism, articulateness in English, Palestine, and kindness, is the epitome of revelation, truth, virtue and redemptive potentiality. The narrator, conscious of the Shylock stereotype of the Jew as grasping, money-hungry, and generally odious, reverses the "truth" of this old story with a new, "truer" portrait of the Jewish human being: the doctor, who in reality would be perfectly justified in asking for and receiving a fee for the medical service rendered to the Morrisons, refuses taking any payment for his services. Is it done in order to show these Christian patients how Jews really are?

Or, on another level, is this a negative comment on how one doctor from a plagued ethnic and cultural minority (representing all Jews) seems to feel forced to prove his worth even on his own turf? The mini-story within the story, that of the Morrisons at the Zionist clinic, contains still another story: that of the anti-Semitism, or at times the reverse anti-Semitism, that can be experienced and glimpsed on American soil. The old joke that someone's "best" friends are Jewish (or black) is filled with the ambiguity of intention that the word "best" reveals.

By this point, the Morrisons just want out of this foreign, strange and filthy land. The narrator's/writer's repetition of the word "Zionist" leaves little unanswered. The "Jewish" hotel owner, taking time off from his hotel operations, personally ("of course") brings the Morrisons to the health wing of God's place of salvation, in this location of the redemption-to-come, Jerusalem, in the country-to-be-again in the holiest of land, an Israel-to-be-redeemed.

This is a rather facetious, culturally dialectic, ironic scene of the narrator-as-Lewisohn at home in the Land of his ancestral Biblical inheritance; when all is said and done, he is just a highly knowledgeable, emotionally-connected visitor. Or is he the universal messiah out of place and time? Like the "American Zionist" traveling with him on the ship, the narrator is, yet isn't, at home in the Jewish homeland. He, like that Zionist, is most at home in displacement; at home in the ambiguity of more than one home; and homeless in both/all of them.

Through his desire to accommodate and accompany Mr. and Mrs. Morrison through the Holy Land, the narrator could appear as the shadow of the clandestine German-Jewish boy of Lewisohn's early years who grew up displaced in the American South, hosting on his own turf that type of Christian-American man and woman, husband and wife, whom he tried in his youth to emulate and please. What a turn of the tables now, as the Christian couple experiences a sense of displacement that the narrator-as-Lewisohn had experienced all of his life. This is repeated in the super-hospitality of the Jewish hotel keeper and the Jewish doctor at the Zionist Medical Service.

In truth, the Jewish hotel keeper, the Jewish doctor, the Morrisons and the narrator are all dislocated in/from some place, some ambiguous origin, deeply enmeshed in an impossible-to-read dialectic. The Morrisons are thankful that Mrs. Morrison's vision has not been harmed by the "land" and its strange people; the truth is that her vision has not been affected at all by the holiness and truth emanating from the place. They have not gained any insights on their travels to the Holy Land of their Christian imagination.

As fate would have it, the narrator's omniscience leads him to Nazareth—he is, after all, a sightseer like the others. There he gravitates, of course, to "the Hotel Germania", another homeland connection also very familiar to the narrator/Lewisohn. Always a reader, the writer-narrator peruses the list of hotel guests: "Yes, their names were in that extraordinary hotel register where people are inscribed from all ends of the earth—from New York and Lebanon, from Teheran and Vienna." (19) The narrator/writer is fascinated, delighted, even excited, by the mix of cultural orientations.

He spies the name of Mr. and Mrs. Lew Morrison. "So I would see them in the morning." (19) He retires to his "small, austere, cell-like room. I was tired and slept." (19) As in a scene from a Biblical story, the author-narrator-prophet (does he dream, or is it real?) is stirred in his sleep by something:

> But in a couple of hours I awoke. A wind had arisen, a wild, disturbing wind.
> I threw on my dressing gown and stood before my arched window. I saw a
> wall that looked like the oldest in the world. In the wall was a little wooden

door and over the door swung a dim, sooty lantern. Behind the wall stood
cypresses and their tops swayed in the wind. And the black, swaying tops of
those cypresses seemed to sweep against the sky, against the stars, the incom-
parable stars of Palestine, the low, large, drooping prophetic stars. (20)

The narrator-writer, on a mission of salvation, with the Jewish nation,
even the world cupped securely in his hands, gazes in awe at the vision
of the present (scene) and of a future one. From his lips and eyes spring
prophecy, the mission to save the world through the perfect God-gener-
ated Word/word. With the pre-sight of the visionary forever alert to the
needs of his human charges, he leaves the small, self-circumscribed, solitary place of prophetic transmission, where from his microplace he can
view, in one panoramic sweep, the past, present and future of the world
and humanity. The narrator's instinct leads him in some certain direction:

I went out of my small room into the hall, which had great arched, paneless
windows through which one could see the roofs of Nazareth and the farther
hills. The wind swept through the hall....
Suddenly I heard a gasp behind me. I turned and saw Mrs. Morrison wrapped
in a kimono. Her frightened eyes met mine. "Oh, it's you!" There was a sob
in her voice. I tried to be matter-of-fact. "It's hard to sleep in this wind. Do
you see the car caravan?"
She nodded dumbly. Her hands were clasped in front of her, holding her kimono together. She stood quite still. Her face was tense. Her eyes were full
of a helpless sadness, a childlike confusion.
"What is it?" I asked gently.
She shuddered. "Everything!"
"Didn't you have a pleasant time?" (20–22)

The narrator already knows the answer to the question he asks her.
Hating the land of the Jews, Mrs. Morrison appears to trust four men in
her life: Lew, her dead father, the narrator, and probably still Jesus—that
is, the Jesus in the stories her father told her. This is another scene of
teasing sexuality mixed with prophecy and insight, in which Mrs.
Morrison either cannot digest, or does not recognize, the truth when she
sees it. There in that dark, windswept hallway, in a moment of total clarity, the Jewish male facing the Christian female, the ages-old polemic is
laid on the table:

"Do you know Bethlehem?"
I nodded.
"And the Church of the Nativity? Why, you can't see the stable. It's all over
images and things.... And everywhere there're Arabs and Jews. Oh, please

don't be offended. I don't mean nice Jews like you and the doctor in Tiberias,
but awful outlandish people. I couldn't imagine our Lord or Peter in Tiberias,
on the lake, you know. I can't imagine anything anywhere—anywhere. I'm
asking Lew to leave as soon as we can. I want to get away; I want to get out
of this terrible dago country."
She sobbed.
"But this is the Holy Land," I said....
"It's all so different, so, so foreign...."
"Jesus was a Jew," I said quietly, "and a son of this ancient land." (22–23)

Ignoring her ethnic slur of dark, swarthy types in the word "dago",
the narrator seems intent on bringing the truth home to her. She resists,
clinging to her fantastic, fake version of a savior: the Jewish one is too
culturally strange for her to digest. Mrs. Morrison will look for salvation
and her savior in Liberty, Wisconsin, the United States of America, while,
as Melnick asserts: "In the 'Holy Land,' Ludwig had said his final good-
bye to the world of his assimilating youth and to the woman with whom
he so clearly identified it. Never again would either appear so benign."
(Melnick I: 393)

Background Discussion II

Ludwig's love for Thelma Spear represented the new direction he was
taking in his life. He had parted ways with a desire to make himself into,
and then to preserve himself as, a Christian-American Gentile. Thelma
was to have been the antithesis of the Mary-Mrs. Morrison of his strife-
ridden past.

By the end of the second decade of the 1900s, it was possible to perceive a transformed face, a feisty fighter for Jewish identity and existence
in Lewisohn's voice, demeanor and mindset. Stuart Sherman, in 1920, for
example, attacked Lewisohn for the latter's broadside attacks on English-
American society and culture. In his reaction to Lewisohn's 1919
publication of *A Modern Book of Criticism*, Sherman notes that the purpose of Lewisohn's book is to show us that America is an uncultured,
uncivilized place. Referring to what Lewisohn calls the "shivering young
Davids", that is, Lewisohn and his "young people", and the "army of
Goliaths" they face, Sherman sarcastically remarks:

One doesn't blame our Davids for their inability to connect themselves vitally with this line [Twain, Whitman, Thoreau, Lincoln, Emerson, among others] of Americans for their inability to receive its tradition or carry it on. But one cannot help asking whether this inability does not largely account for the fact that Mr. Lewisohn's group of critics are [sic] restless, impressionists, almost destitute of doctrine, and with no discoverable unifying tendency except to let themselves out into a homeless happy land where they may enjoy the "colorful" cosmic weather, untroubled by businessmen, or middle-class Americans, or Congressmen, or moralists, or humanists, or philosophers, or professors, or Victorians, or Puritans, or New Englanders.... A jolly lot of Goliaths to slay before we get that "civilised cultural atmosphere".[66]

Lewisohn's relationship with Thelma would produce his only child, James. When he published *Up Stream*, he had just turned forty years of age. Thelma represented not just unbridled sexual expression—which he had erroneously believed he had found in Mary—but also the freedom to be sexual with a woman who would not ultimately enslave him. As well, she was his muse, his poetic voice which was so absent from the early years of his life with Mary, who represented for Ludwig the shallowness and sham of a pure Gentile existence and life-style. As Melnick declares, Thelma "of a Jewish father and Christian mother", may well have stood for "a halfway stop on his road to fully accepting himself as a Jew." (Melnick I: 316)

With the completion of *Up Stream*, Lewisohn entered the Third and final Period of his life and work, from 1922 until his death on December 31, 1955. The writing of this Period consists of eight different kinds of work:

1. Novels, plays, short fiction, including that group of fictional works on the general theme of unsatisfied love—*Don Juan*, 1923; *Holy Land*, 1925; *The Case of Mr. Crump*, 1926; *Roman Summer*, 1927; *The Defeated*, 1928; *Adam: A Dramatic History in a Prologue, Seven Scenes, and an Epilogue*, 1929; *Roman Summer*, 1930; *Stephen Escott*, 1930; *The Golden Vase*, 1931; *The Last Days of Shylock*, 1931; *The Romantic: A Contemporary Legend*, 1931; *An Altar in the Fields*, 1934; *Trumpet of Jubilee*, 1937; *For Ever Wilt Thou Love*, 1939; *Haven* (written with Edna Manley Lewisohn, Lewisohn's third wife and 26 years his junior), 1940; *Renegade*, 1942; *Breathe Upon These*, 1944; *Anniversary*, 1948; *The Vehement Flame*, 1948; *The Tyranny of Sex* (*Crump* in paperback), 1949; *In a Summer Season*, 1955.

2. German literary criticism—*Modern German Poetry*, 1925; *Judaism and its Heritage—Israel*, 1925; *A Jew Speaks*, 1931; *This People*, 1933; *The Permanent Horizon: A Search for Old Truths*, 1934; *The Answer; The Jew and the World: Past, Present, and Future*, 1939; *A Jewish Commonwealth in Palestine: Our Contribution to a Better World*, 1944; *The American Jew: Character and Destiny*, 1950; *What Is This Jewish Heritage?*, 1954.

3. Autobiography—*Mid-Channel*, 1929.

4. Literary criticism, English/American—*The Creative Life*, 1924; *The Romantic: a Contemporary Legend*, 1931; *Expression in America*, 1932; *The Magic Word: Studies in the Nature of Poetry*, 1950.

5. Social and cultural commentary—*Cities and Men*, 1927; *The Man of Letters and American Culture*, 1949.

6. German literary criticism—*Modern German Poetry*, 1925.

7. Translations from German to English.

8. Introductory essays to books of others, essays for periodicals, journals.

The first category of novels consists of stories of personal unfulfillment, creativity, independence, freedom, and sexuality which greatly contrast with his conservative image of the First Period.

The last period of his life finds Lewisohn tied to the Gentile Mary Crocker Childs (married, 1905; divorced, 1937) through alimony payments; finding a new inspiration that finally sours in the half-Jewish Thelma Spear (their relationship lasted from 1924–1939 and, as mentioned, produced one son); a newer muse in the Gentile converted to Judaism, Edna Manley (1940–1943); and finally, his last and widowed wife, Louise Wolk (1944–1955), whom he had met at the time he was breaking up his relationship with Thelma and had already met Edna.

By 1943, Edna knew of her husband's relationship with Louise, a newspaper journalist. As Edna was ailing with TB in a succession of sanatoriums, Ludwig, now deeply absorbed in his wartime Zionist efforts, met the fully Jewish Louise Wolk and was able to create with this last wife the real Jewish environment and life-style he so craved. As well, he wanted to give James the stability the boy had never enjoyed with the succession of stepmothers and a real mother who was not so interested in caring for him. As Melnick describes, Lewisohn was delighted with his son Jim's "'moral progress.... This is what he needed'," crediting Jim's improvement "'to Louise's unrivalled talent for motherhood'." (Melnick II: 310)

The history and nature of Lewisohn's four marriages reflect the personal transformations in the author's life and psyche: the first wife, Mary, as pure Christian-Gentile, is "killed off" (literally, in the dramatic ending to *The Case of Mr. Crump*); Thelma, half-Jewish but, according to Jewish law, not actually Jewish since it was her father who was the Jewish half and not her mother; Edna, the Reform convert to Judaism, a mix of sincere sentiments towards her adopted identity and her Gentile birth. As Melnick writes, Ludwig felt the need to transform her Gentile version into a Jewish one:

> His own need to maintain the Jewishness in his life never appeared more urgent. For the first time, he spoke unequivocally to Edna of how "it would be another tragedy for me if the woman I loved and trusted supremely were unwilling to share my faith and the fate of my people or unwilling to have our house, a profoundly Jewish house in which alone my son, *our* son, could be brought up." (168)

Lewisohn, during the ensuing Holocaust, had severed moral ties with his Germanic roots for its perverse degeneracy. Nevertheless, as Melnick relates in a poll of authors' reading preferences, specifically the "books that had 'contributed most to the development of your philosophy', elicited from Ludwig 'an odd list... but truth compels me.'" (328) Of the five requested authors or works, Lewisohn chose "the Hebrew Bible and the Talmud" as first and second. Following those were Goethe and Freud. Buber was Lewisohn's fifth and last selection, who "'alas [is] so little known in America, [but] perhaps the greatest religious philosopher of our time for *all* men, despite the Judaeo-mystical center from which he radiates.'" (328) Lewisohn had made a final rapprochement with his Hebraic and Germanic roots in the union here—as symbolized by the choice of three German-Jewish thinkers—of Jewish and German thought filtered through both a secular and sacred Jewish prism.

Like Ozick, Lewisohn's liberalism, unquenchable intellectual curiosity, artistic imagination and highly sensitive, romantic nature were decisive in creating ambiguous boundaries—both unclear, definitively unlocatable, inextricably inter-linked—between his German, Christian, Hebrew, Yiddish, American English and Southern upbringing/affinities. These societal, tribal and nationalistic realms, juxtaposed and co-mingled, are the underpinnings of cultural and personal identity. It is therefore difficult, if not impossible, to define, describe or categorize the intricately entangled and perplexing dialectic which exists but is elusive and ultimately unknowable; irreducible, unsimplifiable; defying categorization.

Add to the above the creative process itself, and an even more complicated picture, a type of non-picture, emerges. *The Case of Mr. Crump* fully exemplifies this ever-shifting medley of complication. Called both a work of fiction and a true documentary account of Ludwig and Mary Lewisohn's marriage, the work balances, or totters, on a tightrope of fact disguised as fiction and fiction masked as fact. *Up Stream* was to be the true account of the author's shift from a counterfeit, fictional personal life to an awakening truth; an integration into a completed identity of self. However, as discussed, it is itself replete with fiction—fictionalized names, factual discrepancies, so forth—which undermine the reader's confidence in it as a factual biographical rendering of Lewisohn's experiences in life. Thus, the perplexed reader is unable to discern, or decide if "Anne Crump" or the "Mary" of *Up Stream* is the real Mary Crocker Lewisohn. On April 8, 1946, when she finally died at the age of 83, the author dryly noted to his publisher, Canfield: "'You observed, of course, in this morning paper the notice of the demise of our old enemy, Anne Crump.'" (331) Firstly, Lewisohn confuses (?) fact with fancy, naming Mary by her fictional name(?). Secondly, *The Case of Mr. Crump* was apparently so factual an account of Ludwig's and Mary's life together that Canfield, Melnick continues, feared a "libel suit against both parties [himself and Lewisohn] by Mary's children. Canfield sent a copy of the book to his attorneys, who advised that indeed 'the book constitutes a libel hazard.'" (331)

The Publisher's Note in the 1965 edition of *The Case of Mr. Crump* states that the book "is now recognized as a literary classic, one of the truly significant naturalistic novels of our century."[67] Thomas Mann, in the Preface, states that the book, non-fictionally novelistic in form, is really a documentary. Save for Anne Crump's murder by her husband in the book's final pages, it is, as Mann characterizes it, a true account of an "inferno of a marriage." (*Crump* vii) Mann praises the book's "cool" detached tone which only serves to underscore the horridness of the unfolding events. Mann says that the book is

> a novelistic document of life…. The book's horrifying and infuriating subject matter—a marriage that should never have been contracted, nor would have

been, save for the man's weakness and youthful inexperience—a marriage which under the protection of cruel social hypocrisy and of a cruel social fear for the abstract institution, becomes an *inferno*—first through the scandalous legal advantages possessed by the woman as such, finally and hopelessly through the passionate crime that brings to ruin the gifted and promising protagonist. (vii)

Mann asserts that Lewisohn's "power to stir and entertain us is very great." (viii) The former may also have been alluding to Strindberg's perennial theme of male-female conflict. Also, this book secures Lewisohn's place at "the very forefront of modern epic narrative." (viii) Mann describes the book's "direct truth" and the humanness of the characters: "Even the woman, Anne Crump, remains human in all her repulsiveness." (viii) Finally, elaborating on Lewisohn's ambiguous mix of fictive truth or true fiction, Mann tell us, "the author declares that the book arose from his determination to tell 'as well as entertainingly as he could the true story of Herbert Crump.'" (viii) Where fictionalized characters are considered true representations of the real flesh and blood people, true biographical accounts are fictionalized, and the people are characters in their own life story, willingly or unwillingly presenting so complex a face or mask—or some kind of combination of both—the reader is left to find the way out of so confusing a dialectical maze. Thus, a reading of *The Case of Mr. Crump* must involve the suspension of a dependence on notions like truth and fantasy, intertwined in the text and dialectically related.

The Case of Mr. Crump

Of all the many works in Lewisohn's varied medley of creative expression, *The Case of Mr Crump*, first published in Paris in 1926, is perhaps the most difficult, challenging and complicated to delineate. The great temptation here is neatly to equate certain indisputable biographical facts of the author's life with the descriptions and delineations found in this novel in particular, and other fictional pieces in general. This incipient difficulty in *Crump*, in view of the numerous factual discrepancies brought to light by recent investigation (specifically that of Melnick), already sets up a slippery environment of dialectical elusiveness. Is it therefore true that Lewisohn's fiction is a cover for the struggles and issues of his real life? As Melnick asserts in relation to another of Lewisohn's works, *The Broken Snare*: "Behind the mask of fiction, he [Lewisohn] could weigh everything without the fear of discovery or the pain of confrontation." (Melnick I: 120)

Is Melnick's assessment, however, a valid one? In this one-to-one parallelistic schema, Ludwig and Mary Crocker Lewisohn are, respectively, Herbert and Anne Crump. Lewisohn's own comments on the novel, as related by Melnick, (414) serve only to drive the dialectical issue of biographical fact versus novelistic fiction into an even deeper muddle. In the quotation described earlier, which relates to *Up Stream* and as recorded by Melnick, Lewisohn asserted that the writing of *The Case of Mr Crump* was an objectification, not of the real facts of his life with Mary Crocker, but a development, even transformation, of the real-life experiences "'into art'". (414) The catch here is that, since Lewisohn describes all biographical fact as a necessary takeoff point and an all-important ingredient in the very process of creating art, art itself is indeed a dialectical meeting ground of truth and fiction. Since an artist cannot create in a mental and emotional void, unconnected to his/her direct or indirect life experiences, it can be argued on one level that it is possible to view any work of art as autobiographical.

"The Publisher's Note: 1965" serves to authenticate the book as non-fiction. As the publisher notes in a tone of high seriousness: "Mr. Lewisohn wrote his novel in the mid-twenties, but for legal reasons involving libel it could not be published in the United States at that time." (*Crump* v)

The naturalistic style in which the book is written obfuscates the line between fact and fantasy even more. In his "Preface" to this 1965 edition, Thomas Mann declares that the novel used fictional characters, describes them and what they do from beginning to the novel's catastrophic end. In this sense, he asserts, the book is fictional,

> a work of art, in a word, in so far as it preserves its coolness of tone, keeps its distance, permits things to speak for themselves and sustains that severe and curbed and almost serene silence which is peculiar to all art and especially to the art of speech, and leaves it to the reader or beholder to draw his own conclusions. (vii)

However, Mann continues, the novel is simultaneously "both more and less than a novel; it is life, it is concrete and undreamed reality." (vii) In contrast, and despite Mann's sympathetic portrayal of Herbert Crump/Ludwig Lewisohn as the unsuspecting victim of the cunning and deceptive woman, this "novelistic document of life" (vii) is anything but evenhanded or scientifically, objectively neutral. *Crump* moves with deadly deliberation to a very preordained and certain end. Its cosmological perspective divides the world into two pure poles of good and evil. As Mann insists, Herbert-as-Ludwig is the undisputed gull of a profound and unjust hoax, set into motion through this "man's weakness and youthful inexperience." (vii) Even more so, at play here is a marriage protected by a "cruel social hypocrisy" and "a cruel social fear for the abstract institution" which gave "scandalous legal advantages" to the wife. The murder of Anne at the hands of her husband Herbert is described by Mann as a "passional crime that brings to ruin the gifted and promising protagonist." (vii) No reader can doubt the claim that the cards are heavily stacked *against* Anne-as-Mary and *for* Herbert-as-Ludwig. Thus, even if the reader views *Crump* as a more or less autobiographical rendering of the real events in Ludwig and Mary Lewisohn's life together, the book is nevertheless a retelling of those events to fit a very specific and prejudicial point of view.

In a certain way, any factual parallels between the book and Lewisohn's life could substantiate the assertion that *Crump* is indeed a true-to-life account in fictional form of Ludwig Lewisohn's marriage to Mary Crocker. However, from the very first page, the narrator dissolves fiction and fact into an ambiguous gel. In Book One, "Anne", Mr Crump is described as Anne's "second husband and nearly twenty years her junior." (3) *Crump*, replete with factual documentation, would appear to call the very nature of truth into question. As Mann states, the author "declares that the book arose from his determination to tell 'as well and as entertainingly as he could the true story of Herbert Crump.'" (viii) How, it must be asked, can the "true story" of a fictional character be told? Is the name "Herbert Crump" a code for Ludwig Lewisohn? If so, is the author using factuality as a cover for the fictionalizing of reality? Is Herbert Crump a fiction or a truth? Is Ludwig Lewisohn playing tricks through artistic underhanded chicanery to hide his true identity? Are the author of Crump and Ludwig the same persona/identity?

Does Ludwig Lewisohn have one identifiable identity? It is clear that more questions than answers can be raised from this discussion. Melnick relates that *Crump*, for example, more accurately describes the Lewisohns' first Washington Heights apartment (511 W. 172nd Street) which he characterized in *Up Stream* as "'dingy by nature—cheap, ugly, abominable.' A more detailed description in *Crump* of their new home pointed to a more positive and, by other evidence, more accurate picture of it." (Melnick I: 127) So much factual detail from reality, combined with the meticulously piled-up fiction parading as factuality; or the reverse—factuality from the "true story" of Herbert Crump and his life— sets up an inscrutable wall of puzzlement and confusion. The reader is enticed by the seemingly straightforward guilelessness of the naturalistic narrative account.

From a biographical point of view, *The Case of Mr. Crump* was written at a time in Lewisohn's life when he was soberly reviewing the earlier years, searching for his true identity, rooting out the lies of his past, sorting out the naive fictions from the harsh facts. For example, as Melnick relates, Ludwig had always been deeply "ambivalent" about Mary. (116)

> If he feared that she might actually hold him to his promises [of marriage], and one day come to Charleston [from New York to where he lived with his parents] as she had so often said she would, he also missed her, and perhaps feared that she might not. (115–116)

Lewisohn, Melnick describes, discussed this ambivalence in *Crump*. Ludwig

> missed her attention, missed her physically, missed his long, uninhibited talks with her. There was, he admitted to himself, despite the closeness of his relationship with Minna [his mother], "no one else in the world with whom he could be so frank, with whom he could so let himself go." (116)

Continuing in the biographical vein, Ludwig's ambivalence toward Mary was reflected in the ever-growing ambivalence resulting from a gradual peeling-off process of self-examination that coincided with his relationship with, and marriage to her. This creates another of the many dialectical issues at play in his life and work. In many ways, the First World War, and the antagonism it inspired between Germany, Russia and America, brought to the foreground the issues that were emerging in Lewisohn's personal life and feelings. As Melnick relates:

> Though hard evidence is lacking, it is quite conceivable that other factors [than the War] influenced Ludwig's thinking at this time. Beyond his support of German cultural and geopolitical interests, there was his renascent Jewishness. (187)

As well, Mary along with her family, had a virulent "anti-German attitude.'"(187) Lewisohn, Melnick continues, had an "almost instinctual opposition to all they [Mary and her family] upheld." (187) Mary began to be openly hostile toward Ludwig's father, Jacques, when in the initial period of war he and Ludwig spoke German together. This friction exposes a number of dialectical snares: German-American, American-European. The friction is manifested not just between Anne and Herbert but between Herbert and his parents/his Teutonic past. Anne was also

> angered by Jacques' use of a little skullcap of black silk, which he wore "to protect his head from draughts." Together, his speech and dress clearly emphasized his alien nature and the newly emerging [Jewish] identity of her husband, which she undoubtedly found ill-advised, if not offensive. (Jacques may also have sought comfort in his ethnic past and worn the cap for reasons other than warmth, reasons that Ludwig could not openly refer to in *Crump*.) (187)

At work on *Crump*, Ludwig was already realizing that the war aided him in focusing on the "important issues" in his own life. (188)

A product of fact, fiction or something ambiguously in-between, the Anne Crump of "Book One, Anne" is a basically detestable figure. Herbert and Anne are posed here in a contrast of chronology and age; the narrator lays her on the operating table to reveal the basis of that vileness. With scientific, naturalistically rendered precision, the narrator describes her awesome loathsomeness, which hinges to a large extent on the age difference between them.

The narration appears to begin to establish the validity of the factual description by discussing Anne in relation to her past. "The fortunes of her family, her mother's life and her own earlier years were among the things about which Mrs. Crump liked to talk." (*Crump* 3) Revealed to the reader is the way she looks:

> Her imperfectly hennaed hair would be carelessly wadded on the top of her head as it had been since morning; she would be dressed in a slightly soiled, preferably yellow kimono. A fleeting touch of peace in her gray eyes, a sense sometimes of the pathos of the past, would soften the lines of the sudden bunchy forefront of her nose and of her formidable jaw. (3)

She tries always to hide the fact that she is nearly twenty years her husband's senior. Under the mask of "artificial light and in evening dress, well rested and not unskillfully made up, she would produce this mathematical misstatement [that she was only 9 years her husband's senior] suddenly, irrelevantly and proudly. At such moments it was not wholly incredible." (4)

Herbert is not uninterested in Anne's familial reminiscing. The maternal side of her family was from Frankfort, Kentucky, and according to her, "belonged to the best people of the town." (4) Anne is always "vague" about "economic questions." (4) The "wah" [war], as she relates the story, left the family poor. "Concrete facts began to emerge with the admitted degeneracy of the family in the generation of Mrs. Crump's mother." (4) Anne's stories of her mother and family are ambiguous at best, and contradictory at worse. Herbert is unable to "solve" the contradictions about Anne's family. (5) For Herbert, Anne has acquired status, intelligence, culture and flair from her father. As for her mother's side, all of the females possess that monstrously huge "Bronson forehead". (4) In the juxtaposition of Anne's ancestry, there is exposed here a dialectic mix of Culture and Philistinism: "With the entrance of her father into the story, Mrs. Crump would introduce a touch of romance. He was an Englishman named Farrel. The Farrels had been in England before the Conquest." (5)

Anne's father was, of course, a writer of sorts, whose "pamphlet" could be found in the New York Public Library. All of Anne's stories about her "past" are a combination of "coarse and vital facts" and "a stale but stubborn romanticism." (6) It is Anne's "English birth" in London that "was a source of endless satisfaction to her." (7) As well, her English birth and ancestry cause feelings of both pride and envy in Crump. Thus another dialectic is uncovered: of America/England, the New World and the Old.

Although it is never stated directly, Herbert perceives in Anne some kind of alien quality: "something coarse and violent in all the women of her blood." (11) The words, "her blood", can refer to her specific familial inheritance, as well as the more general racial stock from which she was born. This coarser, totally foreign quality is balanced out by a more sensitive, cultured English side. English can be viewed as a code for all that is elevated/desirable; cultural sophistication. It is Anne's birth in London which is the competitive edge she has over the suspicious foreignness of Herbert Crump.

Herbert also recoils from the sense of "helplessness" and "parasitism on some male creature" (12) that plagued the maternal side of his wife's family. In general, all that was favorable, pleasant, cultured, sophisticated or desirable in Anne has come from her father's English bloodline. Her mother's side also represents a coarse primitive Americanism that defines American culture. As Herbert perceives it, Anne fought the native "moral evil; the consequences of the reality of the conflict between God and the Devil in the universe" (13) at just one time in her life:

> during her years at high school evil had the least power over Anne Farrel's soul. Her indomitableness was directed toward good ends. She had already eagerly read all printed matter that came her way; she had formed a special devotion for a tattered copy of Bryant's *Library of Poetry and Song* which, unaccountably enough, the half illiterate [second "husband" of her mother] John Toohey brought into the household. She elected the classical course in high school, struggled determinedly with her Greek and Latin grammars, joined the literary and debating society, began to express the pain of her longings and of her isolation in verse. (13)

In short, all the "good" that Herbert sees in the universe is connected to the aesthetic, artistic enterprise—writing and literature, art, culture in general. This is the "good", the "familiar" Anne. This, Herbert identifies with the English blood Anne carries in her veins. However, the coarseness in her nature comes to the foreground when, in puberty, Anne discovers the evil game of male seduction:

> She played upon the fact that Toohey [her common-law stepfather] was attracted by her younger adolescence; she let him hold her on his lap and pet her and she wheedled money out of him. "The money is for you," he used to say. "You're a flower on a dunghill." Throughout this episode Anne was strictly loyal to her mother. She despised Toohey. But she found she could manage men. (14)

Anne's mother, Mrs. Toohey, curses "John Toohey and with him the whole race of faithless and lecherous men." (14) Ann learns this attitude toward men very well from her mother.

In her mid-adolescence, the good Anne has a noble goal that motivates her to study hard in school. "She had made up her mind that she was going to be a writer, establish a reputation and make money and save her mother from the cruelties of a man-made, man-ruled world." (15) This was, in fact, also what Ludwig thought he could do to help his long-suffering, hard-working parents.

As for Anne's physical endowments it is impossible for Anne to be really "pretty. The Bronson forehead could be covered, of course. And in her girlhood she had a great quantity of soft blond hair. But the blunt and too knoblike forepart of her nose, the harsh insensitive jaw could never have been more than softened even by the bloom of her girlhood." (14) Nevertheless, by dressing to attract men, by seducing in obvious and also more subtle ways, Anne learns how to handle them. "She discovered that she was more and more attractive to men." (15) Even more, Anne "led them around by the nose…. She had a strong sexual magnetism for men." (16)

Of Anne's first husband, Vilas, the reader learns that he "had a wild but genuine taste for literature, even for poetry; this was one of the things that had drawn him and Anne together." (20) Vilas was "refined" and "inoffensive"; significantly, he also "had a gift for psychological analysis." (20) But if Vilas wanted to assert a manly protectiveness of his wife, it was an impossible mission. "You cannot protect an engine. It goes over you or you hide behind it and let it go over others." (21)

In addition, as a wife and woman Herbert finds Anne to lack a sense of cleanliness, although one would not imagine it when seeing her in public. In her first marriage, as related to him by her stories, the narrator describes how she never displayed any

> knowledge in even the simplest contraceptive methods and Anne was too slovenly and lazy even to get up to wash. Too happy-go-lucky. She had something of a gambler's hardness and freedom from immediate care. Two glasses of beer and to bed. The rest was left to take care of itself. It didn't, in fact. With the inevitable result of a long series of abortions. (23)

Throughout *Crump*, the narrator relates Herbert's perception of events of the past and the present. Many stories compete for the position of being the true account of events. Herbert through the narrator is the collector, sorter-out, organizer: in short, the literary editor of these stories. Through his aesthetic manifold, he sifts out the truth from the fiction and lies. The physician who attended to Anne's cervix, one "Dr. Vogel, a homeopath of course, fell in love with Anne. A time came when Herbert no longer trusted Mrs. Crump's version of this affair. It was too much like an allegory with the moral directed at him. But for a long time he accepted the legend in all its spurious nobility." (27)

In Anne, therefore, is painted a picture of a selfish, coarse, ethereally Gentile-like sexual vamp or vampiress, who uses her body to first attract, then control men. Is this version of Anne the correct, true one? A dialectical ambiguity emerges from the confusion of not knowing whose story/ stories to believe: Lewisohn, Mann, the narrator, Herbert-as-narrator, Herbert-as-Lewisohn-as narrator, or the reader's own version. Even the so-called biographical details of Ludwig Lewisohn's life are true depending on the ever-mutable version one hears or believes. For example, Lewisohn's relationship with Mary Crocker is never clearly rendered in any of the author's works, and therefore cannot be fully understood. Should the reader believe the "autobiographical" *Up Stream* version of the "facts" of the author's life in general, and life with Mary Crocker in particular, in which he describes her in glowing and loving terms? Interestingly, Herbert appears to despise Anne mostly because she ceased being the artist she once was or could have been.

"Book Two, Herbert" purports to historically trace the ancestry of Herbert Crump (*née* Krumpf) from the German city of Schwerin, where his grandfather was the Lutheran church organist and schoolmaster to the South Carolinian town of Queenshaven. The laborious attention paid by the narrator to the historical facts of Herbert's past could in fact be a trap; to lure the reader into a dialectical snare, into deadpanned lies openly pronounced as if there is nothing to hide, that there is no plot or trick afoot. A curious picture is drawn of the Crump/Krumpf family. Although their habits, turn of mind and cultural identification are unmistakably Germanic, nevertheless the biographical details—if "biography" is a valid term to use here—are selectively rendered. Herbert is vaguely described as an ambiguous figure. The narration describes him as having a temperament unlike his father's: "His was not his father's clear, certain and untroubled spirit." (35) His personality's lack of clarity and certitude uncovers a sense of change, doubt, confusion, ambiguity. In short, Herbert's nature is the very spirit of dialectical mutability.

Certain questions emerge. Is Herbert Ludwig, or is Ludwig Herbert? Does the fiction remake the fact, or is the fact the basis of the fiction? What is the real nature of Herbert's personality? What was the real nature of, and what is the real connection between, Ludwig Lewisohn as Ludwig Lewisohn the writer, and Ludwig Lewisohn as Ludwig Lewisohn the person? Mutability even describes Herbert's last name: Krumpf became the Americanized Crump and "the Americanisation of the name had come to stay." (34) As in the real-life story, the narrator describes how, "after [Herbert] returned to Queenshaven in the early seventies the *Courier* [newspaper] had played up the story of his studies and accomplishments." (34) Lewisohn the person and writer was very interested in music, but became a literary figure and professor. Here, if biography has a voice, he becomes the musical component of his personality. "He became a personality in the little city. He became unchangeable 'Professor Crump'." (34)

Herbert Crump in his innermost self wants something he cannot point to exactly:

> He hungered for the ineffable and the infinite. He too played the chorales of Bach but, as his father declared, without consecration. Science had cooled his head while romanticism had heated his heart. He had read Buchner and Huxley; he had given up his Christian faith. Art was his religion; his words were often bitter and full of romantic irony. He offended old Pastor Muller. (35)

In truth, Herbert sees himself as a true aesthete, a real artist. Even as a small child he was easily "intoxicated" by the "visible world" around him. He remembers one event:

> He was four years old, as his mother told him later, and had followed his grandfather into the cool, slightly musty church one summer afternoon. He had climbed with the old gentleman into the organ-loft. The sonorous vibrations of sound had made the child tremble and turn pale and the ecstacy had become so insupportable that he had dropped sobbing on the floor and had had to be carried home. (36–37)

Besides art, culture and music, Herbert is hopelessly addicted to females and sex. As in the true story of Lewinsohn's life (from his perception), and as the narrator leads the reader to understand, Herbert falls into the sex snare set for him by Anne. Mary's and/or Anne's talents in this direction are well documented by Ludwig or Herbert or the narrator. Besides hungering, as the narrator describes in *Crump*, for what was ineffably and infinitely of another world, Herbert could faint from the erotic excitement females caused him to feel. For example, as a boy, Herbert and his friend Ralph Greene like to play a game called "circus" in the basement of one friend, Hen Hanahan's house:

The pretense at playing circus was brief and feeble. Hen stood on his head in the middle of the floor. Then he sprang up and slammed and latched the wooden door to the street. Silence and black darkness. Herbert thought his heart would literally leap into his throat as he felt the head of Estelle on his shoulder and inhaled the fresh odor of the girl's hair. It was she who found his lips and pushed his hands. After that he needed no guidance. There were giggles; there were jokes. All speech was seemly and calculated to fortify the pretense that there was no harm in this game. Nothing fatal and ultimate did in fact happen. But these children of the South had a strong, dumb, ecstatic eroticism—fierce, earnest, almost exalted. (43)

As the narrator tells it, Herbert, even as an adolescent, has a sincere aversion to just animal desires. In truth, his desire is for "a union of passion and love." (48–49) Furthermore, when they are youths, both Herbert and his good friend, Ralph Douglas Greene, are somehow outsiders. Regarding Ralph, the reader is told that he and his family are rejected for their unexplained social inferiority. Ralph is intent on showing Queenshaven society that it would be paid back in hurt and shame for its rejection of him. The reader thus can also understand that Herbert feels like an outsider as well. The question is why? Why does Herbert feel alien? "For all their brave talk, the boys could not quite conceal the fact from one another that they were constantly troubled and on edge." (49) The narrator links this to sexual desires. The reasons, however, for this remain ambiguously unclear.

The real identity of either Herbert or the narrator remains unclear. Herbert states that he left Christianity. What does that mean exactly? Could one or the other, as an alter ego of Lewisohn himself—or both— be something of a Jew deep inside? At the table of Mr Hasselmeyer, the music critic for a German-American newspaper, there sits Herbert, a youthful man, and "the quiet Jewish lady, an authoress from Berlin in her 'reform costume'." (59) Could this "authoress from Berlin" be the author, Ludwig Lewisohn from Berlin, who mocked (and here is mocking) Jews pretending not to be Jews, who is masquerading (like the author?) as a Gentile?

Tired of Anne, Herbert's weakness for a combination of art and sex flowers once again with Gerda, a transcultural mixture of Hungarian and German background. Commissioned to teach Gerda piano, Ludwig as Herbert, Herbert as Ludwig, or Herbert as Herbert, has of course a deadly sexual attraction for her: "They tried other songs and spoke fewer and fewer words. Gerda, reading verses over his shoulder, leaned her lithe, erected young body against him. They stopped. He let his hands drop from the keys. She turned to face him with her back pressed against the keyboard." (62) Their simmering passion is consummated one night as he lays awake in his Morningside Heights apartment unable to sleep. Listening to the sounds of the night, he begins to perceive another sound of something female approaching near the hallway:

> Soft, small, slippered feet were on the stairs.... Softly his door opened. Gerda came in. Upon her face was the grave earnestness of her desire. She stood still and dropped her kimono in a little silken heap upon the floor. She was like a silver shaft in the moonlight. She whispered. "I'm cold, Herbert." With a sob he stretched out his arms. (63)

Herbert is incapable of having sex without marriage, as it happened in Ludwig's real-life events. Perhaps it is his Teutonic orderliness. While in the heat of this romance, Herbert meets his future wife, Mrs. Harrison Dubose Vilas.

"Book Three, Catastrophe" is Herbert's description—through the narrator—of his fated beginnings with Anne. The narration pointedly specifies that "the year was 1903", (72) the approximate year that Ludwig began his acquaintance with Mary. The narration describes their first social event together: dinner with Anne and her husband. In a scene that is nearly identical to one in Edith Wharton's *The House of Mirth*, the evening and their fledgling relationship is set forth:

> They took the elevated uptown, Mrs. Vilas now and then smiling at Herbert amid the roar. She had drawn a black, dotted half-veil to just above her chin, and under the flicker of the electric lights looks almost young. Herbert felt flattered and befriended by her kindness. She had again succeeded in establishing a psychical understanding, a half-merry, half-pathetic conspiratorial bond between him and herself which was more definite this time since it excluded her husband. (73)

Like Ludwig, Herbert begins to feel the effects of the exciting combination of sex, art and potential success. Mrs. Vilas, like Mary Crocker, is an art patron and wields influence in artistic circles. She is also an artist, although as she states, her married life makes her feel thwarted in her creative work. Herbert, like Ludwig, is greatly attracted to the thought of a relationship with Mrs. Vilas:

Now the echoes of Southern chivalry blended in Herbert's mind with his dream drawn from the fancied lives of continental poets and composers. Now he was in his imagination, both knight and young poet and elegiac worlding. He lost his last faint contact with the things and facts and characters with which he was confronted. (77)

Herbert is writing, or rewriting, the story of his life. He hears her say "that she was thirty-six and he believed her. She did not show herself under the searching light of day." (80) Even in that early period, however, he doesn't like her physical features, like "her nose and chin." (80) Nevertheless his urge for sex overpowers him. "Yes, he had been drunk with falseness and with naked sex hunger." (80) After his first sex experience with her, he knows that "his doom was on him." (81) Ambiguities continue to float up from an impenetrable dialectical sea of question marks. He feels anxious but cannot/does not admit to himself that he loves or doesn't love Anne Vilas. He becomes morally shocked by the elicit complicity between Anne and her mother in their progressing love affair in the husband's house.

From this alone, a whiff of moral corruption should have reached him. Steeped in his false romance, persuaded by his nobler pity for Anne to find or make excuses, lulled by the harem ceremonial of the hour [for the attention that Anne and her mother were bestowing on him], he hushed the monitions of his soul. (86)

Doubt and ambiguity are everywhere to be found. Herbert begins to feel the strangeness of her language, being and ways. He grows more fearful, anxious, and perplexed. He is sinking deeper and deeper into a dialectic of uncertainty. After listening to a wrenching description of a physical confrontation Anne had with her husband: "Even in his fear and confusion Herbert was struck by another of those grotesque phrases which Anne evidently brought from some world of experience to which he had no key." (89) He cannot decide what was real or fake, truth or lie:

It was that tenderness in her voice that stayed with him, that would not let him see the fangs of the trap. A trap consciously set? Deliberately sprung? On this single point Herbert always reserved judgment. Perhaps it was an ultimate vanity in him that forced him to do so, a disinclination to believe that in his twenty-fourth year he was an utter fool. But even though, with the passing of the years, the knowledge of Anne's instinctive duplicity, of her boundless

treacherousness, would its tight serpent coiled about his breast, he continued
to want her and hence to strive to believe that during these early and fatal
days, she was impelled by a sincere emotion and was the victim, not the mis-
tress of events. (90)

The disfigurement and derangement Herbert perceives in Anne's
physical appearance is reflected in her moral, spiritual, and emotional
selves. Nevertheless, "he let Anne drug him. He met her more than halfway. He wanted to be drugged." (96) He has a growing disgust of
everything about her: "Even Anne's body, though youthful for her age,
bore definite traces of her history. After one of her confinements she
must have been inadequately bandaged; she had nursed all her children
from the same breast." (96)

Herbert can no longer distinguish what is real from fantasy. Wanting
so to be drugged by her, "the boundary between dreams and hard realities
is obliterated." (96) At the same time, when Herbert flees to his parents
in Queenshaven for comfort, he falls into a deep dilemma:

A subtle fear worked in him like a poison, an instinctive, intellectually unreal-
ized perception of Anne's true character. Yet he missed her too, there was no
doubt about that. He missed her attention, missed her physically, missed his
long uninhibited talks with her. There was no one else in the world with
whom he could be so frank, with whom he could so let himself go. (110)

At times seemingly taking on Herbert's point of view, at other times
the narrator seems to know things that Herbert doesn't. In fact, the narration sets up a contrast between Herbert and the narrator, Herbert and
Herbert, and of course, Herbert and Anne. With the first three sections of
Crump, the complex mesh of doubt, dialectic and ambiguity is established in the conflicts of youth and old age, New World and Old, the
inherent antagonism of America and Europe, European High Culture set
against American primitiveness and philistinism. A highly ambiguous
dialectic of foreignness and blood congeniality, of Jew and Gentile, of
alienness and compatibility, is set into motion by the narration.

Another dialectic is imposed, when in "Book Four, Early Years",
Herbert's early married life to Anne is juxtaposed with Herbert's own
parents, individually and as a couple. Anne is seen in contrast to
Herbert's mother, and in contrast to the father's and mother's Old World:
Germanic European values are contrasted with Anne's raw Americanism,
philistinism, coarseness and foreignness. There is also the jealousy Anne

feels from the attention Herbert and his father show to his mother. Mothers are also contrasted and compared:

> "And what's to become of my poor mother? She's down there in Little Rock
> with Uncle Anthony without a penny."
> Herbert shrugged his shoulders. "I am sorry. I don't know."
> "Well, I guess I'll send for her to come here."
> He looked at her more calmly. "I think you're crazy, Anne."
> "Oh, am I? I guess my mother is as good as yours. The way you and your
> father jump after her makes me sick at my stomach." (123)

Contrasts of femaleness and parenthood combine in a paradoxical tapestry of difference and sameness. Just what is the reality? Where is the truth? The narrator, detective-like, is in search of it. Herbert is enslaved first by his own Achilles Heel of sexual desire, a Teutonic sense of responsibility and a soft heart. He is secondly under the harsh whip of a wife who forever demands that more materiality be showered on her. She is shown as an endlessly unsatisfied, constantly ungrateful witch, despite the filial warmth and care shown to her by Herbert's parents. Not once, from even the beginning of their marriage, does Herbert threaten her with physical violence. He is revolted by her comparison of her mother with his, and the intolerably demeaning way she speaks about the elder Mrs. Crump. After he warns her that she will be hit, her reply is: "'Strike! Do you think I'm afraid of you? I thought it was my house as much as hers anyhow.' 'Not as long as you shirk all responsibility and all work.' 'Oh, I see. Your mother has been complaining to you behind my back.'" (123)

Herbert simply feels like "perishing of the shame and sordidness of it all." (124) He enters the kitchen to speak "to his mother who was busy— strong, grave, immaculate—baking a cake and felt, although he could not see, Anne listening stealthily in the hall above." (124)   Herbert's mother's goodness and even tribal type of superiority is contrasted here with Anne's utter and total detestableness. Herbert and his parents enter a "silent conspiracy to soothe and please Anne." (124) As liberal and egalitarian as the Crump family is, in spite of Anne's enviable paternal English bloodline, Herbert more and more begins to sense a kind of genetic superiority over his wife, who is herself a dialectical mix of cultural, genetic, linguistic and other forces.

What constitutes her real being? What is her real history? The shrewish Anne can give way to a good humored one who "looked gentler and younger." (124) Her very walk changes with her mood:

Anne had begun to tell him the stories of her past and of her family and Herbert, though he believed himself to be democratic in every instinct, was beginning to suspect that blood, training, origin and the resultant habits had much to do with the quality of the soul and with the conduct of life. (124)

The fact is that both Anne and Herbert use sex as a tool and a weapon. After another in a series of her rude and ugly outbursts, Herbert, with his parents now also held hostage to his marriage due to their living arrangement under the same roof, realizes again that there is only one way to calm her:

He must placate Anne and there was still one way of placating Anne—just one. He got up heavily and went into the dim bedroom where Anne was lying on the bed staring at the ceiling. He lay down beside her. He put his hand on her bosom. "Try not to make life so difficult for me, Anne." She did not answer but turned and sought his lips with her own.... No sooner had the act of his prostitution been accomplished than Eileen's shrill voice [Anne's grown daughter] sounded in the hall. (127)

The narrator-as-Herbert exudes the self-assured attitude that Herbert's superior sexual prowess can tame even Anne—albeit temporarily. No reference or self-perceptive remark is made here of Herbert's possible overestimation of his capabilities or lack of modesty.

The dialectic of pasts (Herbert's and Anne's) proves too difficult to get a handle on, to form into a coherent whole. Herbert resents Anne's attempts at synthesizing one past with the other. Herbert's mother tells a seemingly harmless story about Herbert as a little boy. Anne makes an immediate connection between Herbert as a boy and her son, Bronson. Herbert finds it impossible to control himself and tells her that they want to hear about her early years and not anyone else's:

Anne jumped up. "Well, I guess my son Bronson Vilas is as well worth hearing about as anyone around here and a good deal better too, I'd have you know. And now you can go to your God-damn concert with your God-damn family." (128)

Herbert's enslavement to his own sexual drives causes a cycle of fraud, deceit and self-deceit. Each party hides his/her head in the sand of not-knowing: Anne justifies her behavior by bringing the needs of her children and mother into the picture; Herbert insists he is the victim of his own innocence in a relationship with a cunning and shrewish Eve.

Herbert wrings his hands and says: "No one but a born fool could have gotten into such a mess." (127) However, the reader is not totally convinced that he really believes it. In truth, Herbert plays the child tossed from parent to parent to parent. Herbert's strong love for his mother invokes the possibility—especially in light of his own enthusiasm for psychoanalysis—of Oedipal intrigues. Surely his marriage to a woman nearly twenty years his senior, and therefore chronologically old enough to have been his mother, justifies this assertion. Anne's behavior toward the elder Mrs. Crump, who is more or less of Anne's own generation, could then be viewed as pure and simple jealousy.

Anne resents the respect that she sees given to women of Herbert's cultural background. The positive supportive and loving matriarchal household which is the virtual polarity of Germanic patriarchal, authoritarian homes, uncovers an entirely different view of women, men and marriage from Anne's life experience and social-ethnic-cultural tribe. Where Anne had to learn to use sex, physical attraction, cunning, wiles and stick/carrot incentives, she sees with the Crump family an entirely different perspective. Anne equates her mother with Mrs. Crump. Herbert becomes derangedly furious at any comparisons Anne makes between herself/her people and himself/his people.

> "Take still another thing," she [Anne] went on. "Your mother is really a very dear woman. Don't think I don't appreciate that. But when I see how you and your father care for her and defer to her, I can't help thinking, can I, of my own dear mother, old and forsaken out there and with no one but poor, drunken Anthony Bronson to look after her, can I?" (131)

On the other side, Mrs. Crump would appear to be hiding her true feelings under the cover of Germanic tact, politeness and orderliness. Of anyone, Mrs. Crump should have been able to read her son's true feelings and mind better than anyone. Mr. Crump, following his wife's lead, carbon copies her behavior and attitude. Mrs. Crump says as much in an undercover, secret conversation she has with Herbert: "She spoke to him in German so that the maid would not understand. 'Tell me nothing. I know too much already. I'll help you all I can. Just go now. She doesn't like us to talk together alone." (128)

Herbert becomes trapped by the apparently convincing stories he has invented or told about Anne to his family. Outside of these stories, told to boost her image in their eyes, he avoids discussing the real story of Anne:

> Never, never—how well he understood this in the course of time—would he be
> able to communicate his story and his thoughts. For this shame eating into his
> soul, originally tender and realistic, resulted in a constant terror lest others
> know concerning the brutal sordidness of his fate. (132)

The elder Crumps maintain their conspiracy of silence about the truth
and do nothing to help Herbert escape from the terrible tragedy that has
enslaved his life. At the same time, Anne falsifies the facts about herself
and her life with Herbert:

> The implication that he had "curried favor"—another phrase that Anne
> loved—with Bronson in order to win her was one more of those retroactive
> falsifications that Anne was beginning to indulge in at this time. Free of
> Queenshaven and so of the incontrovertible evidence of her pursuit of Herbert
> and of her trapping him into marriage, Anne began immediately to build up a
> legend of their relations and adventures which, in an incredibly short time,
> had lost all contact with the facts of life. In this legend she believed, or
> feigned to believe, with a deep and romantic ardor. Any doubt thrown upon
> its exactness she treated as a foul affront. (135)

Soon after they move to Manhattan, Herbert's first help and work
with his music comes from the owner of a small music house, Mr.
Nathaniel Joffe: "A tall Jew, indefinably elegant, a little cynical and dep-
recatory, the soft eyes of a dreamer behind his spectacles. A smile that
had no intention of being wistful and yet was so." (137–138) Except for
the positive and sympathetic portrait of this man, the narrator's and
Herbert's true attitude and feelings are kept hidden. Joffe himself is
descried as a kind of masked personality: he is a "dreamer" (138) masquerading as someone else. Herbert likes Joffe; "the two men understood
each other immediately." (139) Elsewhere, Anne reveals her attitude
towards Jews in an interchange with Herbert. She asks Herbert for a
quarter to buy something for her son, Bronson. Herbert, not wanting to
argue, nearly throws the quarter at her.

> Herbert flared up. "What has that fellow to do with my poor earnings?" She
> looked at him with that gesture which resembled the reception of an evil odor.
> "You knew I had the children when you came around making love to me!"
> Herbert controlled himself, but the effect was severe. "Don't drive me too
> far, Anne," he warned her. "Drive you? What in hell do you call driving?
> What do you think you are, anyhow? You love your money, don't you? There
> must have been a pawnbroker among your ancestors." She stood before him
> ugly in her jeering malevolence, and for the second and last time in his life he
> struck her full in the face. (144–145)

It is a mystery here why Anne invokes so crude an anti-Semitic remark in relation to her husband and why his response is so extreme. What, in fact, is the real story of Herbert?

Herbert isn't able to understand or believe what he has become capable of doing and saying. At the same time, Anne begins to create a new story about Herbert. Who and what is the reader to believe in all of this ever-deepening dialectical mire?

> If anyone had told him only a year ago that he was capable of such an action he would of course not have believed it for an instant. The action in fact was so out of character that he seemed to himself to be living in a phantasmal world in which all ordinary laws were suspended. And this impression of the fantastic was deepened by Anne's reaction to his brutality. (145)

As the narrator relates to the rest of the world Herbert's terrible predicament, it is dreadfully clear to everyone with whom the former sympathizes. Anne and Herbert are aliens to each other; "these two people walked, each in another and a separate darkness." (151) More and more elucidated is a growing estrangement, not just by virtue of their chronological difference, but also through the dialectical frictions created by the ever-widening gap of their tribal and cultural origins. Herbert becomes good friends with Joffe. From here Herbert is introduced to another Jew, Mrs. Goldstein, Joffe's "old friend, awfully good sort who is one of the really generous and sincere patrons of music in New York. 'I want to bring you together with Mrs. Goldstein. I've shown her your stuff and she thinks highly of it.'" (151) Anne instinctively hates Mrs. Goldstein. When Herbert is forced to tell her about his new art patron, Anne replies: "So you have to curry favor with rich Jews to get on. I [can't] see myself doing a thing like that." (155)

To what is Anne referring? Who are the "rich Jews"? In their respective views of Herbert, Anne Crump and Jennie Goldstein also reflect and represent a dialectic of female cultural/ethnic attitudes. After a tense exit from the house on their way to Herbert's piano recital at Jennie Goldstein's house, "In the cab Anne patted his knee. 'I know my boy will do booful [well].' He nodded." (159) In contrast, with the Jewish Jennie Goldstein as his art patron and friend, Herbert feels in his element; the man he really is, potent, vital; in short, a font of creative outpouring. When the Crumps arrive at her house, Jennie skillfully maneuvers Anne away to the "place reserved for" her in a clever way of both tacitly honoring and erasing any significance Anne might feel she represents or deserves. (159) This is a double humiliation for Anne, since she was Herbert's art patron and help when they first met and he was beginning his musical career. Jennie is the key to the self that Herbert longs for: freedom, art expression, latitude. With her he can drink "a glass of port" if he should want and smoke a cigarette (159)—two culturally forbidden, code activities of rebellion against American, Puritan-Gentile culture. Jennie leads him into the smoking room and Herbert begins to reflect:

> He sat down and closed his lids. What in the eternal world of art, did this woman [Anne] matter who had her claws in his flesh and nerves? She must not be permitted to have power upon his soul. He would play for the honor of art which as his grandfather used to say, is the honor of God. Jennie Goldstein reappeared. "Ready?" He smiled into her eyes. "Quite." "Good man." (159)

The contrast of Anne's "boy" versus Jennie's "man" sums up the dialectic of Jewish/artist/creativity freedom, mixed with America/ cultureness/living death/Gentile Puritanism which is the confused/confusing blend of Herbert's life and attitudes.

In another such dialectically blended scene, Anne sits as an outsider with Joffe, the kindly Jewish music businessman, Jennie Goldstein, his good friend, and Herbert. Where does Herbert belong in this dialectic of Jewish/Gentile/American/artist? On their way out, after making a nasty remark in front of them about Herbert,

> "Well," Anne said, "I didn't know you were such a liar. So you had luncheon with that vulgar woman. Maybe she'd like to go to bed with you. I didn't see her husband anywhere around. Maybe that Joffe sleeps with her too. I've always been told that Jews are vulgar. But they seem to suit you. Why don't you go and live with them?" (161)

Anne senses something alien and different about Herbert and locates him in another place of the dialectic. His identity, life, thoughts, directions are in a dialectical muddle. Helped by his Jewish friend, Joffe to obtain employment as a college music professor in Ohio, as in fact occurred in the life of Ludwig Lewisohn (minus the Jewish-friend part of the story), Herbert travels there alone to set up a home for himself, Anne and her family. He fights a battle in himself between his Germanic sense of duty and responsibility, and his desire to be a high-soaring artist.

"What was he to do?" (181) With a war raging inside him, he nevertheless

> fled to duty, old palliative gray, murmuring nurse who lets us see life bleed to
> death with a good conscience. His first inner gesture was this: his duty to
> himself as a man and an artist would have been of course to break the false,
> muddy accidental molds of his personal life, to forfeit his position in Central
> City [Ohio] and to refuse to return to Anne. What power the habits of consent
> and suffering and the thousand involuntary enchainments of life had left him
> of translating this decision into action—that was a problem which he chose to
> dismiss. (181)

The more slovenly and dishevelled Anne becomes, the more Herbert
hates her. She feels protected by the positive myth she has created about
their marriage for the public. This private Anne is a polarity of the public
one:

> Before strangers she still appeared well made-up, well groomed, in order to
> sustain the legend of her elopement at fifteen and of her nine years' seniority
> to Herbert. At home she let herself go with an unheard-of abandon. She never
> combed her hair until night; soiled underwear showed beneath her dingy
> kimono; she scratched her head and then cleaned her fingernails with a tooth-
> pick. (192)

Anne is caught between jealousy about Herbert's unclear relationship
with Eileen (are Herbert and Eileen secret lovers?) and her anxiety over
the frail emotional health of her other daughter, Luella. Despite his com-
plaints to the contrary, Herbert is after all the male rooster in a henhouse
of females vying for his body, money, support and/or attention. There
seems to be no other reason for his hatred of Anne's son, Bronson.
Another male in the house detracts from Herbert's position as king of the
roost. Herbert and Anne are in sharp disagreement over exactly what tactic to follow with Luella. Ironically, it is Anne who first breaches the
subject of murder in relation to the illness of Luella. Anne enters
Herbert's study and accuses him of not caring about the state of Luella's
mental health. Herbert shows off his psychological prowess and his great
forbearing patience with her wholesale lack of understanding:

> He explained his attitude quietly. "Isn't it better to treat her naturally than to
> grovel and by that very act to communicate one's fears to her ?"

Anne's face swelled again. "Oh, you know all about it, do you? You and Eileen! Maybe you're in love with Eileen. You act as if you were. Well, let me tell you, it's I who have gone through Luella's illness with her and have been in consultation with the doctors. Everybody in this house will do about her as I think best."

"In other words," he said, "we're all to regulate our actions according to Luella's whims."

She was beside herself. "You damned fool! If you drive Luella mad again, I'll murder you. It's not enough that you killed my mother—" (195)

Herbert at once feels the dialectically jumbled forces inside him. Anne, and everything she represents, seem so alien and strange to his perceptions. He feels as if he is stranded and alone in unfamiliar territory. The study where he can create art and have his own undisturbed world— or nearly so—is the only place he can be himself: "He took her by the shoulders, pushed her out of his study and locked the door." (195) This place is sacred to him, for it is not part of her territorial influence or reach. He thinks of the evil and good sides of his life. Anne, with the "English-American" culture she represents in all its alienness, seems now to be outside of his understanding or interest.

He sat down with his head in his hands. His thoughts drifted to [his parents in] Queenshaven, to Joffe and Mrs. Goldstein, to Andrew Black and Hans Breitner. Thank God there were sane and kind and just and charming people in the world. Perhaps he too would not be condemned forever to this. (195)

The dialectics of his life tumble around American, English, Gentile, Puritanical, German, intellectual, artistic and Jewish influences. He experiences difficulty sorting all of them into some orderly form.

It is ironic that it is Anne who first speaks of the subject of murder. As the chaos in his life mounts, Herbert, as the rooster with his harem of hens, perceives it in real terms as well. As the dirt and disorder grow, "Herbert quietly begged Eileen to dust his desk and piano occasionally." (196) Apparently, it never occurs to Herbert that he could dust his own desk and piano. Eileen is herself a dialectic of a mix of forces. She quickly agrees to dust Herbert's study. Like Herbert and his mother, he and Eileen

were afraid to speak to each other [in front of Anne]. For herself and for Luella, Anne was jealous of the fact that Eileen's youth—she at least might have been his little sister—her affection for his parents, the clearness of her awakening mind, made her seem to Herbert the most natural, kindly, and human being in that house of his shame and despair. (196)

Herbert is caught in an unbearable dilemma: He doesn't love Anne (or does he?) and thinks he never did (or did he?). Everything is bathed, or drowning, in ambiguity. At the same time, Herbert's creative, emotional and financial life is being sustained by the Jewish part of the dialectic, Joffe and Mrs. Goldstein; and the German part as well, Black and Breitner. He digs deeper, deeper into the heart of the truth or the lie of his life. As far as he and Anne are concerned:

> They patched up the economic situation with a lie. They patched up the emotional situation with a lie of darker cast. Anne came to Herbert in her most tragic mood.
> "You didn't mean what you said about not loving me, did you Bertie?"
> He sat like a stone. No words would come to him. Yet he saw, clear-minded here too, that this conversation could have but one result. For if he stuck to the cold truth that he did not love Anne and had, in fact, never loved her, the grotesqueness and unnaturalness of their present situation, from which neither could escape, would assume ghastly shapes, shapes unbelievable and unendurable—shapes that meant madness or crime. The fiction that he loved her had become necessary. (205)

Anne's American, English affiliations deeply resent Herbert's Germanic cultural affinities. When Herbert's mother dies, the elder Mr Crump comes to their house to stay. As in Melnick's previously quoted comments about the very same scene,

> Anne professed a great pleasure at welcoming her father-in-law. But on one pretext or another she prevents the two men from being alone together, discouraged Herbert from pressing the point by private threats of an open and vulgar quarrel, resented the attachment between Eileen and Mr. Crump.... She wanted her father-in-law to take off the little skullcap of black silk which he wore to protect his head from draughts; when Brietner called, she harshly and insultingly resented the use of German in her house. (230)

Interestingly "the skullcap" Mr. Crump wears is the "kippah" that religiously observant Jews wear as well. Why is he wearing it? To which world does he belong? Melnick states that after Ludwig Lewisohn's mother died, Jacques Lewisohn took to wearing this head covering. If he wore it for draughts or was not Jewish, why should Anne be upset? On another occasion, the narrator describes Herbert's new friendship with a woman, Mrs. Gloria Haliwell, whose husband is a musical society director. The narrator describes her through Herbert's eyes: "Her face was set and had its slightly swollen air. Gloria melted into her most winning ways. They might, Herbert thought, have temporarily placated a Moloch." (251) Moloch, the Canaanite god of child-sacrifice referred to here, known and used by astute readers of *Tanach*, would seem to reveal in Herbert a more in-depth knowledge of *Tanach*. In fact, there could be another reason for hiding the possibly Jewish identity of Herbert Crump. Stuart Pratt Sherman's attack on Lewisohn's writing, as previously noted, was not just motivated by aesthetic considerations. In Sherman's remarks about "the house of Jesse" (Sherman 22), Lewisohn was quick to recognize the charge of another time and place in his life, and in the lives of his ancestors. Anti-Semitism, heightened by the growing nativism and isolationist sentiments that fed easily upon theological traditions connected with those of Sherman's literary universe, had begun to rear its ugly head by 1919. (Melnick I: 281) At least some ambiguity in Lewisohn's writing is to avoid causing anti-Semitic backlash against his work. Nevertheless, there is no real textual evidence for connecting Herbert with a Judaic background. Published just two years later, *The Island Within*, so overtly Jewish, puts *The Case of Mr. Crump*, with its sparsely emitted references to some kind of Judaic content, in stark relief.

Here can be witnessed more ambiguous dialectical twists and turns. Who are the Crumps? In a story either based on factual events or not, with biographical details, as Melnick laboriously documents, woven into the woof and warp of *Crump* itself, what at the end, is the reader to believe? What in fact were Lewisohn's true identities? Most critically, in the realm of creation, art and writing, is there such a thing as "truth"? All the players in *Crump* vociferously insist on telling the true account of things, but also slide into attacks of wholesale silence when the facts are blatantly revealed. The elder Mrs. Crump, knowing the truth, kept silent. Herbert's father hides under the cover of his Teutonic propriety. Herbert, knowing or not knowing what's true, both overstates and ambiguously hides its significance from public scrutiny, or from himself for that matter. Eileen, Luella, Bronson and their father are players as well in this hoax of dialectic; the manipulation of fact and fiction, truth and lies. As for Mrs. Crump: "Anne did not grasp either Herbert's mood or the probable implications of the whole situation. She was too ignorant and too self-centered." (*Crump* 241)

In addition, is the narrator (as player and/or perpetrator) also caught in this ruse? What is the writer's responsibility in this sham of mercurial ambiguity? Finally, who is Ludwig Lewisohn, and what is/was his identity in the multifarious folds of dialectical intrigue here and elsewhere?

By the near-end of the *Crump* story of many stories, Anne and Herbert sling muddy diatribes and dialectics at each other. The narrator, as usual, takes no neutral course. He hates Anne as much as Herbert does:

> Anne tried her best to undermine Herbert's belief in himself, in the sincerity of those who appeared to like or admire him, in his personal implication with his career. Herbert, stung by this on account of the insecurity and newness of his emergence from obscurity and from enslavement to the Vilases, would characterize the past, strip Anne of her pretensions, stigmatize her history, person, family. "God, you're a disgusting cad!" Anne would shriek. "You didn't talk that way I notice when you came gum-sucking around me on Sixty-First street." (241–242)

As for Herbert, his side of the bitter quarrels revolves around the same text: "'You trapped me when I was a boy. You stole my youth. You robbed my father and mother of hope and life. Then you made me the servant of that Vilas brood. I hate and despise you so that I sicken all over.'" (242) By the end, Herbert appears to also do a turn-around regarding his (?) Christian faith. In relation to Anne, Herbert ponders reward, punishment and the afterlife: "From her treatment of his father, for instance, one could almost arrive at the necessity of punishment in a future life. The trouble with historical Christianity was, of course, its absurd identification of nature and freedom with evil." (256)

At the same time, Herbert begins a kind of ambiguous romantic liaison with a Jewish musician, Rachel Cohen, who "was enormously intelligent. He felt so at home with her." (264–265) With Anne, it is all a different story. He could never feel completely close to her. Herbert gets a preview of what could be in store for him from another, a "married man who went astray" story of Dr. and Mrs. Wick. The narrator gives the reader both sides of the issue, but it is clear that the narration is tilted heavily in favor of Dr. Wick's interpretation, his side of the story. The Wicks' stories—oddly similar in feeling, image, tone and content to one in Ozick's short story, "Rosa"; (that of the newspaper headline, "Woman Axes Own Biz")—are mirror reflections of Herbert and Anne Crump's stories told through Herbert's (Ludwig's?) consciousness. The narrator/

Herbert has a vision, a hallucination in its clearness of the headlines about himself

> with an unbearable inner shrinking, with maddening shame and powerlessness. *Wick calls love-nest only refuse... Mrs. Wick spurns compromise... Why Wick went astray... Wick's notes to sweetie convule court... Wick's wife defends home....* The newspapers trampled on the man's soul; they threw him to the mob and the mob, half lecherous, half envious, sinister, revengeful, unclean, triumphed. (284)

This is a warning to Herbert. Anne, of course, capitalizes royally on the Wick story/stories. Fearful and in dread, Herbert keeps the luncheon date he has made with Anne after their separation. Ambiguous, even as the end nears, the narration states that Herbert "had half agreed to meet Anne at luncheon." (286) When he arrives, he finds Anne posed with a studied casualness, holding her reading material: her glasses in one hand and "a newspaper in the other." (286) She, of course, asks questions that she already knows the answers to.

> "Have you been following the Wick case?" Anne asked quietly. He nodded. "It just goes to show," she said, "that men can't always get away with their dirty lechery. What right had that girl to take Wick away from his wife? He says he stopped loving his wife twenty years ago. A fine excuse, I must say. I wonder Mrs. Wick didn't sue him for desertion long ago. If he had known he'd lose his job he might have gone back home before he had a chance to meet this dirty little trollop. But women are so slavish. They make me sick. He wanted new flesh, I suppose. That's about the size of it. Well how do you know Mrs. Wick wouldn't have liked that too? But did she take a lover? No! She was too decent. Oh! I think men are disgusting." (286)

Herbert has a wholly different interpretation of this story. He knows Anne (and for that matter the majority of the American public) to be a liar; false, deaf, dumb and blind to moral truth and artistic veracity. At the same time, he feels a spark of hope, the sense of ambiguity. Perhaps there is a mistake in all of these things. Maybe there are more decent, humane Americans than he thinks. Herbert tells Anne his side of the Wicks' affair:

> He spoke: "Wick is a friend of Markowski's [a mutual friend of Herbert] and I've gotten some insight into the story. Long ago Wick turned over all he had in the world to his wife; long ago there had ceased to be any love or good or blessedness in their union. Say it was the fault of both, or say, if you prefer,

that it was a fatality and the fault of neither. Now why should either one of
these human souls want to wound or disgrace or hound the other? Why should
either want to rob the other of such flickers of happiness as may still
come?" (287–288)

However, Herbert's language, his story, does not convince Anne. She
is a shrewd and unconvincable reader. "Anne looked up. Anne spoke.
'You're very eloquent, Bertie. And maybe you think I don't see through
you. But your subtleties don't confuse me.'" (288)

Herbert is trapped in the iron claws of the sad story of his misguided
life, and the story he himself created for the world. The tragic end to the
stories of Dr. Wick and Markowski are no consolation to him: Wick com-
mits suicide and Markowski, profoundly affected by the tragic end of his
dear friend, is in failing health from the shock of it all. He is also
adversely affected by the bitter war between his motherland, Germany,
and his naturalized land, America. These friends' stories are a reflection,
re-reflection and warning for Herbert.

Also Herbert's career is becoming successful, even as his personal
life is becoming dismally unsuccessful. He wants out; total freedom from
Anne's vulturous hold on his life. He is served with court papers, not for
a divorce but for a legal separation. He reads the distorted and lie-filled
text of the story of this court order. It describes—from Anne's perspective—the facts of their marriage in 1906 in Queenshaven; his
temperamental artistic personality; his gross insensitivity to his "devoted
wife" when he begins his lecherous pursuit of one young female after
another. Herbert is beyond himself; out of control of all reason, logic and
common sense. She screams that she would hound him to his or her
death:

"And by the time I'm dead or too weak to crawl after you, you'll be old and
you'll both [he and his new love, Barbara Trent, an opera singer] be so jaded
that you'll curse the day you met and the day on which you were born!" Her
yellow teeth were bared like fangs. He trembled so that the chair on which he
sat shook under him and shook the room. "And now go!" she shrieked suddenly. "Go to your God-damned who—" (332)

Unthinkingly, as if to exterminate any trace of ambiguity and dialectical contradictions, Herbert grabs the brass-handled fire poker. It is as if
his mind and sense have snapped, but it's not clear if they have snapped
out of, or into, place:

He knew nothing until he heard the grinding impact of his blow and saw Anne crumple and then tumble forward and strike her forehead against the fender. Slowly blood came forth from the bald center of her skull and oozed slothfully over the gray of that dishonored head. (332)

So closely do the facts of Ludwig Lewisohn's life correspond to the narrative details of *Crump* that Melnick regularly employs it as a biographical reference; as for example, in his account of the early years of Ludwig's life: "In *The Case of Mr. Crump*, Ludwig's fictionalized account of these early years, he (Herbert) [Ludwig] recalled how this life had ultimately broken his father (Herman) [Jacques]." (Melnick I: 39–40) In many ways, *Up Stream*, on the other hand, is a more fictionalized, which is to say *untrue*, account of the author's life; it is much less consistent with the facts of the author's life. Thus, this scene of the murder of Anne-as-Mary takes a macabre twist forward in time. There is an eerie realization of the "truth". This is a scene of wish fulfillment in and through the real life of Ludwig's real son James. In a conversation, James Lewisohn described in detail the act and circumstances surrounding his (James') real murder of his own wife, for which he was imprisoned. As he stated: "I didn't know what happened. I saw my wife who I loved lying on the floor dead."[68] In another eerie parallel event, James Lewisohn also described his early embrace of Judaism when he studied at the Jewish Theological Seminary, Manhattan; and then his later and present rapture with Catholicism. When I told him that his father would turn over in his grave knowing this, he laughed. He explained to me the importance of Jesus as a father and savior for him. He also talked about his mother, whom he termed "a lunatic", and his father, whom he called "a genius" but who was always too busy travelling, writing or lecturing to give him the time and love he wanted.[69]

Afterward, Herbert perceives that he has murdered Anne as an act of self-defense, of moral courage; a cleansing act. He has now set the universe on its right course.

Herbert Crump trembled no more. Quietly he went to the window and opened it and looked up at the stars. If the universe was a mere mechanism and we, but accidental crawlers on this planet's crust, neither deeds done nor undone mattered and love and hate and cruelty and mercy and rancor and justice were indistinguishably one. But if this were not so, if—were it only by a slow process of becoming—the universe strove, like man himself, for values beyond the dust, then he had helped to re-establish the shaken moral equilibrium of the world, to save cosmos from chaos, to make justice to prevail. Though his body would be imprisoned, his mind would be free. (*Crump* 332)

With one deft blow, Herbert—at least temporarily—kills both Anne and the dialectical quagmire which his life with her had become.

Background Discussion III

Sigmund Freud, as well as Albert Einstein, roundly applauded *The Case of Mr. Crump*. Freudian thought, itself filtered through Freud's own German-Jewish being—along with Lewisohn's earlier deep admiration of Arnold and his writing—brought out in Lewisohn a strong chord of naturalism, benign and guiltless, and anti-Christian reflections and attitudes toward the body and sexuality. As Walter Sutton states,[70] Freud "was the most important of the psychological influences upon the [literary] criticism" of the 1920s. Freud's influence on the American literary scene came chiefly from *The Interpretation of Dreams* (1900) and *Three Essays on a Theory of Sexuality* (1905). Freud's concepts kindled enthusiasm for experimenting in "dream symbolism and stream of consciousness narration." The popularized forms of Freudian psychoanalytical theory emphasized, Sutton continues, "the libido and reinforced the social revolt against Victorian or Puritan mores." (Sutton 6)

Significantly, the first reference to Freud that can be found in Lewisohn's work is in the section of *Up Stream* that describes Lewisohn's receipt of the crushing letter from Columbia University's Brewer. Lewisohn then thinks of his fellow Jews around the world and adds that "the subconscious self has a tough instinct of self-preservation. It thrusts from the field of vision as Freud has shown, the painful and the hostile things of life." (*Up Stream* 123) Seymour Lainoff asserts that Lewisohn discovered Freud in Vienna during the period of his expatriation in Europe.[71] This is probably incorrect, since Lewisohn's first known reference to Freud, in the preceding quotation, was published in 1922 and therefore written even earlier. It wasn't until 1924 that Lewisohn left America to live in Europe with his lover and soon-to-be wife, Thelma Spear. Indeed, as Gillis states in his book published in 1933, much closer in time to the appearance of *Up Stream*, the work was completed in 1920,

"after many hesitations and much earnest search for inner guidance."
(Gillis 48) Freud began to psychoanalyze Lewisohn in Vienna in 1925.
The process was broken off by Lewisohn, however, as Melnick relates,
because the latter feared "the loss of his anxieties and thereby the destruction of what had driven him as a writer." This, Melnick states, was
related to him by Stanley Chyet who was told this by Lewisohn himself.
(Melnick I: 389)

Melnick asserts that Lewisohn was certain that there existed a "'Par-
allelism of Zionism and [the] new Psychology.'" He wanted to create a
system of thought to describe a "psychological concept of history" that
could bring about a return to one's Jewish heritage. (559–560)

In his Introduction to a 1919 work edited by himself, Lewisohn
describes "the proverbial Philistine", lacking in "humane sympathies; in
stubborn defiance of all gentler influences"; the insistence on mechanical
values; the steely ferocities of business competition.[72] Equally important
is his "moral indignation over a literary or dramatic treatment of sex",
which Lewisohn Freudianly ascribed to "his own furtive grossness or
embittered self-repression." (*Modern* i) In his essay in *A Modern Book of
Criticism*, "Literature and Life", he discusses the Roman poets, Cicero
and Horace, and the negative changes that Christianity brought to the
heroic world of the classics by bringing rigidity, "moral dualism" and the
ill-interpretation of "reality". (174–175) Lewisohn, as well, was deeply
struck by Freud's concept of the "creative Eros"—the very
antithesis of Christianity.

In *The Golden Vase*, Lewisohn uses the character of a writer who is
told by his doctor to take a voyage to Europe. He leaves behind his
"excellent wife and superlative mother of his children, who was known to
herself and to all their children as the ideal comrade of a writer as severe
and uncompromising as himself."[73] There is, however, one big problem:
he doesn't love this wife, Katherine. "He had tried…. But his marriage
seemed to doom him to barrenness as an artist." (*Golden* 29) For many
years in his desk he had "kept the fragments" of the time in his life with
Dagmar Robbins, "an angel", (29) a "wise child", (30) a "little wench
[who] had an instinctive knowledge of art and the artist, and a wry, vul-
garized, but genuine instinct for the creative life." (30)

Freud thus created three avenues of discovery for Lewisohn: that of
his Jewish history and heritage in the examination of, in Freudian terms,
the repression of the past to shed light on conflicts in the present;
Lewisohn's creative drive, what Freud called creative "Eros"; and feel-

ings of, and towards, sexuality, heretofore repressed and confused by Christian teachings and attitudes toward physicality and the body.

Martin Buber was perhaps the most well-rounded composite thinker who most influenced Lewisohn's life. In Buber, Lewisohn found a perfect union of Teutonic high culture, Hebrew Scriptures, Western philosophy, poetic expression, and humanity. In short, Buber personified Lewisohn's own complex dialectic, but in another twist of emphasis. His thought also gave Lewisohn a system, a language, a code for deconstructing the language of Christian-Hebrew typology, the kind of rhetoric that Lewisohn once had apparently accepted in Arnold's work. From Buber, Lewisohn gained an understanding of the dichotomy between the historical and Pauline Jesus.

Lewisohn's essay on Buber[74] focuses on Buber's philosophical anthropology and on the philosopher's essay, *The Knowledge of Man,* which the latter defines as "the wholeness of man". Buber's Germanic poeticism, belief in God, mysticism, and Enlightenment emphasis on the existential predicament of the human essence alone with his/her choices greatly attracted Lewisohn's interest. In another essay in *Menorah Journal,* as Melnick describes, Lewisohn details the discovery he made of "the 'psychological' elements of 'inner unity... [and] salvation through action' reasonably argued as the essence of Judaism." (Melnick I: 398)

In "What Is Man?" Buber defines "philosophical anthropology" as the study of "the wholeness of man" and he lists the following as among the problems "which are implicitly set up sometimes by this question":

> Man's special place in the cosmos, his convergence with destiny, his relation to the world of things, his understanding of his fellow man, his existence as a being that knows it must die, his attitude in the ordinary and extraordinary encounters with the mystery with which his life is shot through.... [This is] the essence of man.[75]

Humanity partakes not just of the finite, Buber said, but also of infinity. Each human's unique individual existence, so small and alone as it is, is paradoxically made large through his participation with God. More importantly, Buber's work also transmitted to Lewisohn the essence of Jewishness, which emphasized the soul's blank slate—as opposed to Christianity's concept of Original Sin—with which each human essence is born into the world. In *Between Man and Man,* Buber also described Judaism's sense of the dynamic interplay of every human choice in his/her inter-existence with God. He speaks of the freedom of man and the reality of evil. This potentiality also underlies his distinction between cosmological time, in which the future is determined as far as we are concerned, and "anthropological time" in which the future is undetermined because it depends in part on our decisions.[76]

Buber's essential Judaism can be seen in contrast to the Christianity of Kierkegaard's philosophy, with whom Buber contrasts his own work. In Buber's view, Kierkegaard mistakenly believed that the essentially basic relationship to God cannot be forged, as Kierkegaard believes, "by renunciation of the relation to the whole being", but has to contain as well all of the human being's interactions in the world. Buber concludes his essay, "What Is Man?", by asserting that what is unique in humanity is "to be found not in the individual nor in the collective, but in the meaning of 'I' and 'Thou'." (*Between* 161–162)

For six years, Buber had lived among the *Chassidim*, an Orthodox Jewish mystical group which follows the *Ba'al Shem Tov*, Rabbi Israel ben Eliezer. To a large extent Buber, and then Lewisohn after him, absorbed a great deal from Chassidic teaching, specifically the obedience to God's Law combined, in equal measure, with a devotional love of humanity. Both Lewisohn and Buber absorbed a romanticized sense of what they perceived as Chassidism's human-centered attitude toward humanity's relationship to humanity and to God. The apparent influence on Lewisohn increased after the 1920 publication of *Up Stream*. It was in 1927 that a Lewisohn essay on Chassidism appeared in *Cities and Men*. Chassidism believes that in each person, as well as in all of God's creation, is God's divine spark. Chassidism is messianic, joyful, ecstatic. As Lucy Cohen describes in her "Foreword" to Martin Buber's work on Jewish mysticism, God is seen as totally complete, "alone"[77] before He created the world. From nothing, He created all that is, and in so doing, His *Shechina*, or holy presence, became part of everything in the created universe. In each human is the spark of God's holiness and deliverance. Redemption will come when each "spark" becomes one with its Creator. Through his/her actions, each human can help bring about the Final Redemption of humanity by choosing good and not evil. Each individual can usher in the Messianic Age of Redemption. The *Ba'al Shem Tov* teaches that each person must be in the process in his/her own unique way, always "keeping", Cohen describes, "his individuality intact." (*Ba'al* xiii) Buber's work, therefore, brought Lewisohn in profound contact with exactly what he so long had been searching for. By the end of *Up Stream*, he could ask:

> What Anglo-American has lived with the poets who are the sources of his great tradition more closely than I? What Anglo-American has a deeper sense for the beauty of his own tongue than I? But when, in the old days, I desired to translate my Americanism in that high and fine scene of action, I was told that I was not wanted. Yet I was to be Americanized. I am even now to be assimilated. Suppose I intend rather to assimilate America, to mitigate Puritan barbarism by the influence of my spirit and the example of my life. (*Up Stream* 237)

The writer's anger, it would seem, is directed at those who insist on perceiving his place and identity at the opposing pole. In the complex dialectic of the author's life, he insists that they view him as an "Anglo-American" of the purest type with finely enculturated mastery of the English language; as a gentleman of blood and breeding. Nevertheless, they sought to make him over in their own way—not his. At the same time, to what fact or meanings do "my spirit" and "my life" refer? Is "Americanism" not part of the dialectical package that constitutes the author's "spirit and life"? The preceding quotation from *Up Stream* does not represent a preference of one culture/religion/ethnic background or national affiliation over another, but with Arnoldian undertones, jeremiacally denounces Puritan barbarism as the adversary of the finer things of life such as culture, art, and a generally aesthetic life-style and perspective. Arnold can be discerned here in Lewisohn's call for all to be *mainstream* and homogenized, but in the context of Judaism. Lewisohn would appear to be calling for the redemption of the world and America by/through the writer and art.

The Island Within

What is the "island" shut up inside, and what surrounds it? The title brings to mind John Donne's lines, "No man is an island." The human individual cannot stay isolated. He/She is both an individual and a member of the cultural, social, ethnic and national forces that give his/her life its base. Perhaps the title alludes to some unknowable paradox of being, or multiple beinghood that is forever in flux. Perhaps the title appears somehow ill-fit to the writer's growing social, ethnic and identity-linked consciousness. In fact, as Melnick relates, Lewisohn disagreed with his publisher's decision, preferring the title, *The Torch*, "believing it more representative of the content." (Melnick I: 448) In 1928, at the time *The Island Within* was ready to be released to the public, and in light of the biographical and anecdotal facts and stories about Lewisohn's return to his people and to Judaism, the author was nevertheless still demonstrating his earnest opposition to subscribing to any one pocket of the inscrutable dialectic of his being and life. The year that *The Island Within* was being readied for release, at a 1928 New Year's Eve party thrown by Ludwig and Thelma in Paris, one literary friend, Myron Nutting describes the event:

> "His party, of course, was not as riotous as the ones that I had been passing up coming to his. The first thing I remember about that evening was Ludwig taking me up to a splendid ham. He said, 'Have some estimable ham, Myron. I think it is a most estimable ham.' I thought that was a funny word to apply to a ham, especially at that time. He'd been raised an Episcopalian [sic], but he'd gone back to the faith of his father quite vigorously. He was studying Hebrew and I think that he was keeping up the Jewish celebrations. And to be offered an 'estimable' ham by him struck me as rather quaint." (455)

Ludwig Lewisohn, the man (not to mention the writer) was full of inscrutable contradictions, as Nutting points out.

The text that was finally named *The Island Within* appeared on the American scene as a Jewish thorn in a Gentile nation's side. In the twenties, America was undergoing rampant anti-Semitic sentiments. Set against this particular American landscape, the book becomes a sore point in contrasting Jewish and Gentile worlds. Ludwig was fearful for its life and well-being in this decade of anti-Jewish hostility. In fact the book was first released as *The Defeated*. (453) Thus even the title of the book was born in ambiguity, although it was to express a very polemical point of view.

There is a complex mesh of dialectics at play in this work. It is not only full of the contrasts between Jewish and Gentile, but also of barbaric, uncouth philistinism and the refined aesthetic sensibility and freely-roaming consciousness of the poetic cultured soul, the latter of which is the basis of the America-England conflict in Lewisohn's work. This is related further to yet another conflict, that of a New (American) World in contrast to an Old (English-European) one. As well, *The Island Within* examines the conflicting forces within Judaism itself in the struggle between the "Mithnagdic" and Chassidic points of view. As each generation of the Levy family sheds its past cultural baggage to take up a new cultural frame, conflicts develop in the clash between the cultural norms and expectations of the new and old frames. From this springs a cacophonous medley of conflicting pasts which in turn yields yet another contrast of flux and adaptation to an ever-changing world, and the inclination to preserve what is or was.

A contrast of the New America and the Old World of England and Europe is immediately identifiable. As the writer excoriates fellow-Americans for their forgetfulness of the past, several contradictory messages can be slowly discerned:

> Until the other day we Americans lived as though we had no past. There were old families in Eastern cities who worshipped ancestors and played with heraldic devices in a quiet fashion. But the children of the many millions swept past these in the public schools and began the world all over again with Lexington and Bull Run and Valley Forge and the Declaration of Independence. Would that those happy and innocent days could have endured![78]

The relative pronoun, "those", in the last sentence of the quotation is confusing. To what past does "the other day" refer? Is the author playing a trick on the unwary reader? As well, while the word, "we", would appear to count the narrator/writer among the "Americans", the word, "past", seems to simultaneously overturn that possibility. Nearly three-quarters of a century ago when this book was written, an America of the "past" is indicated which was only a century and a half away from the cultural, linguistic and social affinities with a British motherland. The narrator/writer wants to cover all ground, to keep all doors open, to make every possibility an attainable mission. Through the veils that cover and suddenly disclose, emerges a complicated and contradictory picture. The "aristocratic ears" in both American and England—which, is to say the (now) Americans who still maintain their traditional habits and Old World way of life in that terrain of a wilderness across the ocean; and the English of the socially, well-connected upper class—are safely above those of "inferior natures". (*Island* 3)

As attractive as aristocracy is, or all things English (to which no Jew could gain entry, even one of German descent), nothing can beat the "unexampled freedom of this refuge of the refuge-less, this home of the homeless, this haven of the oppressed." (3) It doesn't matter that the champions of that American land of freedom are "crude, premature." (3) The writer champions the victory of his homeland, America, and its hard-won independence which vanquished "the British lion", mocked "emperors", "kings", (3) "priests" and snobs; all "inhuman arrogance" both "dangerous and grotesque." (4) Instead of the past that is England, America must salute its "Golden Ages" when "hard adventurers heaped up unmeasured fortunes" (4) but had democratic rather than oligarchic attitudes to direct them. Yes, there was "raw vulgarity", but there was freedom. That, rather than the Britain of their ancestors, was the real past of America and true Americans. Is the narrator referring to the kind of Americans like the writer? One can't be sure. In this dialectic of identity and lack thereof, is the writer or narrator being named an American as a way of leading the reader on the right track, or off it? What, in fact, are the facts? In "Book Eight", Arthur Levy has a curious interchange with his wife, Elizabeth Knight, daughter of a Protestant minister:

> He took her unawares:
> "Elizabeth, am I an American?"
> She was still warm and preoccupied with her work. She wiped an inky finger on her hair. "What did you say? Are you an American? No, of course not." She wandered about the room. Suddenly she stopped. "What were we talking about, Arthur? I really was not thinking. I was full of my story. It's going fine. Did you ask me whether you were an American?"
> "Yes."
> "What a quaint question! And did I say you weren't?"
> "You did."
> "Oh well, I wasn't thinking. Certainly you are. Oh, but I'm tired. I'll drop right to sleep. Good night." (289)

Although Elizabeth says that she wasn't concentrating on what Arthur was saying, she is able afterwards to recall every word that he said. Arthur plays through multiple identities: the patient and *Herr* Psychiatrist, the Jewish husband of a Gentile wife, the American—which is to say that he feels himself with no place, displaced, or of every place. Catching his wife unaware, answering as she truly or unconsciously feels, Arthur reveals the sense of dispossession he feels at the core of his being. By definition, he is an American, for he was born in America. However, his question reveals the sense of misplaced being that he feels when he compares his inner self, behavior patterns, attitudes, expectations and value system with that of his wife's Gentile-Christian community around him. Elizabeth, on the other hand, is truly caught up in the "story" of her identity. She is at home in America in the deepest recesses of her being. She is obviously too uncomfortable with the issue to give him a straight answer, and in a classic avoidance tactic she pleads tiredness and goes immediately to bed.

Lewisohn's story is indeed epical. It consists of seven "Books" with a short didactic chapter preceding each "Book", the didactic narrative summarizing the central ideas of the remaining "Books" and the narrator's perception of them. The remaining "story" parts are written in a detached, fairly nonprescriptive style. This epic novel traces one of the author's most fundamental and highly scrutinised dialectics, the process of a pathogenetic assimilation of the Mendel (Levy) family into Christian-Gentile culture through five generations and three countries (Poland, Germany, and America); it then goes full circle back to homeostasis and hope of a secure Jewish identity. Because of the complexity of his background, sensitivity and intellectuality, Arthur knows this journey of self-disclosure will be difficult, but he must go on:

> He could not turn back. He must not, on that account, deceive himself as to the difficulty of going forward. Barriers of ignorance, of inhibition, of fear were to be overcome. Such moments of revulsion as he had had the other day in the presence of Elizabeth might come again, would come again. They were part of the price one had to pay. The withdrawal of one's earlier self and of one's immediate ancestors from Judaism—a phenomenon which doubtless had had its legitimate function in the historic process—this withdrawal created inevitable difficulties. (321)

The dialectical process means that certain cultural, personal connections will be made more important, emphasized while others will in some way be wedded to or melted into others in the crucible of self. Arthur understands that he will always remain the sum total of all of his life experiences. The child born from the Jewish-Gentile union of his and his wife Elizabeth's being is itself a testimony to the complexity of cultural dialectic in Arthur's, his child's, and even Elizabeth's life.

The novel is a type of naturalistic medical report detachedly laying out the significant details that transformed a healthy organism into a diseased and dying one. Dr. Arthur Levy is the investigative figure of the doctor/writer and reader/narrator, who studies the pathology of anti-Semitism in self and family.

This novel is not just epical. It is also a naturalistic rendering of the raw, ugly and brutal facts of Jewish existence—and nonexistence—from the year 1096, as set down then by Arthur's forefather, Reb Efraim ben Reb Jacob, transcribed from the Hebrew to English in the present time, and given to Arthur's Chassidic acquaintance and newly discovered relative, Reb Moshe Hacohen. This text is a historical record of Jewish existence, its history, and the facts pertaining to that history. Reb Moshe goes to Arthur's home to speak with him:

> "Here," Reb Moshe Hacohen tapped the roll of paper, "I have brought you something. When the Russians sacked the house of your great great-grandfather, Reb Eliezer Hacohen, he gave an old chest that contained family papers to my great-grandfather, his brother, the *Chassid*. Have you heard the story?" (323)

The transcribed document, and Reb Moshe's remarks, described in the last Book of the novel, thus fleshes out millennia of Jewish history from the year 1096 of the Common Era, through the Crusades of the Middle Ages. "Book One" begins in the year 1840, after the Enlightenment has already begun raging through the European continent. The year 1840 describes Vilna in the time of Reb Mendel ben Reb Jitzock,[79] his wife Braine and their two children, Efraim and Rifke. The generation of Efraim and Rifke is then described in "Book One" especially the marriage of Efraim Mendel and Hannah Bratzlawer in 1850, when the family name, Mendel, is changed to Levy. The children of Efraim and Hannah are born. In this generation are Tobias (1851), Samuel (1855), Bertha (1856), Rose (1858) and Jacob (1861), the last the father of Arthur Levy. Jacob emigrates from Germany to America on 2 August, 1879, and marries Gertrude, Arthur's mother, in 1891. Arthur is born in 1893 and his sister Hazel in 1895. Arthur marries the daughter of a Protestant minister in 1919. A son, John, is born in the same year.

After the tractate that begins "Book One", the writer breaks through the illusory space that ordinarily separates the story from the reader by reversing the point of perspective, and the "space" that each traditionally occupies—addressing the reader directly: "'But we have paid two dollars for a story, not for a treatise!' Have patience, reader; the story is coming—a story not poor, perhaps, in the significant elements that make up the fate of man." (5) What precedes this writer-reader intimacy is, we are told, not yet the story. The writer moves the story's frame as he sees fit. If the story hasn't yet begun by this point, then it is also possible that the "story" began before the book called *The Island Within* was opened to the reader's eyes.

So many dialectics of contrast, and the melting of one into another to form yet another dialectic, intrude on our consciousness as we begin the book. Is the writer American? Why does he care so much to tell us that he is? Is the writer an aristocratic "snob" who wants to be some combination of all cultural possibilities? If the writer can't be English and an aristocrat, although he would dearly love to be, then let him enjoy the freedoms of democracy that protect his possible foreignness—a Jewish foreignness—from wrathful Gentiles. If "Book One" is in truth not a story, but the "truth", then what exactly is the truth that the reader is being told here? What's more, the writer asks the reader "What, in fact, is a story?" (5) In all urgency, he forces our attention to his destination, or so it would seem:

> Are we beginning to see the courses of things? Then, in God's name, let us tell wiser, broader, deeper stories—stories with morals more significant and rich. Yes, morals. If a story does not teach by example it is no story; it has no truth. For let men see truth and they will hasten to apply it to themselves. (6)

These "wiser" stories are, however, not without inconsistencies. Although, as the narrator asserts, "metaphysical truth" (6) cannot be refuted, consciousness and experience give that play, that Derridean "difference" if you will, which paradoxically negates any absolute truth. Lewisohn's (or the narrator's) "margin of freedom" (6) opens the text up to an indeterminacy without a centre; minus borders, without a frame to cage its wonder and flights of fancy. Can we discern that what is implied is the writer's full authority to create texts that can't be framed, closed in on themselves; texts that are centerless and open? The bard, the writer, is the designated voice of prophecy; the messiah to lead us through all the correct expectations to the unalterable truths in life. The writer—that is, one who is secure of identity—is the only one to lead the vulgar, untutored masses to the truth. However, the writer also openly asserts that all he says is logically, inherently implausible, a dialectically, impenetrable maze: "A flat contradiction? But you will find a flat contradiction at the end of every train of human thought. The ultimate wall of mystery is built of antinomies." (7) All is paradoxically unresolvable. Contradiction is at the heart of language itself.

Lewisohn ends his introductory non-story by urging his readers to take faith in the epic nature of stories. To do that, humanity must be able to grasp the paradoxes inherent in the metaphysical dialectic that has both historical continuity and discontinuity, its essential existential existence found in the true nature of all things, for the great epical "adventure" between life and death.

By beginning the text with the date 1840, the name Reb Mendel ben Reb Jitzock, and the place Vilna, Poland, the narrator would appear to be underscoring the story's historical accuracy. He tells the story of Reb Mendel who, like Cynthia Ozick's pagan rabbi, is curiously drawn to the forbidden world of nature. Like Ozick's Rabbi Kornfeld, Reb Mendel's "dark secret was that, despite his later brilliancy as a Talmudist, he was dry of heart. There was no glow in his study and no fervor in his prayers." (14)

What great fervor he does feel is while standing in the synagogue courtyard and listening to "the wind rustling in the single ragged tree that stood among the cobblestones." (14) He performs this act almost each evening and cannot perceive how strange and wrong his behavior is to the others around him. However, as Reb Mendel defensively asserts, the greatest of Talmudic scholars, the *Gaon Elia*, did not disdain study or interest in the physical world and even encouraged the study of geometry. But because he is responsible for the care and support of his wife and little children, and could lose his teaching job because of his socially prohibited inquisitiveness, he decides not to push the issue into open controversy. He, therefore, makes a solemn decision:

> He must not linger under the tree. Was it the "evil instinct" that often drove him from within—that had driven him on that unbelievable day, two years ago, when he had suddenly left the children whom he was to teach and had run and run out beyond the gates of the Ghetto and found himself in a green green field under a newly-washed sky? His warning had come to him at once. He had heard a discordant chanting more like the snorting, it had seemed to him, of unclean animals. (15)

The resemblances between the Ozick story and this one of Lewisohn's, as well as other stories by Lewisohn, are perhaps too striking to be coincidence. This issue is discussed more fully in the Ozick section. On the other hand, the rational *Mithnagedim* (those against the

Chassidim) tradition in mainstream Judaism, unlike the mystical Chassidic approach, sharply disdained all interaction with the world of nature. This gave rise to tales and occurrences in Jewish life and lore that focused on a brilliant-to-average Talmudic or Biblical scholar of the Mithnagedic approach (with which Cynthia Ozick identifies her family), whose internal dichotomies lead to madness, a severing of Jewish ties or worse.[80]

Some time later, Mendel is surreptitiously handed a book by Shimon the Crooked in the synagogue (of all places!) which included the entire history of the Jews "as proof" that even "pious and holy Jews had in all other lands and ages cultivated profane science and philosophy and been no less acceptable to God." (16–17) The narrator continues the tale of Mendel and his family: how Mendel begins to work for a rich Jewish liquor maker, and with all the freedom of his new life, feels more and more dead inside. Braine secretly vows to herself to emigrate to Israel some day. When Mendel dies of some undisclosed illness, with her heart broken long before by the pain of Mendel's and her son's fall from piety to crude business interests, Braine puts her daughter in the care of the son and leaves for Israel.

Lewisohn describes the very first stages in the anatomy of assimilation. Interestingly, he appears indirectly and partially to attribute this fall from Judaic tradition not just to the tragic lures of Enlightenment thinking and the concomitant slow but sure dissolution of Ghetto life, but also to that type of hyperrational perception and interpretation of sacred texts and Talmudic Law that followed the dispersal of the Israelites after the destruction of the Temple in 586 B.C.E. (*I Kings* 6; *II Kings* 25; *Jeremiah* 52); and then again, at the hands of the Roman general Titus, in 70 C.E. (*Mishnah* "Middot"). Thus in the Diaspora, there was a strong influence on the Israelites to impose a strong rationalism on worship and the interpretation of sacred texts, first by the wider Gentile-Roman culture, and also by the necessity of preserving Hebraic culture and belief during the many calamities that befell the Israelites down through the ages.

Lewisohn's epical novel brings into full view the raging conflict between the rational Mithnagedic and mystical Chassidic streams in Judaism that split the Occidental Judaic world in half. In one very real sense, this battle described, and continues to describe, a polemic of harsh contrasts between the mystical and rational traditions in Judaism. However, in this contemporary time, where the exoticism of Oriental thought has seeped into the thinking of a younger generation of Jews, what can be seen is a mixture of these two strains of Judaism, rational and mystical, in the present interest in Kabbalah, the Zohar and other mystical Judaic texts.[81]

Chassidism (also spelled "Hassidism") is a movement that began in approximately 1750 through a handful of followers of Rabbi Yisra'el ben Eli'ezer, also known as the *Ba'al Shem Tov* (meaning the "owner of the good name"), a humble teacher from a tiny Polish village. By the early eighteenth century, the period in which Lewisohn's novel begins, the movement had grown in popularity and numbers. Its main sources of discontent were/are with the *Mithnagedim*'s elitist sentiments towards study of the sacred texts, and with what it perceived as a too-narrow interpretation of Kabbalistic thought. The search for some other option that could blend the two brought many followers to the *Ba'al Shem Tov*'s point of view, which focused on several basic points. One is that God is everywhere and anywhere in the world, in places not usually associated with God. Another is that by training one's inner sense of observation, it is possible to see God's divine energy/light that constantly seeks out Jews for redemption. Still another is that it is the responsibility of every Jew never to turn from the physical world. Instead, he/she must love and enjoy everything around him/her and bring all into devotion and prayer. Thus all the lost sparks in the whole of the material world will be channelled through the Chassidic believer and eventually find their way to the Eternal Source of Light and Love. As well, Jewish souls which have fallen can be redeemed through others' prayers. In this way the Jewish sparks in search of home can find their way back to God. As Arthur Green states:

> These acts of reuniting the world with God constituted a typically revivalist simplification of complex Kabbalistic doctrine, which Hasidism made accessible to ordinary and even unlettered Jews. The *Ba'al Shem Tov* taught that God needs to be served in all ways, not only through the prescribed commandments but also in every act that a person performs and every word that he speaks. (*Religion* 304)

Lewisohn's text evinces a number of examples of this Chassidic-Mithnagedic aspect of dialectic. One instance is in the description of Braine and the distinguished scholarly family into which she was born:

> She was the daughter of a good house. For many generations her fathers had been learned men and hence belonged to the *jichess*, or intellectual aristocracy, which is the only class distinction among Jews. Her father, moreover, had been a rich man at one time and had therefore gladly given her in marriage to the penniless Mendel, then a brilliant *Yeshiva-bocher*, or student at a Talmudic university. (*Island* 8)

Except for the century and a half difference, this is exactly the world of Ozick's pagan rabbi. Like Braine, Rebetzin Sheindel Kornfeld, the pagan Rabbi Isaac's wife, albeit born dead centre in the Holocaust, was the spiritual and intellectual heiress to a great Talmudic dynasty. Thus she is a member of the *jichess*, the intellectual elite of modern New York City, America. Braine's aristocratic line is a subject of discussion with her husband, Mendel:

> Efraim looked up. "And how far back did you say the family tree went?"
> Braine shook her head with proud mysteriousness. "Who knows? My mother—*Selig*—said it went clear back to King David. But my father—peace be upon him—said that was only a story, but that it did in truth go back to the great Raschi of Worms, the light and guide of Israel." (13)

To have been from the family of "Raschi" (Rashi), one of the greatest Jewish scholars of all time, would have been enough, and also nearly unbelievable.

Like Mendel, Isaac Kornfeld is also a brilliant Talmudist. Both Mendel's and Kornfeld's families are *Mithnagedim*. Thus a serious, strict (even stern), rational approach rules their lives. If the frame of Orthodoxy were not enough, these *Mithnagedim* also create a world with strict borders, in order to protect and preserve their lives and the Jewish future. A strong fence is erected against all forms of what they perceived as irrational and wild thinking. Thus the extreme actions of Rabbi Isaac Kornfeld and Rabbi Mendel are perceived by their respective communities as outrageous, pagan, Goyish (Gentile), and possible grounds for social ostracism, even excommunication.

Mendel tries to reason with his wife concerning his desire to take a more active part in worldly things. She is horrified, calls him a nonbeliever, and on the memory of her dead antecedents calls him a traitor to his people:

> He had shaken his head in despair. He had tried to get her to understand the distinction between the law, both written and oral, which was eternal on the one hand, and the customs which had arisen in certain lands and periods of the dispersion and which had no binding force. (21)

Mendel tries to get Braine to understand that showing interest in the world and nature is not against God or the Holy Scriptures, but she will not listen. Her defence is that, in whatever way her great father perceived the world, so will she view it. One night, on Reb Mendel's way back from a meeting with Shimon the Crooked, Mendel sees a group of *Chassidim* standing outside, near his house:

> All the motions and gestures of these people had something tense and rapt, as though they had just completed, or were about to begin a grave and mystical dance. They were poised between ecstasy and ecstasy. "*Chassidim*," Mendel murmured a little contemptuously to himself. But he stopped; he listened. (18)

In one way the story he hears the Chassidic Reb Menasche telling parallels his and Braine's problem child, Efraim, who is not a good Talmudic student. When Mendel tells her that not all boys or men are suited for deep intellectual activity, Braine's response is to weep "herself to sleep." (22) In the grip of this ever-encroaching contrast of change between the status quo—be it Chassidism or the world at large—Mendel and Braine represent, respectively, two different sides of the polemic:

> When Efraim, a year after his *Bar-mitzvah*, suddenly left the *yeshive*, the Talmudic university, Mendel merely looked at his son with grave and inquiring eyes. Braine stood beside them, flushed and desperate. Efraim looked little sullen.
> "I had set my hope on him!" Braine cried. She turned to the boy. "What will you do, *shegez*, worthless one?"
> Efraim looked at his father. "Reb Bratzlower [Mendel's employer] sent for me. He heard I could speak Polish and do sums."
> Mendel nodded. He could not command or even advise his own son. The conflict within him had robbed him of certitude and thus of power. Braine turned upon them both. (28)

Braine's only solution, after Mendel's death, is to spend the last days of life in Israel. She likes to tell her children stories of her past. They especially love to hear about the "old carved wooden chest" which stood "under the great *Chanukah* lamp." (12) No one, not even little Braine's grandfather, knows the age of the chest. All they know is that

It had always been in the family, long before the days of the Jewish migration to Poland. It came from the west. It was dark brown and showed cracks in the wood and had an old, old lock with a huge key. No one dared open it but grandfather and he opened it only once or twice a year on very solemn or very joyous occasions. (12)

The chest is an integral part of Braine's ancestry. It contains marriage contracts, *ketubot*, of many family members; a heavy old gold ring; "and bundles upon bundles of parchment exquisitely written by hand in... spare Hebrew letters." (12–13) One of these parchments, "[a] very mysterious one, was an account written long and long and long ago, of Jews who died somewhere in the west a death of martyrdom to sanctify the ineffable Name." (13) When Efraim asks what happened to the chest, Braine answers that it was nearly the sole thing that they were able to salvage when the Russians burned down their house. Braine's grandparents ran to a village inn, where Braine's grandfather turned the chest over to his brother:

> "His brother, the *Chassid*?" Efraim asked.
> Braine nodded. Her voice had a tang of bitterness. "Why a man from such a family should join the *Chassidim*—not of us be it said—that goes beyond my understanding! And why father gave him the chest!" (14)

Braine Hacohen Mendel's father and the great grandfather of the *Chassid* Reb Moshe Hacohen, who attaches himself to Arthur Levy's life, were brothers. This magnificent "chest" is now in the safekeeping of Reb Moshe. Is it Lewisohn's intention to say that only Chassidism can preserve the Jewish past? Does the contempt that the *Mithnagedim* have for the *Chassidim* somehow spell doom for the former? Lewisohn himself was greatly attracted to Chassidic thought, as described in the Introduction to this study. This occurred either before, or as a result of, Lewisohn's English translation of Martin Buber's story of Chassidism, *Gog and Magog*, in 1943. (Melnick II: 285) Melnick makes a number of allusions to Lewisohn's own personal interest in Chassidic writers and thought. As Melnick describes, the *Menorah Journal* editor

> [Henry] Hurwitz suggested that they place one of [Thelma's] pieces at the end of Ludwig's forthcoming article on Martin Buber in whose retold Hassidic tales Ludwig had discovered the "psychological" elements of "inner unity...[and] salvation through action", reasonably argued as the essence of Judaism and the instinctual response of a Jew to the idolatrous worship of

things, ideas, places, and institutions—what, in sum, had been Ludwig's own
response to the Puritanism of America and to the dangerous pagan nationalism
of Europe. (Melnick I: 398)

This was published by Hurwitz in 1925, which proves that Lewisohn's interest in Chassidism preceded the publication of *The Island Within* by a number of years.

When Reb Moshe Hacohen and Arthur Levy discover that they are related through Braine's father, Reb Eliezer Hacohen, Arthur Levy informs him that he is "extremely" interested in hearing this, and even "very glad to know it." (*Island* 309) Reb Moshe Hacohen is then compelled to tell Arthur that there is "an old division in our house. My great-grandfather joined the *Chassidim*. His older brother, Reb Eliezer, a learned Talmudist who traced the descent of the family from great scholars and pious men of the Middle Ages, considered this a disgrace." (309)

Reb Moshe Hacohen then tells Arthur a story of the *Chassidim*, "the pious or holy ones" and the *Mithnagdim*. In the story, a man goes to the Chassidic rabbi and asks if the Messiah, upon his coming, will be a *Chassid* or a *Mithnaged*. The rabbi quickly answers that, for certain ones the Messiah will be a *Mithnaged,* because as a *Chassid* the *Mithnagedim* would turn their backs on him. The *Chassidim* will receive him no matter from what group he emanates. After learning that Reb Moshe Hacohen is a *Chassid*, Arthur Levy asks him if he believes "in the coming of the Messiah". (309) The Reb replies: "I believe that active love will gradually build a better world, a world of brotherhood and peace. When that world is completed, the Messiah will be among us." (309–310)

As with the figure of Reb Moshe Hacohen, *Trumpet of Jubilee*'s Peter Lang and Jehuda Brenner each represent both the same and different emphases and manifestations of cultural dialectic. Each is a union of opposites or contrasts, which paradoxically complements or unites with the other's characteristics to form yet another composite of their shared friendship and experiences. As a real Christian (which is to say, a Gospel Jewish-Christian), Peter Lang—kind, ethereally sensitive—embodies all the nobleness of a true Jew like Joshua/Jesus, except for an inability to see the world realistically. Simultaneously, Jehuda Brenner is a true Jew because he embodies the spirit of real compassion, love, intellectual acumen, aesthetic sensibility, and a tolerance for all cultural differences. Like Jehuda Brenner, Reb Moshe Hacohen accepts all humankind, particularly "Real Christians" who "are capable of Jewish actions." (315) That is to say, they are capable of Jesus-like acts. As such, Reb Hacohen, a type of synthesis of the culturally complementary figures of Lang and Brenner, voices the same point of view and attitudes as *Trumpet of Jubilee*'s protagonists who are two forms of the same type. Lang and Brenner represent not enmity, but acceptance and love.

It is interesting that Reb Moshe Hacohen and his Chassidic ancestry are responsible for having kept the text (the Book/book) safe through more than a century of threatened extermination by the enemies of the Jewish people. In *Trumpet of Jubilee* where Lewisohn's theme of messianic redemption will be continued and extended, it is the writer, Gabriel Weiss, who is among the few survivors to tell of the great Israelite nation. In the same way, Arthur Levy's tree branch where Braine's father, Reb Eliezer Hacohen, sits at the head, has faded out through Tobias, who became a baptized Christian. The assimilation cycle comes to a halt when Reb Moshe Hacohen enters the book with the "book", the texts and records which have kept Jewish history and the past alive so that it can rekindle in Arthur Levy the sparks of his Jewish soul.

In describing the pathology of assimilation, the author recounts the stories of the generations after that of Braine and Reb Mendel. Their son Efraim and his wife Hannah (Mendel) Levy emigrate to Germany from Poland to continue and expand the distilling house business of Chaim Bratzlawer, his father-in-law. Even before his emigration, and after he begins working for Reb Chaim, Efraim is always kind and good to his mother:

> He performed all his devotions correctly as a good Jew should. But he turned up one day with his earlocks clipped off and on another he had discarded his *caftan*, the long coat of the Orthodox, and appeared in a German suit of the period. (29)

When Efraim and Hannah decide finally to go to Germany, Efraim chooses the name Levy, as he not very clearly explains, so as not to bring disrespect to "the great Moishe Mendelssohn and his descendants." (37) The reader can almost assume that perhaps he already knows that his life will take a more extreme assimilatory turn. He will now be known as Efraim Levy, indicating that his father is from the tribe of the Levites.

They arrive in Insterburg, Germany, in the year 1850, to begin a new life. From the beginning, Efraim's and Hanna's relationship has always been different from others who began their lives through arranged marriages. For one thing, they freely and independently chose each other without, as was the custom, the parents' choosing their partners for them. Like Lewisohn's own parents, having chosen each other,

> they found that a strange community of ideas existed between them. They wanted in their lives neither Mendel's devotion to mere study, nor Reb Chaim's business bustle and superficial piety. Were not new Jewish voices coming out of the west? Could not one be a European *and* a Jew? (36–37)

Hannah's father makes a very expensive and fun-filled wedding for them with violin players and even "a jester". It is a very "merry" affair. This wedding brings to mind the lusty, lively one attended by the narrator of "The Pagan Rabbi" and his Gentile wife, Jane. As well, "a group of *Chassidim* came in uninvited. But who would take upon himself the sin of turning away any Jew on such an *unbeschrigen*, happy and auspicious occasion." (38) The presence of the *Chassidim* at the wedding seems like a divine angel from above who swears never to leave this young couple's side.

Grandmother Braine dies in Jerusalem when Efraim and Hannah's children, especially the apostate Tobias, are still very young. In all, Hannah bears five children: Tobias, 1851; Samuel, 1853; Bertha, 1855; Rose, 1858; and as a surprise, Jacob, 1861. On a personal level, life in "the west" is advancing peacefully enough. However, Reb Chaim Bratzlower's ideas of creating a Kummel distilling centre in Germany does not fare well. When Hannah finally has to write and ask her father for a loan for their faltering business, he surprises them: firstly, by refusing, and secondly, when "he, once the man of advanced thought, added that he wondered whether the blessing of God was on Efraim's business in view of the stories of apostasy and impiety that came to him daily from the west." (44)

The Levys gradually have less and less contact with their homeland and "its customs". (44) Whenever they receive a letter from Poland, the problems and subjects of discourse seem "quaint" to them. They are in a new Western world and have left behind the rather unimportant woes of their native ghetto. Efraim's sister Rifka writes that the *shochet* (the butcher who kills permissible animals in the ritually kosher fashion) was found to have been in a conspiracy with the Gentile butchers and to have sold nonkosher animals as koshers ones. Not surprisingly, the Jews were horrified that such a thing could happen. Nevertheless, it cannot be said that the Levys approve of such behavior either:

> The Levys themselves had not, to be sure, abandoned the observance of the law of Israel in any single respect. Sabbaths and holy days were kept and celebrated. They would not have dreamed of eating *trefe* [unkosher] meat; they went duly to the synagogue. And it was an orthodox synagogue. (45)

The Levys firstly have no interest in a reform German synagogue with its Gentile-like practices. Secondly, they would not have been made to feel very much at home there, being from Poland, an east European country that German Gentiles and Jews alike ridicule as being backward and uncultured. In the Levys' migration to Germany can be found the same parallel as that of migrants to America. In the new immigrants' zeal to be accepted, to find a place, to negate displacement, there can slowly seep into the deepest recesses of the mind a process that is so gradual as to be almost imperceptible:

> No, the Levys were good Jews. Only into all their thoughts and observances there had stolen a laxness and a tinge of compromise, and a rigid observer— had there been such an one—would have wondered whether ancestral piety rather than any profound personal conviction were not the force that kept their orthodoxy in its state of decorous correctness. (45)

One example of this lack of vigilance comes from the continual presence of two Gentile German servants, "ruddy, peasant girls", in the lives of their growing children; like Lewisohn's accounts of his own childhood where Aryan, German fairy tales were read to and by him, rather than the Biblical stories of his people. The early stories heard by children, Lewisohn remarks in *Up Stream*, create the strongest impressions and effects:

> Little Tobias, a dark curly head of four with the clear passionate brown eyes of his grandmother Braine, would sit on a low stool in the spinning room and listen to the songs and tales of the spinsters. Into the waking dream of his impressionable childhood came to echo and to croon forever this speech and these airs and the piercing poetry of this Germanic world. (46)

The children are taken for walks through the lush German "fields and forests, with the blend of speech and song", which creates a deep-seated love of German culture in them. When Efraim suggests that Tobias is already five and must being to "learn", Hannah says that "there is time enough for that." (47) Hardly perceivable is "the shrug of Hannah's shoulders and a faint line that deepened between her eyes." (47) Thus, as he grows into manhood through the gradual and barely perceptible stages of assimilating culture, attitudes, thoughts, behavior and training practices, Tobias is able to "read" the semiotic messages his parents have laid out for him and the other children in the family. In due time, he will sever all connections with his Jewish roots, become baptized a Christian, marry into high German society and leave all traces of his past life behind. As well, Efraim is slowly becoming introduced to Gentile German society. When he goes out with Gentile friends for something to eat, he orders also. Eating unkosher food and sending Tobias to a German school become natural activities of life for them: "Once or twice his mother's warning and prophetic despair stole into his mind. With an inner tremble he thrust from him these memories. The strong current of life was not to be resisted." (51)

Jacob Levy, the youngest, has always been "a problem" for his parents. (70) Of all the Levy children, only Jacob has blond hair. Jacob, like Tobias before him, hates to go to *cheder* (children's Hebrew school). Unlike Tobias, Jacob is a very poor learner and barely manages to learn the *Torah* portion that he must read to mark his thirteenth year, his *bar-mitzvah*. Jacob "is a hopeless *shlemihl*" (inept). (70) Hopelessly unsuited to German society, there is only one thing he can look forward to now: the military, which is no real option for the Levy family. Jacob therefore decides to leave Germany. "'We are treated like dogs here. I want to go to a free country.'" (72) Jacob then boards a train on his way to America: "He had $310 when he landed in New York on the 2nd of August, 1879. With a sense of release, of hope, almost of consecration he set his foot upon the soil of freedom." (73) In the same way that his parents left their restrictive Polish ghetto life, so does Jacob flee from what he perceives as the bitter harshness of German culture and society.

In the tractate introducing "Book Three", the section devoted to Jacob's life in America, the narrator describes the genesis of Jewish feelings of inadequacy that have dogged the Israelite nation from earliest times on. He builds a case for how this nation of pacifists, as he describes them, deniers of hatefulness and brute aggression, exalting kindliness and piety, have always been inept at physical combat. Whenever battles were won they gave the glory to God only, since "defeat and contrition were their habitual bread." (78) Thus they grew to hate oppression and to love the freedom that their essentially passive natures enjoyed. Israel stood outside the interests and value system of a war-driven universe by refusing to accept that these values existed at all. Pinning Israel's fate in a brutal world to its repulsion of aggressive physicality, Lewisohn fleshes out yet another aspect of the dialectic: of Jewish intellectual sensitivity, humanitarianism and the primitive, heartless brutality of the pagan-Gentile world around them. He then cites those few Jewish personalities who were totally able to transcend this dialectic and make of it a positive, constructive force in the world of nature and humankind:

> But the process [of transcending the warring values of the world] is an infinitely gradual one and comes to completion only in isolated individuals: Jeremiah, Isaiah, Jesus, the martyrs of the Crusades, the early *Chassidic* rabbis, pacifists and lovers of freedom here and there. (79)

Putting Jesus, "the Rabbi Jehoshua of Nazareth", in the same "place" as the Jews brings the contrast of Christian and Judaic into a kind of synthesis that immediately becomes its own dialectic; for there are "good" Christians and "good" Jews as well as "bad" ones of both groups:

> The Rabbi Jehoshua of Nazareth, even as the late and clouded and confused legend portrays him, had cast out fear. The Law that was the stay of Israel's integrity was to be kept. But to at least an equality with it were to be raised those written and oral precepts, reshaped with the force and poignancy of genius, by which Israel had already from age to age denied hate and force and exalted love and humility and peace. And those precepts were to be deepened and men's actions were to square with them to the uttermost—to complete nonresistance, to faultless charity and loving-kindness. (79)

Thus Joshua/Jesus, as the eternal, exemplary Jewish soul, died for those qualities that the Israelites held dear to them and which were an inseparable part of their being. In this way, a new contrast, of Gentile-Christian and Jewish-Christian, is created. The latter, descended directly by blood and the teachings that have come down to the Israelites from Mt. Sinai to Jesus/Joshua, find "place" together under the wing of the God of Abraham, Isaac and Jacob. "Outside" are the Gentiles professing a belief in this Jewish prophet, but whose nature and souls are alien to the culture and sacred Texts from which he evolves.

Calling forth another dialectical aspect, Jacob, now safely at "home" in America, remembers

> The terror and the shame of the last episodes of his life in Europe [which] had burned themselves deeply in Jacob Levy's soul. He identified this terror and this shame with Europe; he identified the prudence and the circumspection that arose from that terror and that shame with America. He always insisted in later years that his luck had changed the moment that he set his foot on the soil of the United States. (80)

Jacob remembers his father Efraim as "honest" and "able", who was for his entire life a slave to a livelihood that eked out a poor existence for the family. "He had died a poor man." (81) This is what Jacob takes as an instruction for his own new life in America, for here the case is entirely otherwise:

> If a man was honest and decent in America it didn't matter what he did. He was respected. And more important even, a man could try one thing and then another and see what he was fit for. He didn't have to become an apprentice for three years. He was no one's slave. (81)

As Jacob sits searching in the newspaper for a job, a kindly, rich, old German-American-Jewish gentleman who likes to help new immigrants sits down beside him. Jacob soon finds himself employed at Friedenfeld and Cohn's lower Sixth Avenue department store. As time moves on, and since Jacob has no ambition or ability for introspection, he slowly forgets the world of his birth and even to some extent his parents. Like Ludwig Lewisohn, by degrees Jacob becomes assimilated into American society and culture: he eats nonkosher food and socializes with Gentiles. Ironically, however, here in America he becomes more German. He feels more comfortable among people of his own native culture. He would not marry someone who is not Jewish, but he hates Jews who speak Yiddish. He feels strangely separate from other Jewish immigrants. When he marries, it is to socially climbing Gertrude Oberwarter, from a German-Jewish family which is Jewish in name only. Having gone into business with a Jewish partner (he would never go into business with a non-Jew), Nathan Goldmann, and now (in 1891) ready to marry Gertrude, Jacob's life seems to virtually encompass the life all immigrants dream of. Gertrude was born in America; Jacob has filed for citizenship, and his children will be American citizens as well. On the question of Judaic practices, all seems quite clear: "Neither he nor his wife ever debated the question of any religious observance. Gertrude knew, of course, that her husband's parents had been observant Jews; so had her grandparents been. All that lay in a scarcely imaginable past behind her." (94–95)

Jacob's business is successful; he slowly adopts Gertrude's "American" attitudes. He himself is happy to forget his painful past in Germany. A son, Arthur (1893), and daughter, Hazel (1895), are born. Jacob doesn't like the names Gertrude picks for their children. In fact, the children's names are a kind of Gentile-Jewish synthesis of the names of Gertrude's parents, Abram and Hannah. Taking the first letter of each name and combining them with names Gertrude gleans from her reading of Tennyson, the chosen names perfectly symbolize the synthesis of two cultural forces. Jacob gently convinces his wife to circumcise Arthur. "To Jacob it never occurred that his man-child should not be circumcised." (100)

Arthur and Hazel grow up as free as can be, Americans unencumbered by any past. They are barely conscious of the Jewish world of their predecessors. When Arthur asks his mother what a *mezuzah* is (the traditional small scroll containing the devotional Hebrew "*Shma*" prayer, never missing from the entrance of a Jewish household), Gertrude stops to think for a moment, then answers: "'I believe, sonny, that it was a sort of a little metal case with the Ten Commandments in it that old-fashioned people used to nail to their door and kiss when they entered the house.'" (128–129)

However, this is not to say that from their earliest conscious thoughts, Arthur and Hazel haven't always known they are Jewish. This is a curious fact, since "in the house [was] no visible symbol of religion and of race." (103) When Arthur is six years old, in the first days of school, from the seat in front of him,

> there was suddenly turned a small round screwed-up gargoyle face, red, freckled, pug-nosed, blue-eyed, with crimson tongue stuck far out and hot against the lovely, fair chin. Then the tongue slid, like a quick little round animal, back into its hole and he heard a hot whisper, "Sheenie!" Was it again the voice of the blood? For Arthur was sure that he had never heard that word before. But neither had he any doubt as to its meaning and character. (105)

Arthur is so wounded by the incident, and his home is so insulated, secure and peaceful, that he tells his mother that he met "a nice little boy" (105) named Georgie Fleming. Other anti-Jewish incidents occur to

Arthur as he is growing up. He refuses to take gymnasium for fear that the Gentile boys will see that he is circumcised, since at that time circumcision was performed for religious reasons only.

Arthur begins university and his studies in psychology. He reads Freud and decides to study German as well, his parents' cultural and linguistic background. Arthur, in his studies of psychology, and in accordance with the normal tenor of his personality, is always introspective, questioning the motives and reasons for things. Strangely, the family is thrown into a crisis because Hazel has decided to marry a Gentile, the brother of Georgie Fleming. While Arthur and Gertrude are ambiguous about Hazel's plans, Jacob is grief-stricken and asks for his son's opinion: "His father's face bent closer, almost touching him; his father's soul tugged at his own. 'Do you like it, my son?' Relief and liberation come to Arthur. He could answer that question honestly. 'No, I don't.'" (149) Hazel, greatly disappointed in her brother's answer, calls him a hypocrite. Jacob regards "her sternly yet appeasedly. 'Arthur is no hypocrite. He is a goot Chewish son!'" (150)

But when Hazel admits that she feels a "need of a religion" and plans "to become a Catholic" (151), even Gertrude is shocked. Both parents admit that they would "rather see her dead" than become a Christian. The matter is settled, and Hazel is dissuaded from this dangerous idea. For a family which to all outward appearance seems anything but Jewish, the Levys stand surprisingly united against Hazel's plans. Like the "Jewish sparks" that the *Chassidim* describe, the family members seem to feel some connection deep inside themselves. Lewisohn, in this tractate to Book Five (again in lines similar to those used by Cynthia Ozick in one of her texts), waxes poetic and philosophical when he asserts: "For Jewishness is like that Hound of Heaven described by the poet. It tracks you through the universe; it lies in ambush from without and from within." (162)

Arthur continues to swing back and forth in his dialectical quandary of Christians and Jews:

> Jews... Jews.... He loathed the very word. And as for the Jews from Russia..., he had seen them on Grand Street and Norfolk Street and once in a Yiddish theatre to which Joe had dragged him. Utter aliens to himself, these people—repulsive, in fact: dirty, sunk in superstition, loud, Oriental without being picturesque, jabbering in a mongrel jargon, smelling of garlic.... Why he should take their part... he simply didn't know. (167)

It is when Arthur becomes a psychiatrist assigned to intern "at the Hospital for the Insane on Drew's Point, Women's Department" (178) that his perceptions about Jews begin to solidify, mature and deepen. With "his instinctively diagnostic eyes" (182) he discovers, to his horror, that many of the "foreign" female patients are

> Jewesses, Jewesses, Jewesses.... More and more and more.... His heart contracted.... Suddenly he was afraid. Afraid for these women of his people in the hands of the contemptuous doctors and attendants.... Good God! What nonsense! He was a scientist. An American. The Poles and Italians and Germans were in no better case.... Yes, they are, something within him said, yes, they are. (182)

When Dr. Arthur Levy has a discussion with Dr. Kirke, the latter, without using the word "Jews", describes them as "neurasthenic". (183) Dr. Levy concurs with Kirke's judgement and answers by saying: "'Why didn't you say "Jews", Doctor? I wouldn't have been offended. There is a high percentage of nervous and mental disorder among Jews.'" (183)

The true tests, and perhaps final lessons about his own identity, come when Dr. Arthur Levy realizes that "the mechanism of the Jewish anti-Jewish complex was precisely analogous to the mechanism of insanity.... He had felt this urge toward flight himself, flight from a reality that had no inner meaning, from a burden that seemed irrational." (187) It is exactly at this juncture in his life that Arthur meets Elizabeth Knight, the Gentile daughter of a Protestant preacher. Again there are parallels here with the content in at least two of Ozick's stories, specifically "The Pagan Rabbi" and "Levitation", in which the Christian wife of the Jewish husband has a Protestant-minister father who is as purely religious and God-seeking as his Jewish son-in-law.

The narrator in the tractate preceding "Book Six" describes the confusion that brews in the mind and heart of sensitive, perceptive, well-educated, Jewish Dr. Arthur Levy when he meets the attractive, well-educated, Gentile young woman Elizabeth Knight. He feels irresistibly drawn to her and confesses his love to her. His life is in upheaval. In a painful crisis of consciousness, his head tells him one thing, but his heart says something else: "All his Jewish experiences from the days of Georgie Fleming on had been negative. All he wanted was to be left alone and function freely within the society into which he had been born." (220)

He and Elizabeth are now "friends and lovers". (220) A virgin when they first make love, he realizes now that Elizabeth's "ultimate inhibitions" haven't yet "broken down." (220) Her only answer to this problem is the wistful comment: "'I suppose I can't get out of being a parson's daughter and granddaughter.... The repudiation of the body and its instincts is rooted deep.'" (220–221) He wonders if it's because he's a Jew. She brushes off his remark as "silly". (221) However, Arthur doesn't consciously react to this first sign of a Christian mind-body dilemma, while Cynthia Ozick's narrator in "The Pagan Rabbi" makes very vocal mention of this same problem in his wife, Jane.

When Arthur and Elizabeth sit down and tell each other stories of their childhood, Elizabeth can communicate the poverty of her family and, like Mrs. Morrison's parson father in *Holy Land*, the saint-like forbearance of her kind father. Her childhood seems for Arthur to have a "breath of poetry" in it. However, when Arthur begins to describe his own early life to her, he stops:

> He found that he couldn't break down the inner resistance that kept him from telling her these things [about the anti-Semitism he had experienced in his life], and that resistance evidently communicated itself to much else, so that his words came slowly and conventionally. He tried to communicate to Elizabeth something of the quality of his mother and father and sister and the atmosphere of his home. She shook her head. "I don't get the feeling. I don't seem to see clear." He groped his way along a psychical wall of glass. (223)

In point of fact, he can't speak to her about his inner thoughts and being. The more Arthur speaks with Elizabeth, the more he realizes that she doesn't share what he considers a fundamental Jewish reverence toward one's parents. He actually reveres and adores his parents; in contrast, she has an "affectionate" but entirely disconnected feeling for her father, void of any strongly based "subconscious instincts." (225) Arthur secretly dreads the time when Elizabeth will meet his parents. It comes soon enough when Elizabeth tells him she is pregnant.

Only a minute before that, he tells her, in a flush of heartfelt love, that she should marry him. As a feminist, Elizabeth dislikes feeling that Arthur wants to take "possession" of her, to master her and reduce her "'on account of this accident [of pregnancy] to the status of a nurse and a slave.'" (228) This is the second important sign of their potential incompatibility. Arthur, nevertheless, moves forward in his relationship with her, especially now that she is pregnant with their child. Elizabeth then informs him that, now that she has found out she is pregnant, "'I'm not even sure that I love you any longer. I only feel trapped and caged. I'm sorry. But, it's so.'" (230) They marry anyway, at a magistrate's office. But Elizabeth insists on maintaining her own little apartment with "an icy, desperate passion." (230–231)

Arthur knows he must inform his parents soon about the profound changes going on in his life. He knows that they will not be happy. "It was evident, therefore, that somewhere in his mind lurked an agreement with his father's and mother's disapproval of exogamic marriage." (233) Jacob, heartbroken at the news, tells Arthur that neither he nor Elizabeth will be happy in this marriage. Then their son John is born.

Perhaps because Elizabeth is a writer and Arthur is a psychoanalyst, the communicative, poetic, quality in her can create a foundation on which to build their lives. As well, Jewishness becomes a kind of synonym for writer/writing. He is very impressed by her writing talents. As with the other of Lewisohn's prophet-writer personalities, this talent can be considered "Jewish" in and of itself. She becomes a writing celebrity in New York literary circles:

> That world took to Elizabeth with a kind of passion. There are very many Jews in it, Jews who never speak of themselves as Jews and try hard not to think of themselves as such. Elizabeth being a Gentile, but being married to a Jew, was bound, aside from her personal charm and talent, to be much-beloved. (247)

Like Lucy Feingold in Ozick's "Levitation", Elizabeth is caught in a dialectic of a writer who is either a Jewish writer, or a Christian writer married to a Jew. Jews are somehow attracted to this Christian writer as if she were Jewish. In any event, being a writer in literary New York turns one into a kind of a Jew.

After Arthur and Elizabeth finally visit his parents, an event filled with much tension and the feeling that things are somehow out of place, Elizabeth tells Arthur: "'I didn't know you were so Jewish in your feelings.'" His retort to her is, "'You are a little Puritan.'" (258) For his part, his life is "becoming more confusing for him from day to day." (258) When they begin to live in the same apartment, Arthur discovers, like "The Pagan Rabbi" narrator with his wife Jane, that Elizabeth has more than Puritan attitudes; she is sexually frigid. When he confronts her with his perception, she tells him: "'I don't really think that that side of life means much to me personally.' After that she was careful to create occasions once in a while and to give herself to him. But it was a weary and deliberate and joyless process." (259)

The Christian-Jewish contrast becomes painfully clear for Arthur, and he considers what the reason could be that he didn't rebel earlier. Arthur has ignored all the signs; he hasn't listened to the feelings and thoughts within him. He even finds himself trapped in another dialectic in which he plays no part: that of the American Puritanical view of woman as a sex-slave to be subjected, overpowered and repressed, *versus* the liberated (feminist) anti-Puritan female in full rebellion against that suffocating (Christian) culture:

> And Arthur knew that if he protested, she would take immediate fright; she would think that he was protesting from the point of view of that old Puritan notion of marriage which had crushed her mother, from the point of view of the dominant Gentile male. And how was he to tell her and, above all, to convince her, that what he had in mind was something different, was a third kind of condition or estate which he felt to exist but which he himself could neither precisely define nor describe. (259)

It is perfectly clear to Arthur that with Elizabeth in his life, he cannot break out into that "third kind". He needs a sensitive, literate, educated, Jewish wife for that. Arthur begins to think seriously about all the Jewish families he knows:

> He knew no Jewish home in which the children were not brought up in equal obedience and respect for both parents in function, wisdom, worth, [which] was not silently and fundamentally taken for granted. But that was not all. There was an indefinable element. As women grew older among Jews, they were instinctively treated as though they were repositories of some special grace or wisdom. (260)

Close to a final split, Arthur and Elizabeth discuss how their child John should be brought up. Elizabeth mentions that, during her recent visit to her father, he expressed the fear that "John's soul won't be saved." (276) Arthur says, to her great surprise, that he is also concerned about saving his son's soul. He explains: "'You're saved, Elizabeth, because you live in a stream of tradition that is native to you. The stream changes. You don't believe what your father believes. But the stream is the same. You are an American Protestant.'" (276) Arthur the Jew, on the other hand, as Lewisohn discovered, is not and cannot ever be part of that stream. This is why as Jews "'we live in a void, in a spiritual vacuum.'" (276) He doesn't want his son to be pulled and ripped apart by the Christian-Jewish polemic that his body and genetic makeup already bear. As he tells Elizabeth, with the name Levy, John could never get along in a Protestant world. The alternative is simple to guess. Arthur desires his son to be raised as a Jew. The Gentile-Jewish contrast has synthesized into a Jewish identity for a child whose mother is Christian and father is Jewish. John even looks "in "colouring and expression, [like] a Jewish child." (278)

Arthur begins examining the history of his people and the Bible. He begins working in a Jewish hospital and starts feeling more at home with himself, more in place. It is at this point that he meets Reb Moshe Hacohen, who finally opens up and presents the text of Arthur's past, bringing Arthur back into the fold of his people. At last, Arthur has come home. His great great-grandmother, Braine, can finally rest in her grave, and Arthur can come ashore from the island within himself. As the story ends, the numerous conflicts find some meeting ground, a paradoxical point of rest. Arthur's son, the living synthesis of a dialectical marriage, finds his place on the Jewish side of his cultural life, although by Jewish law he is not considered Jewish.

Reb Moshe Hacohen, a redeemer and spiritual leader, artist of a kind, and keeper of the Text, brings Arthur back to his past, his history and the text/Text of his life and people. Signified by Reb Moshe is the spirit of the true Jew, the man of God, guide of humankind and poet-savior of his people. In and through him, there is the hope that all conflicts can somehow be mollified, laid to rest.

Background Discussion IV

On his way to Jerusalem, the writer of "The Return to Jerusalem" tours Egypt and Cairo. Standing in the Cairo Museum, Lewisohn describes how he contemplated "the remains of an elaborate and splendid world.... Into this civilization, as in many another since, the children of Israel were invited." ("Return" 725) Here the Israelites "prospered and increased in numbers." (725) Continuing the identification with his people's tortuous history, he asserts that they "were good Egyptian subjects, loyal and patriotic", (725) as the ten-year-old Ludwig had been when, as he states in *Up*

Stream, "my emotional assimilation" into Southern American culture "was complete." (*Up Stream* 51)

According to James, the author's son, his father strongly supported the Jews in Palestine's War of Independence against the British, in particular, and the Jewish people as a general entity, to the point of "fighting me on every point if I challenged any of his assertions." James Lewisohn added, "My father would have been a very strong supporter of Bibi Netanyahu [the former Israeli Prime Minister]."[82]

There is another aspect to the complex dialectic in Lewisohn's life and work. In the author's bitter musings at the Cairo Museum and elsewhere, over the emotional, moral, psychic, spiritual and physical enslavement of Jews, historically and at that present time, Lewisohn, quoting from the Jewish Bible, *Tanach*, declares:

> The fear was expressed [by the Egyptians] that these strangers would become "too many and too mighty" for the natives of older stocks and... the Israelites were reduced to the status of slaves.... [Yet] no doubt there were Israelites of wealth and position who... saved themselves. ("Return" 725)

In reading the next part of Lewisohn's article, one gets the strange and distinct impression that he identified himself here not just *with* Moses, but *as* Moses. The Germanic Lewisohn, like Moses, was of a cultured, seemingly privileged and comfort-filled upbringing in a comfortable house and lived a privileged life. Both Moses the Israelite, whose Hebrew identity was hidden from the Egyptians after the decree to slay all newborn male Israelites was instituted, and Ludwig Lewisohn the Jew, whose Hebrew identity was hidden from the Lewisohn family's consciousness in opting for a better life as successful people, and thus as assimilating Jews, were born into Jewishness but more or less raised as something foreign to their birth heritage. As if describing himself and the rebirth of his life, Lewisohn, quoting from the *Torah*, declares:

> But when "he was grown up he went out unto his brethren and looked on their burdens." He slew one of their Egyptian tormentors, despite the recorded meekness of his nature; he fled, only to return as the leader and savior of his people, steadfast, majestic, greatly enduring, careless of happiness, or content for himself, destined to die... after that one glance from Nebo across the glistening waters of the Dead Sea to the Judaean Hills beyond. (725)

In the same way, Lewisohn had set himself out to help free his enslaved brethren, to bring them the Word/word, to set their lives on the right and redemptive course—a savior of his people whether they liked it or not. Now he, like the prophet Moses or Jeremiah, would fight to save their souls, as he would labor twenty years from the time "The Return to Jerusalem" was written, to help save their bodies from the Holocaust enslavers and tormentors of his people. He asks if this story of Moses, be it

> history or fable—is it not the eternal symbol of a recurring fate? The arguments that the Egyptians used against the Israelites, do not the Poles and Hungarians and Rumanians use it today?.... The story is the symbol of the fate of Israel; the fate of Israel is the symbol of an ultimate necessary redemption of all of mankind in the Final Days of the coming of the Messiah. (725)

His voice of prophecy, his voice as a self-declared prophet of his people, called them back, urged their return home. The Jewish people was the source and way to redemption of all humanity with the *Torah* as a light unto the world:

> Thence springs a meaning deeper than I dreamed from the words of that Chassidic rabbi who exclaimed: "Lord of the world, redeem Israel! But if thou wilt not, redeem the Gentiles!" The redemption of Israel and the redemption of mankind are [one]. (725)

Through the creative enterprise of the word/Word, and the establishment of the Jewish state, the Israelites and the world can find the salvation promised by God.

A 1925 article in *The Nation* exhibits Lewisohn's by now apparently full immersion in Zionism, Palestine and his people. He describes, quoting a leader of the mass construction in progress all over *Eretz Yisrael* (the Land of Israel), how for the first time, Jews are involved with labor that is "creative" instead of enslaving. "In other words, where we were outsiders, we worked for others and always in external conflicts. Here we do not [have to] combat anti-Semitism. We are quite freed from that external conflict. Our conflict, our struggle here is an inner one: How to become a productive people."[83]

A year before his death (1954), nine years after the Holocaust ended, Lewisohn writes:

The pattern of [the Jewish people's] history is violently abnormal. It knew defeat and desperate catastrophe over and over again. Yet from each historic grave it re-arose; it survived; it lived to reaffirm its changeless character and historic function. What was the source within history of that power of survival and renewal which has taken place from age to age, down to that birth of the State of Israel from the ashes of the six million martyrs, an event within the memory of the youngest Jew now living and seeking to interpret his destiny and its meaning.[84]

Dr. Arthur J. Lelyveld, a contemporary of Lewisohn and one of his Brandeis University colleagues, speaking in a February 14, 1956 Brandeis memorial address for the by-now-dead Lewisohn, pronounced:

Those of us who hold the memory of Ludwig Lewisohn in profound affection need not be disturbed by the fact that he was not always loved and not always understood. He would have rejected popularity as evidence of the shallowness that was the target of his unremitting attack, and he would have scorned being too easily understood as he scorned the imprecise word and the easy half-truth. For Ludwig Lewisohn was a man with a mission—he was... a preacher—exhorting, correcting, berating "the average intelligent American Jew," striving to awaken him to the perplexities and crisis of the times in a dimension equivalent to the intensity of his own commitment.[85]

More exactly, Lewisohn was a writer who expressed, as he viewed it, the word of God in the various forms of the creative communication: essays, novels and speeches, which he employed to convey the word/ Word of God's servant, the Jewish writer who is firmly rooted in the history and life of his/her people, and thus has the authority to speak. In the spirit of this view, with the slippery dialectic at play in every point of contact in his life and work, Lewisohn began writing *Trumpet of Jubilee* (1937), the novel which Elliot B. Gertel describes in a 1982 article as "the first significant and 'messianic' novel by an American-Jewish writer."[86] It is, he adds, "an apocalyptic novel whose like has not since been dared by an American-Jewish writer." (Gertel 154)

Trumpet of Jubilee

The writer announces what would appear to be his final unalterable divorce from the masses of Christianity in one of the prefatory quotations, this time in French by Andre Gidé, with its accompanying English translation that opens the book: "Is it not amazing that the Christian peoples alone should have been capable of creating the civilization that is the remotest from the precepts of the Gospel, the most contrary to any form of Christian life?" (*Trumpet* "Prologue") The quotation brings to the fore two major contrasting issues: Judaism/Christianity and Civilization/Barbarism.

Another related issue is that of true Christian (one who lives in the full spirit of the Gospel) *versus* those bestial examples of humanity who call themselves Christians. The Holocaust represents the macabre arena in which the real Christians could be separated from the counterfeit ones. For those European Jews of High Culture and Civilization, the Holocaust was also the Nazis' tragic crucible for the revelation of true Jewishness that included several eagerly forgotten generations of full Jewish being. With the frightening entry of the Nazi machine onto the world's stage, the Holocaust tested in the same way the level and nature of truth or lie in the Jewishness of America's Jews, which lay buried, dormant or ready to be formed in their hearts and minds.

In this book written in 1937, four years after the rise of Hitler and a year or two before *Kristalnacht* (November 10, 1938, that Berlin night in which all hopes of full Jewish assimilation into Gentile German society were smashed), Lewisohn would seem no longer to harbor idealistic delusions or internal conflicts as to the fundamental question of a Jewish or Christian identity. With the Holocaust in motion, and plans for the Final Solution no longer in the planning stages but nearing active implementation, his prophetic warnings about Gentile antagonism against Jews and the dangers of losing one's Jewish history, self and *Torah*, were coming to horrifyingly full fruition.

Having passed the first stage in the three-phased process of redemption (personal, national and universal), Lewisohn would appear to be in a fully active mode for disseminating the word/Word to all who will lend an ear, Jewish and Gentile alike. In the ensuing war between good and evil, the word of God, spoken through His Book the *Torah*, and given for safekeeping to His people the Israelites, must be spread to all corners of the world through the writer as Hebraic prophet, and his message must be heard and heeded.

The book title is from *Va'yikra* (*Leviticus*) 25:9: "Then shalt thou cause the trumpet of jubilee to sound. In the day of atonement shall ye make the trumpet sound." ("Title Page") The translated version used here by Lewisohn lacks the substance of the Hebrew original.[87]

The significance of the translations and versions of the original underscore the conflict of language and its significance in the text's linguistic messages. Thus biblical interpretations, especially those made from translations of the original texts—more specifically, Hebraic biblical texts—can be interpreted or reinterpreted based on a specific theopolitical agenda. In place of the word "trumpet",[88] which designates a brassy, metallic musical resonance, an instrument in Christian lore also symbolic of "proclaiming the message", the original Hebrew word "*shofar*" is used also in English. The *shofar* (ram's horn) was/is blown on specific holy days, for celebratory and condemnatory occasions. The horn could also be taken from other ritually clean animals, except for the cow because of the "Golden Calf " idolatrous episode in Jewish history. It is blown to signal the anointing of a new king, to declare war, for the commencement of the High Holy Days and the conclusion of *Yom Kippur* (the Day of Atonement), for excommunication, and in modern Israel, for proclaiming a new president. The sounds of the *shofar* consist of three specific kinds of notes, in a specific order: the *Shevarim* sound, a series of short, broken sobbing-like sounds; the wailing *Teru'ah* sound; and the long, unbroken *Tekiah*. The ram's horn produces a natural woody sound similar to that of any wooden musical instrument but wilder.

Directly related to Lewisohn's book title, and the quotation that explains it, is the Jubilee year (in Hebrew, *yovel*); designating the fiftieth year of "rest" that concludes a cycle of seven seven-year time periods. This fiftieth year (which the modern state of Israel celebrated in 1998) is coupled with laws of redemption: those in servitude must be freed, and those who have lost their property to debt must be given the opportunity to reclaim it. Beginning on Rosh Hashana (the New Year), the Jubilee designates the year of opportunity; the final reparation of self, country, the world and all that pertains to them. The *yovel* year offers the chance for freedom, opportunity and progress to all, irrespective of social standing, education, economic level and the wheel of fortune. As Baruch Schwartz explains, God's intention in the *yovel* is to show that He, and not the landowner or slaveholder, is the Master of the universe; that all of humanity has the freedom to find ultimate redemption and the opportunity to advance on any and all levels of existence—from the material to the spiritual. (*Religion* 755)

The book, *Leviticus* (in Greek terminology, as opposed to the Hebrew, *Va'yikra*, meaning "and [God] called"), is the story contained within the story that Lewisohn calls *Trumpet of Jubilee*. *Va'yikra* is, in fact, the story/text intended for the High Priests of the Israelites, the *Kohanim*, containing the instruction and laws for them and the Levites; thus the Greek word, *Levitikon*, meaning "pertaining to the Levites", the tribe of the Israelite High Priests. This is the third of the Hebrew Scriptures' five books. The *Tanach* also includes the entire corpus of sacred Jewish literature: the Books of Moses, *Joshua, Judges, Samuel I and II, Isaiah, Jeremiah, Ezekiel, Joel, Amos, Zechariah, Kings, Psalms, Proverbs, Job, The Song of Songs, Ruth, Lamentations, Ecclesiastes, Esther, Daniel, Ezra-Nehemiah,* and *Chronicles I and II*.

One of the more significant examples of dialectical issues is that the "Trumpet of Jubilee" and the term "ram's horn" are used interchangeably, showing conflicting Hebrew and Christian images; as in Lewisohn's description: "He has blown the ram's horn, the Trumpet of the Jubilee." (*Trumpet* 345) As well, the story is replete with the juxtaposition of other Hebrew images, names and allusions with Christian ones. In spite of what many would call its Jewish message and content, the final sentence of *Jubilee* contains the word "Christ". The book on all levels is a playing ground of conflicting forces and cultural perspectives: Jewish and Christian; good and evil; revelation and ignorance; poetic vision and cultural barbarity; civilization and crudeness. Lewisohn's story, a reflection contained in *Leviticus*, both reflects, and is reflected by, all the texts contained in the Sacred Writings (*Tanach*). As such, Lewisohn's text would seem to be an attempt to reimpose or reassert the fundamental Hebraic character of the Book's message; that is, to impart a Hebrew signification to Its words, to make a clear distinction between Judaic and Christian, and also to reveal, through the explanatory English words the author employs ("trumpet" and others), paradoxically Gentile forms of expression. Thus, in one way or another, on whatever level, Lewisohn's story displays some ambiguity of message.

There is another type of dialectic in the form of a psychological chain. Through the central figures in *Trumpet*—those like Kurt, Lewisohn himself, Gina, the book's author, Gabriel, the narrator and Betty—there can be found a chain of action and reaction, a dialectic of conflicted human consciousness and perceptions, a type of deterministic link-up in which each player has his/her role and understands it. Gabriel's drive to succeed as a writer is not only for the sake of the salvation of humanity.

The drive that one might define as ego-centered, helps propel him into a relationship that mimics the primal one with his mother. Betty is both the perennially defamed *shiksah* (female Gentile) and the Jewish being who adores Gabriel and is a patron of the arts. Thus Gabriel justifiably can take his place in this symbolic psycholinguistic chain, described by Muller and Richardson's rendering of Jacques Lacan, and Jacques Derrida's analyses of Edgar Allen Poe's "The Purloined Letter". Each link (person) in the chain has its private fantasized version, its artistic point of view, its reading of enfolded and enfolding events, its special role.[89] As they state in their prefatory essay, each "becomes an observer observed in turn (by our own imaginary vision at least), without being obviously aware of the fact." (*Purloined* vii)

Such a multiple fantasy, doubled and redoubled on itself in relation to the language used to express it, would suggest (in ways which Lacan and Derrida explore) a connection between the unconscious and the production/creation of language. In all stages of the dialectic-like chain—when the author observes the narrator observing the characters observing each other, and with the vigilant reader observing them all—there is a type of detection process in which one desires to discover the other, yet both falling prey to yet a third; in a seemingly endless chain of this dialectical process of discovery. The author of *Trumpet of Jubilee* frames and unframes, discloses and hides, reveal and thwarts, ultimate knowledge. Thus there is revealed the displacement not just of real geographic place (Germany, France, America), but of a psychic, emotional and linguistic displacement of the text: *Trumpet of Jubilee*, through the words the author employs to tell this/these stories which the text encompasses, and which in turn encompass the text. Such dialectic of textuality, or intertextuality, is transversed by the multiple dialectics of nationality (Germany, France, America, Israel, Poland), race, (Julian's "white" people, or Gentiles, *versus* Jews), language (English, Hebrew, German, French, "good" English, "bad" German; Mme Levi-Bloch's use of French instead of German; or one level of adequacy or inadequacy in language production), creed (Christian *versus* Jewish; "good" Christian *versus* "bad" Christian; "good" Jew *versus* "bad" Jew), High Culture *versus* Low Culture (European *versus* American cultures), and the artist-writer *versus* the imaginationless masses, or "business" people. In the dialectical processes that describe their relationships, contrasting forces continually displace one another to form an intricate lacing of consciousness.

Nevertheless, all seems to follow an unwritten law inherent in the dialectic chain itself. There is a symbolic order that runs its course. Like the oppositions in the dialectic chain, Peter Lang, Jehuda Brenner and Andrew Saracen appear, disappear and reappear. The narrator, author, characters—one of the three or the other, the reader—are detectives in this dialectic of disclosure, concealment, suppression, expression, repression. The net result is bewilderment and perplexity. For example, what is the message of the crucifix imagery in Kurt Weiss's death? Is Peter Lang Jewish or Christian? Is Jehuda Brenner Jewish or Christian? Where and who is Andrew Saracen? What is his place? Where is the trick—if indeed there is one—which dupes us (or doesn't), that is set on its course, on one level, by the psychoanalyst-narrator-detective? Is there a trick somewhere, a "sense of mystification" (33) as Lacan asserts in his essay, "Seminar on 'The Purloined Poe'", "sufficient for us to discern in this tale, on the contrary, so perfect a verisimilitude that it may be said that truth here reveals its fictive arrangement"? (34)

Indeed, the language of Lewisohn's *Trumpet of Jubilee* tricks the reader into sharing in its ratiocinative "strategy", in which can be perceived yet another dramatic event, a story with its own intrinsic dialogue. Thus is created a complex maze of dialectic on dialectic, in relation to another text Lacan refers to as the language: "The dialogues themselves, in the opposite use they make of the powers of speech, take on a tension which makes them a different drama, one which our vocabulary will distinguish from the first as persisting in the symbolic order." (34)

This symbolic order, the end product of the unconscious dimension of language, and the imaginary process to which language-processing, that is, writing belongs, "holds" the dialectic on its paradoxically, ever-dissolving and appearing reference point/points, the frame. Thus the dialectic, on one highly complex level, can be said to be, as Lacan asserts, "the very foundation of intersubjectivity." (35) Lacan illustrates all of this with the joke told by Freud, which Lacan refers to as "a Jewish joke": "'Why are you lying to me?' one character shouts breathlessly. 'Yes, why do you lie to me saying you're going to Cracow so I should believe you're going to Lemberg, when in reality you are going to Cracow?'" (36)

Such is the problem the reader of *Trumpet of Jubilee* confronts in attempting to discern what it is saying. The net result is a barrier to logic:

disputatious mazes, paradox, self-contradiction, and jokes that undermine, trick and put one to "sleep", to dupe us into unawareness. How often does the narrator or a character reveal the "truth": that underneath the legerdemain is still another trick? Indeed, there is deception everywhere in the text. Through all of it, as Lacan states, is an endless "parade of erudition": (37) that of the narrator, Peter Lang, Andrew Saracen, Jehuda Brenner, Gina Weiss, Gabriel Weiss, Kurt Weiss, the Nazis, German Jewry, the author and the book itself—and even the reader's believed sagacity in perceiving all of this. Is the assertion of facts and historical documentation, used to disclose, or to conceal? Or is the truth being revealed in such a way as to seem a lie, as in the "Jewish joke", to trick us into not knowing what to believe? Once deluded, we can no longer know who or what to believe.

There is an inherent revulsion in finding this in a story about a horrific subject like the Holocaust, the facts of which are so easily verifiable by historical data. With Derrida's *différance*, characters and texts are interwoven into an ever-transmitting textuality in which nothing either exists or doesn't exist, nothing is present or absent. Instead (but in all places), will be found "differences" and the traces of traces. As Derrida asks in his essay, "The Purveyor of Truth":

> What happens in the psychoanalytic deciphering of a text when the latter, the deciphered itself, already explicates itself? When it says more about itself than does the deciphering (a debt acknowledged by Freud more than once)? And especially when the deciphered text inscribes in itself *additionally* the scene of the deciphering? When the deciphered text deploys more force in placing onstage and setting adrift the analytic process itself up to its very last word, for example, the truth? (174)

Indeed, if anyone reins supreme in Lewisohn's text, or in any other text of his, or of others, it is the poet in all facets of concealment. Who is Gabriel? Is he the poet-messiah of his Jewish people, sent to redeem them? Or is he the writer as Christ-Messiah whose father died for the sins of the world, the very dialectic of the true, Jewish Joshua/Jesus messianic figure who continues the history of the Jews through Joshua/Jesus within *Torah* and Law? Is Joshua/Jesus, then, the embodied form of both the Old and the New in the same way that Peter Lang and Jehuda Brenner unite to form—a real, Jewish Jesus devoid of a fake, hatemongering church; the world, whole again; the redemption of all humankind?

Trumpet of Jubilee is divided into four sections: "The Prologue", "Burning World", "Apocalypse", "The Epilogue"; and begins by mapping out the central forces at work within it. The book, the writer tells us in the "prologue", is not fictive because it is based on "truth". It is also not exactly fact because, as in other works, the writer is often masked, as are views expressed by other characters representing varying perspectives of cultural dialectic. One example is Dr. Grunfeld who operates in the book "both as a psychiatrist and as a Jew," (*Trumpet* 16) and who both describes and interprets the events and people contained in the larger narrative frame. Through his eyes, the larger narration is sifted, channelled and organized. He ferrets truths: psychological, emotional and moral; he is a composite of writer, perceiver, moral guide and intellectual. As well, it can also be said that the signposts of the writer are the "Jew", as the receiver of God's Book (and therefore eternally at home in the book); and the psychiatrist, as the perennial uncoverer of encoded messages, the weaver of fragments of the unconscious, subconscious, conscious thoughts and memories, through a past perceived either as a maze of disconnected images, or as a continuity of historical realities.

However, this writer is not just any writer. As with Cynthia Ozick, the writer is not only the aesthete at work with words, arranging them into some heavenly form; perfectly rendering ideas and perceptions that are at once mental, physical and spiritual as if to bypass a human element in their creation. Rather, the writer is also the protector and preserver of the past in the continuity from remembered historicity and memory in the present, to the hope of continuity in a time yet to come. Thus "the word", perfectly rendered, guides its way in the present through the past, and points the way to the messianic redemption to come. The psychiatrist as Jew—Freud as the great prototype — renders signification through language, pieces together the past, present and future into a perfect text of the self. Freud is part of the long Hebraic tradition beginning with the biblical Joseph, the interpreter of dreams through *Merkavah* mysticism in the process of hermeneutical discovery, the search for meaning and love of interpretive interplay. The Jew as psychiatrist follows language on the path to self-discovery and ultimately, therefore, redemption; the first step, through a national redemption of a peoplehood, on the way to final Salvation through the artist as messiah. As the writer explains: "It follows that the teller of stories which were convincing because they were true had to be deeply rooted in the life first of his clan and folk, next of mankind itself." (3) Thus the psychiatrist creates an artfully coherent text from the patient's memories, that is, the past. Similarly, the artist-writer creates art from life, as the Jew creates his/her life from the Word. In this way, the art created from life is less a matter of feigning than a real art. The narration continues:

> For his creatures are both concretely and symbolically more real and more secure from time than beings of mere flesh and blood. They are creatures— created things. Not, to be sure, created out of nothing. Agonized observation, pity that scorches the heart, aspiration that rends the sky, identification of his own hunger, passion, frustration, prayer, with those of his fellows—such are the elements out of which the artist fashions his creatures. He knows their secretest thoughts and has paid dearly enough for that knowledge. He has, in truth, come by it so hard that he may well be believed. (4)

In this discussion of the writing process, the polemic of truth and fiction is brought to the foreground. Can the characters that, so to speak, are brought to life by a skilled writer be considered alive? Does suffering render art true, authentic? The artist, this writer says, can be believed because the writing came through a process of pain and agony. In this way, all writing is biographical/ autobiographical. The writer's characters are simply a manifestation of the painful personal life process and therefore must be real and believable. However, is all art full of truth? Are Philistine art creations also true? True art necessarily conforms to a truth that is more true than even factuality, reality or historicity. It is therefore questionable if the writer or the narrational voice warrants belief when it is written:

> Yet there are three men that must be told of in the story which follows who live and breathe whom I have seen and known, with whom I have held converse in more than one city and, in fact, on more than one continent. How many times? Not many. Nor were any of the three commonly given to quick intimacy or self-revelation. Luckily and naturally I am not the only one who has known Peter Lang and Jehuda Brenner and Andrew Saracen. People have spoken to me concerning them in Boston and Hamburg, in New York and in Constantine, in San Francisco and Jerusalem. Thus I have been able to add glimpse to glimpse and detail to detail. And all facts about these three were pregnant with meaning. (4)

The piling up of factual details serves to lend weight to the argument that these three men are indeed true flesh-and-blood people. The three, whether real or fictional, represent a trinity of faces, forces and value systems. Peter Lang is the force of a real Christian who shows true piety, humility, respect and love for all of humanity. Jehuda Brenner ("Jehuda" is neither its Hebrew original, "Yehuda", nor the proper English equivalent, "Judah"), born and raised as a Jew, has tested secularism but found it wanting. He is a complex mixture of warmhearted kindness, devotion to his people and God, and pungent intellectuality. The third, Andrew Saracen,[90] morally depraved, is one time a baiting Communist and another a rabid Nazi. He is without pity or kindness in his heart. No one know about his past. "The origin of Andrew Saracen remains impenetrably obscure. He himself sneered at the notion that one's kin and country mattered." (20) Everyone tries to guess Saracen's origin. One account of his past comes from a Jules Satije, who is himself, as the narrator explains, someone no one trusted and whose own background is highly ambiguous:

> He spoke with the unctuous pleasure and release of one who, having found another more treacherous of soul, more basely equivocal than himself, paints that other in the most lurid colours as an act of self-exculpation. And laughs softly and continuously while he does so.
> "André? André Saracen? *C'est un sale type, vous savez!* I could show you the stinking alley in Tunis where his father, Ali ben Radjeb, kept a pastry-cook's shop. His mother was a reddish Berber woman from a mountain village near Michelet." (21)

Peter Lang represents the true Christian of a doctrineless faith in Jesus of the Gospels. He reflects an aspect of the young Lewisohn moved by the great passions of both body, soul and mind. As Brenner comments:

> "[Peter] wants the Word to change and redeem the world on the instant. If it doesn't do so his soul sickens and there overcomes him the old, old despair of the Aryan-speaking peoples, which you find in the Upanishads and subtly worked into the Gospels, too, and above all in that Aryanizing, upside down Jew, Paul. Life and the world have no true worth. The will to live is a corrupt will; it's a disease in an otherwise respectable planet." (9)

Jehuda Brenner has grown up as a devout and untiring student of *Torah*. When he enters the story, he is a Jew of the *Haskalah*, the Enlightenment, a freethinker who has abandoned the poverty and piety of his youth for wider horizons. Nevertheless, he retains the sensitivity and feeling of his early education and is endowed with a strong aesthetic sensibility. He also is seen as the type of real Jew who dazzlingly combines intellectual curiosity, cosmopolitanism, pure-heartedness, kindness, an essential Jewishness, true spirituality, humanity, tolerance, level-headedness, *Torah* learning, common sense and a keen aestheticism; a perfect Renaissance (Jewish) man. He is, in short, a virtual bundle of cultural dialectic who perhaps most reflects Lewisohn as the writer and the man. The first-person narrator quotes from a letter written to him by Peter Lang about Jehuda Brenner, which illustrates the high esteem which Peter Lang, Dr. Grunfeld and the narrator hold for Brenner:

> "I had good old Jehuda Brenner up home here in Castleton for a week. He and my father took to each other tremendously. At very first Dad was a bit shy at the idea of a foreign Jew who used phylacteries and a prayer shawl and kept his head covered during meals after he had added a Hebrew blessing to Dad's grace. But when Brenner agreed with him that the precepts of the Gospels were to be obeyed literally without so-called adaptation and sophistication and matched every command and every beatitude of Jesus with exact parallels from Talmudic sources—why then Dad begged him to occupy his pulpit and they took long walks together, and Dad ended up by thanking me for bringing Jehuda here and said he had had the time of his life." (19)

Through the force of Jehuda's personality and cultural sophistication, there is the hope of bringing all dialectical parts and conflicts to a final rest. He can be seen as some potential of synthesis and appears to want to forge a messianic dialectic of all cultural, racial, ethnic, national, social and religious possibilities into a cosmic, apocalyptic, messianic and paradoxical union of differences, in a humane and tolerance-filled whole. Only the devil incarnate, Andrew Saracen, can threaten this lofty goal. Jehuda and Peter represent both the same and the opposite ends of the dialectic of love-hate and Jew-Christian respectively. The Gentile Peter Lang, unlike the Jewish Jehuda, Brenner is ultimately unable to effectively deal with the world as it really is, a dialectical cacophony of evil and good, love and hate.

It is Dr. Grunfeld who helps birth the story of Jehuda through the larger narration. Grunfeld relates to his listeners the story Jehuda related to him: specifically about how, once a year, Jehuda shares his life with the Chassidim:

> "'All year long I touch things made with hands — things made to be beautiful in space. And then I go to the west and see museums and shops full of painted canvases and bronzes and brocades and images cunningly wrought, and my eyes grow blinded by the pagan beauty of things and my heart becomes sur-

feited and ill at ease. I come here each year to purge my eyes of sinful seeing and my heart of error. Here men do not know the difference between beauty and ugliness. If they see a tree they do not pause to say how beautiful is this tree, for fear of forgetting during even that instant the Eternal and his Law.'" (17–18)

At the other side of the dialectical maze of love and hate is Andrew Saracen, who hates beauty, goodness, truth and kindness: "What Andrew Saracen really wanted was revenge - revenge upon all mankind except those dark masses whom he conceived of as the instrument of his revenge. He wanted destruction; he wanted chaos." (23) He seeks the false messianism of Socialism, Communism or Fascism. Saracen's undefined background matches his desire to destroy his past, the past—all history—to build a new social world order devoid of all individual distinctions.

While Andrew Saracen searches only for destruction, Peter Lang and Jehuda Brenner seek messianic redemption. They are the true artists: their creations are products of their devotion only to the Almighty. On a more subtle level, Jehuda Brenner ultimately believes that he and Peter Lang are philosophical opposites. As well, Jehuda could view himself as a truer manifestation of the Joshua/Jesus of the Gospels, through his Jewishness by birth and practice. In reverse, Peter can be considered more Jewish for his belief in the Gospel than, for example, Kurt Weiss, who is unable to identify with anything Jewish. Brenner can maintain his humor, his realistic if not sardonic appraisal of events and people around him. He perceives a different type in his good friend, Peter Lang. The latter, too kind for the wickedness of the world around him, becomes emaciated and consumed by its horror. With both feet firmly planted on solid terrain, Brenner is a true survivor:

> Brenner stroked his small, pointed black beard. His hands were slender and beautifully articulated, neither bony nor too padded. "The whole business [of the politics and extermination of people] nearly killed Peter. He couldn't then, he doesn't even now, [realistically] accept life as tragic—inherently tragic, I mean. He wants miracles, ethical miracles—sudden salvations, the Messiah around the corner. What he 'discovered' in Russia some of us wouldn't even have had to go to ascertain. (9)

Saracen's desires are fulfilled in the Europe of the 1930s. The world is on fire. A Holocaust is raging. Peter Lang, Jehuda Brenner and Andrew Saracen would each appear to desire the obliteration of the opposing life-force designated by the other two. However, Peter Lang and

Jehuda Brenner, respectively representing the Christian and Jewish ways in the ideological divide that separates them, both standing seemingly unconnected from the religious institution they can be said to represent, can find a common ground in kindness, piety, humility, good acts and the search for ultimate redemption. They are spiritual-aesthetic entities, defying the accepted rules of normal behavior and belief. As true spiritual forces, they seek only justice, order, truth and beauty in a humane world. God-embracing, the two represent the most civilised and human forces their respective creeds offer, standing united against their opposite, the dark world of Nazi horror and Andrew Saracen. They listen to Saracen explain the revolutionary ideological platform that his own life and belief system represents:

> He said that in order to establish a new order, any new order, certain very
> deeply rooted notions and reactions of men would have to be eliminated. But
> since these historic ideas and reactions were concretely embodied in people,
> in people too stupid and too slothful to change, it was necessary to eliminate
> these people themselves. By execution. By starvation. By exile to waste
> places. By the destruction of morale and physical stamina in labor camps.
> This, he said, had been and was the method of the proletarian revolution and
> would necessarily be more or less the method of any radical revolution in
> modern times, whether this radicalism was "rightest" or "leftist". (24–25)

Saracen wants to destroy history, along with every and any spiritual, moral and behavioral "weakness" the average person represents, by physically destroying the people themselves. This description of abject evil, so aptly embodied in Hitler, strikes terror and grief in the hearts and minds of Lang and Brenner who, as true Christian and true Jew, stand united against their common enemy—the hatred of humanity.

Thus in this complex dialectic of Judaic and Christian, God and Godlessness, those who represent the love of the world and humanity stand as one against the forces of that which would wage wanton destruction against it. Listening to Saracen explain his evil political platform, and the narrator watching them all, Lang and Brenner fall completely silent:

> They rose slowly, but at the same unpremeditated instant, to their feet, Peter
> Lang and Jehuda Brenner, this Christian and this Jew, and like sleep-walkers,
> unseeing yet unerring, approached each other until they were face to face.
> Then at last they lifted their lids and looked into each other's eyes and clasped
> hands in silence and arm in arm, and with no look backward walked forth
> from that accursed place. (25–26)

As if in a ritual act of solidarity, these true men of God turn their backs on the evil face of perdition. With the lines clearly drawn (not so much between Judaism and Christianity as between Spirituality/God and the opposite force of darkness), they face the conflagration around them, as one. Paradoxically, only because each is truly what he is—without device, disguise or self-invention—they can stand as a common front against the pretenders, assimilators and evildoers. In this way, with so allegorical a backdrop, Lewisohn's book "opens".

In the book's "first" section entitled "Burning World", the forces of what Ozick designates as Pan, are discoverable in places that are otherwise opposed. It is 1933, the year of Hitler's rise to power; he is elected to head the German state on a platform of ridding the Aryan race of the Jews. As the story moves on, the narrative gathers description after description, fact after fact, of how the Jews themselves actively began much earlier, by cowardice or drift, the process of assimilation into Gentile Germanic culture: that is, the process of auto-destruction. The boundary has been drawn across a line of goodness and evil, but where in this map of contradictions do such self-eradicating Jews belong? Certainly they do not warrant being placed in the same category with the Nazi killing machine. Yet they have forsaken themselves and God, and have abandoned the history that made them distinct as God's chosen children. In the three-levelled tier of the redemptive process, these German Jews, removed from their true ancestry, have committed the greatest of transgressions: in losing themselves and their true identity, they have stopped the process of redemption cold in its tracks. Unlike Peter Lang and Jehuda Brenner, who know who they truly are and thus are able to continue to the second level of redemption (national salvation) and on to the top (universal redemption), the German Jews that the story "opens" on, can be nothing that is authentic and true. The three forces represented by Lang, Brenner and Saracen will re-enter the book in various allegorical, flesh-and-body, spiritual or spiritless disguises and faces.

The origin of the book title in *Va'yikra* (*Leviticus*) returns Lewisohn's story to its Biblical frame and to the larger subject of redemption, and also the punishments that will be incurred for disobedience and backsliding. The Book of *Leviticus* sets forth the Laws or Instructions for the Priests which are reflected downward to the Israelite nation as a totality. In a monologue of God to Moses, the Almighty instructs the great Hebrew prophet in the following which, from early spring of each year until the Holy Day of *Shavu'ot* (the giving of the *Torah* to the Israelites), are set out in ten weekly portions that are read on each Sabbath preceding *Shavu'ot.* These ten portions were divided into specific subjects related to prohibitions and commandments regarding foods, sacrifice, holiness, offerings, property, charity.

Almost as important as forgetting the priestliness and order explicit in their birthright as Jews, the Jews of Germany have forsaken the German-Jewish High Priest of self-awareness, *Herr* Doctor Sigmund Freud, who could have led them through the sacred process of self-discovery. Thus these errant Jews of Germany are threefold betrayers: they have forsaken the divine psychoanalytical journey that might have set them free—as the year of jubilee promises; they have severed all ties with their past, betrayed their Creator, His Promise to them and theirs to Him; and finally, they have aped a civilization not their own. On all three counts, personal, national and universal, they have shunned salvation and any hope for a real future. They are caught in a complicated cultural dialectic web of their own creation, and Hitler's savagery toward them brings their double existence cruelly into the forefront of their lives. As the narrator reminds the reader: "They had hardly remembered in those days that they were Jews." (56) They have only to hear the ram's horn calling them back, setting them free from their masquerade of a shameless bondage to a nation not their own.

Dr. Kurt Weiss, his wife Gina from the wealthy, upper-class Jacoby family, and their son Gabriel live the (decadent) life of moneyed, cultured, assimilated German Jews. Bearing strong similarities to the young Ludwig, this seven-year-old child is precocious, perceptive and highly sensitive: "A throbbing started in Kurt's throat. He saw Gabriel's eyes upon him, large, intense, full of a strange innocent and yet unchildlike wisdom." (37) The child has the makings of an artist, a prophet, an angel of God, for his name holds great biblical significance. Gabriel and Michael are two of the mightiest angels in God's Court. Their job is to secure well-being for humanity and to protect Israel from its enemies.

Little Gabriel refuses to attend school now because, as his father, Kurt, explains to his wife: "'They insult and humiliate him there. Because they wound his child's soul beyond measure and beyond belief. I envy your indifference to the dreadful fate that is overtaking us. Do you hear nothing? Do you see nothing? They torment Gabriel because he is a Jewish child.'" (39) Later in the text, as the Holocaust fires begin engulfing Europe, Peter Lang is desperate to find those who can bring harmony and redemption to the world. Lang describes the conflict between the forces of "primitive barbarism" and "civilization" that are vying for control and then:

> He turned to Gabriel. "What do you do specifically?"
> To Gina's slight astonishment Gabriel answered at once, "I write—mostly verse."
> The older man and the youth looked into each other's eyes.
> "Poets are needed," said Peter Lang. "There are few. Is any of your stuff mature enough to be heard?"
> "I doubt it," Gabriel answered. "It's not my own yet. But I've translated some Rilke, Mummie's favourite poet, to show the trend. He died many years ago. People loved his poems but didn't listen to their meaning. He prophesied all the new meanings." (211)

Here Rilke is seen as the prophet-poet par excellence. Lang urges Gabriel and all his poet-compatriots, as if they were an army, to prepare to save the world through the Word/word, Book/book. Then Gabriel adds: "'Many of my generation know the answer and the meaning now,' Gabriel said. Peter Lang nodded. 'Even in my generation some did. They were too few. I pray God that you and your comrades are not too late.'" (212)

Gina's upper-class upbringing and insularity from the world around her effectively shuts her out from redemption at this point. Kurt, on the other hand, can see "as in prophetic vision monstrous and unheard-of things. Terror clawed at his vitals." (34) He understands the price the Jews of Germany will ultimately pay for severing their ties with their past:

> "The modern world said to us Jews: be modern men and all differences will be forgotten. We accepted that bargain. We accepted it honestly. We became Germans. We gave up all we had had before. We forgot it. We no longer know what it was. I didn't know there were Jewish catacombs in Rome. We have nothing; we are nothing; if we can no longer be Germans we are finished, we are destroyed; we have lost all." (61–62)

These German-Jews have lost various parts of the dialectic itself. No longer culturally Jewish, and now forbidden to be culturally German, they are without place or identity, adrift in forgetting even something they vaguely knew. As well, "sedulously most of them had avoided the political implications of Zionism." (79) Turning against themselves, they also shrank from their ancestral land.

Peter Lang reenters the narration as a helpmate and savior of the German Jews. His German language skills, described as "quite foreign but fairly fluent", (92) encode him as the writer-prophet, a type of new Moses who comes to save the (German) Israelite nation from certain destruction, and hopefully lead them to the Promised Land. As if to underscore his biblically Hebraic affinity, he takes from "his inner pocket" a copy of *The Judische Rundschau* (*The Organ of The Zionists*), (94) and shows it to Kurt (who doesn't know of its existence), and another German Jew, Ernst Simon. Even more so, he engages Weiss in a polemical discussion regarding the latter's Jewishness. When Peter Lang insists to them: "But you are Jews," Weiss can feel only annoyance eating away inside of him. His retort to Lang is:

> "I have never denied it. And it has often seemed to me that not denying it was a grosser lie than denying it would have been. You can tear open my breast and my brain and you will find nothing that is specifically Jewish, that is specifically different—generically different—from other men. Now you ask me suddenly to make a new content of life of something that is a figment." (94)

Instead of following the custom of nearly two millennia, trying to proselytize to these errant Jews, Lang feels genuine disappointment and sorrow at Weiss's reaction and begins to wistfully speak of his good friend, Brenner:

> "I wish my friend Jehuda Brenner were here. I asked him to come. But he said that he was not needed here. He said the German Jews would find their Jewishness in their souls and learn to be Jews again without any help, just as certain Christians in Germany were learning to be Christians again and were gladly taken upon themselves the Cross of Christ." (94–95)

It is only the fake Christians, that is, the Nazis and their sympathizers, who are killing the Jews. As well, the Jews who believed themselves to be fake Jews (or even non-Jews) are learning who and what they in fact really are. Lang describes his friend as "a great Jew and a great human being" who "has taught" him "by what he is, what a great and precious thing it is to be a Jew." (95)

He creates yet another dialectical side here in his polemic here: of unredeemed individuals—from the extreme poles of Nazi Stormtroopers to the assimilated Jews of Germany—and those redeemed in a true love of humanity and total faith in the Creator. Weiss, on the other hand, is stateless, peopleless, Godless, without "refuge, nothing on which to lean." (101) As a German-Jew, Kurt's desire is to melt into the spirit and soul of German culture. He does not realize that he, like other German-Jews of his time, has put into motion his own holocaust of identity, and has ironically become the unwitting ally of the Nazis. What the German Stormtroopers in this tale seek to do to Jewish bodies, Kurt and his Jewish compatriots seek to do with their own souls. Kurt, like the others who ostensibly see civilization, beauty, High Culture and aesthetic appreciation, has in fact descended into a grave of selfhood he will never have the opportunity to climb out of again.

Gabriel, Kurt's progeny, named after one of the highest angels of God, was born as if sent by God to bring the Israelites back to the fold; to lead them to their final redemption; to bring civilization and love back to the world through the Word/word by eradicating savagery and hate in its wake.

Dr. Kurt Weiss meets his downfall when his Gentile secretary, wanting to entrap him with the Stormtroopers (and in an act that clearly demonstrates how vulnerable the Jews of Germany have become), enters his office half-undressed, and flings herself on him. Immediately the Stormtroopers, who have been waiting just outside, enter the room, call him a "Jew swine" (104) and take him into custody. They eventually torture and then kill him. The scene of Kurt and his secretary repeats a much earlier one, the biblical story of Joseph and the wife of Potiphar, who also attempted to seduce the Israelite and to bring about his downfall by publicly accusing him of rape. In both cases, the Hebrew male ultimately remains loyal to himself and his Hebrew nation.

With the help of her father's French connections, Gina and Gabriel flee Germany for Paris. On her very painful journey of self-discovery, Gina meets Mme. Levi-Bloch, whose family are friends and business associates of the Jacobys, Gina's family, and who have helped her and Gabriel escape from Germany. The irony implicit in Mme Levi-Block's behavior toward her is driven home. Like *The Cannibal Galaxy*'s Hester Lilt, the Madame's French is laced with the unmistakable intonations of

a heavy German or Alsatian accent. So if the woman wanted to be kind, why didn't she speak German [Gina knows very little French]. As Mme. Levi-Bloch continued her carefully Parisian exclamations the purpose of the comedy came flamingly to Gina. These rich French Jews were now taking the same line in regard to the German Jews which the rich and cultivated German Jews had

taken until just the other day towards the Russian and Polish and Romanian
Jews: inferior people living among barbarians whose fate could in no wise be
conceived of as having any bearing upon their own. (120)

Implicit in this irony is yet another dialectic of civilized, cultured Jews
and the uncouth, uncultivated ones.

Jehuda Brenner reappears as the nephew of Gina's father's wealthy
Jewish Parisian friends, who are instrumental along with the Levi-Blochs,
in helping Gina and Gabriel. When asked by Gina where he is from,
Jehuda replies, "from the East, Aunt Bionca, from *misrach*. I am and we
ought to be." (132) This is a clear allusion to Zion, Israel, and his deep
Zionist sympathies; Jehuda doesn't miss an opportunity to air his views
about the Holy Land.

As Gina's Jewish (personal) consciousness grows, she slowly begins
to understand the meaning of Zionism and her people. It is at the warmly
gracious house of these Brenner relatives, the Meyerheims, in attitude,
graciousness, kindness and sensitivity diametrically opposed to the con-
descending and pretentious Levi-Blochs, that Gina meets the first real
Jews in her life. This brings to the foreground the theme and conflict between real and fake Christians and Jews. The people who gather there are
on the way to being personally, nationally and universally redeemed.
They are trying to recover, or construct, meaning in their lives. All who
speak to Gina have seen through the falseness of believing one could be
German, French or whatever, without addressing their Jewish core. The
practice of religious observances and customs, Gina hears Jehuda explain
to a young woman, is not so Jews are enslaved to something that binds
them. It is in order to preserve who they are as individuals. It is "a double
obedience: obedience to the law of our being, obedience to the Law of
God. For Jews these two obediences are one. There are higher and
greater ways of practicing that double obedience than by removing leaven
from our houses at Passover." (140) Brenner is describing the sense of
self, rather than its abandonment, in the "other" which is protected and
maintained through the practice of ritual customs, adding: "We threw
ourselves away; we threw ourselves under the feet of any who chose to
trample on us; we invited them to trample." (140)

However for some inexplicit, ambiguous reason, when Gina asks
Brenner to which country it would be best for her and Gabriel to emigrate, he tells her:

"I don't think you are ready for Palestine, nor is Palestine ready for you." His words were very slow and very deliberate. "I think in fact I'm sure, that you and your child could go to America. There are Jewish masses in America; there is a Jewish future in America—there, at least, if anywhere in *Golus* [Exile]." (141)

Uncovered here is yet another conflict between being Jewish in Palestine and being Jewish in America. This conflict brings to the fore the polemic of the Promised Land of Palestine (Israel) as opposed to that of America.

Jehuda's identification of himself as "a simple Jew from Poland" who wants only "to serve our people", brings deep consolation to Gina's soul. The narrator describes the scene and Brenner's words as having "pierced her heart"; and for the second time, at least, she thinks of her dead husband Kurt, their Jewish folk, and her son's future with a rather strangely complicated image: "His people and hers and Gabriel's—above all, Gabriel's, and the people of Kurt who had died upon a cross because that people was his people, too." (142)

Employing, not for the first time, the crucifix image—which is to say the scene of Jesus on the cross—the writer once more yokes together its counterpart in the spiritual union of the truly Christian Peter Lang, and the genuinely Jewish Jehuda Brenner (from whose Hebrew name, "Judah", the word "Jewish" is derived). Thus in the closing of the circle, or the reflected image in a mirror, Jehuda and Peter are two sides of the same thing: one the reflected image of the other. Through each knowing his own true self-identity, the "other" can be embraced in full acceptance and humanity. The oft-evoked crucifixion scene not only sets the Christian-Jewish polemic on its head, but would appear firstly to de-Christianize, and secondly to describe, a historical continuity of the Israelite nation, through and including Joshua/Jesus. In the "Prologue", as previously described, the narrator quotes from a letter describing Jehuda's visit to the Lang home, and how Brenner was able to close the circle of Jewish-Christian belief and its perennial conflict, and also to find a constructive and viable common denominator in Jesus/Joshua as a Jew, for both Christianity and Judaism. Thus the writer's contrast of Jewish-Christian would seem in this instance to be one of counterfeit Christian and real "Jewish", and *vice versa*. Real Christians, the writer seems to be saying, can easily accept Jews for who they are, of the genetic family of Jesus/Joshua, and God's chosen people.

By the conclusion of "The First Book: Burning World", Gina and Gabriel, on the unexplained advice of Jehuda Brenner, have left France and Europe for the new promised land, America, like the young Ludwig, where the now eight-year-old Gabriel appears to be destined to grow into a full blown prophet-artist/writer of his people in a new "Israel". While still a young man, Gabriel could already discern the role he would play in the world:

> So his great Jewish meaning, Gabriel told himself, was also a universal meaning. Only, would that meaning create a form for itself through him in the English language on this unstoried Middle Western earth under these yet unanimated skies? He wanted a form that was plastic; he wanted a form that was dense. But he wanted that dense and vibrant and plastic form to be not art, but message; and thought in great humbleness, yet with often a sudden incandescence in his heart, of that last nameless prophet who called himself *maleach* (messenger) or *maleachi* (my messenger) and also of those unrivalled verses of his old favorite Rilke in which that modern poet, though in a happier and more hopeful age, had prayed that he might be the dancer before a new Ark of the Covenant, the herald and the baptist of a new Messiah. (234)

Gina's and Gabriel's first impressions of America are like those described in *Up Stream* of the young Lewisohn and his family, upon their first entry into the New York harbor, where they are overwhelmed by the strange speech and sounds. It is this speech in the English language which Gabriel, as writer-to-be (like Lewisohn), will not just make intelligible, but learn to render in prose as if it had been his own mother tongue. They go to Ozark City, home of an Americanized relative of the Jacoby family who is, of course, a banker, wealthy, and most graciously helpful to them. Gina notes to herself that "there is nothing about him in his easy, well-made American clothes to mark him as Jewish." (*Trumpet* 148) Here in the place of contrasts, America and Europe, as well as Christian and Jew, Gina begins to piece together the meaning of being Jewish in America—the home of the free; far from the fires of Europe, but yet not the historic homeland of her people, Palestine.

Gina quickly learns of the Ozark City family's great wealth and influence (as it had been in Germany as well); its upper-class life-style; the patriotic Americanism of Albert Jacoby, her uncle and benefactor; the definitive Jewishness of Albert's wife. Gina Weiss is, however, also growing increasingly aware of something that is missing there. Although she feels very satisfied that Gabriel has kind and friendly playmates in a school that positively impresses her, there is something she cannot understand: "What was it that puzzled her? What was it she missed and began to long for? 'There is an emptiness,' she said, articulating to herself, 'a great emptiness.'" (153) Gina decides, therefore, that she and Gabriel must leave the Jacoby house, where everything "seemed to her like the gyrations of a farce about a centre of nothing in a void." (153)

She soon finds the cause of her unhappiness. This Jacoby home, although financially very secure, is without the High Culture that was so much a part of her and her husband's life in Germany. When all is said and done, she is living in American culture. One evening Albert drifts into Gina's room and sees the books of Goethe, Rilke, Mann and Kant in her bookcase. He is in total amazement. He can't imagine that people would "still read Goethe" and has "never heard" of Rilke. He remarks that if Kurt had read Kant, his mind must have been "most unusual". To this Gina replies: "'I cannot truthfully say that.... At least all of his friends, whether Jewish or Gentile, read philosophy and tried to find a *Weltanschauung* of their own.'" (154)

Yet another dialectical can of worms is opened, as Gina's High German culture is contrasted with Albert Jacoby's (naturalized) American Low Culture. Albert laughs, trying to diffuse the growing tension between them, but Gina cannot be stopped. She openly (and rather rudely) describes, as she sees it, the meaningless life he has, "manufacturing paper boxes and buying real estate low and selling it high." (155) Albert responds that Gina had "better get rid of some of her high falutin' European notions." (156)

The first meaningful Jewish contact Gina makes is with the Frosh family who observes the laws of *Kashrut* (kosher dietary laws) and sends their child to a Hebrew Day School, whose name, Ge'ulah, as Sara Frosch explains, "is the Hebrew word for redemption—the redemption of our land and the redemption of our people". (171) Gina, at Gabriel's request, decides to send him to the same school. Gina's (and by extension, Gabriel's) "ultra-modern" life in the "atmosphere of the Weimer Republic", a life "soaked with psychoanalysis and expressionist literature", forged in her and in her upbringing of Gabriel "a definite realism of the interior life." (173)

Gina meets the spirit of Andrew Saracen in Albert Jacoby's son, Dr. Julian Jacoby. A self-hating Jew, he desires, like Saracen, to create a new order in the world without the "hocus-pocus" of real Christians or Jews.

He is bitter, malcontented, hateful, loathing of all things '"foreign", and also addicted to alcohol and drugs. Gina tells him that "since you hate the Jew in yourself, you hate all Jews." (175) Gabriel's assessment of Julian is that "'Uncle Julian is a wicked man.'" (182) The child would appear to be, as in Lang's vision, the perceptive, true Hebrew prophet-writer growing into his fully mature form. Through him it is possible to redeem the world. As the narrator describes, Gabriel's is "a tranquil soul," able to "summon... images at will"; (185) or else they come "unsummoned, at the fragrance of lilac or of fresh-baked rolls." (185) As well, he slowly begins to understand "the world around him." (186) The "Second Book: Apocalypse" is the story of Gabriel's maturing into the apocalyptic Jewish writer. The word "apocalypse" describes a number of unnamed Jewish and Christian prophetic and visually symbolic texts of the second century B.C.E., principally pertaining to the impending annihilation of the wicked and the redemption of the righteous on the final Day of Judgment. From Greek, the word is also synonymous with revelation. Interestingly, as Martha Himmelfarb states: "While prophetic literature consists primarily of the words the prophets hear the Lord speak, the apocalypses place their revelations in the context of narratives." (*Religion* 54)

Apocalypses describe prophetically predetermined plans *vis a vis* the coming Day of Judgment. As Himmelfarb adds:

> The eschatology of the apocalypses is more deterministic than that of prophetic literature [in general]. While the prophets hope to persuade their listeners to repent and thus avert catastrophe, the apocalypses view the coming judgment as the inevitable conclusion of a plan formulated long ago. The goal of pious behavior is not to head off disaster but to secure a place among the righteous at the last judgment. (55)

A specifically Christian text, *The Revelation of St. John*, contains prophetic pronouncements in the image of seven golden candlesticks and the trumpet.

The gift of prophecy and vision can be seen in Gabriel early in his life. This comes to him in a mix of artistic sensibility, a taste for High Culture, supernaturalistic intuition and his Jewishness. In the same way as Lewisohn describes in *Up Stream* the facts or the fact-like information of his own life, by the age of fifteen Gabriel has mastered five Shakespearean plays and parts of *Paradise Lost*. Also Gabriel is an intricate picture of cultural dialectic: Jewishness, poetic vision, High German Culture/Germanic modes of thinking, intellectual curiosity, a life in America, Europeanism, scholarly achievement on all fronts and a facility with all aspects of language. Gabriel finds the secret of existence, "the solution of a central mystery, the mystery that he must know and live in order to be at all," (*Trumpet* 197) in the poetry of Rilke whose aspects of his own cultural dialectic are re-reflected in Lewisohn and Gabriel. This young man Gabriel often stops under a favorite "faintly exotic tree" and feels the divine music of Rilke's poetry in his very soul:

> The boy under the tree in the park murmured: "No victories can make him free." Jacob had wrestled with the angel. Because he [the Angel] had been de-feated he [Gabriel] had been called Israel. To wrestle with the Angel and to be defeated, that was to be an Israelite. That too, was to be a poet. By a sud-den impulse he looked at his watch. He laughed at himself. It was past the time for the meeting to start. He had hurried forth so bravely and ardently. He had stopped to dream by the wayside. Luckily Dr. Aaronson, the Young Judean [Jewish youth organization] leader for the Ozark City district, under-stood him. He had been late at the last single Unit meeting and Aaronson had laughed and quoted: *'Hineh, ba'al ha-chalomoth!'* ("Look, the master of dreams!") He had asked if they had not better call Gabriel Joseph here-after. (198)

He has the sensitivity and the gift of insight that can foresee the coming of messianic redemption, the final Judgement and End of Days. As Gabriel grows into young adulthood and with "the thinker's forehead", (192) he, like the narrator who is both a Jew and a psychoana-lyst, decides he will study psychology. Gabriel, also a writer of verses, has read much literature: Milton, Virgil, German poets, Yehuda Halevi and Bialik, all in the original Hebrew, Latin and German tongues: "Rhythm had quivered in him early and words had been incantations to him as far back as he could remember. It was not until he was sixteen that he knew that he wanted to be a poet." (204)

Another facet of the dialectic, that of Time, is marked by the book's structural organization into two parts which are thrown into relief by the "past" of the "First Book" and the "Future" of the "Second Book". In the "First", the past divides into a series of "pasts". There is the far past of the historical Israelite nation; of Judaic antiquity that lies in wait to ambush the soul and all misguided hopes for "success" and "progress" in the present. In most cases it is a suppressed past, better forgotten. Then comes the past of the generations of grandparents, great-grandparents, back to several more generations that lived religiously, then intermarried and climbed high up the ladder of social, educational and economic attainment. After that is the "past" of the German life that was just lately, in the "Now", snatched away with no warning (or at least a warning the eyes and ears saw and heard but refused to believe). Finally comes the past of discontinuity and placelessness, when there is no longer any past, present or hope of a future. This section corresponds respectively to the geographic locations of: Canaan, Egypt, the Sinai Desert, Mt. Sinai, Israel; Poland, Germany of the Weimar Republic; Hitler's Republic; France (Paris); America-New York City; Ozark City of a past, present and future.

"The Second Book: Apocalypse" is a narrative recounting the events that will transpire in the future. In itself, the Second Book is an Apocalypse, a prophetic text outlining the predetermined events that have been set on course. In this way the writers (both the writer of the text and Gabriel), as re-reflected writers of this present apocalypse, are being read by the reader. This simultaneously connects the three areas of prophet, writer and Jew into the same singular human form making the text, writer, prophet and Jew synonymous and inextricably intertwined. Thus, this "Second Book" is a description of the Jewish (read) prophet (read) writer in the process of mastering the craft of writing. Gabriel also painfully remembers the past, specifically his father, Kurt, the sacrificial lamb "crucified" by the Nazis. With Kurt out of the picture by the "Second Book" (except in memory), Gina, like Lewisohn's own mother Minna, can focus all her ambitions, desires and dreams for an authentic new life and a future of hope and total redemption.

The life, word and person that is Jehuda Brenner re-reflects the Jewish voice of prophecy of the budding writer that is Gabriel Weiss. Brenner has labored hard and long to prick the consciousness and memory of European Jewry, and with Hitler at work at his grim task of eradicating them, the assimilation of Europe's Jews has come to a dead halt. Now Israel, as the old-new place of hope, the ancestral homeland, is within reach of becoming a fact, a reality again after so many years of wandering. Jehuda, as a near-allegorical figure representing the Jewish nation, has gone to Palestine to make a life for himself. His work is done. In a talk with Peter Lang in Ozark City, Gina inquires about Jehuda:

Peter Lang sighed.

"I haven't seen him in a long, long time. He lives in Palestine; he travels much less than he used to. You see, no one is needed in Europe now except the relief and immigration agents for the Jewish people. There isn't a Jew in Europe to-day who doesn't want to go to Palestine, except those in England and France and Scandinavia, and the people in these countries are all Zionists, too. History has done Jehuda's job for him. (209–210)

Lang then tells Gabriel that he is now what his father would have been if he had been alive today. Kurt did not have the chance to live a full life. Gabriel, however, will take Kurt's place as a fighter for purity and aesthetic beauty in the world.

Andrew Saracen's perversity of soul and moral nature is reflected in Julian Jacoby, who has been incarcerated in a mental institution. This brings to mind Dr. Arthur Levy's later comment of the high incidence of mental illness in Jews, especially self-hating ones. Julian has wanted Gina to marry him, or to be at least his constant physical companion. She has rebuffed him and is now emotionally married to her son, Gabriel. A case could be made for the similarity of Gina and Gabriel's closeness with that of Lewisohn and his own mother, Minna.[91] Gabriel has become as close to his mother as is possible without passing any forbidden sexual boundaries. More so, perhaps, Gabriel seems to serve the role of a messiah (as Jewish mothers can view their sons!), a type of detypologized Jesus (now Joshua) figure, born not from a sexless union, but the issue of a parent's highly sensual, physical attraction, based on shared loved and respect. This relationship is the type that Dr. Arthur Levy wishes he could have with Elizabeth Knight. His father Kurt having been crucified by the forces of evil, Gabriel is now the risen son, his father's proxy. Thus the writer describes Gina as if Gabriel were her husband and not her son. The phrase, "learned husbands" here instantaneously equates Gabriel with the role of husband to his mother, and invites an Oedipal interpretation of its content:

As the years went on and her knowledge of her people was increased by reading and by conversation, she had become accustomed to saying that she understood those Jewish women of another day who by either inherited means or personal activity had supported learned husbands whose studies were quite without worldly value, wholly *l'shmo*, that is, for the glory of the Ineffable Name. (213)

Gina's and Gabriel's life begins to descend into divisive conflict when nineteen-year-old Gabriel, like Lewisohn, falls in love with a widow nearly twice his age. Unlike the youthful Lewisohn's Mary, who was thoroughly Gentile, Elizabeth Warner, born Elizabeth Cohen, is Jewish on her paternal side. Betty, as she is called, adores Gabriel—or is it that he personifies the youth she wants to recapture through him? Could it also be his talent for writing? Interestingly, nowhere can a comment or incisive psychoanalytical remark be found about Gabriel's perhaps too emotionally intimate relationship with his mother, that now appears to have been transferred, so to speak, to Betty Cohen.

As well, Betty could represent both conflicting differences (Jewish and Gentile) and a synthesis of these differences into a harmonious new entity of being. Betty's strong interest in the arts and culture, according to the equation of culture/art with Jewishness and the Word of God, would turn her into a one hundred percent Jewish being. In addition, her adoration of Gabriel bears a strong resemblance to the descriptions of the writer of *Up Stream* and *Crump* of both Anne Crump and Mary Crocker's early admiration for the budding young composer/writer, Herbert / Ludwig; this would nullify any possible conflicts borne from cultural differences. Gabriel's secret love, Elizabeth, is the very essence of dialectic:

> Her maiden name was Kohn, since Mrs. Warner, far from wishing to conceal the fact, made it perfectly plain to all fitting hearers that her father had been a German Jew of the extremist assimilatory type who had never consorted with his fellow Jews and who, able and successful in America almost from the day of his landing, had forty years ago married a Christian girl very much as a matter of course. She and his only child and later heiress had been brought up in the Episcopal communion. No one had thought of Betty Kohn as Jewish. (214)

She addresses him as:

> "Dear Poet!" Of course he had melted; of course he had glowed. Of course he carried the image and the moment in his heart. Of course upon that altar in his heart he laid his daily taciturn offerings of verse, music, memory, adoration. When others spoke of her he would not speak. Even when others praised her he was silent. He and his inviolable secret stood apart. (215)

This rich benefactress picks Gabriel from all of the aspiring young writers who are invited to her salons.

Gabriel's college education, like the "Dual Curriculum" of Joseph Brill's school in *The Cannibal Galaxy,* is also the very model of a duality of Gentile and Hebraic: his major course of study is English Literature and his minor, philosophy and Hebrew Literature. He is growing into a more mature artistic voice, and with Elizabeth as his lover, he has grown into a man. Without comment the narrator describes Gina in the shadows stewing in her jealousy:

> It came upon her suddenly that her man child was no longer wholly hers, that he who had come out of her womb and had now for so many years been her only vindication and her only triumph was seeking for himself the womb of woman. She was too intelligent to hope to halt the cycle. She had built rationalizations about her feeling drawn from the specific circumstances. Tensely she had watched Gabriel's comings and goings. One night she had sat up for him very late and out of her sufferings flung at him, when he returned, an accusation not against him but against Elizabeth.
> "It's unscrupulous in a woman of her age to seduce a boy." (230)

Morally and emotionally, Gina is quite correct about Elizabeth but fails to see, or doesn't want to see, that she has been doing exactly the same thing. Each of the three, Gina, Elizabeth and Gabriel, is playing the fool with themselves and one another. Gina and Gabriel—so usually alert to every sign, gesture, word—dupe others and are themselves being duped; they are blind and deaf to this near comedy of Oedipal struggle. When a weeping Gina asks her son if he still loves "Mummie", Gabriel reassures her: "'Nothing has changed between you and me, Mummie—nothing, nor ever can.'" (231)

In Gabriel's relationship with Gina, and in the struggle he suffers inside him because of it, he is torn between the pole of a counterfeit life with Elizabeth and a total commitment to himself to his people. As a prophet-poet-leader of his people, being completely true to oneself is synonymous with total commitment to one's art. In the end, Gabriel chooses the Jewish course. He leaves both his mother, his mother substitute and his *shiksa* behind and marries Eve, a young woman his age and burning with the history of their people. Their son, David ben Zion is born, and history and the world go forward into a rosy future—or do they?

The final chapters of *Trumpet of Jubilee* are strange indeed. Gabriel announces that he is needed in Palestine to help defend against the forces of evil that want to see the destruction of the Jewish people. When Eva resists giving him her blessing, Gina tells her:

"Let him go, my daughter. It is more than twenty years now since his father died. And I know that retribution belongs to God. But perhaps Gabriel and the many thousands like him are being forged by God into the instrument of his justice. Let him go, Eve. Let him help strike the blow. It may be that then our little David will never have to strike any blow. It may be that then *his* world will be a world of peace." (327)

Gabriel and those poet-prophets like him must sound the trumpet of justice and spread the word of God.

However Lewisohn's/the writer's true visionary dream has not been made clear. As Elliot B. Gertel asserts: "Once more, the psychological complexity of his [Lewisohn's] messianic yearnings is veiled by a seemingly definitive statement" that 'The Second Book: Apocalypse' ends with." (Gertel 157) What sort of a messiah does Lewisohn/the writer envision; and what kind of a world will follow the Armageddon, the apocalyptic war of wars? In contrast to Gina's ideals for the vanquishment of Israel's enemies by the forces of Good, and the implicitly understood messianic age such victory will bring in its wake, the "Epilogue" finale depicts a post-third-war world filled with bestial primitives; a war waged in the land of Israel itself:

Long long ago the year two thousand had sunk back into the mists of time. How long ago? The people who lived in the old concrete-and-steel catacombs which had been built during the third world war under all the cities and all the lands of the continent of Europe did not know. Nor did the peasants know who here, where disease was no more virulent nor the soil forever ruined, scratched shallow furrows in the earth and brought forth meagre crops. (*Trumpet* 331)

The poet-messiah-prophet implicit in the "First" and "Second Books" was meant to save the world from such barbarity. As the writer's quotation from Paul Valery describes:

We have come to see that the abyss of history is deep enough for all. We have come to feel that a civilization is a fragile as a single life. Circumstances which may well send the works of Keats and Baudelaire to join those of Menander in oblivion are no more inconceivable at all. We read of them in our daily papers. (329)

When the forces of evil rule the world, the poets descend into oblivion. In the same way, the opposite is true. As God's Word fills the world, the poets surface to spread the Word/word of God which their art is synonymous with.

Lewisohn's book thus ends as it begins: in bestiality and cruelty. There is some goodness left in the world, mirrored in the preserved stories of the Almighty and His people Israel, and other legendary tales that mingle Jewish and Christian culture. It is the teller of stories who incorporates the prophetic-messianic figure. In the guise of the storyteller reside the prophets or prophet-helpers of Israel. As such, the writer of *Trumpet of Jubilee* would seem to ascribe the full measure of messianic might to the writer who punitively wields his pen like a sword to cut down those who would despise the poet's power, and the High Culture that was able to give it birth. In a veiled comparison of God's law with the story or "tale", the narrator describes the time before and after God's law: "Of all the tales told among the people of plain and mountain, of riverbank and seashore, this was the first to be written down. It was written down in various places by men who spoke diverse tongues." (339) This appears to be a description of the various biblical texts; of the different religions. The narrator describes how many versions of this tale are written, and there is debate as to which one is the truest. The phrase, "those three oldest ones", (339) would appear to mean Judaism, Christianity and Islam. "This tale" is told throughout the world when the forces of evil set out to annihilate the world and the messengers and minions of the new brutal rulers

> sought out all copies of the Book of Zur, as that favourite legend and evangel had now long been called, and destroyed them and hunted and hounded men who sought to tell the tale again by word of mouth or to rewrite it from memory or to bring in copies written in the still free lands of the free people. (340)

Like Andrew Saracen, the "Epilogue" would appear to condone a new world order—this time based on the absolute power of the writer. Gabriel leaves for Palestine and seemingly resurfaces in the "Epilogue" in the person of Jehuda Brenner, the figure who haunts the book's end: "one tall, slender, bearded" (344) figure who stands blowing the ram's horn to mark the end of the day of Atonement. The otherwise undescribed character, "Malcha" calls out: "'He has blown the ram's horn, the Trumpet of the Jubilee. Now is the hour.' And she lifted up her voice and cried aloud: 'We would have peace and know God's law. Bear us the Christ, again!'" (345)

The cry, "Bear us the Christ again!" are the final words of Lewisohn's book. The words are clearly there on the page, but the message is not. The dialectical maze sinks down into itself. It appears to be indecipherable. The question still remains: For what kind of Jubilee of freedom is the trumpet being blown, and for whom?

Conclusion

Ludwig's son, James, in an article describing his late father, depicts him as having "experienced his Abrahamic dream—dying in his sleep with all his faculties his own, and leaving nothing still to be completed."[92] James adds that his father was fully ready to die and a decade beforehand, "he embraced a kind of neo-Hasidism with the spiritual ferocity of a *Ba'al Shem Tov*." ("Father" 48) Asserting that his father was "a difficult man to get along with", (49) he added that he was neverthe-less "a very distinguished writer, intellectual and prophetic Jew." His father believed that "the Jews [were] the chosen tool of complete redemp-tion for an unreclaimed world.... [This] consumed the man [Ludwig] who, with a truly Renaissance mind, had mastered many literatures and cultures." (49)

As James observes, his father, however, fell into a very great predica-ment. Probably no longer able to trust the ethical reliability of the Western world after the unspeakable event that wiped six million Jewish brethren from the face of the earth, he forced himself to stop reading "Nietzsche and the other German idealist writers." (49) Having grown from his very young years to love the beauty of Western art, from the Greeks onward, "he could not... ignore the so-called pagan anti-Semitic voice." Like Cynthia Ozick, Lewisohn was at constant war with the pagan demon, caught in the inextricable grip of a complicated, culturally dialectical puzzle.

Lewisohn also mourned the loss of posthumous fame, as Milton Hindus writes in his Introduction to Lewisohn's *What Is This Jewish Heritage?*, published shortly before the latter's death. He had never "gained the Jewish people. Have I gained their support and their memory?" (*Heritage* xv) Hindus quotes Lewisohn as having said, "Time will show."[93] The author's final years, as Hindus describes them, were filled with great embitterment from the constant verbal and emotional abuse of Jews who felt highly insulted by his attacks on the ease with which they were assimilating; and the Gentiles who were stung by his assaults on the various hypocrisies in American culture. Lewisohn, Hindus emphasizes, was plagued by the sense of "homelessness in the universe." (*Heritage* xviii). He was a thorough modernist in the sense of "metaphysical terror", as Hindus expresses it, that followed him to the end of his days. He stood in (at least) two worlds, one modern and pagan, the other in the tradition of his people, carrying the Covenant of God with the Israelites in his very bones.

The artist-as-prophet in him was, however, the strongest element of his being. He warned us like Jeremiah, Hindus declares, quoting a *Midrash*, that "when the Jews followed God's word, the Creator blessed them with plenty; but when they were arrogant, stubborn and derelict in their duty to Him, he punished them with a quick and heavy hand." (xxii) Hindus adds that he himself heard Lewisohn disparaged because his own spiritual observance was found wanting. Most especially, as Hindus quotes Lewisohn:

> "The artist doesn't have to make any special effort to BELONG—he belongs naturally, to the marrow of his bones." Home for him, as for Frost's "Hired Man"—in words which Lewisohn liked to quote with approval—was "'something you somehow haven't to deserve." (xiii)

M. Merowitz sums up the view of Lewisohn as a man of many cultural influences, faces, identities: in short, the cultural dialectic that constantly shifts from one realm to another. He appears as a paradoxical mix of cultural, ethnic, personal, social factors so intertwined that it is impossible to know who the real Ludwig Lewisohn is. Merowitz asserts that as "an individualist and an artist by temperament", Lewisohn's life, personality and work created "a rather interesting picture: the German as American, the Zionist as humanist, and the artist as a... Jew."[94]

Of himself, Lewisohn believed he knew "America and the American people." He attended school and college with Americans, and had "close and dear friends among American liberals." (*Answer* 158) Continuing, he asserts: "Again and again... liberal Christian American clergymen come to me, a conservative nationalist Jew with a *yarmelke* [skull cap] ready in his pocket and a *mezuzah* [a *Torah* scroll] on each door of his house, for advice and help." (158)

He viewed himself, it would seem, as a propagandist like Jeremiah, an artist on a holy mission. "[A]ll communication of art," he explains, "science, religion and philosophy is propaganda.... Jeremiah was a propagandist." (160) As Gertel asserts, Ludwig Lewisohn is one excellent example of that unique combination of America-Israel neo-messianism that, as he explains, has fired Jewish-American writers—either through abject denial or zealous affirmation—into this "dream" of a prophetic artist-leader of the Jewish nation, and the world in general, based on *Torah*, God's written word. "Their visions," Gertel continues, "are no less passionate than those of the ancients, but they reflect individual and group concerns that are as American as they are Jewish." (Gertel 153)

Jewish-American writers like Lewisohn and Ozick, in their writing or rewriting of the "book", show a chronicle of belief—or make-believe—in the process of being made. Lewisohn was more than a Jewish-American writer. As Hindus describes it, "he erupted into the consciousness of the Jewish people and the world, at the very moment [that] he came into the consciousness of America itself." (Hindus x) He nevertheless brought the complexity of his variety of secular, cultured Berlin, German-Jewish lifestyle and the multiple influences that played on, or bedeviled, his sensitive, artistic nature.

Notes

46   Hayden White, "Introduction: The Poetics of History", *Metahistory: The Historical Imagination in Nineteenth Century Europe*, (Baltimore: Johns Hopkins University Press, 1973). White's ideas were first presented in a lecture at the Comparative Literature Colloquium, Yale University, January 24, 1974. This lecture was then elaborated on in "The Structure of Historical Narrative", *Clio* I (1972) 5–20. See also "The Historical Text as Literary Artifact", *The Tropics of Discourse: Essays on Cultural Criticism* (Baltimore: Johns Hopkins University Press, 1978).

47   Ludwig Lewisohn, *Up Stream: An American Chronicle* (New York: Boni and Liveright, 1922) 9. Also (London: Richards, 1923). Revised edition (New York: Modern Library, 1926). Corrected revised edition (New York: Modern Library, 1926).

48   Ludwig Lewisohn, *Mid-Channel* (New York: Farrar, Straus and Giroux, 1929; reprint New York: Arno Press, 1975) 288.

49   *Authorized Bible* reads [*Mark* 15:34]: "And at the ninth hour Jesus cried out with a loud voice, saying, '*Eloi, Eloi, lama sabachthani?*' which is being interpreted, 'My God, My God, why hast Thou forsaken Me?'"; also *Matthew* 27:46. (*Authorized Bible*)

50   An acronym from the Hebrew words for *Torah*, Law; *Nevi'im*, Prophets; and *Ketuvim*, the sacred Writings; also a synonym for the Jewish Bible. (*Religion* 673)

51   Adolph Gillis, *Ludwig Lewisohn: The Artist and His Message* (New York: Duffield and Green, 1933) 1.

52   Melnick's biographical account is consistent with the facts of Lewisohn's life, whereas Lewisohn's own so-called autobiographical account in *Up Stream* is not consistent with the facts. (Melnick I: 27)

53   Georg Hirschfeld, *The Mothers,* tr. Introduction Ludwig Lewisohn (Garden City: Doubleday, 1916).

54   He is called Ferris in *Up Stream*. Again, facts are different. Melnick identifies "Ferris" as Lancelot Minor Harris. (Melnick I: 55)

55   Ludwig Lewisohn, "A Study of Matthew Arnold", *The Sewanee Review* (October 1901) 442–456 (April 1902) 143–159 (July 1902) 302–319.

56   His real name. (Melnick I: 83) Lewisohn calls him Brewer.

57   Sacvan Bercovitch ed, *Reconstructing American Literary History* (Cambridge: Harvard University Press, 1986) viii.

58   Werner Sollars, "Region, Ethnic Group, and American Writers: From 'Non-Southern' and 'Non-Ethnic' to Ludwig Lewisohn; or the Ethics of Wholesome Provincialism", *Prospects* 9 (1984) 441–462.

59   The German in this case and hereafter translated by Jane Statlander.

60   Ludwig Lewisohn, *Gegen den Strom: Eine Amerikanische Chronik* (Frankfurt: Frankfurter Societats-Druckerei GMBH Abteilung Buchverlag, 1924) "Frontpiece".

61   Ludwig Lewisohn, *Trumpet of Jubilee* (New York: Harper & Bros., 1937) 234. Melnick would appear to wittingly or unwittingly be drawing the identical conclusion when he states, "Ludwig was now determined to go forth like Abraham the Patriarch, 'clothed in the new strength and beauty of perfect wisdom', without fear for himself and without doubting the righteousness of his cause." (Melnick I: 75)

62   Ludwig Lewisohn, "The Return to Jerusalem", *The Nation* 119/3104 (December 31, 1924) 724.

63   Identified by Melnick as a statement made in a letter written by Lewisohn to Milton Steinberg, February 26, 1950.

64   Ludwig Lewisohn, *Holy Land, A Story* (New York: Harper & Brothers, 1926).

65   Ludwig Lewisohn, "Holy Land, A Story", *Harper's Magazine* (October 1925).

66   Stuart Pratt Sherman, *Americans* (New York: Charles Scribners, 1922) 22.

67   Ludwig Lewisohn, *The Case of Mr. Crump* (New York: Farrar, Strauss & Giroux, 1965) v. First Edition (Paris: Edward W. Titus, 1926); (New York: Henderson, 1930); (New York: Farrar Straus, 1947); (London: Bodley Head, 1948).

68   In a November 12, 1998 conversation with the present writer.

69   In a conversation with the present writer on December 2, 1998.

70   Walter Sutton, "Early Psychological Criticism", *Modern American Criticism* (Englewood Cliffs: Prentice Hall, 1963) 6.

71   Seymour Lainoff, *Ludwig Lewisohn* (Boston: Twayne Publications, 1982) 19.

72   Ludwig Lewisohn, ed., *A Modern Book of Criticism* (New York: The Modern Library, 1919) i.

73   Ludwig Lewisohn, *The Golden Vase* (Hamburg: The Albatross, 1932) 11.

74   Ludwig Lewisohn, *Cities and Men* (New York: Harper, 1927).

75   Martin Buber, *The Knowledge of Man*, ed. Maurice Friedman, trans. Maurice Friedman and Ronald Gregar Smith (London: George Allen & Unwin, 1965) 13.

76   Martin Buber, *Between Man and Man*, trans. Ronald Gregor Smith (Boston: Beacon Press, 1955) 140.

77   Martin Buber, *Jewish Mysticism and the Legends of Baalshem,* trans. and Foreword by Lucy Cohen (New York: Block Publishing, 1931) xii.

78   Ludwig Lewisohn, *The Island Within* (New York: Harper, 1928) 3.

79   Native German speakers like Lewisohn pronounce words that begin with a "J" as if it were a "Y". This is the reason for the (mis)spelling of the name "Yitzchack", which is a more appropriate English phonetic spelling of the

original Hebrew name than "Jitzock". One could infer from this that the German language was continuously closer to Ludwig Lewisohn's speech processing than English.

80   The *Mitnaggedim* opposed Hassidism on a number of grounds: (1) the general democratization of Judaism and its observance, by substituting millennia of Talmudic scholarship for unschooled piety; (2) a more flexible perception of when, how and where worshipers could pray; (3) a new method for slaughtering animals according to Jewish Law; (4) too much emphasis on fun and lighthearted behavior; (5) free use of alcohol; (6) an unpleasant similarity to the mystical movement of Shabbetai Tsevi (1636–1676), a pretender messiah who nearly single-handedly destroyed Judaism as it was known at that time — as Josef Kasteen relates, "Shabbateanism was the last major messianic movement in Jewish history and left a long and bitter legacy." (*Religion* 625); (7) the attribution of supernatural abilities, God-like attributes and worship of /to their Rebbes; (8) the ascendancy of curious ways of thinking; (9) finding God in both good and evil in the world, an idea which closely resembled pantheism. (*Religion* 473)

81   Even in Tel Aviv, the most cosmopolitan and secular city, there exists an active and well-attended Center for the Study of Kabbalah and Jewish Mysticism in the heart of the city, at Dizengoff Center.

82   In an interview with the present writer on January 3, 1997.

83   Ludwig Lewisohn, "Workers in Palestine", *The Nation* 123 (September 16, 1925) 301–302.

84   Ludwig Lewisohn, *What Is This Jewish Heritage?* (New York: B'nai B'rith Hillel Foundation, 1954) 2–3. Rev. ed. (New York: Schocken, 1964).

85   Arthur J. Lelyveld, "Ludwig Lewisohn: In Memoriam", *American Jewish Archives* xvii/2 (Nov. 1965), 109–110.

86   Elliot B. Gertel, "Visions of the American Jewish Messiah", *Judaism* 31/122 (Spring 1982) 153.

87   *Authorized Bible* has this passage translated as: "Then shalt thou cause the trumpet of the Jubilee to sound on the tenth day of the seventh month; on the Day of Atonement shall ye make the trumpet sound throughout all your land."

88   The word "trumpet" is found in *The Revelation to St. John* (*Authorized Bible*) 1:10: "I was in the Spirit on the Lord's Day, and I heard behind me a great voice as of a Trumpet." The same source states in 4:1: "...of a trumpet talking." In this usage and sense, the word "trumpet" is connected to revelation and the final Apocalypse. The earlier *Authorized Version* of 1611 omits the word "I" in this quotation.

89   John P. Muller and William J. Richardson, ed., *The Purloined Poe: Lacan, Derrida and Psychoanalytic Reading* (Baltimore: John Hopkins University Press, 1988) vii.

90   His name is an ambiguity in itself: Andrew is a Christian name, while Saracen

has Moslem connotations. In a historical context, the name can be associated with the Crusades.

91   See Melnick's *Life and Work of Ludwig Lewisohn* for detailed descriptions and discussions of Lewisohn's close relationship with his mother, Minna.

92   James Lewisohn, "My Father, Ludwig Lewisohn: A Personal Reminiscence", *Midstream1, A Monthly Jewish Review* XII/9 (November 1966) 48.

93   Quote from Ludwig Lewisohn, *The Answer; The Jew in the World: Past, Present and Future* (New York: Liveright, 1939) 341.

94   M. Merowitz, "Ludwig Lewisohn's Zionism", *The American Zionist* LXI/2 (October 1970) 38.

Chapter Three
Cynthia Ozick

Introduction

Ludwig Lewisohn and Cynthia Ozick, whose lives overlapped for some twenty-seven years, both represent examples of the so-called genre of Jewish-American writers. In a letter to the present writer, Ozick explains:

> My own connection to Lewisohn is, I'm afraid, nil. I once heard him speak at Brandeis [University, Massachusetts] (in 1952, I think) and, well before that, I had read *The Island Within*. Otherwise I know of no similarities or affinities.[95]

However, as this study attempts to demonstrate, "similarities or affinities" do exist between Lewisohn and Ozick in their lives and writing. The most basic affinity is in their cultural Jewishness, which—through the complexities and stages of aversion, denial, attraction, repulsion—deeply binds their common fate, characteristics, imagination, mind-set, cosmology. As well and to varying degrees, their lives and work were/are punctuated by the deep and undecipherable oriental dialectic, *pilpul*, that is an underlying part of Jewish thinking itself.

Of any Jewish-American writer alive today or in the recent past, Cynthia Ozick is considered to be the most vociferous, and perhaps the only, spokesperson of Jewish-Diaspora return to traditional Hebraic values. In a significant way, this could be said to be true. However, on the deepest interactive levels of language and cultural discourse, it is, if not blind, both a shortsighted and naively simplistic perception. In this same letter, Ozick continues by saying:

> I wonder if I might take the liberty of pointing you to the preface of *Metaphor and Memory*, one of my essay collections, in which I plead that my essays not be employed as interpretive instruments to be applied to my fiction. As a writer of fiction, I am utterly uninterested in sermons, tracts, polemics, moral positions, piety, and so forth. Lewisohn, as I understand, ended as a hot polemicist. A polemicist in a good cause [produces] a valuable critique; but a polemicist is not a literary artist.

Ozick's rhetoric discloses a number of interesting avenues of thought. First, she negates all facile solutions or definitions of personal selfhood in her art. Secondly, her comment at its heart exposes a dialectical message that is both elusive and paradoxical. To call her, in view of her essays, a polemicist for Jewish causes and Judaism itself, as her own comment suggests, is not to say that she is not an advocate for the Judaic enterprise. Rather like Lewisohn, Ozick, so enmeshed in the very thinking/ language structure of *pilpul*, Jewish dialectic itself (unlike the antithetically yoked dualism inherent in Western-Christian thinking), reveals a form of negation that is both a puzzling affirmation of its opposite, as well as the very essence of linguistic or metalinguistic subterfuge. On still another level, Ozick's mini-essaic plea to discount polemicism in her art can be no more true or no less false than her polemical essays that jeremically call for the return of Jews to their traditional cultural roots. All of the above possibilities may be, to some degree, both true and false in meaning as Derrida and *pilpul* understand the nature of language to be. Thus it falls into the open gaps of linguistic discourse.

On yet another level, Ozick as a polemicist points out that she cannot be considered to be, as many assert, ahead of her time as a spokesperson for Judaism. True, in her 1970's essayist voice she was on the American literary landscape as a lone, non-typologized Jewish Jeremiah, calling for a return to traditional Jewish values and Torah, and even assimilation— this time of Gentiles into the Judaic cosmology. In fact, Lewisohn, in his essayist voice, had done all of that five decades earlier in the 1920s, when even greater courage was needed in that pre-libertarian world.

In her 1971 essay, "Esau as Jacob", first published in *Commentary*, and later, in *Art & Ardor*, Ozick, musing over why a widely-read writer falls into literary oblivion, ambiguously or reproachfully, comments on Lewisohn:

> That a hitherto frolicsome entertainer-novelist is of Jewish origins is not very remarkable in itself—we have seen it once before, in Ludwig Lewisohn, who turned from the kind of fiction that made him a popular novelist (*The Case of Mr. Crump*) to the passionate tracts (the novel *The Island Within*, the lyrical prose essay called *Israel*) that returned him to obscurity.[96]

Ozick would seem to be saying here that Lewisohn, not having been a serious writer to begin with ("frolicsome entertainer-novelist"), merely perpetuated his literary "obscurity" after beginning to write didactical tracts. Also, she would seem to be contradicting her own assertions in a complexly spun web of ambiguity and contradiction. The depreciation of the Lewisohn-as-creative-novelist, that is, the artist adept at the art of fiction, goes hand in hand with depreciating the value of the Lewisohn who is, like one part of Ozick, the moralizing polemicist. Which part/s of whom and what is to be believed?

Indeed, like Lewisohn, Ozick herself could be considered a very feisty polemicist for Jewish return. Both writers address the issue of not only Jewish being, but also of being Jewish in America (with Lewisohn having directed much thought, as well, to Jewishness in Germany and Europe). Both can be said to distinguish between the ontology of Gentile versus Jewish beingness; the latter rooted in both the wider, cosmic rootedness of the historical covenant and promise.

Unlike Lewisohn, Ozick does not call for a return of Jews to Israel but for readers to return to the "covenant with God".[97] If Diaspora Jews desist from returning, they will disappear from literary history, if not from memory in general. Interestingly, like Lewisohn, Ozick sees the death of artistry in the death of one's (Jewish) identity. Literature-as-word is tied to both history as Word and self-history as authentic beinghood. Echoing Lewisohn's own words, she affirms that:

> Literature does not spring from the urge to Esperanto [universalism] but from the tribe…. The fact is that nothing thought or written in Diaspora has been able to last unless it has been centrally Jewish. If it is centrally Jewish it will last for Jews. If it is not centrally Jewish it will last neither for Jews nor for the host nations. ("America" 168–169)

Thus it would seem that history, or Jewish history, in and of itself is less important than a (Jewish) history bound to language, the text, the word, which is identical to the Word of God. This urge to create would seem to vie with God's greatness in creating the universe in the spirit of an impeccable morality, purity of vision, and absolute love for the created world. Ozick's deep sense of disquiet, as manifested in her discussions of idolatry, belie an urge to create not for the sake of Jewish history, morality or truth, but for the sake of creating in and of itself. In one essay, Ozick jeremiacally condemns Bloom for what she describes as "the perverse idolatry in which he has, in effect, a vested interest."[98] Substituting the word "idol" for that of "poem" as the latter word as found in Bloom's book,[99] Ozick declares:

A Jew is someone who shuns idols, who least of all would wish to become like Terach [the biblical Abraham's father who fashioned idols from stone] the maker of idols. A Jew—so Jews are taught to think—is like Abraham who sees through idols. But Bloom is both: he is both Terach and Abraham. He is a system-builder who is aware that a closed, internalized system is an idol, and that an idol, without power in itself, is nevertheless a perilous, indeed a sinister, taint in the world. ("Idol" 188)

There are, Ozick continues, four fundamental qualities of an idol. One is that it, as a self-enclosed scheme, has only itself as a point of reference, rendering it passive to God's created universe and humankind. An idol is similar to "a toy" or "a doll" and seduces humans to duplicate it, to be as it is. It sets up a dehumanizing process; it becomes "dead matter". The second quality is the inherent presumption that the idol pre-existed the one who shows devotion to it. It therefore reeks of authorial power and precedence. The third characteristic is that, because of its inertness, it "cannot imagine,... create or alter history." (190) The final quality Ozick describes as "the most universally repugnant," due to the fact that "the power of the (powerless) idol—i.e., the powerful imaginations of its devotees, can root out human pity." (190) Thus the catastrophe comes, as in Auschwitz, "when art is put in competition, like a god, with the Creator, it too is turned into an idol." (190–191) Ozick then blasts poets for being "dangerously strong imaginers, vampirishly living on the blood of earlier imaginers, from Moloch to Moloch [a Canaanite deity the worship of which employed child sacrifice]; no Jew ought to be a poet." (193)

Ozick's characterization of Harold Bloom fashions him as a cultural hermaphrodite. As she asserts: " Bloom, then, is a struggler between Terach and Abraham." (195) This is to say that Bloom, like the writer Ozick herself (and Lewisohn as well), is both a Biblical Terach, the father of Abraham who made idols (statues), and Abraham who was an idol-smasher, destroyer of such pagan objects. Thus Ozick derides a moral uncleanliness in Bloom which mixes unlike things into some new synthesis of being and attitude. This is, in fact, as this study asserts, the very essence of Ozick's notion of a "New Yiddish" which is itself an example of mixing the Jewish and non-Jewish, cultural alchemy, dialectic.

In the "Preface" to *Bloodshed and Three Novellas*, Ozick affirms her belief "that stories ought to judge and interpret the world."[100] American Jewish writers, she adds, have a very special problem: her generation is the first one since the liberation of the Israelites from Egyptian bondage that thinks speaks and writes completely in English, a Gentile language which is, by its nature, a language devoid "of the Jewish Idea". (*Bloodshed* 10) Thus all stories of Jewish writers written in English are, from the beginning, devoid of the Torah that naturally breathes through anything written in Hebrew. Her story, "Usurption (Other People's Stories)", (129–178) is posited on two essential questions: should Jewish-American writers writing in English "be storytellers" (10) at all, in the face of the Second Commandment's injunction against idolatry?

Believing in storytelling without redemption and healing constitutes idolatry; and this form of idolatry is a belief in magical forces. Telling stories, as she insists all writers are aware, is a type of magical performance, but The Muses, she continues, are a Greek concept, not Hebrew.

In "Innovation and Redemption: What Literature Means," she concludes that literature has to be part of a kind of cultural dialectical process:

> My conclusion is strange, and takes place on a darkling plain. Literature, to come into being at all, must call on the imagination; imagination is in fact the flesh and blood of literature, but at the same time imagination is the very force that struggles to snuff the redemptive corona. So a redemptive literature, a literature that interprets and decodes the world, beaten out for the sake of humanity, must wrestle with its own body, with its own life.... Cell battles cell.[101]

The idea is a kind of "Eucharist, wherein the common bread of language assumes the form of a god." (*Bloodshed* 11) Paradoxically, Ozick's story, "Usurption", is a story that stands opposed to the creation of stories; for the story points out that, although a story can be redeeming and moral, the writer's real primary, honest (and profane) first impulse is the exercise of his/her "wild" imagination, which the Second Commandment forbids. Thus the tension generated by writers who are also Jewish is predicated on a cosmological struggle between what Ozick refers to as the Greek/Hebrew, "Pan-Moses" conflict. However, as this study asserts, it is this strife that represents not a dualistic war of opposites, but the inherent paradox of *pilpul*; the lacework of intellectual gymnastics and artistry that accompanies the very way the cultural linguistic framework of Jewish thought/thinking manifests itself. In "Usurption", a Jewish poet's ghost prefers to be with the old cannibal gods of Canaanite idols over "the genius of Abraham and Moses." (11) The central Western belief system, Ozick asserts, has as its focal point "human sacrifice", which it offers as a virtue-filled norm. This is the same stuff that the lyrical—as opposed to the moral—imagination consists of. As Ozick rhetorically asks: "Why do we become what we most desire to contend with? Why do I, who dread the cannibal touch of story-making, lust after stories more and more and more? Why do demons choose to sink their hooves into black, black ink? As if ink were blood?" (12)

Ozick's essay on Virginia Woolf was written in response to Quentin Bell's biography of his aunt, Virginia Stephen Woolf, and relocates Ozick's Pan-Moses obsession into another context. Here, Ozick tells the story of the courtship, marriage and life of Virginia Stephen Woolf and her husband, Leonard Woolf. What Leonard lacked for her in his genetic/ social background and history, he made up for in his devotion to, and meticulous care of, her every physical and emotional need. As Ozick describes it, the Virginia Woolf that Bell recreates is not Virginia as writer or daughter of the very rich and well-placed Gentile-English Stephen family, but "about a madwoman and her nurse", Leonard Woolf.[102] For Bell, Leonard had no background of consequence, no lineage, no native habitat: "Cambridge was not natural to him, Bloomsbury was not natural to him, even England was not natural to him—not as an inheritance; he was a Jew. Quentin Bell has no 'authority' over Leonard Woolf, as he has over his aunt; Leonard is nowhere in the biographer's grip." ("Woolf" 31) In courting Virginia, Leonard didn't know and wasn't told that she was only intermittently sane. Her sister Vanessa and brother Adrian never gave Leonard a true, detailed and explicit account of Virginia's illness, or told him how deadly serious it was (since insanity ran in the Stephen family as well). (32) However, on the other side, as Ozick intimates, Leonard was led into the trap because of his desire to be more than his Jewishness: "'I was an outsider to this class, because, although I and my father before me belonged to the professional middle class, we had only recently struggled up into it from the stratum of Jewish shopkeepers. We had no roots in it.'" (33)

As Ozick points out, Leonard mistakenly thought that his only problem was his class—coming from the middle and not the upper class. In fact, he was blind to the fact that, *vis a vis* English society, being Jewish and upper-class was a contradiction in terms. In a letter to Virginia during their courtship, Leonard begs her "to love him." (33) Her answer, Ozick describes as "oddly analytical": (33) "'Of course, I feel angry sometimes at the strength of your desire. Possibly, your being Jewish comes in also at this point. You seem so foreign.'" (33) Ozick then relates another strange incident described by Bell. It was in 1935. Leonard and Virginia had travelled to Rome by automobile. Bell's reaction to this incident, as reported by Ozick, is that Leonard

> always thought of himself as wholly an Englishman.... "I was astonished then (I am astonished still)... that Leonard chose to travel by way of Germany." They were on German soil three days; near Bonn they encountered a Nazi demonstration but were unharmed, and entered Italy safely. What prompted Leonard Woolf to go into Germany in the very hour Jews were being abused there? Did he expect Nazi street hoodlums to distinguish between an English Jewish face and a German Jewish face? He carried with him—it was not needed, and in the event of street hooliganism would anyhow have been use-less—a protective letter from an official of the German embassy in London. More than that, he carried—in his "bones and brain and heart"—the designa-tion of Englishman. It was a test, not of the inherited fragment of spiritual steel, but of the strength of his exemption from that heritage. If Quentin Bell is twice astonished, it may be because he calculated the risk more closely than Leonard; or else he is not quite so persuaded of the Englishness of Leonard Woolf as is Leonard Woolf. (35)

In an essay on E. M. Forster's "Morgan and Maurice: A Fairy Tale", Ozick continues with her rubric of the Greek-Hebrew conflict through a recurrent Forster theme, homosexuality. Sprinkled through Ozick's work is a *leit motif* of homosexual, transsexual, nymphomaniacal and other types of behavior which she views not so much deviant in and of them-selves as Hellenic. For her, Hellenism perfectly describes the very nature of deviance from the norm, which is to say, Mosaic law. The icing on this Pan cake, for Ozick, is that Forster "remained... attached... to Christian morals."[103] Ozick's sense of both estrangement from America—Gentile America—and her great attraction to it, is explored in her discussion of Bernard Malamud's "Literary Black and Jews". For her, estrangement or its lack—no matter how "happy" one may be, living in America—is related to the degree of connectedness with American soil that one either feels or doesn't feel:

> Few Jews, even of the third or fourth generation, will recognize in themselves this sort of at-homeness with the land, whereas even urban Poles and Italians have land-memory to draw upon. What emerges... is a Gentile ease in America.... It is almost as if the Jew can do nothing but cultivate ideas.[104]

What it means to be Jewish generally, and Jewish in America specifi-cally, is explored in a broadsided but kindly attack on John Updike's

Bech. Ozick accuses Updike of portraying Jews as "a silliness sans comedy... empty data."[105] It's not that Updike's portrayal of Jews is false, she says, it's that his portrayal is not false enough. It is not unreal enough, which is to say not "imagined, mythically brought up into truthfulness." ("Bech" 121) The reason is that Updike's Gentileness causes him to turn the focus and scene of his book into an American Dantesque *Inferno*. (122) "Updike is our chief Dante: America is his heaven and hell.... It is as if he cannot *imagine* what a sacral Jew might be." (122) In any event, as Ozick explains in a long footnote, Updike has no notion of what "Jewish Peoplehood" means. (122) On another level, Ozick's deconstruction of Updike's deconstruction of Jews and American Jews can itself be deconstructed.

In truth, Ozick as an American writer of distinction who is also Jewish is criticizing Updike as an equal or even as, from her perspective, his superior. She is writing for Americans—Jews or Gentiles—in a language that is not only English but, more specifically, an American New York English: that is, first and foremost, a cultured Jewish, east-coast, Manhattan, American intellectual, post-Holocaust, European-Covenant Jewish history—a connected elite class of one, plus a relative handful of others. She, like Lewisohn, practically fits into no group, anywhere. She is on the American cultural literary scene, but not of American soil. Her Yiddish soul-roots are in the Russian Pale—but what Jew can have roots in the Russian Pale? Czarist Russia was only a place from which Jews wanted to escape. Her roots are certainly in Israel, but it is the Israel of Hebrew Scripture, not of the modern state that scorned her "Jewish dreaming",[106] her love for the present state of Israel notwithstanding. Her life is rooted in cultural dialectical contrasts and contradictions.

Ozick accuses Updike of "silliness" in his portrayal of American Jews, but Updike at least belongs somewhere. Ozick is always on the run and landless. From her soil, also, spring only ideas. If, as Ozick says, Bech is a Christian's perception of what a real Jew is, then what can be said of the Jewish soul that has no real home anywhere?

Ozick's only answer is to be forever watchful: "to be every moment in history, to keep history for breath and daily bread." ("Esau" 132) Ozick's characterization of Mark Harris, "born Finkelstein", (130) and main character Westrum in *The Goy*, are people who have never fully entered Jewish history. He is an amorphous chameleon of identity and culture. As Ozick says: "Cultural impersonation is an ancient artistic risk." (133) In fact, the essay's very title, "Esau as Jacob", restates the very same cultural dialectic in Ozick's personal and professional life and mind; and by extension, in those of her characters. It is difficult, she says in an untitled article, to be Jews

> just merely by being alive. This is the most exhausting and difficult thing. We can't fall asleep even for a split second. Gentiles can just be. I begin to feel irritation with so much emphasis on differentness, on marginality, on narrow dedication—on SURVIVAL—and a kind of easeful sloth invades me, and I want to slide off into every-ness and everyone-ness. It is not so much that I am lured by the Gentile world—this is for me by and large no longer true—as that I become worn out by the demands of thinking, thinking always about historical resonances, and by being always on the alert, and by always analyzing and judging, and interpreting according to Jewish valuations.[107]

Just as in the Biblical story, Jacob, wanting to steal Isaac's blessing from his twin brother Esau (the earliest prototype of non-Jewish values), pretended to their nearly blind father to be Esau, so they are an intact continuation of (what now in retrospect is) Jewish history, and are not a manifestation of rupture. At the end of her essay, Ozick significantly reminds us:

> And what makes *The Goy* such a societally pressing book is that it reflects with static precision a mentality we had thought the freedom of America—and certainly the advent of Israel—should now have wiped out: what the Shtetl used to call "fear of the *goy*". Harris retains that fear; though a child of America, he has not lost the tremor of suspicion that characterizes an immigrant five minutes out of steerage. It is a nervousness that is probably not atypical of any Jewish Americans; and it is hard to decide whether it is Jews or Gentiles who should be more ashamed by its presence. ("Esau" 137)

The Holocaust for Ozick is the greatest, most infamous monument to idolatry that the Gentile world has so far produced. It is the cannibalism of Moses by Pan. In one essay she harshly condemns it:

> The Holocaust—the burnt offering of the Jewish people in the furnace of the German Moloch—is an instance of aberration so gargantuan that it cannot leave wary nature (which understands its prerogatives and guards them against facile mutation) unshaken. Killing for the pangs of hunger, nature always celebrates; killing out of rage or fear or lust, nature often claims; but killing for Spirit, on behalf of death, nature abhors. It is for the sake of life that nature allows its creatures to become instruments of death. Jewish bone meal is a slur on a planet given over to life: a disorder that contradicts nature's means and calumniates its ends.[108]

In connection to it, and for the sake of memory, Jewish history and history itself, only "a morally responsible literature" has ethical permission to be written. The comment of one writer who told Ozick, as she relates, that "'For me, the Holocaust and a corncob are the same'", ("Innovation" 244) represents the mainstream of the Art-for-Art's-Sake Movement that comes down from Greek culture: "Art for its own sake, separated from the moral life." (245)

For Ozick, as she says here and elsewhere, art must be synonymous with moral living, for the stories we cherish are like Hassidic tales: they "touch on the redemptive." (245) This is to say that these tales teach and guide us to choose good over evil, "the singular idea that is the opposite of the Greek belief in fate; the idea that insists on the freedom to change one's life." (245) As well, and most importantly, the ability to change is predicated on the ability to make choices that can redeem us. A literature that redeems is one "that interprets and decodes the world, beaten out for the sake of humanity." (247) It must, like Jacob wrestling with the angel, "wrestle with its own body, with its own flesh and blood." (247)

The question for Ozick has been: how does Jacob make peace with Esau? How can, or should, Pan be joined with Moses? How can one resolve an insoluble dialectic? This is the conundrum that has always disturbed her.

Like Lewisohn, Ozick began her adult life with the totally absorbing mission to become a writer. As she describes in one of her essays on Henry James: "I felt myself betrayed by a Jamesian trickery. Trusting in James, believing... in the overtness of the Jamesian lesson, I chose Art."[109]

She didn't grow up in an assimilated house; her uncle was a well-known Israeli poet, her father was a scholar of Hebrew and wrote Hebrew prose; her grandmother, "Bobe",[110] read Hebrew Scriptural *Aggadah* to her as bedtime stories. Ozick spoke and learned Yiddish from her home; her grandmother took her to Hebrew school to learn when she was five-and-a-half. The family was Jewish by virtue of its closeness to its shtetl roots, but it was also very open to, and appreciative of, Western culture and art—which is to say that of the Hellenic-Christian world. Ozick's family, in short—although to a much lesser degree than the German cultural, elitist Lewisohns—succumbed to the same types of pitfalls, excesses, humiliations, feelings of inferiority and culture shocks that every Jewish immigrant family experienced in the painful and difficult process of absorption into American culture and society. As Joseph

Lowin describes, Ozick's family experience was that of immigrants in New York City:

> Her parents came to America from a more severe northern climate, the north-west region of Russia. Most important for an insight into Cynthia Ozick's temperament, they came from the *Litvak* (Lithuanian) Jewish tradition of that region. That is the tradition of skepticism, rationalism, and anti-mysticism, opposed to the exuberant emotionalism of the Hassidic community that flourished in the *Galitzianer* (Galician) portion of Eastern Europe. This information explains, perhaps, why the Hassidic rebbe in Ozick's story "Bloodshed" is such a reasonable man, almost a *Litvak*. Ozick herself, she does not tire of repeating, is a *mitnagged*, an opponent of mystic religion. In her stories, however, she wallows in mysticism.[111]

Although it was to a very Jewish New York that they came, it was nevertheless a secular Jewish New York. She was born there in 1928, just before the Great Depression that began with the 1929 Stock Market Crash. Cynthia Ozick, a first-generation American, interestingly led an extremely happy, peaceful and secure childhood and adolescence during the 1930s and '40s, through the Depression and while the Holocaust was ravaging the Jews of Europe.

At age 25 (Lewisohn had been 40), Ozick made a revolutionary and startling discovery about herself, life and her people: she found the work of Leo Baeck, whose book *Judaism and Christianity*,[112] and specifically the essay called "Romantic Religion", set her on the thematic and philosophical course that would dominate her life and work to this day. There are perennial echoes of Baeck in nearly everything she says or writes. Of him Ozick observes that he "is a consummate polemicist, but only once (though that once is a pinnacle), in his essay "Romantic Religion".[113]

Leo Baeck wrote from at least two perspectives. The first was as a scholar (and ordained rabbi) of Hebrew Scripture and its commentaries. The second was as a German-Jewish Holocaust survivor. This for Ozick was the bittersweet combination that could help her first to comprehend, then to construct, an edifice on which to build a new canon of Jewish-American writing. German-Jewish thinkers, and Baeck in particular, were seen as sacred voices able to understand and speak the language of the secular world, to be certifiably Jewish in surviving the Holocaust fires, with the added insights and knowledge to initiate in others a return to Covenant and wholeness. As Walter Kaufmann describes in his prefatory essay to Baeck's work:

When Leo Baeck died in 1956, he was widely hailed as one of the most saintly
men   of   our   time....
Baeck was equally at home in Aristotle and in the Talmud, in the Bible and in
German literature: He was the heir of the best the world could offer him—and
a rabbi. The way in which he fused this multifarious heritage was inimitably
his own....
In these men [Moses Mendelssohn and Leo Baeck] Judaism lost the narrowness of the ghetto and recovered the scope it had always had when it was
free—without ceasing to be Jewish. The major reason for the wide appeal of
these men and their impact was that they were not eclectics, nor primarily
apologists.
There was something serene and irenic about Baeck, and no man could have
been more polite than he could be. But he had fire and originality and was at
heart an iconoclast. (Baeck 3, 5)

Baeck, as Kaufmann relates, was a scholar with few peers. He had
command of four languages and painstakingly did his own research from
the original sources:

Baeck's erudition is never secondhand, never a matter of being able to cite
some dubious tract that comes in handy, never an abstrusely learned way of
saying what we knew anyway. He read the Hebrew Scriptures in Hebrew, the
New Testament and the Greek philosophers in Greek, Tertullian and Augustine and some of Luther in Latin, and of course German literature in German;
and instead of producing convenient but questionable excerpts, he used quotations that came to him from an intimate knowledge of the sources. Since he
always made his own translations, which occasionally involved new interpretations, the translations [into English, a language that Baeck didn't know] in
the present volume often had to deviate from the standard versions. (9)

Leo Baeck launches, in the essays that comprise this book, what
Kaufmann describes as "one of the most important polemics ever
launched against Christianity." (3) Baeck's focal idea is that Judaism is
not only not inferior to Christianity, but in fact its superior. In the book's
first essay, "The 'Son of Man'", Baeck examines this important concept,
indeed the one at the core of Hebrew-Christian polemics. The concept, he
says, typologized by Paul and the early Church from the *Book of Enoch*,
the *Fourth Book of Ezra* and the *Book of Ezekiel* among others, was used
in

the language and teachings of Judaism in the century before the destruction of
the second temple [as an] expression to designate the expected messiah....
Without exception, it designates man in general, as opposed either to God or
to the animals; it denotes the human race, the human kind. (23–24)

Ozick also studied the Hebraic concept of history, mystery and commandment from Baeck. There exists, Baeck states, a dual experience in the soul of every human being: that of "mystery and commandment", (173) which is to say that which is "real" (171) and that which is still to become actualized as real. At the heart of life is mystery, but how humanity lives in the world is "the revealed". (172) Humankind reveres the Creator as something that has no comparison in its enormity. The human being lives life in reality, in the "real", in time and space: this is to say in history. All is set within one total, ubiquitous whole of the Absolute Creator. As Baeck asserts in the essay, "Mystery and Commandment": "Not only the individual's life but history, too, receives its meaning from this. There is history because there is a unity of creation and future. Creation is unthinkable apart from a future." (179)

Equally important, Ozick was to understand from Baeck that Judaism is not a faith that stands separate from the world and reality. In one essay, Ozick explains what the Ordinary is as opposed to the Extraordinary. "And this is the chief vein and deepest point concerning the Ordinary: that it *does* deserve our gratitude. The Ordinary lets us live out our humanity."[114] Judaism fosters the sense of the social interconnectedness of life and human endeavour. Baeck and most of Ozick's characters grapple, in some degree in their personal lives, with the concept of the Ordinary. Its importance rests, as Ozick states, on the following: "For the sake of the honing of consciousness, for the sake of becoming sensitive, at every moment, *to* every moment, for the sake of making life as superlatively polished as the most sublime work of art, we ought to notice the Ordinary." ("Ordinary" 56–57)

Leo Baeck initiates his polemical critique of Christianity for what he describes as its romanticism, its "poetic imagination". (Baeck 53) He begins with an analysis of the Hebrew and Aramaic term, "son of man", the Hebrew *ben adam, bar enosh*. Christianity, he states, kept the same phrase but completely changed its significance. Thus, between the words appearing in the original and their typological form in the "Greek Gospels", the meaning was converted into something entirely foreign to Hebrew philosophy and thinking. As Baeck states, the term signifies generic man and not anything else. This conversion of the term's signification occurred, Baeck asserts, between the first two centuries C.E. when it changed from a simple, oft-used expression meaning humanity, to something "apocalyptic"; an "intensification of the [Hebraic] messianic idea into something supernatural." (32) In contrast, the Gospel is inseparable from the history of Judaism and is "a testimony of Jewish faith." (42)

The typological process from the Hebrew Word (the Bible) to its usurpation in the "New" form was, Baeck states, a reflection of the early (Pauline) Christian Church's thinking and "poetic imagination." (53) In typological renderings into the original word/words/form, new meanings are exchanged for the original ones; new significations are added, injected, converted into new subversions of traditionally understood words, phrases, terms. As Baeck describes, citing the Christian Bible,[115] a miracle-birth tale is inserted:

> The genealogy which is intended to exhibit Jesus as a *ben David*, a progeny of David, has been extended by Matthew back to Abraham to show Jesus as the heir of the promise made to Abraham. Luke even extends it back to Adam to let Jesus appear as a new Adam. Both ideas are Pauline. (104)

Paul's ideas, Baeck declares, were affected by the then-contemporary "mystery cults and creeds." (156) As Baeck explains, Paul's "background was that of the Jewish people. But his vision, and the certainty it gave him, received a new significance." (156) As such, there was created a dichotomy of the "classical religion" of Judaism, versus the "romantic religion" of Christianity. Baeck defines "romantic" using the words of Friedrich Schlegel, as the former applied it to the "romantic book": "'It is one which treats sentimental material in a phantastic form;'" (189) that is to say, the self-engrossed or opinion-based attitude which is steeped in anti-reason; a feeling or emotion that is set into an illusion of reality more akin to non-prophetic dreams or a feverish hallucination. Moreover, Baeck continues, romantic faith generates passivity in its believers. Paul's phrase "obedience of faith" invokes a duality of submissiveness and willfulness—the experience of Christianity's "immediate" transcendence, *versus* the mediated, indirect Hebraic one. The Christian romantic experience of faith created a split between the faithful and the faithless, and needed an "external authority" of the elect to lead the way:

> That kind of faith which is merely accepted remains purely passive. The only freedom which it can grant is that of moods and experiences, such romantic freedom as has wholly subordinated the individual's own aspiration and thinking, while seeking compensation in the consciousness of the finished man. (232)

Thus in the Church, "authorities" were needed and "created". There were, Baeck explains, two forms of authority: a hierarchical frame of priests in ascending levels of power and prestige, and a hierarchical system of dogma in the form of layered statements that are created to be accepted "on faith" and not through reasoning or logic:

> The dogma comprehends and grants the knowledge of faith, even as the priesthood with its sacraments possesses and dispenses the experiences of faith. Both of them embody, and transform into a body, an originally spiritual content of faith. If romanticism began by finding knowledge in such seizure and transport as come over man through meditation and ecstasy and let their waves close on him, now all this floating and flowing become condensed. Dogma is frozen feeling; clotted, petrified mood. Billowing knowledge becomes firm, tangible acknowledgment. (234)

Truth and falsehood thus receive significance and legitimacy from ecclesiastic authority and dogmatic doctrine, and must be followed on faith rather than through one's personal sense of "conscience", ethical responsibility, or reason. Christian dogma is to be accepted as received through obedient faithfulness. "Truth" becomes synonymous with the ecclesiastical truth; the "lie" is a digression from Church doctrines. "Religion" thereby replaces ethics and conscience.

Thus, for the sake of art and morality, humanity is enjoined to see, know and absorb the Ordinary. As well, when we absorb ourselves in the Ordinary, that lone moment does not preclude exclusion from the human world, humanity. As Baeck taught and Ozick echoes, the Jewish belief system is predicated on a societal community of human interchange. Ozick's Joseph Brill in *The Cannibal Galaxy*, Lars Andemening in *The Messiah of Stockholm*,[116] Ruth Puttermesser in the *Puttermesser Papers*,[117] Rosa in "The Shawl" and "Rosa"—the list is long: each one is a deformity of the human heart, thwarted or unable to connect with the consolation, support and interaction within the social frame of the material world. Each finds herself/himself alone in a solitude of thoughts that can never mesh with the reality of life as it is lived. Even more so, each is caught in a culturally dialectical quagmire: how to arrive at what is "true" within the ongoing conflict of opposing realities? Rosa's Warsaw life was amputated from her. In its place, in succession, was first the culture of the death camp with its barbed wire and black-booted message of perpetual nightmare; then Manhattan as a new immigrant-refugee of the

Holocaust, to be absorbed into yet another matrix which held no meaning for her; and finally, absurdly, Miami Beach, the place where retirees go to live out the last years of their lives.

In "Romantic Religion", Baeck distinguishes between two basic belief types: the classical and the romantic, with Judaism representing the former and Christianity the latter. Romantic religion creates myths out of fantasy. As Baeck asserts: Its world is the realm in which all rules are suspended; it is the world of the irregular; the extraordinary…, that world which lies beyond all reality." (Baeck 190) This world is, in short, the world of the German soul where all melts into feeling, and all events are just "moods". The world is totally subjective, and thinking is not separate from feeling. The romantic impulse thrives on ecstasy and rapture for its own sake. Even the highest delight is equal to "the deepest pain". The romantic "enjoys his wounds and the streaming blood of his heart." (190) More importantly, Romantic religion abhors law and everything "that legislates": all commandments and their morality. The Romantic religious worshipper "believes that he can become certain of himself only in self-contained feeling, in emotional self-contemplation." (193) This state of being, Baeck explains, only negates emotional expression. There is only self-introspection. The Romantic views the past as an "ideal", a time of perfection, and "does not want to create but to find again and restore." (194) Thus Rosa, Joseph Brill and the others prefer the dream—not of a Jewish future of hope and redemption—but of what belongs to the past or a self-created idea of the past. Ozick's characters are balanced between the Jewish life on the one hand, a present reality pointing to a hopeful time to come; and on the other hand the fantasy, solitude and "enthusiastic flight from reality" (196) that assimilation into the wider, more attractive Hellenic-Christian culture has to offer. The tragedy of Romantic religion and absorption into the cultural milieu it engenders is that "however much romanticism lives in the past and reexperiences it, it still cannot attain the idea of history as a power which makes demands on human life…. Romanticism does not know *Geschichte* living history, but only *Historie* dead history—a mere story." (217–218)

This story that Baeck tells of Christianity and Judaism would seem to be re-reflected in the stories Ozick tells of the tragic lives of Rosa, Brill and the others. Without history—or the overwhelming burden of history that one wishes so much to forget—there is a history of death. Truth lies somewhere outside of it all. Life is represented, as in Joseph Brill's "Dual Curriculum", as dogma and repetition. Joseph Brill recites the tenets of his "Dual Curriculum" like a catechism. It lacks any human connection, social dimension, truth or feeling. He lives a lie that he calls "truth". The human entity is hopeless and helpless. Guilt is unconnected to social and human interchanges. (245) In place of humane behavior by human to human, there is a religion of dogma, which is to say the mindless repetition of unconnected amoral behavior. Joseph Brill can treat Beaulah Lilt unkindly, inhumanely, because she doesn't fit into his dogmatically constructed educational schema. Like Joseph Brill, Rosa is the pure Baeckian romantic type. Her ideal is to be beyond everything. Wrapped in her dead child's shawl, she is solipsistic and passively so. She has relinquished her will to be. (276) As Baeck says:

> The hermit who is exclusively preoccupied with himself, and whose experience of activity in the human sphere is confined solely to the things which a man does for himself, can therefore be regarded here as the great representative of sacrifice and hence as a saint. He is truly the egoist of piety: he lives for himself. (279)

Baeck's ideas can be summarized as the following:
1. The institution of Christianity, as derived from (Greco-Gnostic) Pauline philosophy, faith-centered, romantic, is a religion which manifests itself in fantasy, supernaturalism, paganism, sentimentalism, predestination, Original Sin, and extremes of feeling.
2. Judaism, as classical religion, combines faith, which is to say, mystery, with commandment, law. Thus humankind must choose either to fulfill God's commandments through good acts in the world or to do evil.
3. Anything other than the direct worship of the Creator of the universe, without intermediaries, is idolatry. Thus the adoration of Jesus as a deity is idol worship.
4. Anti-semitism, as it has been manifested through the Holocaust, has its roots in official church doctrine.
5. The concept of history as the movement of time through past, present and future, is the very fabric of Hebrew Scripture. Thus memory (as past) and redemption (as future) are temporal directions we can imagine and recall in the present.

Ozick's fictive world is peopled with misfits, hermits, dreamers, idolators, assimilationists, universalists and Pan-worshippers. In spite of their ability to speak Yiddish, and having survived the Holocaust, they have nevertheless lost their Jewish cultural heritage. They have no memory, but the past is worshipped in their fantasy or ever really existed.

Before Rosa's death-camp existence, she was in a life steeped in Romantic culture, Gentile values and unreality. Ozick's characters maintain a fantasy of the ideal life of the past which is the opposite of an imagination of redemption that can envision the promised future. They have no hope because they have no imagination to envision what is their birthright. Not being in the "details", the "Ordinary" of life and everyday experience, they show adoration for some universalist ideal through which they will be what they could never be. Each, coming from the Holocaust fires of Europe and "Jewish" by cultural affinity and definition, longs for either a culture now lost or some dream of an ideal life. Each presently exists in a culture he/she refuses to be integrated into. Each lives the solitary life of Pan in rejection of Moses.

For Ozick, the creation of art and storytelling is probably the most perplexing and slippery conundrum with which she is forced to grapple. So enamored was she in her years "as" Henry James with "dreaming", making art, that she deserted her youth and life. As she has stated on numerous occasions, storytelling has always been an unavoidable compulsion—from an early age she knew that writing was her calling.

In relation to *Aggadah*, Ozick also takes Matthew Arnold to task for what she believes to be a misinformed duality he sees between Hellenism and Hebraism, as described in *Culture and Anarchy*. Arnold defined Hebraism incorrectly, she believes. Even

> that very phrase, "sweetness and light", as well as its halo of "aerial ease, clearness and radiancy", shows how much of Arnold's notion of Hellenism came from conventional Victorian idealization of Greek ideas and society. Plato is Greek, but there is little in Plato that is sweet. The mystery religions are Greek, and there is little in their obfuscations that casts light. And Arnold's definition of Hebraism is limited by his sense of the English Bible, surely a grand and vital service road, but hardly, for Jews, the main highway; moreover, it was the English Bible strained through the sieve of Puritanism. Nor did Arnold appear to have any inkling of the *Aggadah* side of Hebraism.[118]

There is one *Aggadah* which perfectly captures the spirit of Ozick's life and art, and the essence of cultural dialectic that permeates them. It is a Hassidic tale about the *Baal Shem Tov*, the creator of the Hassidic movement in Judaism, a story-within-a-story that begins exactly on the day that this great Hassidic master dies. As the final moment nears, all of his disciples are called to his side. Every one of them is given an individual and special task to accomplish in each one's

> lifetime. A few were dispatched to different masters; some were made into leaders; others were simply sent away without any special task. However, one of the Master's more treasured disciples was assigned an odd mission: The Master instructed Reb Jacob Joseph to spend his life as a wanderer, earning his livelihood as a storyteller. Hearing this, Reb Joseph was very frightened and shaken. The Master patiently explained to him that the purpose of this assignment was to bring healing to himself and the world. As a result of fulfilling this mission, the Master told Reb Joseph, he would become very famous and wealthy.[119]

Art as storytelling and the language it employs constitute a slippery adventure into ambiguity. Through *Aggadah*, the art of storytelling can be both a secular enterprise and the instrument for transforming and redeeming the world. The process of doing art, storytelling, is akin to moral mission.

In a conference paper delivered in 1970 at the annual American-Israeli Dialogue on Culture and the Arts (Weizmann Institute, Rehovot, Israel), Ozick begins by attacking George Steiner's address there two years earlier. The crux of her attack is that he had come "out of Diaspora to this place and offered Exile as a metaphor for the Essential Jew and himself as a metaphor of Exile. He came, he said, 'as a visitor.'" ("America" 264) Ozick, on the other hand, wants to make a distinction between the word "visitor"—which he was—and the word "pilgrim" as she described herself. In their coming to the Holy Land and leaving it, she says, they are exactly the same. However, whereas the visitor "arrives" and sees the sights as any tourist might, "a pilgrim is restored." The "visitor passes through a place" but "the place passes through the pilgrim." (264) For Ozick, Steiner has committed one of the unpardonable sins. Not only did he not ideologically feel and see Israel, Jerusalem, the Promised Land, as "his", but he first elevated his Exile into an ideology, characterizing it "as an arena for humankind's finest perceptions, free of 'lunatic parochialism' and finally—questionably—he concluded that to be most exiled is to be most exalted; that a sensibility most outside the commonality of Jews is most within the 'genius of Judaism.'" (264) For Steiner, Ozick says, "this is the very opposite of 'cultural disaster' since he perversely inverted the concept of outside to signify 'cultural opportunity.'" (264) Comparing himself to the cream of Jewish intellectuals, Steiner, Ozick says, believes that if Marx's body is entombed in Highgate, Freud's in Golders Green, and the ashes of Einstein are now somewhere on the coast of New Jersey, then why not revel in homelessness?

In another essay, Ozick, using Baeckian terminology, describes Steiner as "Romantic." Ozick discusses romantic excesses in relation to Steiner:

> He may seem momentarily Romantic in that special sense when he speaks of "Montaigne's tower, Kierkegaard's room, Nietzsche's clandestine peregrinations." But Steiner himself warns us not to mistake his meaning for mere Romanticism: "...one need not mouth romantic platitudes on art and infirmity, on genius and madness, on creativity and suffering, in order to suppose that absolute thought, the commitment of one's life to a gamble on transcendence, the destruction of domestic and social relations in the name of art and 'useless' speculation, *are* part of a phenomenology which is, in respect of the utilitarian, social norm, pathological."[120]

Ozick also criticizes Steiner for his romanticism regarding, as she describes it, "the necessary isolation and antisocial pathology of genius." ("Steiner's" 93) Ozick is unable to agree with Steiner's characterization "of the artist as a kind of shaman or holy figure, set apart from the tribe by special powers and magickings." (94) Rather, as this study maintains, the artist as synonymous with Jew is part of the tribe and thus part of the intercommunication of the humanity in that tribal group (of readers).

In phrases reminiscent of Lewisohn's description of the wealthy American-Jewish woman who invited to her mansion only those Jews who never associated with Jews, Ozick rails against what she sees as Steiner's ridiculous association of himself with all other homeless Jewish intellectuals. Indeed, the commonality of such a homelessness ironically made of them a parochially specifiable community whose identifiable common characteristics were (a) their Jewishness and (b) their comically perverse attempts to swim in the greater universe of humanity, which is to say, to be culturally assimilated. Lewisohn also railed against this tragic comedy of "enlightened" Jews, most especially his own parents. They are each, like Ozick's portrayal of Steiner in her quotation from his text, "'a wanderer, a *Luftmensch*.'" ("America" 264) Homelessness itself has become their home. They are "'marginal... unto the elements...

free.'" (264) This, Ozick says, paraphrasing Steiner, is what he believes being Jewish really means.

The Steiner Ozick portrays here is one of the familiar Jewish types whose very denial of themselves as Jews clearly and paradoxically distinguishes them as Jews. Both Lewisohn and Ozick minutely dissect this phenomenon of what could be termed self-erasure, or the syndrome of feeling, on some level, out of step with the (Gentile) environment around them.

Ozick speaks of a new Jewish fictional type called

> the liturgical novel [that] will not be didactic or prescriptive: on the contrary it will be aggadic [biblical storytelling], utterly free to invention, discourse, parable, experiment, enlightenment, profundity, humanity. ("Yiddish" 175)

As for Ozick, the Diaspora where she lives, works, raised her child and where, as she describes, "I shall undoubtedly will die,... is full of humps." ("America" 267) In describing her street in New Rochelle, New York, "and how I live in it, or do not live in it", she says that hers is "the Jewish house" among the Italian, Lithuanian, German ones. She is thus "marginal" and lacking a true sense of "liberation". She has, rather, "a worrisome buzz in back of my mind." (267) Cutting the grass around her house, she realizes that she "will not let myself love the clover too much", because even the clover can "deceive me." (267) Contrary to what Steiner asserts, Ozick states that Diaspora does not speak to her sense of universalism, and being marginal does not give her freedom. It does exactly the opposite: "It makes me tuck them [these marginal feelings] away when the neighbor's Stars-and-Stripes smothers his porch on Flag Day." (267–268) She wants to avoid having polemical discussions with her New Rochelle neighbors—to conserve her energy for her religion of art. She has to read and write quickly before the "American pogrom" comes: "How much time is there left? The rest of my life? One generation? Two?" (268) Jews are not shocked by this pessimistic attitude but will tell her that she exhibits "the craven ghetto mentality of the shtetl"—"'America is different.'" Perhaps it is, she implies. But what isn't different is the sameness of every universalist or Diaspora Jew "full of fear, masking as hope." (268) All American-born Jews, even leftist ones, identify the government as the enemy because they have the Czars of their grandfathers' bellies in their souls: "And so, like me, they dream old nightmares of the Czars—without knowing they dream these nightmares *because they are Jews*. My Russian-born father had a plain word to signify a certain brand of moral anaesthesia: *Amerikaneergeboren*." (268) Of her life in America, she asserts: "It seems to me we are ready to rethink ourselves in America now; to preserve ourselves by a new culture-making." ("Yiddish" 174)

Like Lewisohn in his battle with the Reform Jews of his time, Ozick asserts that the universalists pay "dues to the Reform Sunday School to promote the teachings of Jewish universalism." ("America" 269) The young Jews of America see themselves as romantics, "zany and strange", (269) but "they are only the de-Judaized shadows of their great-grandfathers in the Pale, whom they have excised from memory." (269) In Diaspora, Jews are either one extreme or another; either cowards or full of aggressive "revulsion". (269)

It is in keeping with Jewish ontology, as Baeck also pointed out, to jump or bathe in the pool of human reality with great passion and enthusiasm, and to not remain separate from it. In this Judaic cosmology, foundational are the sense of covenant, moral conduct and the commandment against creating idols. Therefore, to stay Jewish in Exile is to acknowledge that one is, in fact, in Exile. Jewish-American writers who acknowledge not just their Exile but also their Jewishness must, by definition, pay great passionate concern to humanity and all of its myriad levels of reality. Only the Greeks could contemplate "pure form", not the Jews. (273)

Every Jewish-American writer must understand "that nothing thought or written in Diaspora has ever been able to last unless it has been centrally Jewish." (275) By this, Ozick means "whatever touches on the liturgical… [which] is in command of the reciprocal moral imagination rather than of the isolated lyrical imagination." (276) Thus, in a 1986 article, she is able to distinguish between a bad imagination of romantic excesses and a "good" imagination of morality. In the latter, it is metaphor that links art to memory, pity and life. "I want to argue," she insists, "that metaphor is one of the chief agents of our moral nature, and that the more serious we are in life, the less we can do without it."[121]

Ozick, however, goes much farther than all of this, in first paradoxically praising and then proposing not just a benign American Diaspora, but in fact a "Jerusalem Displaced". This she calls "Yavneh"; to have a Jerusalem-in-America because American Jews have not ingathered to

Israel due to their "spiritual self-centeredness". ("America" 278) As she states: "Perhaps [it's] 'our destiny' [to be] in another place: that America shall, for a while, become Yavneh." (278) As she proposes, for the time being there should be two parts: a "Diaspora Israel and Jerusalem Israel", combined with the Jewish-American "makers of literature just now gathering strength in America." (279)

Realizing that this idea sounds like a ridiculous contradiction after what she had just said about the Diaspora, and also that this literature would be written in a "Gentile language", she proposes that American-Jews "learn to speak a new language" which she calls "New Yiddish". Why not, she muses? Finally, of all the Jews living in this world, nearly half of them live in America and speak English. Why haven't Jews ingathered to Israel? She answers that Jews are "in love with the American Idea"—and with America, because America loves them. Yet even after that is said, there is still something not quite right. A "cultural regeneration" can't be complete, just as Yiddish was the "temporary" language until the Diaspora disappeared and reappeared in Israel. Until that time, she must try to put the puzzle pieces together so that the image will be the face of America. How else could she expect to exist on her street in New Rochelle?

She also knows that she has to keep the bitter taste of "marginality" in her mouth, and to constantly fight to keep uppermost in her mind who she is. It is very difficult. Which other country in the history of the world ever loved Israel or accepted Jewish culture more than America? There is, however, a trap inherent in this acceptance, as well as a trap inherent in Ozick's explanation and rationale for all of it: as a writer who is driven to write for an audience in the English language, she is left with little choice. Irving Howe states that in the early twentieth century, the American idea of the "melting pot" was a favorite metaphor for minority cultures like the Jews. Everyone always knew "who would melt whom."[122] As Woodrow Wilson said in 1915, Howe reminds the reader: "'America does not consist of groups. A man who thinks of himself as belonging to a particular national group in America has not yet become American.'" (*World* 411) Therefore, the best Ozick can accomplish as a committed Diaspora Jew is what she relates in a 1975 essay, reporting an encounter between two writers, the Jewish American Saul Bellow and the Israeli Shai Agnon:

Agnon: "And have you been translated into Hebrew?"
Bellow: "Yes."
Agnon: "Good, then you are safe."[123]

In Ozick's 1978 essay, she summarizes the linchpins of her intellectual and aesthetic concerns: How can one stay connected to "human feelings"?[124] How can one retain his/her Jewish identity? How can the idolatry of the congregation members be remedied? How can any Diaspora Jew explain or justify life in Diaspora? ("Four" 21) One can also add another question: How can one be a writer and Jewish as well?

Cultural dialectic, so ambiguously decentered, puts all into question. The answer, if indeed there is a final definitive one, is yet another question: how far can dialectic, *pilpul*, be stretched until a Jewish writer ceases to be Jewish? The solution or rejoinder can be found imbedded somewhere in a story like "The Pagan Rabbi".

"The Pagan Rabbi"

The polemical issues at work in "The Pagan Rabbi" lack certitude and are therefore a challenge to examine and define. Ozick circumscribes, names and signifies her global, oft-pronounced Pan-Moses theme through the self-contradictory story title itself. The juxtaposed words, "pagan" and "rabbi", put the reader's anticipatory perception of the subject on alert. The message appears to be a duality of Hellenism and Judaism.

Building on this, the epigraph from the *Mishnah* (The "Oral Instruction" serving as the textual basis for Talmudic law and tradition), *The Ethics of the Fathers*, can be said to be within the story's frame. Serving as a kind of abstract of a philosophical essay, it is possible to see it as an encapsulating summary of the Rabbi Isaac Kornfeld story. The Mishnaic quotation, Josephine Z. Knopf says, is a miniaturized version of the story itself.[125] The Mishnaic passage reads: "'Rabbi Jacob said: 'He who is walking along and studying, but then breaks off to remark, "How lovely is that tree!" or "How beautiful is that fallow field!"—Scripture regards such a one as having hurt his own being.'"[126]

Through the incorporation and juxtaposition of the Mishnaic quotations within a new context (that is, Ozick's story, "The Pagan Rabbi"), and the story it describes about a Hellenizing Judaic scholar, Ozick thereby reinterprets/interprets the Mishnaic passage. In parallel, within its applied rabbinical and scholastic jurisdiction—specifically that of Rabbi Yehuda HaNasi and his interpretation's broadly based approval and implementation—Mishnaic (oral Law) interpretation, as Abraham Walfish and other Mishnaic scholars have observed, changed from "focusing not on the mere formulation of the Law, as in *Mishnah*, but on the *dialectical* and *hermeneutical* principles on which the Law is based." (*Religion* 472, emphasis added) Thus, the inclusion of a Mishnaic text itself, and Ozick's use of it in the service of her art, meet in the identical intersecting dialectic of Torah and Art, Moses and Pan.

This "chosen" Mishnaic text could appear to assert one truth, but because of its very open-endedness, any assertion is invariably and unceasingly undermined by the hermeneutical dialectic that is itself the very substance and open-ended methodology of the Mishnaic text that Ozick quotes. Thus, the "meaning" of the Mishnaic text that begins "The Pagan Rabbi", itself ambiguous, shifts its meaning (its meaning is always shifting) in its new contextual base in the Ozick story. The Mishnaic quotation would seem to maintain the dichotomous course of the story title. A Torah scholar "walking along... studying", suddenly stops to admire a tree of nature or an unplowed field. At face value, according to Scripture, this learned man has "hurt his...being"; he "breaks off" from his study of sacred Scripture to wonder at nature. It is also possible to understand that the Torah scholar could indeed have observed the beauty of nature *if* he had only first thanked the Creator for creating it. The words, "but then breaks off", could signify the possibility of a permitted transition from Torah to nature; the scholar, however "breaks off".

The word, "but", signals both textual contradiction and the effectiveness of a shift from Moses to Pan, Pan to Moses, bringing to bear Gertel's image of Rabbi Gamaliel, submerged, so to speak, in "Pan", but, in the core of his being, unchangeably "Moses". As Gertel implies, and as Avigdor Miller, Aubrey Rose, Marc Swetlitz and other Torah scholars state[127] regarding the concept of nature *vis a vis* Hebrew Scripture:

The concept of nature as a system operating according to fixed laws of its own derives from Greek philosophy rather than from the Bible. The biblical writers, while evincing an appreciation of the regular workings of the universe ([*Psalms*] 104 and 148), are nevertheless primarily concerned with the acts of the Creator and his permanent and direct responsibility for the cosmic order (...[*Psalms*]19). In fact, there is a natural order, but it exists not by itself but is owed to God's covenant with his creation (...[*Genesis*] 8.22 and...[*Jeremiah*]

31.34, 33.20, 33.25). The rabbis held a similar view: the regularity of natural
phenomenon was an expression of God's will, just as were "miracles". Some
medieval thinkers (e.g., Bahya ben Yosef ibn Paquda') held…that admitting the
existence of nature and an autonomous natural law was tantamount to denying
the sole and exclusive role of God's will and providence [and therefore a supreme sacrilege].… Whereas most traditional systems agreed that God was
'outside'—namely, 'above'—nature, some modern 'naturalistic' (that is,
antisupernaturalistic) doctrines take a different view.…[that is,] Spinoza's pantheism identified God with nature. The ancient rabbis and medieval thinkers
insisted that the contemplation of nature led to a recognition of God, and
Abraham is said by the Midrash to have become convinced of the existence of
God by speculating on the nature and origin of the universe. He therefore, possessed a natural religion, arrived at by natural theology, even before God
manifested himself to Abraham, and introduced him to the order of revealed
religion. (*Religion* 496)

Because of the uncommon relevance of the above quotation to the central
focus of this study—that of a Pan-Moses dialectic, not duality, which permeates Ozick's writing—it has been included here in its entirety from
biblical commentary sources. Nature with its varied and splendid beauty
is thus created by, separate from, subservient to, and a manifestation of,
God's love for His willfully created universe. As well, and most importantly, beholding and reflecting on the glory and loveliness of nature
could merely serve to confirm the existence and greatness of nature's
Creator. The quotation from *The Ethics of the Fathers*, representing a
group of signifiers that can be understood to represent "nature" or "God",
serves also to mirror (as macrocosm to microcosm) the beginning of the
Ozick narrative.

Relatedly, the story called "The Pagan Rabbi", like much of Ozick's
fiction, can be visualized as a story within a story within a story, to a
seeming infinity of smaller and smaller (or larger and larger) circles of
circumscribed tales about tales about tales. As Sheindel says to the narrator: "'I'll tell you a story.… A story about stories.'" ("Pagan" 13) Thus
the "first" paragraph of "The Pagan Rabbi" story frames itself beginning
with, "When…" contains the set of word-signifiers of nature (Pan) such
as: "Kornfeld", "brains", "hanged himself", "public", "park", "tree". The
second set of signifiers of "God" could be listed as "Isaac"/"piety". The
last name, Kornfeld, from the German, meaning literally "cornfield"[128]
parallels the words, "fallow field" in Ozick's chosen Mishnaic quotation.
The next word, "brains", points to the idea, as Sheindel expresses it:

"The more piety, the more skepticism. A religious man comprehends this. Superfluity, excess of custom, and superstition would climb like a choking vine on the Fence of the Law if skepticism did not continually hack them away to make freedom for purity." (25)

Moreover, the image itself of a "vine" climbing on the "fence" of Torah would appear also to suggest and mirror the difficulty inherent in maintaining a clean and clear separation between Pan and Moses. The (biblical) hermeneutical, spiralling-out process, allowing for a free flow of imaginative thinking and discourse about Torah, can at times exceed customary borders. Indeed, the greater and deeper the scholar's intellectual capacity, the more chance there is to go beyond the most liberal and creatively extended Halachic borders. The act of suicide and the image, "hanged himself", on its most literal level, flies in the face of Judaic thought and Scripture. In *Genesis* 9:5, [God says:] "With certainty, for taking a life, there will be a reckoning from me."[129] God will punish murder of any kind, even self-murder.

Sheindel tells the narrator that her husband "scaled the Fence of the Law." (24) Rabbi Kornfeld "scaled" the Law's Fence as he also "scaled" the tree. Ozick's imagery perpetually plays on an inseparable mesh of the worlds of nature and Torah. Another such image is in the narrator's desire "to see", and his subsequent act of journeying to the scene of the "crime", paralleling the quotation, "is walking along and studying", in its sense of motion and momentum to an unclear destination and for even a less clear reason. There is also the ironic ambiguity in the notion of Isaac killing himself using a tree *and* his prayer shawl in a public place, a park. This image would appear, in reverse, to reflect/inter-reflect, the original scene-story of God giving the Torah at Mt. Sinai—even after the abominable idolatrous transgression of the Golden Calf—and the community of Israelites receiving it. As the only people among all of God's nations to agree to accept God's Law, the Israelites stood alone at the foot of the mountain where Moses spoke "face to face" with the formless Creator, in the Sinai desert's awesome stillness. That great historical moment in Israel's history is in stark contrast to the image of Rabbi Isaac Kornfeld, alone in a public place of nature, swinging, from his prayer shawl, dead. Is he dead because he displaced, replaced, changed or forgot what that historic commitment of his people meant? What did the giving and receiving of the Torah signify as a historical process? Is Isaac's death the end of that process? As previously stated, the act of having hung himself, combined with the text as a whole, consciously or not opens up more questions than it answers. By the story's end, the reader does not feel a sense of finality and closure.

On the other side, the world of Moses, are the words, "Isaac", and "piety". The latter denotes the high degree of Torah dedication the narrator ascribes to Isaac. The biblical name, Isaac, in stark contrast to the rabbi's last name, invokes the sense of sacrifice fundamental to the biblical story. The name in Hebrew, *Yitzhak*, meaning "to laugh", derives from the delighted surprise of Sarah when, in her advanced years, God told her she would bear a son who would be heir to the covenantal promise God made with Abraham, his father. The biblical story of the Sacrifice of Isaac (*Genesis* 22:1–19) is a narration of Abraham's and Isaac's absolute faith in, and attention to, God's command to sacrifice the son he (Abraham) had waited so long to sire and whom he so dearly loved. The biblical Isaac, with full trust in God's word and command, and virtually no resistance or fear for his life, allowed himself to be tied to the altar on Mt. Moriah in readiness for his own sacrifice. This biblical story, also set in the still majesty of God's nature, finds human beings simultaneously torn, pulled and attracted: their personal lives, private feelings and thoughts poured through the sieve of transcendence.

Ozick's story of Isaac reflects the larger story. Like his biblical counterpart, Isaac Kornfeld is also a sacrifice. Perhaps he is a sacrificial lamb to Art, or serves as Ozick's warning (and God's) to not cross limits. As well, the narrator and his story function as a "double" to both the biblical Isaac and Ozick's Isaac. Ozick's story, as a reflection of the biblical one, resonates with the theme of fathers and sons threatened by, or threatening, disruption, discontinuity; or its opposite.

Another theme, that of voice/voicelessness, gauges the level of power/powerlessness that brings continuity/discontinuity. The narrator describes a visit from Isaac when the latter was in his ascendancy as Professor of Mishnaic studies:

> We sat under scarlet neon and Isaac told how my father could now not speak at all.
> "He keeps his vow," I said.
> "No, no, he's a sick man," Isaac said. "An obstruction in the throat."
> "I'm the obstruction. You know what he said when I left the seminary. He meant it, never mind how many years it is. He's never addressed a word to me since." (5)

Thus the narrative, as Horowitz asserts, "symbolically conflates darkness and muteness…linking voicelessness with hopelessness, moral emptiness, anguish, and death, and light with life, voice, truth, and agency."[130] When the narrator and his Gentile wife, Jane, go to the wedding of Isaac and Sheindel, the narrator describes the encounter there with his own father:

> I…covertly looked for my father. There he was, in a shadow, apart. My eyes discovered his eyes. He turned his back and gripped his throat.…
> "He doesn't speak to you."
> "A technicality. He's losing his voice." ("Pagan" 8)

Apparent here is the contrast between voicelessness, losing one's voice, speaking and storytelling.

The death of Isaac is the event that binds and brings focus to all the stories that intersect in the story, "The Pagan Rabbi". That death, as a kind of crime that needs solving, sets into motion a motif of "detectives and detection" in search of the "facts" related to a nearly-thirty-six year-old, creatively brilliant Professor of Mishnaic History and rabbi, a father of seven daughters, husband of an equally brilliant and beautiful wife; who had an orgiastic, ecstatic but brief love affair with a dryad, in the form of a tree on which he was found hanging by his prayer shawl, dead. The events, state of mind and thoughts leading up to that death are first vocalized in the stories Isaac tells his children at bedtime; then recorded in a notebook which Isaac destroys. What remains is a notebook and a letter summarizing what can be described as the dead rabbi's dialectical Pan-and-Moses arguments, questions, refutations, answers—in short, inextricably complex analyses brought down from himself, Torah, *Mishnah*, *Talmud*, Western philosophy, "the old man carrying heavy tractates" (his Jewish soul), Iripomonoeia (the dryad), and so forth. Thus the reader accompanies the narrator on a journey to detect and solve the mystery of the text, of himself, of Ozick, of Isaac; in the absence of any apparent sense of grief or remorse on the narrator's part for the untimely and (what would seem) tragic death of Isaac. After going out to visit the crime site, the narrator pays a visit to Isaac's widow, Sheindel:

> She returned. "My girls are all asleep, we can talk. What an ordeal for you, weather like this and going out so far to that place."
> It was impossible to tell whether she was angry or not. I had rushed in on her like the rainfall itself, scattering drops, my shoes stuck all over with leaves.

"I comprehend exactly why you went out there. The impulse of a detective,"
she said. Her voice contained an irony that surprised me. (10)

As a curious double for Isaac, the narrator has travelled a long distance
"to that place" even in weather "like this", as if to repeat or mirror Isaac's
own tracks, geographical or otherwise. The narrator, as though he were
Isaac himself, is not sure if Sheindel is angry with him. He knows she's
angry with her *husband*. She says: "He was a pagan." (22) The narrator,
as well, in some torrent of natural spontaneity has "rushed in on"
Sheindel as if he were something of nature, "the rainfall itself", with
leaves "stuck all over" his footwear. Ozick continues to mix inseparably
the elements of nature with that of the sacred, Pan with Moses. Sheindel
reads Isaac's "love letter" to the narrator:

"What follows is beautiful, I warn you."
"The man was a genius."
"Yes."
"Go on," I urged.
...
She read:.... "'I discovered thee. Loveliness, Loveliness.'"
...
"Is it hard for you?" But I asked with more eagerness than pity.
"I was that man's wife, he scaled the Fence of the Law. For this God pre-
served me from the electric fence [of the concentration camp]." (23–24)

Isaac's "art", inspired by "genius", is exquisite to hear but nevertheless
forbidden and pagan. Sheindel's life was saved, ironically, only to witness, as she sees it, her husband's descent into abominations. Paul
Theroux in his essay "On The Pagan Rabbi" says:

The rabbi is torn between scripture and sensuality, and his body, made light
and airy [he becomes disconnected from his Jewish soul] under Pan's influence, regards his soul (personified by a dusty old man with his nose stuck in a
book) as something futile. [The story]...can be seen as a serious philosophic
effort, but ultimately... fails, partly because it depends so much upon classical
fantasy, and mainly because it is insufficiently dramatized and unpersuasive as
a story.[131]

Theroux expresses disappointment with the story as a failed effort to
demonstrate, in dramatic terms, Isaac's either-or choice between covenant
and paganism; he both reiterates and, like others, falls prey to the generally monolithic critical canon that insists "The Pagan Rabbi" must be a

text of stark contrast-duality. In fact, he unwittingly underscores its greatest strength as an ambiguously complex tale of complex people hopelessly trying to separate the wheat from the chaff in the Pan-Moses conundrum.

Thus Sheindel's use of the words, "that place", both pinpoints and obfuscates: Has Isaac come full circle somehow? Has he fallen into abject abomination? Has he broken through, or out into, some yet-unheard-of artistically creative realm; and can this "art" bear witness to his past and the past of his people? The continuity and connection between the narrator and Isaac is fleshed out through the former's narrative description, which again seems to underscore the sense of added factual detail in order to solve some puzzle about the text. The narrator explains that he and Isaac had been not friends, but

> classmates in the rabbinical seminary. Our fathers were both rabbis. They were also friends, but only in a loose way of speaking: in actuality our fathers were enemies. They vied with one another in demonstration of charitableness in the copious glitter of their scholia, in the number of their adherents. ("Pagan" 3)

In the same way that the fathers were identical or "doubles" (both were rabbis, friends, enemies, charitable, competitive, biblical commentators and important rabbinical leaders with a following), so were their sons alike, even though they expressed certain aspects from opposite directions, so to speak. Both were rabbinical students—Isaac completed his studies but the narrator didn't. Ironically, like their renowned fathers, they both appeared to cross borders of decency, humility, kindness and/or Torah Law. They each appeared to have an attraction for Gentile-Greek thought, to the exclusion (so their fathers thought) of the Jewish Idea. Along with Torah studies, they read Greek and western philosophy, but each at a different point in their lives: the narrator did so much earlier, Isaac at the end of his life. Both fell prey to the *shiksah*, with that word's embedded message of release, freedom, choice, instincts, the natural, externality, the forbidden, excitement: the narrator chose Jane; Isaac chose a dryad, Iripomonoeia. The narrator, standing in the park where Isaac is found hanging from his prayer shawl, tells the reader: "I had none of Isaac's talent... and marveled that all that holy genius and intellectual surprise should in the end be raised no higher than the next-to-lowest limb of a delicate young oak." (4)

Isaac's talent notwithstanding, both men, at different points in their lives, nevertheless fell—as the image describes—to a low point in the expectations of their families, their Jewish lives, their people's history, and themselves. Even to the end, for example, Isaac seemed to believe that he could fuse the world of nymphs with his Jewish essence. To state it another way, he, as Gertel asserts in a related context, could be nothing else but the Jewish soul that he was anyway. In his conversation with the dryad, Isaac states:

> """My soul is free? Free entirely? And can be seen?"
> ...
> """Free. If I could pity any living thing under the sky I would pity you for the sight of your [Jewish] soul. I do not like it, it conjures against me."
> """My soul loves thee," I urged in all my triumph, "it is freed from the thousand-year grave!" I jumped up out of the ditch like a frog, my legs had no weight; but the dryad sulked in the ground, stroking her ugly violated eye. "Iripomonoeia, my soul will follow thee with thankfulness into eternity."
> """I would sooner be followed by the dirty fog. I do not like that soul of yours. It conjures against me. It denies me, it denies every spirit...it denies all our multiplicity, and all gods diversiform, it spites even Lord Pan, it is an enemy, and you, poor man, do not know your own soul. Go, look at it, there it is on the road.""" (34)

As in the Holocaust, when the Jews were so ironically reminded by their archenemies of their true identities, so the dryad sees Isaac as foreign, different, "an enemy" to her being and way of life. Although Isaac mimics the world of nature by jumping "like a frog", the dryad remains unconvinced, seeing him only as the "other". The dryad has told Isaac to look at his soul:

> "'I scudded back and forth under the moon.
> """Nothing, only a dusty old man trudging up there."
> """A quite ugly old man?"
> """Yes, that is all. My soul is not there."
> """With a matted beard and great fierce eyebrows?"
> """Yes, yes, one like that is walking on the road...."
> """And he reads as he goes?"
> """Yes, he reads as he goes.... His prayer shawl droops on his studious back. He reads the Law and breathes the dust and doesn't see the flowers and won't heed the cricket spitting in the field."
> ...
> """That," said the dryad, "is your soul.""" (34–35)

Isaac, aping the natural world, scuds to and fro in the moon's light, trying hard to be something he's not. Wanting to be of the world of Beauty, the soul of Isaac is, in reality, just "ugly" and "old". Mirroring the quotation from *The Ethics of the Fathers*, the dryad tells Isaac to look at his Jewish soul "walking" and studying as he walks. In reverse, Isaac's Jewish soul—the old man—either doesn't see, or refuses to see, the natural splendor around him, and thus does not "hurt his own being." The dryad tells Isaac to look at the old man walking down the road who refuses to "heed" the natural world around him. This is why she hates Isaac. For her, Isaac is merely the sum total of his soul.

The mirroring, reversing, reflecting and re-reflecting is further re-reflected in the scene of the narrator, as he stands in the park looking at the tree of Isaac's "crime" and thinks how it "looked curiously like a photograph—not only like that newspaper photograph I carried warmly in my pocket, which showed the field and its markers." (5) The photograph in his mind mirrors the newspaper photograph of the scene where he is now standing. It would thus seem to represent images, stories vocalized or written, and muteness or voice which give movement, context and flow to the stories that collectively are the story called "The Pagan Rabbi". Images as photographs interconnect fantasy and reality, romance and history, Pan and Moses. Thus, at the site of Isaac's death, the reader learns of the reflections of the narrator, who himself becomes part of an imaginary photograph tying fantasies of romance between himself and Sheindel, Isaac's widow:

> It seemed to me I was a man in a photograph standing next to a gray blur of a tree.... I ran that night to Sheindel herself.
> I loved her at once. I am speaking now of the first time I saw her, though I don't exclude the last. The last—the last together with Isaac—was soon after my divorce; at one stroke I left my wife and my cousin's fur business. (5)

Mirrorings, reflections, repeated images, and doublings reflect a myriad of levels, as this passage illustrates in microcosm. The narrator, divorcing himself from Pan, that is, a Gentile wife and the world of nature in his "cousin's fur business", runs to Sheindel, or Moses—but once there, he isn't sure why he came. In a related passage, the narrator describes a past conversation with Isaac about his wife, Jane:

> "And Jane?" Isaac asked finally.

> "Speaking of dead animals.... If you share a bed with a Puritan you'll come
> into it cold and you'll go out of it cold."
> He said nothing then. He knew I envied him his Sheindel and his luck. (6)

Ostensibly, Sheindel is, for Ozick, the most "kosher" of women: religiously observant and a Holocaust survivor. She is also a beauty. Unlike the narrator's account of his wife, Jane, and his sex life with "a Puritan" (which, ironically, warrants belief in "miracles"), Isaac instinctively didn't like the narrator's wife, calling "her a tall yellow straw." (7) The narrator contrasts each of the women he and Isaac married, and their respective fathers' reactions to

> my marriage, which [Isaac's] father regarded as his private triumph over my
> father, and which my father, in his public defeat, took as an occasion for de-
> claring me as one dead....
> I went with my wife to his wedding.
> ...
> Now Sheindel was dancing with Isaac's mother. All the ladies made a fence,
> and the bride, twirling...lost a shoe and fell against the long laughing row.
> The ladies lifted their glistening breasts in their lacy dresses and laughed....
> Sheindel danced without her shoe and the black river of her hair followed
> her. (6–8)

Like a mirror to the lusty scenes of Isaac with his dryad, the Jewish wedding scene reverberates with the biblical injunction "to be fruitful and multiply" in the natural lustiness of (Jewish) women in all their physicality; and becomes a foil and contrast for the coldness of Pan women as exemplified by the narrator's description of his conjugal bed. When the narrator and his Protestant wife, Jane, go to a Jewish wedding, they sit watching the guests dance:

> "Look, look, they don't dance together," Jane said.
> "Who?"
> "The men and the women. The bride and the groom."
> "Count the babies," I advised. "The Jews are also Puritans, but only in
> public." (7)

On another level of significance, the writer/narrator can be addressing the cultural dialectic in disclosing that in American society in general Jews are one cultural identity in private and another (Gentile mainstream one) in public. As well, in a subtly maneuvered logical association, the writer couples Hellenism with Christianity or, in Jane's cultural context,

Puritanism, in this contrast between the Mosaic life-involved lustiness of Sheindel and the Pan frigidity of Jane. In a twist of cultural perspective, the writer turns the commonly accepted (Christian) sense of Pan (paganism) as sexual licentiousness on its head. The reader is forced to reevaluate the meaning of Pan and to relocate its place in a Hebraic point of view.

In Hebraic philosophy, law and rabbinic commentary, especially Talmud, sexual activity between a male and a female (as husband and wife), occupies an important place. In the Talmudic section called *Ketubbah*, specifically the subsection "*Onah*", the sexual rights of males and females are meticulously outlined. A woman, for example, can be granted a divorce from her husband if he fails to fulfill her sexual needs. As David Biale explains, Judaism, like Islam, in contrast to Christianity, in no way values sexual abstinence. In addition, the *Tanach* is replete with scenes, references, and discussions about barrenness and fertility. (*Religion* 623) One of the central biblical commandments is "to be fruitful and multiply." (*Genesis* 1:28) There are strictly defined laws that define the lines between legal and illegal sexual activity (*Leviticus* 19–20) such as incest, adultery, homosexuality, sex with animals and with a woman who is menstruating. Biale comments that these prohibitions were probably associated with fears of reduced procreation as well as the moral repugnance involved with such acts. Sexually metaphoric images are commonly found throughout all of the sacred writings and commentaries, for example in the Israelites' relation with God. Idol worship is execrated as an adulterous act against the Almighty, (*Hosea* 1–2, *Ezra* 16) and God is often described as "a Jealous God."

In the late ancient period of widespread Hellenistic influence and assimilative practices, rabbinic authority began to view sex on more uncertain grounds, seeing it as a basic drive that could incur problems. Nevertheless, the rabbis generally concluded that constructively and positively directed sexuality was the most fundamental ingredient for life activity in its totality. The multitude of psychological, sociological and cultural dialectical agendas and issues brought to bear on the whole subject of personal and interpersonal sexuality are the basis of Sigmund Freud's revolutionary work. As it is stated in the Talmudic and rabbinical commentary, *Genesis Rabbah*: "Were it not for [sexual *yetzer ha-ra*] inclination, no man would build a home, marry a wife, or have children." (9:7)

The Kabbalists, who occupy a central role in Hassidic philosophy, "celebrated eroticism through their erotic theology." (*Religion* 623) The *Zohar* of the thirteenth century and the Kabbala are saturated with "powerful erotic images." Generally speaking, Biale continues:

> Mainstream rabbinic culture in the Middle Ages viewed a healthy sexual relationship between husband and wife as the primary protection against illicit relations and fantasies. Jewish popular culture and folklore also contain rich speculations about erotic matters. (623)

The Mosaic Sheindel is superior to the Gentile Jane in every way:

> Isaac had told me something of Sheindel.... Her birth was in a concentration camp, and they were about to throw her against the electrified fence when an army mobbed the gate; the current vanished from the terrible wires.... She had no mother to show for it afterward..., she had no father to show, but she had, extraordinarily, God to show—she was known to be, for her age and sex, astonishingly learned. ("Pagan" 7)

The world of Pan fractures, and has its own fence that also robs humans of their freedom and ability to express and act on their private interests, their lives as a totality. Pan's fence kills, annihilating the past and future together in one great swoop. Ozick creates a slippery interface of Pan and Moses, not as two distinct entities but almost complementary forces. There is God, but It is the God of nature; there are fences on both sides of the line between Pan and Moses; Isaac thinks he's truly Pan but the dryad hates him for his true Jewish soul; the narrator fantasizes about a Jewish life with Sheindel but has a sudden desire to run from her. There are many such paradoxical examples throughout "The Pagan Rabbi".

Ozick portrays Sheindel as a character in her own story. Moreover, Isaac and Sheindel are detectives in (a) potentially tragic, or potentially redemptive Jewish mystery story(ies). They attempt to reconstruct a factual past and the meanings they bear in their individual and collective lives. Two intermixed worlds loom in the balance. The world of Pan, in its pure form, is the world of nature; its most extreme manifestations for Ozick are in the Holocaust, the extermination of Jewish existence from the world's memory, and assimilation, the auto-extermination of Jewish existence from the world's memory. The world of Moses is manifest in Sheindel's and Isaac's wedding, which is itself a marriage of sensuality and the sacred, pointing to a future redemption and the issue of Jewish fertility in their seven daughters. The number seven is esoterically significant in numerous ways, most overtly in its relation to God's creation of the natural world in six days, reserving the seventh as a sabbath day, signifying separation of what is mundane from that which is holy. The mystery surrounding God, creation, and various symbols such as the number seven, is reflected in microcosm through the acts of detection that weave in and out of "The Pagan Rabbi".

There are as many levels and manifestations of detection, crime victims, crime perpetrators and mystery in Ozick's story, as there are difficult-to-discern distinctions or similarities between Pan and Moses. In these interwoven Pan-and-Moses realms is the first level of the narrator, Isaac, Sheindel, Jane and Ozick-as-character. Next comes that of the fathers (and mothers) and a dead Isaac. Following this is the level of the seven daughters; then come the (real) police investigating the mystery and crime. After that are the dryad, Iriponoeia, and Isaac's soul as the old man. There are, as well, other, transcendent players: Pan, Moses, God, Hebrew Scripture, Art, Nature, American (and English) literature, western philosophy, Sigmund Freud, the detective genre, Sherlock Holmes, and Edgar Allan Poe's detective prototype, Dupin.[132] Liahna Klenman Babener discusses Poe's use of "ratiocinatization", as employed in crime detection and the Freudian psychoanalytic deductive method, both of which flesh out the "structural unity" of the story. Besides the stylistic structuring of Poe's trilogy of stories of which "The Purloined Letter" is one, both Poe himself, as Babener sees it, and Babener herself admonish against forgetting that the story's detection-structure is not an end in itself, but masks a lower level to be discovered by the reader, which Babener, quoting Poe describes as "'an undercurrent of suggestion.'"[133] Babener's discussion of the double motif in Poe's work has interesting potential application for this Ozick story, and others of her stories as well. The use of this doubling process, Babener says, is highly excessive in Poe's trilogy of stories, in that its overuse is not essential to describe Dupin's investigatory methodology

> that stresses detection through psychological identification with an adversary. Rather, the prominent pattern of doubles suggests that the protagonist and his foil are moral duplicates and may ultimately be two phases of the same mind. (*Purloined* 323–324)

Even the purloined letter in Poe's story doubles on itself. The detective in "The Purloined Letter" must solve a binary conundrum: finding a solution to the crime of the letter(s) and dealing with (an) extremely shrewd thief (or thieves). More complexly, Babener suggests that "Poe's persistent duplication" may also represent two parts or the composite of one human being. As she concludes:

> Poe's persistent duplication suggests yet another possibility: that the two characters somehow constitute a single person.... All these factors then tend to interfuse the two figures into one singular character whole and point ultimately to the suggestion that the tale is, in its deepest implications, a study in the oneness of pursuer and pursued.... Further, the emphatic double pattern encourages the inference that Dupin and D___ may be brothers and suggests finally that the two may constitute a singular composite being. In this ultimate sense, then, the double becomes a metaphor for the variant phases—hunter and hunted—of the human mind. (332–333)

There are strong parallels between "The Pagan Rabbi" and "The Purloined Letter". A full discussion of these is not within the scope of this study, but only as it bears on the dialectic at work in Ozick's stories. Suffice to say that the various players and levels of Ozick's story both double and serve to represent, in their ability to ensnare, some aspect of the mysterious and the ambiguous. The reader, the writer, and any of the story's players are constantly entrapped, frustrated and subverted in their attempt at "analytical mastery". In her essay on Poe, Barbara Johnson[134] comments that it is not certain how many texts "The Purloined Letter" contains. Poe's Seneca epigraph, like Ozick's *The Ethics of the Fathers*, is also a text. As in Ozick, Poe's tale contains texts within texts. As Johnson states in her discussion of Poe's text and of Jacques Lacan's and Jacques Derrida's reading of each other's and Poe's text:

> A literary text that both analyzes itself and shows that it actually has neither a self nor any neutral metalanguage with which to do the analyzing calls out irresistibly for analysis. When that call is answered by two eminent French thinkers whose readings emit their own equally paradoxical call-to-analysis, the resulting triptych... places its would-be reader in a vertiginously insecure position.... It is the *act of analysis*... and the *act of analysis of the act of analysis* which in some way disrupts that centrality. In the resulting asymmetrical, abyssal structure, no analysis—including this one—can intervene without transforming and repeating other elements in the [unstable] sequence. The subversion of any possibility of a position of analytical mastery occurs in many ways.... Poe's story not only fits into a triptych of its own, but is riddled with a constant, peculiar kind of intertextuality.... In addition, an unusually high degree of apparent digressiveness characterizes these texts, to the point of making the reader wonder whether there is really any true subject matter there at all. (213–214)

Those critics who feel a sense of mastery over the meaning of "The Pagan Rabbi" are victims of the crime of Ozick's diversionary strategies, which constantly undermine even themselves. Any possibility of systematically exploring the route of the letter that has been purloined in the Poe story is consistently frustrated; so also with the texts in Ozick. The juggling of temporality in Ozick's story, for example, combined with the complicated profusion of texts, has to be questioned and seen as perhaps a strategy (deliberate or not) to confuse rather than clarify; and as a fence against perceiving Pan and Moses as pure and unmixed realms. The "true subject" of the Ozick text-of-many-texts is constantly deferred, lucidly demonstrating, in Johnson's words, "the fallacies inherent in any type of 'presentation' of a text." (214) All of the "letters" and texts Ozick presents in "The Pagan Rabbi" appear not to elucidate but to conceal. Letters and texts get waylaid, lost, misplaced, destroyed. The narrator in "The Pagan Rabbi" describes his reading of Isaac's notebook given to him by Sheindel:

> In my own room, a sparse place, with no ornaments but a few pretty stalks in pots, I did not delay and seized the notebook. It was a tiny affair, three inches by five, with ruled pages that opened on a coiled wire. I read searchingly, hoping for something not easily evident. Sheindel by her melancholy innuendo had made me believe that in these few sheets Isaac had revealed the reason for his suicide. But it was all a disappointment. There was not a word of any importance. After a while I concluded that, whatever her motives, Sheindel was playing with me again.... The handwriting was recognizable yet oddly formed, shaky and even senile, like that of a man outdoors and deskless whose scribbles in his palm or on his lifted knee or leaning on a bit of bark; and there was no doubt that the wrinkled leaves, with their ragged corners, had been in and out of someone's pocket. There was even a green stain straight across one of the quotations, as if the pad had slipped grassward and been trod on. ("Pagan" 15–16)

These "leaves" of the notebook are a code for writing and reflect the "leaves" as a code for nature, that stick to the narrator's shoes as he enters Sheindel's house. The profusion of detail describing the notebook only serves to conceal its contents. The narrator, feeling "cheated", represses his "anger" and returns the notebook to Sheindel. (17) The narrator, like all the others, is frustrated at every turn. As he stands next to the tree that Isaac was found hanging from, the narrator thinks to himself: "I would stand through eternity besides Isaac's guilt if I did not run." (5) What, the reader must ask, is the guilt, and who or what is/are the perpetrator(s) of the crime? Through the word, "besides", the reader understands that the narrator somehow shares in Isaac's crime. After carefully reading the notebook, the narrator finds in a handwriting more "deliberate and readily more legible than the rest,...three curious words: "'Great Pan lives.' That was all." (17) The narrator assigns these "three curious words" (17) to insignificance, and the reader is left to interpret Isaac's meaning.

However, more curious is the narrator's blindness to some kind of connection to Isaac's "message", since their lives have intersected in so many ways. Sheindel's role as one of the principal players is highly equivocal as well, although the reader has been given to assume that as a highly religious woman, born in a concentration camp, believing in God, now sorrowfully a widow, made into a rival by a dryad of nature named Iripomonoeia, her reference point in relation to Pan and Moses would be completely clear. Thus mystery surrounds her also. There is, for example, the curiously Poe-like statement of mystification spoken to the narrator: "[Sheindel] was waiting for me. 'I am sorry, there was a letter in the notebook, it had fallen out. I found it on the carpet after you left.'" (17) Beginning to read the letter together, they become absorbed by its brilliance; and as the narrator says of Isaac: "I saw that he was on the side of possibility: he was both sane and inspired. His intention was not to accumulate mystery but to dispel it." (23)

Isaac, it could be said, was an artist in search of worlds that were still to be created. At Isaac's funeral, "his teacher... said of him that his imagination was so remarkable he could concoct holiness out of the fine line of a serif." (4) Isaac's imagination was so fertile he could magically transform pure art into something sacred. As an artist—more specifically, a writer—Isaac's genius could transform the slightest mark of the pen into the purity of the holiest of hallowed texts. Isaac's artistic genius was so remarkable that the college president of the dead rabbi's *alma mater* "was criticized for having commented that although a suicide could not be buried in consecrated earth, whatever earth enclosed Isaac Kornfeld was *ipso facto* consecrated." (4)

In Ozick's complex rubric of imagination, the moral Moses and the amoral Pan, the fine line between paganism and obedience to Law, can be unwittingly crossed. Left unclear is whether Isaac's imagination was moral or not. His ability to "concoct" something holy out of the stroke of the pen of creative genius cannot be said to describe someone with a moral imagination. Ozick's choice of the word, "concoct", which denotes the fabrication of something out of nothing substantial to make it appear as if he had created something of substance (of Torah and Law), appears to put him in the paganizing danger zone. Nevertheless, before his death, he was "at the peak of his renown." (4) Was it his Torah scholarship that was responsible for his fame, or the creative free-play of his mind that could yoke ideas like no one else around him?

However, the college president, like the rest of the Jewish community, as the narrator says, "did not know the whole story". (4) The narrator tries to piece together the mystery of the Isaac story. As he stands at the site of Isaac's suicide he

> marveled that all that holy genius and intellectual surprise should in the end be raised no higher than the next-lowest-limb of a delicate young oak....almost alone in a long rough meadow, which sloped down to a bay filled with sickly clams and a bad smell.... And I knew what the smell meant: that cold brown water covered half the city's turds. (4)

It would seem to be a very unfitting place for a brilliant and creative Mishnaic scholar's life to end. Ozick again yokes the lowest physical plane with the loftiest spiritual-artistic one. In another context, the narrator in a conversation with Isaac says: "What chance did I have? A nincompoop and no *sitzfleish*. Now you, you could answer questions that weren't even invented yet. Then you invented them." (6) Since no one was in Isaac's league, there wasn't anyone to judge how far out on a dangerous limb Isaac was venturing, and see that he would not be able to descend from it. Sheindel had been fooled by her husband's intensity and creative brilliance:

> "I'm speaking of the beginning," said the widow. "Like you, wasn't I fooled? I was fooled. I was charmed. Going home with our baskets of berries and flowers, we were a romantic huddle. Isaac's stories on those nights were full of dark invention. May God preserve me, I even begged him to write them down." (13–14)

Sheindel did not realize that her husband had been gradually descending into the world of Pan. What seemed like something intimate and intact was in fact Isaac's excesses of romantic-emotional ecstasies. His ability to create gems of intellectual genius had fallen into an abyss of "dark invention". Isaac's fantastic virtuosity had crossed from the side of the moral, to the wild, imagination. Sheindel describes to the narrator the club Isaac belonged to which "met under the moon". She felt sorry for his inwardness and scholastic indoor life:

> "I was like you, I took what I heard, I heard it all and never followed. He resigned from the hikers [club] finally, and I believed all that strangeness was finished. He told me it was absurd to walk at such a pace, he was a teacher not an athlete. Then he began to write."
> "But he always wrote," I objected.
> "Not this way. What he wrote was only fairy tales. He kept at it and for a while he neglected everything else. It was the strangeness in another form."
> ...
> "Will you let me see them?"
> "Burned, all burned."
> "Isaac burned them?"
> "You don't think I did! I see what you think."
> It was true. I was marveling at her hatred. I supposed she was one of those born to dread imagination. (14)

Sheindel, however, appears to have had enough imagination to imagine God after the Holocaust. One might infer from the text that this capacity to imagine what is paradoxically unimaginable takes, perhaps, the greatest power of imagination. As stated, after being thrown against the wire in the concentration camp, Sheindel "had nothing to show for it afterward but a mark on her cheek like an asterisk", pointing "to certain dry footnotes [in her life]." (7) Sheindel is also marked as a writer. The writing glyph on her cheek, which signifies a past of discontinuity, could imply that only through art can a fractured past be reconnected and made whole again. Like Hester Pryne in Nathaniel Hawthorne's *The Scarlet Letter*, who is marked by the letter "A" like Sheindel's asterisk, we are pointed to a (moral) imagination and the force of God which help soothe, sustain and bring healing from a past of disruption. In contrast, Sheindel explains that Isaac destroyed the letters with fire, signifying either an end or a phoenix-like beginning. The image mirrors the burning and destruction of Jewish bodies in the Holocaust, which took an extraordinarily perverse human imagination to devise.

Continuously swinging or sliding between Pan and Moses, Ozick constructs for Isaac a treatise—contained in the letter Sheindel reads to the narrator—imaginatively connecting monotheism with "animism: '"I will leave aside the wholly plausible position of so-called animism within the concept of the One God. I will omit a historical illumination of its continuous but covert expression even within the Fence of the Law."'"" (20) Isaac propounds an animistic philosophy, polemically based on monotheism, for which Spinoza, the medieval philosopher, earned wholesale condemnation and excommunication from the Jewish world. The dryad, Iripomonoeia, who catches words literally in her hands, has caught Isaac's "call" and is responding to it. Isaac tells her:

> ""'I too called thee knowingly, not for perversity but for love of Nature."
> ""'I have caught men's words before as they talked of Nature, you are not the first.... So Corylylyb my cousin received it in a season not long ago coupling in a harbor with one of your kind, one called Spinoza."'" (32)

Isaac's imagination has taken its greatest leap in comparing God's fecundity to human invention: "'In God's fecundating Creation,'" Isaac states, "'there is no possibility of Idolatry, and therefore no possibility of committing this so-called abomination [of idolatrous paganism].'" (21) Isaac, from his rabbinical training in taking ideas into realms of imaginative new syntheses, is doing only what he was taught to do. His own creative genius, however, pushes him over the top. In their discussion after Isaac's death, the narrator asks:

> "Sheindel, Sheindel, what did you expect of him? He was a student, he sat and he thought, he was a Jew."
> She thrust her hands flat. "He was not."
> I could not reply....
> "I think he was never a Jew," she said. (12–13)

This debate between Sheindel and the narrator brings up one of Ozick's most painful and complicated puzzles of what exactly constitutes Jewishness. Her controversial interchange with George Steiner was over the latter's notion of Jewishness as universalism, which (so she said) greatly antagonized her sense of Jewishness as a particularist identity. Being Jewish, she says, represented the fragility of the human predicament, and thus had a paradoxically universalist application. As well, Holocaust-related work, or even fiction written by Jews, with its implied polarity of powerlessness and power, muteness and voice is often set within a trope of disruption and discontinuity. Often, as Sara R. Horowitz explains, writers employing this trope perceive their work as a type of enigmatic fictionality—as this study contends is the case with Ozick.

Thus there is a curious kind of make-believe aspect to it, given impetus through the frame of the creative process of making imaginative art:

> The trope of muteness predominant in Holocaust narratives of all sorts, functions in fiction deliberately and explicitly to raise and explore connections and disjunctures among fictional constructs, textual omissions, and historical events. (Horowitz 1–2)

There is, therefore, a quality of fictionality related to both the thinking process and the identity associated with that process. The idea of the private and the public—so fundamental to American literature—in Ozick's story finds itself in a dialectic of "indoors" and "outdoors". Isaac, speaking to the narrator, blames their fathers for not knowing "'how to love'" because their lives are lived "'too much indoors'". ("Pagan" 5) He becomes, however, his father's double, by first living life too much inside, but then totally reversing it to live completely outside. Both sides of the polarity result in disconnection from human involvement. As a kind of perpetuation of a generational deformity, Isaac

> "insisted on picnics. Each time we went farther and farther into the country. It was madness…. And he would look for special places—we couldn't settle just here or there, there had to be a brook or such-and-such a…little grove. And then, though he said it was all for the children's pleasure, he would leave them and go off alone and never come back until sunset, when everything was spilled and the air freezing and the babies crying." (13)

Ozick, through Isaac, plays out one of American literature's most basic struggles: the allegorical drama of the dark forest (or sea) of (romantic) imagination, in contrast to the restraining borders of civilization, reason and law. This, combined with a creative hermeneutics so fundamental to the reading and study of Hebrew Scripture, along with the idea of the Jew as an outsider to mainstream Gentile-American culture, could bring a character like Isaac to the border where sanity-insanity and artistic genius intersect. Thus Hawthorne's Hester Prynne and Ozick's Sheindel Kornfeld are contrasted with Arthur Dimmesdale and Isaac Kornfeld. The men, although winning the love, respect and admiration of their respective religious communities, nevertheless become isolated from that community through an imaginative brilliance that finally finds itself cut off from its past, present and future. Ozick's narrator speaks to Jane about his father:

"I was never cut out for a man of the cloth," I said. "My poor father doesn't see that....
[My father] lost [his voice] altogether the very week Isaac published his first remarkable collection of responsa. Isaac's father crowed like a rooster and packed his wife and himself off to the Holy Land to boast on Holy soil.... A surgeon cut my father's voice out." (8)

Ozick's repetition of the words, "cut out", yokes the superficial public life of a clergyman with the private powerlessness that accompanies it. The Pan-inspired image of the great Hebraic scholar crowing like a rooster, and boasting immodestly on holy soil, perpetuates the complex dialectic of Moses and Pan operating in this story. The images also serve to double for the tragic end of Isaac, and have within them the promise of an end to continuity and the hope of a future. Furthermore, Sheindel draws a parallel between her and her father, and Isaac and their seven daughters. Both Isaac and her own father used Law as an end, and not a means to living a modest and humane life. Isaac frightened his daughters with wildly imaginative stories of animals with human characteristics; of dancing mice, a talking cloud, "'a turtle that married a blade of withered grass,'" tearful legless stones; and most significantly "'of a tree that turned into a girl.'" (13) She then adds that her "'own father used to drill me every night in sacred recitation. It was a terrible childhood.'" (13) As Horowitz points out:

Holocaust fiction goes against the grain. In the ongoing critical discourse about the Holocaust and its representation, the status of imaginative literature as a serious venue for reflections about historical events comes repeatedly under question. Holocaust fiction is seen by many readers as—at best—a weaker, softer kind of testimony when compared to the rigors of history, or—at worst—a misleading, dangerous confusion of verisimilitude with reality. (Horowitz 1)

Like his father, Isaac cares less for the generations of the future than he does for excessive detective-like explorations into the deep wilderness of the imagination, which have carried him to places incompatible with real-life involvement. He becomes Ozick's dreaded imagination-for-its-own-sake artist; possessed (as Ozick feared for herself) by a demonic urge to create, no matter what harm it brings. Isaac's love-letter to the dryad, Iripomonoeia, is symptomatic of an imagination-turned-"abnormal", as the narrator characterizes it; and Sheindel states that her dead husband "had become aberrant in many ways." ("Pagan" 18)

In counterpoint, the narrator describes Sheindel's Mosaic humanness and heart, contrasting it with her frustrated attitude when he at first refuses to listen to Isaac's love-letter:

> She raised her eyes and watched me for the smallest space. Without any change in the posture of her supplicant head her laughter began; I have never since heard sounds like those—almost mouselike in density for fear of waking her sleeping daughters, but so rational in intent that it was like listening to astonished sanity rendered into a cackling fugue. She kept it up for a minute and then calmed herself. "Please sit where you are. Please pay attention. I will read the letter to you myself."
> She plucked the page from the table with an orderly gesture.... Her tone was cleansed by scorn. (19)

Sheindel's vocalizations that remind the narrator of a mouse—like Isaac's father's sounds of a proud cock announcing the brilliant achievement of his son—describe the relative feelings of defeat/powerlessness and triumph/ potency in two different states of dehumanization. In spite of being overcome by the narrator's blindness, deafness and dumbness to her husband's abandonment of sane limits of deportment, her vocal emission (in contrast to Isaac's lack of awareness of how his behavior could affect his seven daughters) is a result of wanting to protect her children. Her reasonable, caring, protecting attitude, her calm balance and ultimate humanity, shock him. She continues to be the exemplary figure of a wholesome, orderly, but also capacious imagination: a true survivor. After the Holocaust and the relatively early death of her parents, and without her husband and left to raise seven children alone, she remains intact. Never has she even wavered in her faith in God.

She begins to read him the letter: "'My ancestors were led out of Egypt by the hand of God,' she read." The narrator asks: "'Is this how a love letter starts out?'" (19) The letter would already appear to contain a number of assumptions. Firstly, Isaac accepts the concept of God as an understandable and indisputable fact. Secondly, he leaves unchallenged his historical ties to his people, the Israelites, and the sense of continuity it represents. Thirdly, the narrator's ambiguously stated question could also be interpreted as a reference to "a love letter" written to God and the Jewish people.

The solitariness and disconnection referred to earlier is manifested and felt by the fathers and sons in the story, shown in its most extreme case in Isaac, who broke through and crossed any and all borders of human-involved interaction. The conclusion is made clear: reclusion and "wild" imagination, creative genius notwithstanding, are the partners in the crimes against humanity, continuity, and a redemptive future. Significantly, Isaac can no longer see people in his imagination, only "creatures". "Earth," he says, "displays two categories of soul: the free and the indwelling. We human ones are cursed with the indwelling." (21) Therefore, the reader must conclude, Isaac no longer wants to be human:

> "'What is human history? What is our philosophy? What is our religion? None of these teaches us poor human ones that we are alone in the universe, and even without them we would know that we are not.... Innumerable forms exist and have come to our eyes.... It is easy to conclude that further forms are possible, that all forms are probable. God created the world not for Himself alone, or I would not now possess this consciousness with which I am enabled to address thee, Loveliness.'" (20)

Isaac's reference to "indwelling" mirrors the earlier statement he made to the narrator regarding fathers who, living excessively indoor lives, haven't the ability to be loving. (5) As well, Isaac's blindness to the fecundity and fullness of his own life shows that his own "indwelling" caused an inability in him to give and receive love. Interestingly, Isaac compares his first sight of the "creature" to his own daughter:

> "'Then I heard what I took to be the animal treading through the grass quite near my head, all cunningly; it withheld its breathing, then snored it out in a cautious and wisplike whirr that resembled a light wind through rushes. With a huge energy (my muscular force seemed to have increased) I leaped up in fear of my life; I had nothing to use for a weapon but—oh, laughable!—the pen I had been writing with in a little notebook I always carried about with me.... What I saw was not an animal but a girl no older than my oldest daughter, who was then fourteen.... All her sexual portion was wholly visible, as in any field flower. Aside from these express deviations, she was commandingly human in aspect, if unmistakably flowerlike. She was, in fact, the reverse of our hackneyed euphuism, as when we say that a young girl blooms like a flower—she, on the contrary, seemed a flower transfigured into the shape of the most stupendously lovely child I had ever seen.'" (30–31)

This quotation brings together many elements. Isaac is lying down or squatting animallike, with little apparent rational sanity left. He doesn't have the slightest expectation that a human form could be approaching him. This being makes nonhuman sounds that, with the strength of a madman in fear, caused Isaac to come to a standing position.

Significantly, as a true writer, his only weapon is his pen. The Lolita-like sexual fantasy he shamelessly associates with his own daughter, imagines a reversed-mirror double of human form. The sexual flowering ascribed to adolescent girls is literalized into the body of a creature that *is* a flower. Isaac's scintillatingly brilliant imagination, now without even a "fence" in sight, has become transformed into what common sense would call insane genius.

The demon of the imagination that has displaced and disenfranchised his soul—a situation that Ozick, remembering her twenty-two-year-old self bedevilled by her Master of Art, Henry James, could have great empathy for—is also the Pan world in the extreme that Ozick's work, on one level, can be said tacitly to presume to have created the Holocaust. Isaac is no longer able to imagine the daughter he sired, thinking of her only for her resemblance to the nonhuman creatures of the world of Pan. Like the monkish young artist Cynthia Ozick, Isaac is a displaced, lost soul, no longer in touch with the essence of what being human means. The imagination that could have been used to arrive at a redemptive future has now become transformed into the force of evil that annihilates all sense of humanity. The great creative genius that could have brought the worlds of Pan and Moses into perfect harmony has left life and the living, to find only death. Isaac expects now to find sustenance and life in a tree he imagines in the form a dryad he calls by the name, Iripomonoeia:

> "'with forehead flat on the tree, I embraced it with both arms to measure it.... A jubilation lightly carpeted my groin.... "Come, come," I called aloud to Nature. A wind blew a braid of excremental malodor into the heated air. "Come," I called, "couple with me as thou didst with Cadmus, Rhoecus, Tithonus, Endymion, and that King Numa Pompilius to whom thou didst give secrets. As Lilith comes without sign, so come thou. As the sons of God came to copulate with women, so now let a daughter of Shekhina, the Emanation, reveal herself to me, Nymph, come now, come now."'" (28–29)

Isaac's dilemma of Moses and Pan leads him to believe that in Pan he can find the ecstasy of the God of Moses, indeed God's *Shekhina,* which means "divine presence". Significantly the Shekhina is God's divine presence specifically in His creation of the natural world. As Joshua Abelson, Gershom Gerhard and other biblical scholars state:

At first sight shekhinah might be regarded as one of the many circumlocutions employed by the Talmud to avoid mentioning the name of God directly. Closer analysis, however, shows that the rabbis used the term in the more specific sense of the manifestation of the divine presence in the life of man or to express the principle of divine immanence in creation. (*Religion* 629)

Isaac also evokes Lilith, a name which occurs once in the Bible, probably that of a Sumerian goddess. This name, similar to the word for night in Hebrew, *lilah*, became associated with "a nocturnal spirit" and the first wife of Adam (before Eve), from whose womb all the demons of the world were born. Interestingly, Lilith is connected to a serial kind of narration of the ninth century called *Alphabet of Ben Sira*, which tells the story of this Lilith

[who] demanded equality with [Adam]. When he refused, she ran away and united with "the great demon". Three angels pursued her by God's command.... They let her go when she promised not to harm.... babies. Following this story, Lilith became a demon who harms babies and young children. She also began to appear as the sexual temptress of pious individuals.... In the kabbalistic system of R. Yitzak ben Ya'aqov ha Kohen of Castile.... Lilith is the spouse of Samael and the feminine counterpart of the Shekhinah in the system of evil powers. (*Religion* 421)

When Isaac's artistic and creative genius completely leaves the human realm, he becomes an evil conjurer with evil powers. Still possessed by his Jewish essence, after his sexual orgiastic ecstasy, he falls into a deep mortification of guilt and is shown his Jewish soul as it is walking on the road nearby:

"'My body sailed up to the road in a single hop. I alighted near the shape of the old man and demanded whether he were indeed the soul of Rabbi Isaac Kornfeld. He trembled but confessed. I asked if he intended to go with his books through the whole future without change, always with his Tractate in his hand, and he answered that he could do nothing else.

""""Nothing else! You, who I thought yearned for the earth! You, an immortal, free, and caring only to be bound to the Law!"

"'He held a dry arm fearfully before his face..., "Sir," he said, still quavering, "didn't you wish to see with your own eyes?"

""""I know your figure!" I shrieked. "....It is not mine! I will not have it be mine!"

""""If you had not contrived to be rid of me, I would have stayed with you till the end. The dryad, who does not exist, lies. It was not I who clung to her, but you, my body.""" ("Pagan" 35–36)

For better or for worse, Isaac is inextricably connected to that "old man". Paradoxically, Isaac believes that he has not just discovered the purest form of God in Nature, but has found the purest form of language in the dryad, Iripomonoeia. Her language, Isaac realizes, is totally physicalized, inseparable from the world of experience: a writer's ideal.

> "'Moreover, by experiment I soon learned that she was not only capable of language, but that she delighted in playing with it. This she literally could do—if I had distinguished her hands before anything else, it was because she had held them out to catch my first cry of awe. She either caught my words like balls or let them roll, or caught them and then darted off to throw them into the Inlet. I discovered that whenever I spoke I more or less pelted her; but she liked this, and told me ordinary human speech only tickled and amused whereas laughter, being highly plosive, was something of an assault. I then took care to pretend much solemnity, though I was light-headed with rapture. Her own "voice" I apprehended rather than heard—which she, unable to imagine how we human ones are prisoned in sensory perception, found hard to conceive. Her sentences came to me not as a series of differentiated frequencies but (impossible to develop this idea in language) as a diffused cloud of field fragrances.... All the same it was clear that whatever she said reached me in a shimmer of pellucid perfumes and I understood her meaning with an immediacy of glee and with none of the ambiguities and suspiciousness of motive that surround our human communication.'" (31)

Ozick's ambiguously stated comments on the art of communicating language leave many doors open and questions unanswered. Is the perfect transmission of language, as a flawlessly created enterprise, impossible to achieve without taking leave of humanity, the world, one's sanity? Is great art possible without Pan? Is great art possible with only Moses? Isaac, like perhaps some aspect of Ozick, does not like his Jewish soul's answer: that it was not Isaac's soul that clung to the dryad but just his body. Ironically, this sets the Jewish soul free to be Jewish and nothing else; but the creative spirit of the artist is compelled to imagine and make art. Somehow, the two must find balance and harmony within the same body—channelling, fencing in the imagination in the service of God, the omnipotent force over all of creation. Isaac, however, is ironically out of touch with the natural world that he worships and believes is a direct manifestation of the essence of God; disconnected from his life, the people who love and admire him; unable to create the great art his great imaginative genius promised.

Hopelessly bogged down in a messy dilemma he is unable to resolve between Pan and Moses, he dies in a scene that perfectly represents this

Pan-Moses dialectic. Unable to be rid of his Jewish soul, rejected by nature in the form of the dryad *because* of his Jewish soul, he seems on some level convinced that it robs him of his ability to be a free spirit. Yet he is ironically so free of borders he is unable to create great art. In the end Isaac is found with his Jewish soul in the form of his prayer shawl wrapped around his neck, hanging dead from a tree, in a meadow surrounded with dying creatures in an excrement-filled, stinking muddy (dead) ocean inlet.

Isaac is angry with the old man, his Jewish soul, for elevating Law above everything:

> "'At this nervy provocation—he more than any other knew my despair—I grabbed his prayer shawl by its tassels and whirled around him once or twice until I had unwrapped it from him altogether, and wound it on my own neck and in one bound came to the tree.
> "''Nymph!' I called to it.... "For pity of me, come, come.'
> "'But she does not come.
> "''Loveliness, come.'
> "'She does not come.
> "'Creature, see how I am coiled in the snail of this shawl as if in a leaf. I crouch to write my words. Let soul call thee lie, but body...
> "'...body...
> "'...fingers twist, knuckles dark as wood, tongue dries like grass, deeper now into silk...
> "'...silk of pod of shawl, knees wilt, knuckles wither, neck...'"
> Here the letter suddenly ended. (36–37)

The sudden conclusion of Isaac's letter nearly coincides with the ending of the Ozick story itself. Israel's singular relationship with the (Mosaic) Creator and Torah Law starkly compares with the image of a brilliant son-of-Israel's profound descent into Pan: from the heights of Sinai represented by the dead rabbi's brilliant Torah scholarship, to the depths of a Pan world that abhors the Covenant. All of this is signified by the story's final word, "excrement", with which "The Pagan Rabbi" closes its story frame.

In "The Pagan Rabbi" Rabbi Kornfeld stretches the imagination to its most dangerous limits, even beyond. His beautifully artful undulations, twists and turns, profound explorations and focus on Talmud and Jewish philosophy cannibalistically search out, find and devour even that which contradicts the very Jewishness of his intellectual and theosophical endeavors. His true being and truer strivings or compulsions are directed at language and thought, to a place beyond *Torah* (although that very *Torah* was his stepping stone) and Law. He betrays his people, God and history by becoming obsessed with the process of language and thought production through the vehicle of imagination, rather than subordinating his creativity to God.

In "Envy; or Yiddish in America", Ozick will explore another facet of cultural dialectic. There we shall find a juxtaposition of Gentile and Jewish being and culture through another type of Kornfeld figure, this time from the other side of the frame, who tries to fit, reconstruct, connect his too-Jewish being into that mix of cultural dialectic quirkiness that defines the writer.

"Envy; or Yiddish in America"

With the very title, Ozick throws down the story's gauntlet of dialectic, first asserting, then undermining. Like the words in another title, "The Pagan Rabbi", "Yiddish" and "America", would appear to negate each other. The conjunction "or"—signaling an alternative, even incertitude, vacillation, ambiguity, obscurity—leaves all doors open. The word, "Yiddish", like the title itself, bespeaks exile: banishment from certainty, identity, nation. Hebrew, on the other hand, is not the language of exile. It describes the sometimes difficult but nevertheless steadily flowing line of Judaic historicity from Mt. Sinai to contemporary Tel Aviv. Thus, *vis a vis* Jews, "Yiddish" as the exilic language finds a place of residence "in" the United States, the Jewish national homeland-in-exile.

More specifically, Yiddish (created from a mixture of Hebrew, East-European cultural elements and high German) is a contradictory blend for a deeply castigated people compressed within a paradoxically vibrant but extinct ghetto counter-life. As such, it finds its existence assured only in the more orderly, sterile, Gentile-transformed American version. The trick in this culturally dialectical sleight of hand is to be neither "Yid" nor "Yankee", and yet both Jewish and American. The state of being one and the other, but not either, creates a profound sense of displacement—a dislocation that is simultaneously emotional, mental, geographic and also linguistic.

The process of "telling the story" defers the end of the process and meaning. Like the Hebrew nation's patient waiting for the Messiah's arrival, the reader waits for the varying levels of dislocation to unwind themselves and uncover the message. Edelshtein, his life, especially his language of Yiddish, and the language which ostensibly is the subject matter on which the story focuses, are all dislocated. The story's opening words, "Edelshtein, an American for forty years",[135] gives, and then relinquishes, its claim to truth and meaning. Identification of nationality is from one's birthplace or adopted home. In truth, has Edelshtein been an American for forty years? What was he before these forty years? Even in the Ukraine, itself displaced by Russia and made part of the United Soviet Socialist Republic, Edelshtein was displaced. With a name that means "noble upper-class gentry", or "a gem",[136] and actually from Minsk, the young Edelshtein

> had been to Kiev, though, but only once, as a young boy. His father, a *melamed* [teacher], had traveled there on a tutoring job and had taken him along. In Kiev they lived in the cellar of a big house owned by rich Jews, the Kirilovs. They had been born Katz, but bribed an official in order to Russify their name. Every morning he and his father would go up a green staircase to the kitchen for a breakfast of coffee and stale bread and then into the school-room to teach *chumash* [Torah] to Alexei Kirilov, a red-cheeked little boy. The younger Edelshtein drilled him while his father dozed. What had become of Alexei Kirilov?.... Only Edelshtein's father was expected to call him Alexei—everyone else, including the young Edelshtein, said Avremeleh.... Today he was a citizen of the Soviet Union. Or was he finished, dead, in the ravine at Babi Yar?.... With his father he left Kiev in the spring and returned to Minsk. ("Envy" 41–42)

Actually from Minsk, Edelshtein and his father "lived" in Kiev in the big house of the Kirilovs. Born Jewish, the Katzes became the gentilized Kirilovs. The young student, whose name was "Avremelah", had to be called Alexei—but only by the *melamed*, Edelshtein's father. All the others could call him by his "real" name. Was Avremelah/Alexei's real identity connected to the Gentile or the Jewish world? Was it connected to both? Where was Avremelah-Alexei now? Was he a Russian, alive, or one of the Jewish corpses of the infamous massacre at Babi Yar, lying at the bottom of the ravine?

The *melamed* was the elder Edelshtein, but the younger one taught little Avremelah while his father napped. There is a constant

displacement of physical place, self, identity, role; an ever-shifting defer-
ment of meaning and truth. Perhaps most importantly, "the language was
lost, murdered." (42) Yiddish, generically standing for language itself,
has been mislaid, waylaid; it is missing from its place, displaced:

> The language—a museum. Of what other language can it be said that it died a
> sudden and definite death, in a given decade, on a given piece of soil?....
> Attrition, assimilation. Death by mystery not gas. The last Etruscan walks
> around inside some Sicilian. Western Civilization, that pod of muck, lingers
> on and on. The Sick Man of Europe with his big globe-head rotting but at
> home in bed. Yiddish, a littleness, a tiny light—oh little holy light!—dead,
> vanished. Perished. Sent into darkness. (42)

The exiled Jews, the wanderings through millennia of grief, made their
home in the Book, the Word of God. Without "place", their only comfort
and hope was in "the text". Yiddish, however, as the language of exile,
became exiled from its exile when the ghettos were emptied by emigration or force. Without the ghettos, Yiddish became an artifact in the
process of extinction, something to display. "Western Civilization"
(Ozick's code for pagan Gentilism/Pan) is the world of Nature's "pod of
muck"; the slimy, sick-clam-filled, bad-smelling, cold, brown, turd-filled
place where the brilliantly imaginative Rabbi Isaac Kornfeld met his
death.

Edelshtein, as the prototypical wandering Jew, is of no place, but
rather carries the entire universe in (or as) his very head, which rots at
home in bed. Those Ozick characters described as being in bed are never
there for sexual purposes or even sleep. Rather, they have become intellectually and creatively impotent human entities. With (his) language lost
or misplaced, Edelshtein's life and being have been rendered useless,
absurd. Edelshtein, who is himself both American and not American, and
therefore Jewish-American and not Jewish-American, hates Jewish-
American writers who are also both but neither—albeit in reverse
proportions. An American for 40 of his 67 years of life, he is European-
born and therefore culturally nobler than his *Amerikaner-geboren* Jewish
counterparts, who are like insects or amphibians of the natural world:
"Spawned in America, pogroms a rumor, *mamaloshen* [the Mother
Tongue, Yiddish] a stranger, history a vacuum." (41)

He hates them and envies them, these writers

> "of"—he said this with a snarl—"Jewish extraction." He found them puerile,
> vicious, pitiable, ignorant, contemptible, above all stupid.... Also many of

them were still young.... He was certain he did not envy them, but he read them like a sickness. They were reviewed and praised, and meanwhile they were considered Jews, and knew nothing. (41)

They are ignorant because of their immunity to the fires of Europe: their culture is really American. They can easily convert their Jewishness to a Gentilized version because they are not European. There is nothing that they have to suppress in themselves or hide. At the same time, because they are born of Jewish mothers, they are Jewish. They have the best of both, but not too much of either. Edelshtein can be neither: his Yiddish culture is a museum piece, and he has not mastered being American. Edelshtein is displaced, out-of-place. There is also a third side to the dislocation:

> There was even a body of Gentile writers in reaction, beginning to show familiarly whetted teeth: the Jewish Intellectual Establishment was misrepresenting American letters, coloring it with an alien dye, taking it over, and so forth. Like Berlin and Vienna in the twenties. *"Judenrein ist Kulturrein"* [being clean of Jews is a clean culture] was Edelshtein's opinion. Take away the Jews and where, O so-called Western Civilization, is your literary culture? (41)

Just as Edelshtein wants to keep the (Yiddish) language pure, its real (Jewish) essence intact, so does the Gentile monolith desire to maintain the cultural homogeneity of American letters. However, Edelshtein carries the universe in/as his head, which is to say that Jewish consciousness is the Western world's consciousness. Western culture is generated, in large measure, by Jews. Without Jews where would the Western culture be? At the same time, Eastern Civilization is both fundamentally Hebraic and yet isn't. Everything is simultaneously in its place and missing from its place.

Ozick ventures here not just into the abyss of linguistic authority. Who is master over the word/Word; who controls meaning? Whose Book/book will dominate? The battle is also cultural, Jewish contrasted with Gentile: will the pure Hebrew word transcend the mucky, lower-world, Pan-Western one?

> [The death of Yiddish] was... was Edelshtein's subject. On this subject he lectured for a living. He swallowed scraps. Synagogues, community centers, labor unions underpaid him to suck on the bones of the dead. Smoke. He traveled from borough to borough, suburb to suburb, mourning in English the death of Yiddish.... They wanted jokes about weddings... and he gave them funerals.

> To speak of Yiddish was to preside over a funeral. He was a rabbi who had survived his whole congregation. Those for whom his tongue was no riddle were specters. (42–44)

Edelshtein must believe that his language (Yiddish) has significance and lives; but hardly anyone understands him, or wants to. Those who can and do are all ghosts, that is, dead. His language died in a holocaust of flame. Ironically, he needs to keep the memory of this holocaust alive, in order to eke out a living for himself, and because it is his past. His language, however, finds no ears that can render meaning from it:

> Sometimes he tried to read one or two of his poems. At the first Yiddish word the painted old ladies of the Reform Temples would begin to titter from shame, as at a stand-up television comedian. Orthodox and conservative men fell instantly asleep. So he reconsidered and told jokes. (43)

His jokes, of course, are about language:

> Before the war there was held a great International Esperanto Convention. It met in Geneva. Esperanto scholars, doctors of letters, learned men came from all over the world to deliver papers on the genesis, syntax, and functionalism of Esperanto. Some spoke of the social value of an international language, others of its beauty. Every nation on earth was represented among the lecturers. All the papers were given in Esperanto. Finally the meeting was concluded, and the tired great men wandered companionably along the corridors, where at last they began to converse casually among themselves in their international language [Yiddish]: *"Nu, vos macht a yid?"* [So, how is my Jewish brother doing?[137]] (43)

In "The Pagan Rabbi", Isaac discovers in his dryad an ability for perfectly rendering language into meaning, free of the flawed intrusion of inept human expression or studied invention; a universal tongue that was at once the most sexual but also an intellectual and artistic experience; in short, a language that is an flawless act of creation, not heard or seen but somehow apprehended. Like Isaac, Edelshtein is searching for that perfect communicative connection. Yiddish is that language, formed from the soul of one thousand years of European Jewish ghetto life. In Edelshtein's joke, Yiddish, as the truly creative communicative channel, displaces the concocted language of Esperanto. In the slippery dialectic that is language, all things are possible; everything is turned bottoms-up and upside-down. After one such talk he gave, he fell asleep in the train on the way home:

He dreamed he was in Kiev, with his father. He looked through the open schoolroom door at the smoking cheeks of Alexei Kirilov, eight years old. "Avremelech," he called, "Avremelech, *kum tsu mir, lebst ts' geshtorben?*" ["Avremelech, come to me, are you alive or dead?"] He heard himself yelling in English: "Thou shalt see my asshole!" A belch woke him to hot fear. He was afraid he might be, unknown to himself all his life long, a secret pederast. (44)

Edelshtein has begun to suspect himself of linguistic, moral, cultural, and now carnal, perversity. The world is reversed: the dead don't stay dead, and the living don't live. Edelshtein dreams of a universe of Yiddish in the language of English. He loathes the plastic, empty Jewish places of worship he is used to identifying by their Yiddish term:

The new Temples scared Edelshtein. He was afraid to use the word *shul* in these places—inside, vast mock-bronze Tablets [of the Ten Commandments], mobiles of outstretched hands rotating on a motor.... Everything smelled of wet plaster. Everything was new.... He read Scripture riveted on in letters fashioned from 14-karat gold molds: "And thou shalt see My back; but My face shall not be seen." (44)

It is forbidden "to view" the unspeakable, ethereal manifestations of God, His frontal presence so to speak. He can be "viewed" only from behind. Edelshtein even reverses this Scriptural inscription in a dream in which it is reapplied to a fantasy of caressing Avremelech from behind. The image of the Holy of Holies' "face" turned sodomizer's face, framed by that of the rectum's opening, that is, to "see my back", is welded into a new commandment of unholiness. Jewish-Gentile, life-death, holiness-unholiness incessantly reverse, melt into each other. In all of it, language is the key that opens the door to another enigma, behind which is an infinite regression—or progression—of enigmatic dialectic: "Later that night he spoke in Mount Vernon, and in the marble lobby afterward he heard an adolescent girl mimic his inflections. It amazed him: often he forgot he had an accent." (44)

Edelshtein is a monument to a dead world in which, as in the apartment of his friends the Baumzweigs, "lives had passed through... and were gone." (45) Like those lives of parents who float through Ozick's stories "Rosa", "The Pagan Rabbi", *The Cannibal Galaxy* and "The Shawl", for reasons of muteness, death, or some generalized sense of dislocation, the Baumzweigs' lives are unable to express what must be expressed, and reach a dead end:

Watching Baumzweig and his wife—gray-eyed, sluggish, with a plump Polish nose—it came to him that at this age, his and theirs, it was the same having children or not having them. Baumzweig had two sons, one married and a professor at San Diego, the other at Stanford, not yet thirty, in love with his car. The San Diego son had a son. Sometimes it seemed that it must be in deference to his [Edelshtein's] childlessness that Baumzweig and his wife pretended detachment from their offspring. The grandson's photo—a fat-lipped blond child of three or so—was wedged between two wine glasses on top of the china closet. But then it became plain that they could not imagine the lives of their children. Nor could the children imagine their lives. The parents were too helpless to explain, the sons were too impatient to explain. So they had given each other up to a common muteness. In that apartment [these sons] had grown up answering in English the Yiddish of their parents. Mutes. Mutations. (45)

The reference the narrator makes to Edelshtein's "childlessness" underscores a highly sensitive point in Jewish life and philosophy, for the state of never having produced a child is considered in Judaic thought to be "the greatest of misfortunes". There are many Biblical examples of the sense of grief and loss from this lack of progeny. Abraham cried out to God: "My Lord God, what will You give me knowing that I go childless?" (*Genesis* 15:2) Or there is Rachel's sorrow over her barrenness:

And when Rahel saw that she did not bear Yakov any children she was jealous of her sister [Leah]; and she said, Give me children or I will die. And Yakov had a burning anger against Rahel: and he said, Am I in God's place, who has withheld fruit of the womb from you? (*Genesis* 30:2–3)

Barrenness aside, as with the respective fathers of "The Pagan Rabbi" narrator and Isaac, Rosa and Stella, Rosa and Magda, Persky and his son (in "Rosa"), the failure of language to form and preserve human ties and history reinforces the cultural, emotional, physical, psychic, linguistic dislocation of the characters. This is set against both the necessity and/or absurdity of historical continuity-discontinuity. The "immune" teenage girl who mimics Edelshtein's Yiddish accent puts her finger on the cultural, emotional, physical and linguistic displacement that Edelshtein represents and feels. Muteness as the Derridean difference in human language, the great yawn of *Yahweh* nothingness, just serves to punctuate the long crescendos of meaningless chatter, imperfect talk, imprecise language and chameleon dialectic:

Baumzweig had a good job, a sinecure, a pension in disguise, with an office, a part-time secretary, a typewriter with Hebrew characters, ten to three hours. In 1910 a laxative manufacturer—a philanthropist—had founded an organization called the Yiddish-American Alliance for Letters and Social Progress. The original illustrious members were all dead... but there was a trust providing for the group's continuation, and enough money to pay for a biannual periodical in Yiddish. Baumzweig was the editor of this, but of the Alliance nothing was left, only some crumbling brown snapshots of Jews in derbies. His salary check came from the laxative manufacturer's grandson—a Republican politician, an Episcopalian. The name of the celebrated product was LUKEWARM: it was advertised as delightful to children when dissolved in lukewarm cocoa. The name of the obscure periodical was *Bitterer Yam*, Bitter Sea, but it had so few subscribers that Baumzweig's wife called it Invisible Ink. In it Baumzweig published much of his own poetry and a little of Edelshtein's. Baumzweig wrote mostly of Death. Edelshtein mostly of Love. They were both sentimentalists. They did not like each other; though they were close friends. (45–46)

Every claim to truth is constantly replaced and undermined by a counter-claim to another truth. Interestingly, the publication devoted to a language of/in exile is produced in an office that has a "typing" instrument for Hebrew, which is in fact the alphabet used to communicate the Yiddish language. It can be inferred that a Hebrew "typer", from which the exilic language of Yiddish is "typed", has sustained the Jews in exile: Hebrew being the language of the Holy Word, Yiddish that of the Jewish soul. As Yiddish was born from Hebrew (among other influences), so is Edelshtein's and Baumzweig's Yiddish the "type" that bears resemblance but is not identical to the American Yiddish born from a newer exile. No one reads this Yiddish periodical written in a completely ghettoized, which is to say pure, Yiddish. As with Edelshtein, who earns a meagre living lecturing in English about the death of Yiddish, so Baumzweig is supported by monies set aside by a now-dead real Jew. Both live off the dead in one way or another. They dislike each other but are still good friends, perhaps mostly because they share the same fate: the seemingly only real Yiddish Jews alive in a world of fake Yiddish and unreal Jews. Another reality ties them together:

Edelshtein's friendship with Baumzweig had a ferocious secret: it was moored entirely to their agreed hatred for the man they called *der chazer*. He was named Pig because of his extraordinarily white skin, like a tissue of pale ham, and also because in the last decade he had become unbelievably famous. When they did not call him Pig they called him *shed*—Devil. They also called him Yankee Doodle. His name was Yankel Ostrover, and he was a writer of stories. (46)

Yankel Ostrover has done the impossible: he has transformed America's consciousness into a Jewish one; or perhaps he has transformed Yiddish consciousness into a Gentile one. It isn't clear which has been accomplished, or even how it was done. American Jews and Gentiles alike (were the Jews really just Americans; the Gentiles, Jews?) enthusiastically read and accepted him as a great figure on the American (Jewish) literary landscape. Was Yankel/Yankee Ostrover writing for the old or the new promise; the new or the old promised land? Was his audience the Chosen people of Israel or America? In which "text" does he find significance?

The words that Edelshtein and Baumzweig use to name this profoundly envied Jewish-American success story carry great signification. Changing one letter of the Yiddish (not Hebrew) name, Yankel (the Hebrew version is Yakov-Jacob), they mutate Yankel's being into a real American "Yankee Doodle", the prototype of Americanism.

This narration has, in reverse, a parallel to another story in Hebrew biblical history: the story of Jacob and his twin brother, Esau, sons of Isaac and Rebekah. These sons appear in the book of *Genesis* as opposing types or symbols for the Israel and Edomite nations respectively, that began from the same historical point—the same womb of the same mother—but developed into totally opposite and parallel directions. Esau took two Hittite women, and later Ishmael's daughter, as wives. The Hittite nation was anathema to God and therefore to the Israelites. Thus Esau's way of life, as represented by the women he took to bear his future children and thus determine the generations to follow after him, signified utter power-lust and vulgarity. Esau's other name (Edom) is the eponymic designation for Rome "and in medieval Hebrew literature for any anti-Jewish regime, Christianity in particular." (*Religion* 232). Jacob's enmity, not with just a brother but with his twin, deepens the dialectic dilemma of Pan-Moses, Christianity-Judaism. Again this enmity is epitomized and re-reflected in the *Genesis* story of the late-night power struggle between Jacob and "a man". After "stealing" Esau's birthright from the bed of their dying father, Jacob flees. Only in the time frame of the following story do Jacob's and Esau's lives intersect once again.

Jacob, after many years of no contact with his twin sibling, must pass through Esau's land, Edom. Full of great anxiety and fear because of the historically ruptured relationship set off by Jacob's displacement of the historical birthright from Esau to himself, and because of the notoriously bloodthirsty character of Esau, Jacob sends messengers ahead to speak with "'my lord Esau'... to make his passage uneventful.... The messengers returned... and said that Esau was coming to meet him with 400 men. Jacob was in great trepidation." (*Genesis* 32:6–7)

Jacob spent the night there in Edom, alone except for "a man" who wrestled with him until sunrise:

> When he realized that he could not triumph over him, he touched the inside of his thigh: and the hollow of Jacob's thigh was [injured] as he wrestled with him. And he said: "Let me leave. The day is breaking." And Jacob said: "I won't let you go unless you bless me." And he said to him: "What is your name?" And he said: "Jacob." And he said: "Your name will no longer be Jacob, but Israel, because you have striven with God and with men and you have triumphed." (*Genesis* 32:26–30)

The *Genesis* story of Jacob and Esau, itself consisting of several smaller texts or pre-texts, recapitulates the envy, the unbrotherly hate and fear, but also the profound divergence of direction that even brothers, born from the same womb at approximately the same moment, can take in their lives. From the same nation can spring the paradox of its own opposition.

The Esau-Jacob story also underlines the very dialectic of the Israelite nation which is re-reflected in the envy, struggle and name-changes Ozick's story contains. Yankel-Yankee Ostrover, renamed by two who envy and hate him, carries the Germanic surname, "Ostrover" which means "one from the East [Europe]".[138] The East-European Jews were despised by the German Jews, and of course by the German Gentiles. Ostrover is thus between the two worlds of Jewish and Gentile, and potentially despised by both.

The Biblical pre-textual story also mirrors the greater Pan-Moses dialectic of Books that is re-mirrored in the story's account of the struggle for literary dominance between Edelshtein *et al* and Ostrover; and between the American Gentile and Jewish literary camps. Jews (and Gentiles) who have a talent for literary chameleonism succeed in the war of control, authority over the word, which is also to say identity and being. Which word, whose word will dominate? Ostrover's genius, and the source of Baumzweig's and Edelshtein's envy, is his ability to be both what he is and isn't; of one Book but also of another; a member of one nation-people and also of the other. Is Ostrover's Yiddish, that is, his language, the purest? On a larger scale, is the Hebrew Word or the Christian-Pan one more dominant? Like the son Esau, twin of the Hebrew nation who became that nation's opposite but still paradoxically remained a son of his birth nation, so is Ostrover both "Yankel' and "Yankee"; Jew and Gentile; of Israel and America. So despised is Ostrover that he is named after one of the most unholy beasts in Jewish Scripture and philosophy, "pig", which for Edelshtein and his cronies is only equal to the word for "devil". Ostrover, they say, writes freakish books in a

> Yiddish [that] was impure.... Or else they raged against his subject matter, which was insanely sexual, pornographic, paranoid, freakish—men who embraced men, women who caressed women, sodomists of every variety, boys copulating with hens, butchers who drank blood for strength behind the knife. All the stories were set in an imaginary Polish village, Zwrdl, and by now there was almost no American literary intellectual alive who had not learned to say Zwrdl when he meant lewd. ("Envy" 47)

Ostrover, as Jacob and/or Esau, Yankel and/or Yankee, has transformed the traditional and generally devout Jewish ghetto into Esau's Gentile, Polish village of Zwrdl. Even

> Ostrover's wife was reputed to be a high-born Polish-Gentile woman from the "real" Zwrdl, the daughter in fact of a minor princeling, who did not know a word of Yiddish and read her husband's fiction falteringly, in English translation.... Her Yiddish had an unpleasant gargling Galician accent, her vocabulary was a thin soup—[Edelshtein and Baumzweig] joked that it was correct to say she spoke no Yiddish—and she mewed it like a peasant comparing prices. She was a short square woman, a cube with low-slung udders and a flat backside. It was partly Ostrover's mockery, partly his self-advertising, that had converted her into a little princess. (47)

Which is the real Zwrdl? Who are the real Ostrover and Mrs. Ostrover? Strangely, Ostrover's grandeur

> was exactly in this: that he required translators. Though he wrote only in Yiddish, his fame was American, national, international. They considered him a "modern". Ostrover was free of the prison of Yiddish! Out, out—he had burst out, he was in the world of reality. (47)

Ostrover, who is himself a crossover from one world's reality to another, needs people who know the exact linguistic formulations for alchemizing Jewishness (Yiddish) into American-English Gentilism, or the reverse: those Jews already Gentilized who can imitate the tongue of the assimilated Jewish-American or Jewish-Gentile mind. This fake story called "Envy, or Yiddish in America" about Ostrover and Edelshtein mirrors a real story Ozick relates in an essay about the author I.B. Singer, who in the following description seems to be a cross between Ostrover and Edelshtein. In describing Singer's own relationship to his translators, Ozick's states:

> After all these years, the scandalous rumors about Singer's relation to his changing translators do not abate: how they are half-collaborators, half-serfs, how they start out sunk in homage, accept paltry fees, and end disgruntled or bemused, yet transformed, having looked on Singer plain. One wishes Singer would write their frenzied tale.[139]

Ostrover's potency is not just creative or linguistic; it has a sexual manifestation. Edelshtein is also a cultural and linguistic intercross, a crisscross, a Jewish cultural transvestite parading as Pan, or a Pan transvestite pretending to be Jewish. In any event, the two, Edelshtein and Ostrover, were destined to live in the displaced Israel, America; more specifically, Manhattan:

> Thirty years ago, straight out of Poland via Tel Aviv, Ostrover crept into a toying affair with Mireleh, Edelshtein's wife. He [Edelshtein] had left Palestine during the 1939 Arab riots, not he said, out of fear, out of integrity rather—it was a country which had turned its face against Yiddish. Yiddish was not honored in Tel Aviv or Jerusalem. In the Negev it was worthless. In the God-given State of Israel they had no use for the language of the bad little interval between Canaan and now. Yiddish was inhabited by the past, the new Jews did not want it. Mireleh liked to hear these anecdotes of how rotten it was in Israel for Yiddish and Yiddishists. In Israel the case was even lamer than in New York, thank God! There was after all a reason to live the life they lived: it was worse somewhere else. ("Envy" 48)

Significantly, Edelshtein left Israel out of disgust for its attitude towards the Jewish ghetto-language of Yiddish, and he continues to remain in America. Paradoxically, and ironically as well, the Gentile country America has embraced (transformed?) an important form of Jewishness, Yiddish, while the Jewish State contemptuously rejected it. An exiled people, like its language of exile, Yiddish, is continuously displaced. Exiled from Poland, itself a place of exile, Edelshtein goes "home" to Palestine—a name later replaced by the name "Israel". Exiled from "Palestine" because it is a stranger to the *mamaloshen* of his Jewish people, Edelshtein finds his way to America. Edelshtein has been searching for the "real" home of his people, that is, of his past, which is in fact just a "bad little interval" between one reality of the Jewish people and another. Like Derrida's difference, Edelshtein's journey is also the search for a perpetually displaced meaning. Edelshtein and his now-dead wife Mireleh were powerlessness itself. She counted her miscarriages, while Ostrover's wife Pesha, meaning "crime" in Hebrew[140] counted her children. Mirelah

> was vindictive about Edelshtein's sperm-count.... Pesha had her third daughter, Mirelah her seventh miscarriage. Edelshtein was grief-stricken but elated. "*My* sperm-count!" he screamed. "*Your* belly! Go fix the machine before you blame the oil!" (48–49)

Unlike the Ostrovers, the Edelshteins' physical childlessness merely serves to emphasize the impotency of their creative potential as well. Edelshtein is doubly punished: not only has his writing eclipsed into oblivion, but when he dies, he will be, according to Jewish tradition, really dead since there will be no progeny to say *Kaddish* (the Jewish prayer for the dead) for him. The agony of childlessness is set out, as Gerald J. Blidstein describes, in the Talmud that addresses "'him who is childless'." (*Ned.* 64b) This Talmudic section states that childlessness is one of "the four categories of living men who are considered as dead." (*Religion* 156)

Edelshtein's and Mirelah's impotency, in reverse, is mirrored in Ostrover's and Pesha's potency. Sexual power or its lack is re-mirrored in the unfortunate or well-placed word. Mastery over the word is power and Law/authority. In a letter to Baumzweig which Baumzweig reads on the telephone to Edelshtein, one of Edelshtein's most cruel opponents, the now-dead Zimmerman, writes:

> Who is the merciless one, after all: the barren woman [Mireleh] who makes the house peaceful with no infantile caterwauling, or the excessively fertile poet [Edelshtein] who bears the fruit of his sin—namely his untalented verses? He bears it, but who can bear it? In one breath he runs from seas to trees. Like his ancestors the amphibians, puffed up with arrogance. Hersheleh.

Frog! Why did God give Hersheleh Edelshtein an unfaithful wife? To punish him for writing trash. ("Envy" 50)

The Law is also the law of language. Bad writing is a blasphemy against the Creator himself; against Creation itself. The Book/book, the Word/word, holds the key to salvation and a messianic future. An important commandment is to write with the inspiration of the angels, as if from God's mouth. To write poorly is the greatest of crimes. This is the crux of Edelshtein's impotence. On the other hand, why did fate choose Ostrover?

Why not somebody else? Was Ostrover more gifted than Komorsky? Did he think up better stories than Horowitz? Why does the world outside pick an Ostrover instead of an Edelshtein, or even a Baumzweig? What occult knack, what craft, what crooked convergence of planets drove translators to grovel before Ostrover's naked swollen sentences with their thin little threadbare pants always pulled down? Who had discovered that Ostrover was a "modern"? His Yiddish, however fevered in itself, bloated, was still Yiddish, it was still *mamaloshen*, it still squeaked up to God with a littleness, a familiarity, an elbow-poke. It was still pieced together out of shtetl rags, out of a baby *aleph*, a toddler *beys* —so why Ostrover? Why only Ostrover? Ostrover should be the only one? Everyone else sentenced to darkness, Ostrover alone saved? Ostrover the survivor? As if hidden in the Dutch attic like the child. *His* diary, so to speak, the only documentation of what was.... Ostrover was to be the only evidence that there was a Yiddish tongue, a Yiddish literature? And all the others lost? Lost! Drowned. Snuffed out. Under the earth. As if never. (51)

Ostrover's writing is as potent as the erect male member. It is, whatever its subject matter, the *mamaloshen* of the Jewish people, which is itself created from Hebrew, the holy language of God. Hebrew language (including Yiddish) is the trope for language itself. Ostrover, born under a lucky star, was saved alive under a heap of dead writers. All other writers are "sentenced"—as if the writing process itself enforces the Law of the universe—to death and darkness. Ozick transfers the idea of Holocaust survival to the life or death of writers, who either are read by others and found "significant", or are sent into the blackness—a terrifying ordeal Ozick herself underwent at the beginning of her career as a writer. Edelshtein's life, for yet another time, has been preserved, it seems, to witness its death.

The messiah is the (Jewish) writer who leads his/her people to the promised land of the book/Book. This is one of Ozick's clearest statements connecting salvation to the writer's creative process of giving life to words. Within the greater metaphorical image of the Holocaust, Ozick shifts the rhetoric from saving Jewish lives to saving (the) language (of the European Jews) and the historical proof of Jewish existence through the Words, the Book. Having wandered millennia without a land, exiled from their God-given place, the Israelites, the Jewish nation, had a homeland in the text, the Book/book, the Word/word. The linguistic enterprise was and is their salve, the reason for their preservation, and the key to their ultimate future redemption. The "place" of the final fulfillment of the promise, however, is not Israel, the object of the promise, but America; for only America has preserved the *mamaloshen*.

The Derridean irony, the paradox, is that only in displacement can the Jewish Word, as language itself, survive. The Word, "out of its place" in America, also requires "readers" to translate its meaning, its significance. Is Ostrover's version the "real" one? The competing truths (of Jewish existence) urge for preeminence. Who will control what is reality? The absurd reality is that Ostrover's "thin little threadbare… sentences" will be the record of the creative, Jewish European ghetto existence, and its expression through its language, Yiddish. Ostrover was not just "in the world of reality"; he himself formulated, for those Yiddishly illiterate "Yankee Doodle" American Jews thirsting for their historical roots, the meaning and reality of pre-Holocaust European Jewish life. His interpretation has been chosen by destiny to signify the meaning of the language of a now-dead displaced life.

At the same time that Ostrover's version of Jewishness is chosen as truth, he also "keeps all his translators in a perpetual frenzy of envy for each other." (55) His readers, that is, "translators", each compete to be the one to interpret his reality; more so, to create "the language Ostrover is famous for." (55) Most importantly, only one who is of both and neither (Jewishness or America) can succeed as Ostrover's translator. In a letter from one of Ostrover's translators, Edelshtein is told:

> You understand me, Edelshtein? He [Ostrover] stands on the backs of hacks to reach. I know you call me hack, and its all right, by myself I'm what you think me, no imagination, so-so ability (I too once wanted to be a poet, but that's another life)—with Ostrover on my back I'm something else: I'm "Ostrover's translator". You think that's nothing? It's an entrance into *them*. I'm invited everywhere, I go to the same parties Ostrover goes to. Everyone looks at me and thinks I'm a bit freakish, but they say: "It's Ostrover's translator." A marriage. Pesha, that junk-heap, is less married to Ostrover than I

am. Like a wife, I have the supposedly passive role. Supposedly: Who knows what goes on in the bedroom? An unmarried person like myself becomes good at guessing at these matters. The same with translation. Who makes the language Ostrover is famous for?.... *Who* has read James Joyce, Ostrover or I? I'm fifty-three years old. I wasn't born back of Hlusk for nothing. I didn't go to Vassar [College] for nothing—do you understand me? I got caught in between, so I got squeezed. Between two organisms. A cultural hermaphrodite, neither one nor the other, I have a forked tongue. (55)

Cultural displacement means linguistic displacement. With meaning out of its place, there is no single truth in language. The linguistic enterprise of writing as creative expression is a perpetual process of (self) discovery. Jews as Americans are of two worlds, culturally both and also neither. Language, writing, as the dislocation of meaning, creates the gap between truth and lies.

Still a stranger in a strange land; out of (his) place in a new cultural, linguistic reality; if he is to survive, if his language is to live on after him, or if he is to be redeemed from his misery, Edelshtein's only hope is to find a translator who can convert his too-Jewishness into some mix of non-Jew/Jew, non-Gentile/Gentile. Unlike Ostrover, Edelshtein doesn't have the slightest clue as to how these two can be combined into some dialectic in which neither is a distinct reality. How did Ostrover, the Pig, do it?

During a visit to Baumzweig's house, as he talks with Paula, Edelshtein himself realizes that everything connected to Yiddish is dead. He leaves their house filled with the grief of his existence. Catching his image in a mirror, he sees "an old man crying, dragging a striped scarf like a prayer shawl." (67) Ozick repeats here one of her most essential metaphors of Pan-Moses identity: the scarf/shawl/prayer shawl image. The mirror, itself an image of reflecting, re-reflecting images, deepens the confusion, makes more slippery the dialectical conundrum of Gentile-Jewish being. Like Rabbi Isaac Kornfeld, re-reflected in the image of the old man carrying tractates of Jewish commentary, this aged figure represents the solid historicity of essential Jewish selfhood. This Jewish "being" is, however, in masquerade, in a costume pretending to be other than what it is.

Edelshtein's perception of himself is of a Jew desperately wanting to conform to find a place; but ultimately, like Kornfeld, Edelshtein is out of place and out of life. The *tallit* (prayer shawl) is a burden, but he nevertheless drags it. He wishes he could be a Gentile, but he cannot. His major problem is that he is too Jewish, and unable to do anything to change it. In addition, he apparently lacks whatever is needed to not just create babies, but also art—to write successfully. He has a real or imagined conversation with Ostrover.

In a dizzying symphony of dialectical interplay, Edelshtein sees the biblical reverberations, re-reflection of God's promise to Abraham of a healthy and vibrant Jewish nation; the world's sky replete with the spirit and body of God's Israelite people. The very *"sky is cluttered with stars of David".* (68) Under this heaven-blest Jewish manifold, or in spite of it, where is the Jew's place in geographic, psychic, emotional terms? What identity should each Jew manifest? What does being Jewish mean? In this slippery rubric of cultural dialectic, there are no unambiguous answers to these questions. Ostrover responds to Edelshtein's open-ended query on personal identity by telling him: "It's only a make-believe story, a game." (68) Ostrover appears to want to debunk Edelshtein's worship of art as an end it itself, as the only point of address in existence. Paradoxically, however, the Ostrover who turns everything into some kind of moral and physical obscenity, is also the Ostrover who distinguishes between the Story/Word/Book that is God's and the relatively unimportant child's play that storytellers partake in: "So what is it [literature], Torah?" (68) Edelshtein wants to be like Ostrover, which is to say, a Jew pretending to the Gentiles that he is the Jew of their conception. Paradoxically, Ostrover somehow has learned how to be what he isn't. He has learned how to play in life and his being. He doesn't just have a good translator: he is himself a translation of himself. He proposes an absurd example in the person of William Shakespeare, reinventing the facts about one of the greatest writers in the English tongue, about whom paradoxically no one really knows the facts for certain:

> "I'll let you in on the facts, Hersheleh, because I feel we're really brothers. I feel you straining toward the core of the world. Now listen—did you ever hear of Velul Shikkarparev? Never. A Yiddish scribbler writing romances for the Yiddish stage in the East End, I'm speaking of London, England. He finds a translator and overnight he becomes Willie Shakespeare." (68)

Like stories, identities can be created at will; all one needs is an interpreter, one who can translate, transform, render, decode, transfer, construct an edifice of dialectical process, the Derridean gap of difference wherein lies art as well. Who one is, is like a story: meaning and significance are open to interpretation. Any good translator can render one identity or story into its opposite: transform fact into fiction or fiction into fact. Also by changing translators, reality shifts. As "readers", translators bring with them their own individual realities.

Edelshtein is just Jewish (an old man dragging a prayer shawl). He believes in all things Yiddish, a consecrated language. What's more, he believes in the sacred:

> Ostrover: Lost soul, don't make Yiddish into the Sabbath tongue! If you believe in holiness, you're finished. Holiness is for make believe.
> Edelshtein: I want to be a Gentile like you!
> Ostrover: I'm only a make-believe Gentile. This means that I play at being a Jew to satisfy them. In my village when I was a boy they used to bring in a dancing bear for the carnival, and everyone said, 'It's human!' They said this because they knew it was a bear, though it stood on two legs and waltzed. But it was a bear. (69)

Edelshtein wants to be the same kind of "Gentile" that Ostrover is, the created fantasy simulating a chosen reality. That life is theatre and art can be the only definitive and unchanging fact of existence. Without a translator, Edelshtein remains just a Jew; too thoroughly, homogeneously, Jewish.

When Edelshtein first meets Hannah, the American-born young niece of his friend Vorovsky, at an Ostrover book-autographing event, he sees her "mooning over an open flyleaf, where Ostrover had written his name. Edelshtein, catching a flash of letters, was startled: it was the Yiddish version she held." (69) The writer, Ozick's Hannah, re-reflects the stories of two biblical matriarchs named Hannah. The first biblical Hannah, eventually the mother of Samuel, one of the two wives of Elkanah, was perpetually tormented by the other wife, Peninah, for her barrenness and Peninah's own fertility; (*Religion* 299) this again re-reflects the story of Edelshtein's impotence and Ostrover's fertility. The second biblical Hannah, a mother of seven sons, re-reflects the importance of Jewish identity even over death, through her decision to have herself and her sons put to death rather than assimilate into the greater Hellenistic culture imposed then on Palestinian Jews by Antiochus IV Epiphanes (167 BCE). (299) In another twist of the complicated cultural dialectic, the Western and Eastern churches "adopted this Hannah and her sons as the 'Maccabean saints' to whom an annual commemoration day was declared." (299)

In the same ways, Ozick's Hannah incorporates, reinforces and reintegrates the line of historicity and continuity through her knowledge of Yiddish, as well as having preserved—even in America—a Jewish identity. In a cultural dialectic of time, language and literature, Hannah, who reads Edelshtein's work in untranslated Yiddish, is amazed that this relatively famous poet, revered by her now-dead grandfather, is still alive. "'I see you read Yiddish,' Edelshtein addressed her. 'In your generation a miracle.'" ("Envy" 69) Hannah knows Edelshtein's poetry by heart. In a pure play of ghetto black humor, Edelshtein apologizes for still being alive: "'I'm sorry,' Edelshtein said, 'Maybe I was young then, I began young.'" (70)

Hannah throws only mockery in his face. All hope is aborted. Edelshtein's barrenness torments him. His jokes merely serve to annihilate, or delay despair. He hates his life, its boring sameness:

> Ordinariness. Everything a routine. Whatever man touches becomes banal like man. Animals don't contaminate nature. Only man the corrupter, the anti-divinity. All other species live within the pulse of nature. He despised these ceremonies and rattles and turds and kisses. The pointlessness of their babies. Wipe one generation's ass for the sake of wiping another generation's ass: this was his whole definition of civilization. (73)

Edelshtein's hatred and despair is also the guilt of the survivor. He feels out of place in a world displaced by such a vastness of death and suffering. Like Isaac and Rosa, he is writing letters that will never be sent, never reach a destination. He addresses them, rather, to the future, and also to the past. In this way, "one does not expect an answer.... Often I have spat on myself for having survived the death camps—survived them drinking tea in New York." (74)

He writes to ask Hannah to resurrect his life, to be his translator. It is, however, a letter that will be waylaid, for it has no expectations of being answered. It is only "the sound of a dead language on a live girl's tongue!" (74) Ozick repeats here, as elsewhere, the mirroring in its oppositions of life and death. In Ozick's schema, and for post-Holocaust Jews, there are a number of levels of being/non-being: There is the death that occurs through a more or less normal course of events, after sickness, accidents or old age; there is the extermination that gives office to the name "death camps"; the "life" of those born elsewhere (other than Europe) but not in America; the "real" life of the *Amerikaborner* like

Hannah; the "life" of the dead that live on in the memory; and the "life" of the living dead that live on in the past.

The term "survivor", which displaces that of "living", has no moral right to sit casually among the "real" living ones, drinking tea in a way-laid place of the promise, the (thrice-removed) Jewish homeland; and perhaps has no right to be "alive" at all. Edelshtein wants to be counted among the living, which is to live in the regular time progression from a "normal" past to a present that can look ahead to a future. For Ozick, it would seem, this can be achieved only through art, the writing process. For Edelshtein, to be translated means to have a future; he and his life can be redeemed; then there is the hope in the redemption that art as "the word" can bring to the world:

> If the prayer-load that spilled upward from the mass graves should somehow survive! If not the thicket of lamentation itself, then the language on which it rode. Hannah, youth itself is nothing unless it keeps its promise to grow old. Grow old in Yiddish, Hannah, and carry fathers and uncles into the future with you. Do this. You, one in ten thousand maybe, who were born with the gift of Yiddish in your mouth, the alphabet of Yiddish in your palm, don't make ash of these! A little while ago there were twelve million people—not including babies—who lived inside this tongue, and now what is left? A lan-guage that never had a territory except Jewish mouths, and half the Jewish mouths on earth already stopped up with German worms.... Whoever forgets Yiddish courts amnesia of history. I call on you to choose! Yiddish! Choose death or death. Which is to say death through forgetting or death through translation. Who will redeem you? What act of salvation will restore you? All you can hope for, you tattered, you withered, is translation in America! Hannah, you have a strong mouth made to carry the future—! (74–75)

Ozick's dialectic of art and Yiddishkeit finds salvation in "the word", that which mirrors "the Word" of God. Edelshtein's call is for Hannah, through her mouth, to circumvent the death of Yiddish and to save the Jewish people. However, in each turn of Edelshtein's mind, and in the creation of beautiful phrases to convince her to be his translator, sits a lie:

> But he knew he lied, lied, lied. A truthful intention is not enough. Oratory and declamation. A speech. A lecture. He felt himself an obscenity. What did the death of Jews have to do with his own troubles? His cry was ego and more ego. His own stew, foul. Whoever mourns the dead mourns himself. He wanted someone to read his poems, no one could read his poems. Filth and exploitation to throw in history. As if a dumb man should blame the ears that cannot hear him. (75)

Is he mourning the death of Yiddish and its perfect ability to wring beauty from language, or his own death, or both? To mourn the death of a language is to mourn also the death of its people. Lie and truth are just the word's beauty, or its lack, on the page. The perfectly rendered text is the greatest—the only—truth; and the only language in which to render that perfection is Yiddish: "The gait—the prance, the hobble—of Yiddish is not the same as the gait of English. A big headache for a translator." (81) In a letter which Edelshtein writes to Hannah but has no intention of sending, he in effect describes the Yiddish language as the antithesis of homelessness, worthlessness and drift:

> *Mamaloshen* doesn't produce *Wastelands*. No alienation, no nihilism, no Dadaism. With all the suffering no smashing! No INCOHERENCE! Keep the latter in mind, Hannah, if you expect to make progress. Also: please remember that when a goy from Columbus, Ohio, says: *Eliohu hanavi*. Eliohu is one of us, a *folksmensh*, running around in secondhand clothes. Theirs is God knows what. The same biblical figure, with exactly the same history, once he puts on a name from King James, COMES OUT A DIFFERENT PERSON. Life, history, hope, tragedy, they don't come out even. They talk Bible Lands; with us it's *eretz yisroel*! A misfortune. (82)

Edelshtein's claim, and probably Ozick's as well, is to the truth and power of the Jewish people by virtue of their linguistic enterprise, and the nearly 6000 years of history comprising it. It is the Hebrew nation's total identification with the Word/Book (of God) that empowers, authorizes and gives them ownership over the Word/Book. Theirs is the Real; the others are the Fake. The Gentilized King James Bible, the typologized version of the Hebrew book, does not constitute the real Word (of God); it is not what it claims to be. Beneath the Gentile Nazis' decimation of European Jewry lies an even deeper crime: in annihilating Yiddish, they killed language itself.

Only through writing/language can the Jewish people be resurrected to their full power as a people of the Word/word, and to their rightful place as the prophets of the Word of God. Through the Jewish message as "the word", the Israelites can usher in the messianic age of redemption. Thus, from within the complex dialectic of Jew-Gentile, American-European, Yiddish/Hebrew-English, America-Israel—using the vehicle of language, the Word/Book of God, the holy writing process—humanity can draw closer to its creator, and the Messiah of the Book can come to bring peace and love to all peoples of the world. But Edelshtein as a would-be messiah is not able to pull it off. He appears on the door-step of Hannah's uncle Vorovsky at 5:00 in the morning:

> "Who is this!"
> "*Yankel* Ostrover, the writer, or Pisher [one who "pees"] Ostrover the plumber?"
> "What do you want?"
> "To leave evidence," Edelshtein howled. (77)

Neither Edelshtein nor the reader is sure if what Hersheleh tells Vorovsky is true or false. Identities appear, disappear and reappear: Edelshtein identifies himself as the Jewish "Yankel" Ostrover, a name that is both Yiddish and also a kind of permutation or mutation of the word, Yankee, the code word for American identity. When Edelshtein is asked again to identify himself he signifies his selfness as the long-awaited Messiah, which is to say, the writer who redeems humanity through the Book/book. The sense here of the coming of the long-awaited Messiah both signals Edelshtein's personal waiting for literary recognition, and also his people's wait for the Redeemer, God and God's Davidic representative, the Messiah. In a complex linguistic coup, the writer melts hope, future, redemption, the story and the messiahship of the storyteller in the same crucible of cultural dialectic.

Edelshtein's appeal is to Hannah, who was "born 1945 in the hour of the death camps. Not selected. Immune. The whole way she held herself looked immune—by this he meant American." (91) His anguish and salve is that by saving him, in other words (his) Yiddish (and language), Hannah will be saving the Jewish people and recovering history itself. The total annihilation of Yiddish is the Holocaust revisited/completed. By saving Yiddish, his Yiddish, history itself will be recovered: "'You'll save Yiddish,' Edelshtein said. 'You'll be like a Messiah, to a whole generation, a whole literature.'" (93)

The story's denouement brings the Pan-Moses contrast into clear profile. Edelshtein pleads with Hannah to give him entry to a world to which he is totally incapable of gaining access on his own; but which is "the world"? Is it Ostrover's and Hannah's perception, or Edelshtein's? With her boots, which stir up in Edelshtein the Nazi nightmare of the past, Hannah becomes the final step in the "final solution" of his life, which is to say his writing (art); the final step in the "selection process" of who (whose language) will live and who (whose) will die. Edelshtein's plea to her is to be his (re)creator; to give him life. Tragically, Edelshtein's world cannot be translated (into something else). As Hannah tells Edelshtein:

> "So pay attention Mr. Vampire: even in Yiddish Ostrover's not in the ghetto. Even in Yiddish he's not like you people."
>
> ...
>
> "God, four thousand years since Abraham hanging out with Jews, God also stinks from the ghetto?"
> "Rhetoric," Hannah said. "Yiddish literary rhetoric." (94–95)

Ostrover, in becoming part of the world, that is, the Pan world, is condemned to life. Hannah's refusal "to translate" Edelshtein, to render him in a Gentilized version, means that Edelshtein has failed. Hannah's refusal to "read" him sends all hope into darkness, and sends Edelshtein, the Jewish nation and language into exile, to tarry longer still for the Messiah-as-poet to come and redeem the world with the word/Word.

Kornfeld and Edelshtein, both trapped in the snares of cultural dialectic through the process of art, attempt to deal with (*must* deal with) the essence of Jewishness (whatever that is): convert, reject, exclude, displace and/or combine it with/by/through the compulsive cannibalism of the artistic endeavour, or of imagination in general. The creative enterprise can be viewed, therefore, as a type of sickness, a malady, the ever-shifting linguistic juncture between all facets, levels, shades of cultural diversity and dialectic.

In "Levitation", Ozick returns to the theme of the writer in yet another twist of cultural dialectic: in a Jewish-Gentile marriage of two writers in which the wife has converted to Judaism, but either doesn't stay converted, or could never really be converted in her being. In all three stories, "The Pagan Rabbi", "Envy, or Yiddish in America" and "Levitation", the writer is seen in spirit, being and/or practice to be in control, or out, in one facet of the dialectic or another; exploring, self-exploring, fantasizing on real or imagined worlds, in or out of their historical frame.

"Levitation"

In apparent defiance of nature's gravity, Ozick's story title alludes to the absolute power of storytelling—which is to say Jewishness—to redeem the world. Through Moses at Mt. Sinai, the Hebrews were chosen keepers of the Book, the Word, and entrusted with the Story of stories, the Holy Writ. Of all the nations, only the Israelites accepted the power and truth of the Word/word, and elected to safeguard and promulgate its message.

The main characters are Lucy and Jimmy Feingold, a pair of novelists, husband and wife, who

> fancied themselves in love with what they called "imagination". It was not true. What they were addicted to was counterfeit pity, and this was because they were absorbed by power, and were powerless....
>
> About their own lives they had a joke: they were "secondary-level" people. Feingold had a secondary-level job with a secondary-level house. Lucy's own publisher was secondary-level; even the address was Second Avenue.... Anonymous mediocrities. They could not call themselves forgotten because they had never been noticed.[141]

Caught in a vice of power/powerlessness, like Edelshtein, they want to break out of their impotence, but either do not know how or simply cannot. Thirsting for first-rateness, in envy of those who arrived to the pinnacles of puissance, they decide to throw a party. The Feingolds draw up

> a list of luminaries. They invited Irving Howe, Susan Sontag, Alfred Kazin, and Leslie Fielder. They invited Norman Podhoretz and Elizabeth Hardwick. They invited Philip Roth and Joyce Carol Oates and Norman Mailer and William Styron and Donald Barthelme and Jerzy Kosinski and Truman Capote. None of these came; all of them had unlisted numbers, or else machines that answered the telephone, or else were in Prague or Paris or out of town. Nevertheless the apartment filled up.... The guests were freestanding figures, in the niches of a cathedral; or else dressed-up cardboard dolls, with their drinks, and their costumes all meticulously hung with sashes and draped collars and little capes, the women's hair variously bound, the men's sprouting and spilling: fashion stalked, Feingold moped. He took in how it all flashed, manhattans and martinis, earrings and shoe-tips—he marveled, but knew it was a falsehood, even a figment. The great world was somewhere else. ("Levitation" 9)

The couple is caught in another vice as well: Jewish-Gentile, which paradoxically seems to cement the attraction they have for each other:

> For love, and also because he had always known he did not want a Jewish wife, he married a minister's daughter. Lucy too had hoped to marry out of her tradition. (These words were hers. "Out of my tradition," she said. The

idea fevered him.) At the age of twelve she felt herself to belong to the people of the Bible. ("A Hebrew," she said. His heart lurched, joy rocked him.) One night from the pulpit her father read a Psalm; all at once she saw how the Psalmist meant *her*; then and there she became an Ancient Hebrew. (3)

Even the name "Jimmy Feingold" is a dialectic of a Christian and a Jewish name. In their dialectic of love and attraction for the opposite, writing is the matrix, the base, the common element, that absorbs any possible friction or antagonism between them. Their writers' imaginations are able to convert what could be antagonism into a kind of harmony—a dialectical harmony. Also, they shut themselves off from the literary world's dialectic: the bickering about character-characterlessness, story-storylessness, do not upset their lives. They are writers, albeit second-raters, who paradoxically ignore the world of the story:

All the roil about the State of the Novel had passed them by.... They wrote not without puzzlements and travail; nevertheless as naturally as birds. They were devoted to accuracy, psychological realism, and earnest truthfulness, also to virtue, and even to wit. Neither one was troubled by what had happened to the novel: all those declarations about the end of Character and Story. They were serene. Sometimes, closing up their notebooks for the night, it seemed to them that they were literary friends and lovers, like George Eliot and George Henry Lewes. (4)

They also agree on leaving the tellers of stories out of their stories, which in most cases is to avoid writing in the

"first person. First person strangles. You can't get out of their skin." And so on. The one principle they agreed on was the importance of never writing about writers. Your protagonist always has to be someone *real*, with real work-in-the-world—a bureaucrat, a banker, an architect (ah, they envied Conrad his shipmasters!)—otherwise you fall into solipsism, narcissism, tedium, lack of appeal-to-the-common-reader; who knew what other perils. (4)

This is also a warning against too much imagination, which creates confusion, a destructive kind of ambiguity, out-of-this-worldness, a lack of humanness, a loss of reality contact; and other perilous pitfalls. Such self-destructive solipsistic behavior and thinking describe the path of Edelshtein, Rabbi Kornfeld and Rosa. As in other Ozick stories, this one is a polemical blend of reality, "facts", and ordinariness mixed with characters torn through by a dialectic of directions and realities. Lucy, for example, writes of domesticity; her husband, Jimmy Feingold, writes of

Jewish survival, and more specifically on the seemingly endless litany of Jewish massacres.

> This difficulty—seizing on a concrete subject—was mainly Lucy's. Feingold's novel—the one he was writing now—was about Menachem ben Zerach, survivor of a massacre of Jews in the town of Estella in Spain in 1328. From morning to midnight he hid under a pile of corpses, until "a compassionate knight" (this was the language of the history Feingold relied on) plucked him out and took him home to tend to his wounds. (4–5)

The story within a story describes how ben Zerach (whose name means "seed" in Hebrew) finds himself alive under a mountain of dead bodies, only to triumph later in life by becoming "a renowned scholar", which is to say a writer:

> "If you're going to tell about how after he gets to be a scholar he just sits there and *writes*," Lucy protested, "then you're doing the Forbidden Thing [talking about writers and writing in their writing work; as Lucy and her husband have agreed not to do]." But Feingold said he meant to concentrate on the massacre and especially on the life of the "compassionate knight"....
> "Solipsism," Lucy said. "Your compassionate knight is only another writer." (5)

Replete with paradox and irony, this is exactly what the writer herself could be doing in this story: The quotation is re-mirrored, on one hand, through the writer, and on the other, through the characterizations of Lucy and Jimmy Feingold. Ozick, reiterating here her oft-stated conflict between "telling the story" and moral issues, again solves the dilemma by ascribing a messianic role to the writer. His compassion and bookishness makes the scholarly knight highly qualified for such an arduous and holy mission. Thus writers are somehow identifiable with Jewishness. To be a writer—that is, a real writer—is to also be Jewish, even if one happens to have been born a Gentile. The reverse is also true: To be Jewish—that is, genuinely and really Jewish—is to have the makings of an authentic writer. Also in Ozick's scheme, even doing Jewish things like showing compassion and humanness qualifies one to be Jewish.

Lucy's major crime is that she feels herself Jewish, but only of the fake Christian typologized kind. She continues to believe, like Mrs. Morrison in Lewisohn's *Holy Land*, in the story version of Jewishness that she learned from her minister father. In this sense, she is a victim of the dialectic manifested by their union. If she truly felt herself Jewish, she wouldn't have wanted "to marry out of her tradition." Together and separately Lucy and Jimmy can neutralize their mediocrity and Jewish-Gentile union through the art of writing; to feel like "literary friends and lovers". In the dialectical disappearing-reappearing act of the fake Jews/ real Jews, those who don't believe in God and Jewishness all gather in one room:

> "Theatre in the dining room," [Feingold] said. "Junk."
> "Film. I heard film," [Lucy said.]
> "Film too," he conceded. "Junk. It's mobbed in there...."
> There were Jews in the dining room too, but the unruffled, devil-may-care kind: the humorists, the painters, film reviewers who went off to studio showings of *Screw on Screen* on the eve of the Day of Atonement. Mostly there were Gentiles in the dining room. (10,12)

These "fake" Jews, having abandoned history, their people, and the reality of who they are, become the reverse-mirror image of the Gentiles wanting to climb socially, who desire to reflect the cultural secular Jewishness that so permeates Manhattan's artistic climate. Thus all the "fakes" are in the dining room; that is to say, the dialecticized ones: Gentile Jews and Jewish Gentiles. This group cannot even hope to attain the stardom they so dream of: like Edelshtein, they haven't a clue as to how to transform themselves into the perfect composite of opposites, of Jew and Gentile, to become truly famous. The case is totally otherwise in the living room, where as if through the force of some chemical magnetism all of the "real" Jews have gathered; which is to say, "fake" Gentiles who are really Jews and seemingly "fake" Jews who are in truth "real" Jews. These are the ones who genuinely wish to preserve (Jewish) history and historical veracity; these are the real human beings capable of appreciating and performing as compassionate human beings; the ones who respect, even worship, at the feet of those touched by the great Calamity of recent (Jewish) history: the Holocaust. There, in fact, sit the potentially "real" writers:

> In the living room, Feingold despaired; no one asked him, he began to tell about the compassionate knight. A problem of ego, he said: compassion being super-consciousness of one's own pride. Not that he believed this; he only thought it provocative to say something original, even if a little muddled. But no one responded. (11)

The potentially real Jews do not react to Feingold's attempts at cultural legerdemain. It is clear that they want authenticity, intact history, true artistic and intellectual depth and dimension:

> They sat down on the carpet in front of the fireless grate. "Is that a real fireplace?" someone inquired. "We never light it," Lucy said. "Do you light those [Jewish Sabbath] candlesticks ever?" "They belonged to Jimmy's grandmother," Lucy said. "We never light them." (11)

Ozick's story returns to the trope of fire and incineration, their relation to Jewishness and its divine incarnation in textuality. Interestingly, this trope operates on two opposing poles: there are also the fires of the Holocaust and Jewish decimation. Since, according to Jewish tradition, it is the woman in the Jewish home whose responsibility it is to light the Sabbath candles, Lucy's veraciously direct statement to their party guest reveals the absence of any "real" Jewish feeling, identity or desire for historical continuity. Jimmy's marriage to Lucy, like Rabbi Kornfeld's fornication with the nymph, and the narrator's marriage to Jane in that story, all signal the rupture of Jewish history. Only when one of the guests initiates it does Jimmy enter the real Jewish realm of his being: "Feingold looked up. 'Can't you light that fire?' said a man. 'All right,' Feingold said." (11)

Only now does it become possible for Jimmy to become who he truly is: Jewish, and thus become the writer he earnestly hopes to be. At one with his Jewishness, he begets his historically Jewish self. Thus he will use writing/storytelling, the Text/text to illuminate the world:

> He rolled a paper log made of last Sunday's *Times* and laid a match on it. A flame as clear as a street light whitened the faces of the sofa-sitters. He recognized a friend of his from the [Jewish Theological] Seminary—he had what Lucy called "theological" friends—and then and there, really very suddenly, Feingold wanted to talk about God. Or if not God, then certain historical atrocities, abominations [in which the Jewish people were victims]. (11)

Writing as Art can illuminate the crossroads of life, the map of existence. In reference to Pan's world of "mappiness" ("street"), Ozick would appear to be telling us that only "the text" can guide us in finding our way through the world; back to our history and the promised redemption. The God who gave Torah, the Text of all texts, is also the God of history and continuity cemented by/in the promise. Imagination is not enough, as Rabbi Kornfeld, Joseph Brill, Rosa and now Jimmy Feingold discover. Imagination adhering to history—which is to say, a Jewish past—is the only road to redemption and storytelling. In fact, stories bereft of history lack the qualities that will deem them lasting "classics", like the Torah text itself. Lucy, witnessing this scene and irritatedly listening to her husband's solemn recounting of the slaughter of Jews, becomes "uneasy with the friend from the Seminary; he was the one who had administered her conversion, and every encounter was like a new stage in a perpetual examination." (12)

Feingold's seminary friend, a rabbi, attempted to "convert" Lucy's Gentileness into Jewishness. This attempt at creating the antithesis of what she was from birth, and could still be, has apparently failed. Listening, watching and feeling outside of the Jewish experience unfolding in their own living room, she begins to question herself: "Was she a backslider? Anyhow she felt tested. Sometimes she spoke of Jesus to the children. She looked around... and saw that everyone in the living room was a Jew." (12)

Lucy, now feeling at the dialectically opposite side of the Lucy-Jimmy Feingold home, begins to blame her husband:

> He was having one of his spasms of fanaticism. Everyone normal, everyone with sense—the humanists and humorists, for instance—would want to keep away. What was he now, after all, but one of those boring autodidacts who spew out everything they read? He was doing it for spite, because no one had come. There he was, telling about the blood-libel. Little Hugh of Lincoln. How in London, in 1279, Jews were torn to pieces by horses on a charge of having crucified a Christian child. How in 1285, in Munich, a mob burned down a synagogue on the same pretext. (12–13)

The Christian text, that is both pre-text and a pretext, for example, to burn "down a synagogue", vies to replace the earlier text of Torah, the real pre-text. The Christian story wants to kill off the Jewish one. Which tale, whose version, will prevail? Feingold wants his stories to be heard, heeded, be taken as strident warning. The fire has purified Feingold's memory. These are tales of his life, his history, his soul. "Feingold was crazed by these tales; he drank them like a vampire. Lucy stuck a square of chocolate cake in his mouth to shut him up." (13)

Feingold is waiting for something/someone to break the void of silence and to reconnect them to history:

The friend from the Seminary had brought a friend. Lucy examined him: she knew how to give catechisms of her own, she was not a novelist for nothing. She catechized and catalogued: a refugee. Fingers like long wax candles, snuffed at the nails. Black sockets: was he blind? It was hard to tell where the eyes were under that ledge of a skull. Skull for a head, but such a cushioned mouth, such lips, such ordinary expressive teeth. Such a bone in such a dry wrist. A nose like a saint's. The face of Jesus. He whispered. Everyone leaned over to hear. He was Feingold's voice: the voice Feingold was waiting for. (13)

Reality continues to slip and to slide. Is the refugee dead or alive? To which world does Feingold belong? Who/what is Jewish and what is not? The reference to "the face of Jesus" underscores Christianity's (pre-textual) conversion of a Jewish Joshua, son of Joseph and Miriam, into a Greek-Christian Jesus. Is Jesus Joshua? Is Joshua Jesus? Is he both Joshua and Jesus; does he have the face of both? One thing would appear to be certain: the Holocaust fires nearly snuffed out not just this survivor and others like him, but Jewish and non-Jewish history—the human essence of humanity itself. In the face of the survivor is the human scene and history of one of the most powerful stories of the world: that of Joshua/Jesus the Jew. Is the story of the world really a Jewish one? Does this survivor's face represent the survival and face of humanity?

The refugee has the power to ignite a fire: his fingers are "wax candles". The survivor of the great Fire of the Holocaust that consumed so many Jewish lives, he carries within him the seed of a future regeneration; the fire of love, redemption, of the Story. Lucy could have seen a Jewish face in the Jesus she surreptitiously chooses to talk to the children about. Instead, she sees only the Christian version of Joshua's face. But because it is a survivor of Pan's great Fire who bears the face, even "Jesus" momentarily becomes one of these "real Jews", a transformation not to her liking.

As well, the refugee reminds Lucy of "her father. She put away this insight (the resemblance of Presbyterian ministers to Hitler's refugees) to talk over with Feingold later: it was nicely analytical, it had enough mystery to satisfy." (13)

Analyzing the dialectics of being is an endlessly mysterious process; it is the writer's addiction. Lucy, as writer, watches the spellbound listeners absorb the refugee's story:

They all listened with a terrible intensity. Again Lucy looked around. It pained her how intense Jews could be, though she too was intense. But she was intense because her brain was roiling with ardor, she wooed mind-pictures, she was a novelist. *They* were intense all the time; she supposed the grocers among them were as intense as any novelist; was it because they had been Chosen? (14)

Are the Chosen people, the Israelites, writers? Are the writers Jews? Lucy dreads what story this unfamiliar (Jewish) Jesus might tell. The refugee turns out to be an arch-storyteller who was witness to

horror; sadism; corpses. As if—Lucy took the image from the elusive wind that was his voice in its whisper—as if hundreds and hundreds of Crucifixions were all happening at once. She visualized a hillside with multitudes of crosses and bodies dropping down from big bloody nails. Every Jew was Jesus. That was the only way Lucy could get hold of it: otherwise it was only a movie. She had seen all the movies, the truth was she could feel nothing.... If there had been a camera at the Crucifixion Christianity would collapse, no one would ever feel anything about it. Cruelty came out of the imagination, and had to be witnessed by the imagination. (14)

The image she sees of Jesus the Jew crucified over and over in the Holocaust, which could have been for Lucy a way out of her Gentile aloneness and into the roomful of Jews, instead becomes a way to Gentilize the Jews she can otherwise not "get a hold of", to fantasize them out of the alien world of Moses and into her own Christian world.

The refugee, as pure (Mosaic) Jew, describes the devastation of Moses by the Nazi forces of Pan. Not only Jews, but writing as redemption, writer-as-Messiah of the Jews and of all the world, are extinguished in one blow:

All the same she listened. What he told was exactly like the movies. A gray scene, a scrubby hill, a ravine. Germans in helmets, with shining tar-black belts, wearing gloves. A ragged bundle of Jews at the lip of the ravine—an old grandmother, a child or two, a couple in their forties. All the faces stained with grayness, the stubble on the ground stained gray, the clothes on them limp as shrouds but immobile, as if they were already under the dirt shut off from breezes, as if they were already stone. The refugee's whisper carved them like sculptures—there they stood, a shadowy stone asterisk of Jews. (14–15)

The Pan Moloch, in killing Jews, kills the text and writing ("asterisk") as well. The Jews are writing itself; their story the spirit of the world's history, of the Story of stories—humanity's prototype. As the living room begins to rise into the air (or so Lucy imagines), she feels

herself alone at the bottom, below the floorboards, while the room floated upward, carrying Jews. Why did it not take her too? Only Jesus could take her.
They were being kidnapped, those Jews, by a messenger from the land of the
dead. The man had a power. Already he was in the shadow of another
tale: she promised herself she would not listen, only Jesus could make her
listen. (15)

Here is Lucy's last chance to go with them: "only Jesus could take
her." But she has already forgotten that her Gentile Jesus has become
their Jewish Joshua, revealed in the face of a Jew leaving with the other
Jews; she has forgotten that the storyteller "kidnapping" these Jews is
none other than Jesus-as-refugee. Without realizing that she has done it,
she appeals to someone she has already refused. Although the refugee's
storytelling ability is very compelling, it is clear to whose story Lucy will
listen: she has fallen on the Gentile side of the dialectic. Lucy

craned after [the room]. Wouldn't it bump into the apartment upstairs? It was
like watching the underside of an elevator, all dirty and hairy, with dust-roots
wagging. The black floor moved higher and higher. It was getting free of her,
into loftiness, lifting Jews. (15–16)

Lucy then imagines, like a film story running before her eyes, a Pan
scene of her and "the children in a little city park." (16) Like the scene in
"The Pagan Rabbi" where Isaac's life ended, Lucy imagines that the children "are chasing birds" which she has forbidden them to touch. Within
this park story is another story, of a boy who lies sick in a coma with
meningitis but whose testicles have descended. There is yet another
switch to a scene of lascivious-like peasants who are in a play in which
they must act like peasants but who refuse, wanting to be "real peasants".
They sing songs that celebrate the Madonna of Love, the

giver of fertility and fecundity. Lucy is glorified. She is exalted. She comprehends. Not that the musicians are peasants, not that their faces and feet and
necks and wrists are blown grass and red earth. An enlightenment comes on
her: she sees what is eternal....
Inside Lucy's illumination the dancers are seething, writhing. For the sake of
the goddess, for the sake of the womb of the goddess, they are turning into
serpents. When they grow still they are earth. They are from always to always. Nature is their pulse. Lucy sees: she understands: the gods are God.
How terrible to have given up Jesus, a man like these, made of earth like
these, with a pulse like these, God entering nature to become god! Jesus, no
more miraculous than an ordinary goatherd; is a goatherd a miracle? Is a leaf?
A nut, a pit, a core, a seed, a stone? Everything is miracle! Lucy sees how

she has abandoned nature, how she has lost true religion on account of the God
of the Jews. (18)

In this schema, by choosing nature gods over the God of the Jews, Lucy
embraces Pan and rejects Moses, revelling in her "redemption" from a
false religion as it were. Joshua has left with the roomful of Jews, and
she still has her Gentile god-man Jesus, now freed from the fetters of
Moses to join the pantheon of gods and goddesses. With Jesus, however,
she can (if she still chooses) imagine that she has both sides of the
dialectic—the Jewish face momentarily appearing on the surface, but the
natural essence belonging to Pan.

Like Edelshtein but in reverse, Lucy wants to be the kind of Jew her
minister father described in her childhood as "an ancient Hebrew". Her
father's stories fired her imagination of this archaic People of the Book.
In the same way, Lewisohn's Mrs. Morrison of *Holy Land*, remembering
her father's stories of this ancient nation, wants somehow to recapture
those stories in the very place and on the very ground that Joshua/Jesus
has lived and died. However, both Lucy Feingold and Mrs. Morrison discover that the reality of this ancient place and people is very different
from the stories created from their fathers' imaginations and re-imagined
by the daughters through language and communicative artistry.
Edelshtein wants to be a reinvented Gentilized Jew. In the same way,
Lucy wants to be a Judaized Christian. Unfortunately, like Edelshtein, she
is too much of what she really is. When the "refugee" Holocaust survivor
tells his story as witness to that great Calamity that befell him and the
Jews of Europe, Lucy is incapable of fitting her conception of ancient
Hebrews to the mountains of (real) Jewish corpses. Her only avenue for
getting a handle on the horrific scene of grotesque Jewish sacrifice is to
transform/translate it into a Christian one filled with a mini-scene of crucified Jesuses. Unlike her father's stories, Lucy is inaccessible to those of
the refugee who "was in the shadow of another tale." (15) Is this tale the
Book, Torah, which is to say the real Jewish version? Lucy cannot imagine the real Jewish Story; does not comprehend the real Jewish Book;
cannot penetrate or be penetrated by real Jewish stories. She therefore
would appear to be beyond any chance of becoming both a real Jew and
(logically) a first-rate writer. She cannot in any way share in any form of
commonality with a post-Holocaust world as true Jews can. Ostrover, a
converted Gentilized Jew, sees his mirror reflection but in reverse—in
Edelshtein who is unable to convert his Jewishness into any magical for-

mula of (feigned) Gentile Jewishness. Lucy is too Gentile, like Edelshtein in reverse, to even be able to imagine Jewishness or herself as Jewish. She only knows the Gentilized version of it as Ancient Hebrews.

To her frustration, Lucy, like Edelshtein, cannot find the special code, the alchemic way to transmute her Gentile self into a Jewish one. She and Edelshtein are both too much and too little of who they are, and they are unable to fathom or create any means for reinventing or transforming themselves. If at least she were able to tell good stories, there would be hope and instantaneous transformation. However, she is very far from being a Jamesian Master Storyteller. Such perceptiveness and writerly craftpersonship automatically confers Jewishness on its owner. She is condemned by the mediocrity of her being and writing. Thoroughly second-rate, she is a true counterfeit, an imitation on all levels in every way.

In "The Shawl", Rosa will pathetically and poignantly try to protect, shield, fence in and out, the Jewish and Gentile worlds—if not just to save her Magda's life—at the same time that she is a convert or would-be convert of Jewishness into Gentileness.

"The Shawl"

While she rarely uses the word, the Holocaust is nevertheless the most important metaphorically and imagistically charged element in Ozick's fiction. With America in the temporal foreground, the Holocaust is the "time before" and the present is the "time after". It is the virtual gauge, the time-line that cuts across the vast divide of the twentieth-century life of Jews. The "time before" is a "life before", when time and place existed in the idyllic reflections and recollections of a happy, peaceful, secure, but above all safe and determinable childhood.

In "The Pagan Rabbi", Sheindel was born into a concentration camp of death, lived parentless and was nearly killed by the electrified fence (if not for the miraculous coincidence of the war's end). She began her life in total displacement. Her seven children, emotionally fractured by their father's suicide, like Sheindel, must begin anew. The pivotal struggle for the male and female parents and their children is whether continuity should be undermined, ripped, subverted, ignored, or perpetuated. Is the line beginning with Moses at Mt. Sinai—a line that also fences in or out—to be maintained, erased, moved, or reinterpreted? In Ozick's *schema*, therefore, the Holocaust is the transcendent point of calamitous collision of the two fundamental cosmic forces of Pan and Moses.

The American Jewish community's connection to the Holocaust, according to Alan L. Berger,[142] can be understood from two opposing viewpoints. One understanding, articulated by Arthur A. Cohen, is that every Jew, whether that person experienced the death camps or not, is a survivor. Berger, quoting Cohen, states that these Jews, belonging to a post-Holocaust period of the establishment of the state of Israel, consist of "'the generation that bears the scar without the wound, sustaining memory without direct experience. It is this generation that has the obligation, self-imposed and self-accepted (however inelectably), to describe a meaning and wrest instruction from the historical.'" (Berger 11)

Expressing another point of view, he quotes Jacob Neusner's somewhat more radical assertion that the "Holocaust-Rebirth myth" (the Holocaust immediately shadowed by the creation of Israel), "is not appropriate to American Jewry's historical experience." (11) The Holocaust, he says, *vis a vis* American Jews, is less a scar than it "is an ethnic identifier, not psychologically decisive, and misleads Jews away from their religious role. Neusner is correct in warning that the Holocaust should not become a surrogate for American Jewry's attempts to express itself Jewishly in a creative way." (11)

Cynthia Ozick's writing falls exactly at the juncture of these contesting points of view. Her protagonists are caught in an intricate conundrum: of remembering and/or forgetting; bearing the scar, with or without the wound; under the self-contracted burden to prevail at any cost; wanting to perpetuate, or extinguish, any remnants of the pre-Holocaust sense of Torah connectedness. If Sheindel, in a post-Holocaust America, is lodged precisely between the continuity of covenant-of-Torah and loss, discontinuity and fracture, then Rosa in "The Shawl" (1989), in neither the "time before" nor the "time after", is ensnared exactly dead centre in Holocaust time. Lawrence S. Friedman, it would seem, misjudges the sense-presence and impact of the Holocaust in and on Ozick's writing. As he states:

> Since, however, nearly all of Ozick's settings are American and contemporary, the Holocaust, no matter how poignantly invoked, is inevitably distanced by space and time. While the Holocaust must retain its centrality for contemporary American Jews, the majority of Ozick's fictional characters have no direct experience of the bloodshed of the title [of the story].[143]

Friedman would seem to imply that the Holocaust's impact on the story would be minimalized unless it were directly brought as one of the players, so to speak. He underestimates the weight and effect that even an unmentioned Holocaust has on post-Holocaust Jewry. Rabbi Isaac Kornfeld's position, as compared for example to that of the Reverend Arthur Dimmesdale in *The Scarlet Letter*, is so much more complicated by the unimaged presence of the Holocaust which, on all levels, informs every aspect of "The Pagan Rabbi". In this story of a Mishnaic scholar and husband of a Holocaust survivor whose too-creative concoctions of Pan and Moses leads to his insanity and suicide, how much greater is the impact of entertaining the notion of, or creating, a kind of Judaism that can absorb and contain elements of Pan as well as Moses. Quoting from Ozick, Friedman suggests that there is another aspect which proves difficult for all writers who deal with Holocaust fiction:

> If storytelling is itself a risky business, ...how much riskier must it be to make art out of the Holocaust. "I worry very much," said Ozick, "that this subject is corrupted by fiction, and that fiction in general corrupts history." Like many postwar Jewish writers, Ozick is torn between the fear of trivializing the Holocaust and the belief in the necessity of bearing witness to its enormities. (Friedman 113–114)

"The Shawl" is Ozick's only story directly set in the Holocaust as a present time, and not as flashbacks of memory. The central gripping image is described in the "The Pagan Rabbi" by the narrator, through Isaac's retelling of the story Sheindel had told him of her birth and near-death in a concentration camp, when "they were about to throw her against the electrified fence." This same scene, repeated in "The Shawl", is the story's denouement. In this scene, Magda, Rosa's baby, is hurled by a Nazi soldier against the electric fence. Of this climactic moment Friedman, quoting Ozick, states: "Fittingly, its genesis is historical, inspired by a single line in William Shirer's massive *The Rise and Fall of the Third Reich* 'that spoke about babies being thrown against the electrified fences.'"[144]

For Ozick, the story's creation was balanced on a moral struggle, as Friedman says, of remembering and never forgetting, together with an apprehension of rendering this calamity insignificant. (Friedman 114) The shawl, seen as a single focal image, seems to serve as a trope for a fence protecting Magda from enemies:

Rosa with Magda curled up between sore breasts, Magda wound up in the
shawl. Sometimes Stella carried Magda. But she was jealous of Magda. A
thin girl of fourteen, too small, with thin breasts of her own, Stella wanted to
be wrapped in a shawl, hidden away, asleep, rocked by the march, a baby, a
round infant in arms.[145]

Like the "fence of the Law" that Sheindel alludes to, a fence not only
divides, but also contains, distinguishes and excludes. The shawl, then,
can be seen as the element that encloses as it protects Jewish existence
from those "without pity". ("Shawl" 5) Like the electrified fence that
keeps people in, not out (for how many would want to steal into a death
camp?), the shawl, in reverse, keeps what's inside it safe from what's outside. The electrified fence reserves Jews for the killing that awaits them,
in contrast to the Law's fence, which protects them, like the shawl, from
death through physical murder or extinction through assimilation. The
shawl, as a great psychological and emotional divide between existence
and eradication, is the barrier between Pan and Moses, separating the
pitiful from the pitiless; the Jewish world of Law, covenant and Torah
from the Greek-Pan world that respects and worships aesthetics—even an
aesthetic of killing—over humanity. From another direction, the shawl
can represent a (Jewish) prayer shawl. Thus both Isaac's and Rosa's
shawls stand for the identical trope of Jewish essence/existence serving as
the cover, shelter, fence and divider between Pan and Moses. In "The
Pagan Rabbi", Isaac, losing balance and sight of any borders or fence,
hangs himself with his (Jewish) prayer shawl. Rosa, in "The Shawl",
seeks to keep her baby safe, covered, protected, hidden and separate from
the external, insane Pan world. Berger states:

Ozick strongly implies that the camps, designed to turn Jews into matter and
then to destroy that matter, although successful to an awesome and staggering
degree, were not able to achieve complete domination of the Jewish soul. The
peculiar aroma of cinnamon and almonds, itself so out of place in the midst of
death, corpses, and wind bearing the black ash from crematoria, evokes a
quasi-mythical image of the *besamim* (spice) box. Jews sniff the *basamim* at
the *Havdalah* ceremony which marks the outgoing of the Sabbath, thereby
sustaining themselves for the rigors and tribulations of the profane or ordinary
days of the week. By utilizing the prayer shawl and spice-box imagery, and
paranormal phenomena usually associated with the mystical clement of
Judaism, Ozick's tale conveys the message that the bleakness of the historical
moment is not the final chapter in Jewish existence. Jewish religious creativity
and covenantal symbolism can occur even under the most extreme conditions.
(Berger 54)[146]

For Ozick the Holocaust, with its Nazi killing-machine, is pure Pan as in "The Pagan Rabbi"; in all other areas, however, there is no absolutely delineated dividing line, no clearly distinguishable polemic between the realm of Pan and that of Moses. Thus, as this study asserts, a dialectic of Pan and Moses creates an ambiguous mix, an interplay, a confusion or complexity of these forces which can appear as one, and then be identifiable as the other—constantly and simultaneously disguising and unmasking itself. Instead, each of the dialectically placed Pan and Moses components has a series of codes delineating what is of Pan and what of Moses. The world of Pan can be characterized by words and ideas such as: cold/coldness, hell, pitilessness, cannibalism, death, muteness, fences, things of nature. The Moses world has words/ideas of: voice, pity, survivor, Yiddish, Israel as the fulfillment of the Zionist dream.

In Ozick's cosmological scheme, beginning with the world of Pan from its purest to mixed manifestations, the institution of the Church, starting with its inception in the period of post-Joshua/Jesus, is the primal scene, so to speak, of the Holocaust. It is the backdrop and forestructure of the Holocaust which is itself a frame in all of Ozick's work. The first two sentences of "The Shawl" initiate the dialectical web that informs the story: "Stella, cold, cold, the coldness of hell. How they walked on the roads together." ("Shawl" 3) In contrast, the Torah is the Mosaic primal scene. Ozick's stories often also display a number of Tannaic characteristics: syntax, structural minimalism, and the ambiguity inherent in the absence of absolute closure. A case in point is an example from *Genesis*: the story of the Sacrifice of Isaac, which reflects the deep love between a parent and child set within a cosmic drama. The Torah portion, translated here literally, with the punctuation of the original biblical Hebrew text, emphasizes these characteristics:

> And Isaac said to Abraham his father and he said "My father" and he said "Here I am my son." And he said "Here is the fire and the wood And where is the lamb for the sacrifice": And Abraham said "God will show him the lamb for the sacrifice my son." And they went the two of them together: (*Genesis* 22:7–8)

The biblical quotation, like the Ozick one, leaves several very important pieces of information unexplained. In the former, most important to know, perhaps, is who or what the sacrifice is. In Abraham's answer, who "him" is isn't made clear. The ending could mean that the lamb is "my son"; "my son" is the sacrifice. In a quotation from "The Shawl", the first line beginning with the word, "Stella" (Rosa's niece), followed by a comma, would seem to indicate that Stella is physically cold, and/or emotionally cold; or, that the place is cold like hell is cold. There is an unclear, ambiguous referential web linking the Mosaic Stella with a characteristic of their Nazi tormentors—"cold and of hell", albeit to a much lesser degree. Thus qualities of Pan are linked with those of Moses. The second sentence does not make clear who "they" are: "they" as the three of them (Stella, Rosa and Magda); "they" as Stella's "coldness of hell" combined with the extremely vulnerable state of her Jewish being. "They" can also refer to the worlds of Pan and Moses which are impossible to keep totally separate.

Stella is compared to disease and the animal world. "Her knees were tumors on sticks, her elbows chicken bones." ("Shawl" 3) In "The Pagan Rabbi", disease, voicelessness and the animal kingdom, skewed on the side of Pan, are constantly replaced and *vice versa* with the opposite characteristics of Moses: humanness, the (human) voice, health, life, pity. Thus in "The Shawl", Stella's tumored body, and the pitiless process of dehumanization the Nazis set into motion, have either rendered her less than human and/or serve to describe certain preexisting qualities that such dire circumstances only illuminated. Rosa, on the other hand, "did not feel hunger; she felt light, not like someone walking but like someone in a faint, in trance, arrested in a fit, someone who is already a floating angel, alert and seeing everything, but in the air, not there, not touching the road." (3–4)

Rosa is not less than human, but more: angelic. Stella's Pan-devilishness contrasts with Rosa's Moses-heavenliness. She no longer has human characteristics. Her breasts, like the supernatural realm she already inhabits, don't produce milk but "Magda sucked air." (3) Her body seems to have etherealized. She doesn't appear to need food to exist. Her body is weightless. She floats above everything from a heavenly panoramic perspective, like a portrait of mythic and eternal Jewish motherhood; Rosa is "a walking cradle." (3)

Magda having been birthed in a death camp, "You could think she was one of *their* babies." (4) No longer a baby, but a child who "lived to walk" (5) Magda, "fifteen months old", (5) lies curled up inside the shawl: "She looked into Magda's face through a gap in the shawl: a squirrel in a nest, safe, no one could reach her inside the little house of the shawl's windows. The face, very round, a pocket mirror of a face." (4) The shawl is Magda's protection and the fence that keeps them out. Magda, however, looks as if she is already one of them: "The face... was not Rosa's bleak complexion, dark like cholera, it was another kind of face altogether, eyes blue as air, smooth feathers of hair nearly as yellow as the Star sewn into Rosa's coat." (4) Magda is already of death. She has only one of her teeth that sticks up from her gums like "an elfin tombstone." (4) The only thing separating Rosa's (Jewish) child from the Pan Nazis outside is the "magic shawl". (5) Like naming some esoteric number, the shawl "could nourish an infant for three days and three nights." (5) In reality, because Rosa has no milk in her breasts: "both were cracked, not a sniff of milk. The duct-crevice extinct, a dead volcano blind eye, chill hole so Magda took the corner of the shawl and milked it instead." (4)

A Jewish future represented by this child cannot be nourished and kept alive in a death camp. Magda has already become *them*: "Rosa and sometimes Stella studied... [the] blueness [of Magda's eyes]. On the road they raised one burden of a leg after another and studied Magda's face. 'Aryan', Stella said, in a voice grown as thin as a string." (5) By degrees, here in the death camp Pan conquers Moses. Jewish existence cannot be renewed and replenished in such a place. Stella is steadily becoming mute. The place could make it seem as if Jews would have to become "Aryan" to survive such a pitiless place:

> and Rosa thought how Stella gazed at Magda like a young cannibal. And the time that Stella said "Aryan," it sounded to Rosa as if Stella had really said "Let us devour her...." They were in a place without pity, all pity was annihilated in Rosa, she looked at Stella's bones without pity. She was sure that Stella was waiting for Magda to die so she could put her teeth into the little thighs. (5)

The shawl is not just a symbol of Jewish existence. In the death camp it can be also a symbol of death. In "The Pagan Rabbi", Isaac's prayer shawl is transformed from a representation of Jewish entity into that of Pan-death. Grabbing it from off the "body" of his Jewish soul, the prayer shawl becomes a kind of grave-marker designating the extinction of Isaac's (Jewish) life. Similarly:

> Rosa knew Magda was going to die very soon; she should have been dead already, but she had been buried away deep inside the magic shawl, mistaken there for the shivering mound of Rosa's breasts; Rosa clung to the shawl as if

it covered only herself. No one took it away from her. Madga was mute. She never cried. Rosa hid her in the barracks, under the shawl. (5–6)

The shawl marks the place of Jewish life which prevails or doesn't. Against all odds, it can also sustain, because it is "magic". It is of (Jewish) body but also of (Jewish) soul. Magda's (Jewish) body is now more dead than alive. No sounds come from her voice any more. Just as Torah has historically helped Jews persevere, so the shawl, reflecting in miniature, gives strength, hope, even cheer. The black humor—the ability to laugh through tears of grief—that emerged from a millennium of Jewish catastrophe mixed with hopefulness is recapitulated in one description of Magda and the shawl:

Magda was quiet, but her eyes were horribly alive, like blue tigers. She watched. Sometimes she laughed—it seemed a laugh, but how could it be? Magda had never seen anyone laugh. Still, Magda, laughed at her shawl when the wind blew its corners, the bad wind with pieces of black in it, that made Stella's and Rosa's eyes tear. Magda's eyes were always clear and tearless. She watched like a tiger. She guarded her shawl. No one could touch it, only Rosa could touch it. Stella was not allowed. The shawl was Magda's own baby, her pet, her little sister. She tangled herself up in it and sucked on one of the corners when she wanted to be very still. (6)

The image of Magda laughing from the shawl blowing—not from the breeze but from the wind made by the huge crematorium fires—emphasizes several possibilities. One is to contrast the utter innocence, the inability to comprehend, and the helplessness of the Jewish babies and little children facing the seemingly cosmic power and torment of hell itself. Another is the aspect of transformation from human to animal form through adversity, and self-generated or other-generated dehumanization. Magda's self-perceived existence has been reduced to the fulfillment of one goal: to keep and protect her shawl. Finally, it is always the children who are ultimately responsible for maintaining the historical continuity of the Jewish people. In messianic times, according to one Jewish mystical interpretative tradition, it is "the children who will teach the parents" about God and Torah, and who will be the torchbearers of tradition.[147]

Pan is everywhere. It is, of course, indistinguishable from the Nazi killing-machine. It is also in Stella, of and like "the coldness of hell." She partakes in specific Pan characteristics: "Then Stella took the shawl away and made Magda die. Afterward Stella said: 'I was cold.' And afterward she was always cold, always. The cold went into her heart; Rosa saw that

Stella's heart was cold." (6–7) Without the shawl, Magda cannot exist: it is her life, food, balance and future. Ozick's Tannaic, minimalist, repetitive style serves to underscore and contrast the surrounding Pan horror.

Stella, Rosa and Magda represent three aspects of Jewish existence. Rosa is the mythos of the "Jewish mother" who protects (sometimes excessively) her Jewish child against the ravages of the outside world. Torah, in the trope of the shawl, thus becomes synonymous with transmission and historical continuity. Magda is the focal point of that continuity. She is fully identified and indentifiable with Jewish existence, which is in turn indistinguishable from Torah. "Rosa... saw that Magda was grieving for the loss of her shawl, she saw that Magda was going to die." (8) Without the protection and life of, and with, Torah, the only possibility is death. Stella's coldness represents the distance Jews can wander in search of the very thing they run from: Torah and historical transmission. She is parentless and will remain childless. "Stella didn't menstruate." (5) Her past destroyed, she has little hope for a future. She is "[a] thin girl of fourteen, too small, with thin breasts of her own." (3)

Rosa already has a future in Magda. Her only desire is to guard and keep safe, keep warm and alive, the Jewish future represented in her. Rosa trusts no one else. "Rosa hid... [Magda] in the barracks, under the shawl, but she knew that one day someone would inform; or one day someone, not even Stella, would steal Magda to eat her." (6) Rosa's angel-like behavior, synonymous with the world of pure Moses, is contrasted with Stella's coldness.

After Stella takes the shawl from Magda, Rosa isn't sure whether to run after Magda or to look for the shawl. Deciding on the latter, "Rosa entered the dark. It was easy to discover the shawl. Stella was heaped under it, asleep in her thin bones. Rosa tore the shawl free and flew—she could fly, she was only air—into the arena." (8)

Stella, too, desires to continue her (Jewish) existence. Only the shawl could warm, protect and keep her alive. Jewish values and the Jewish people itself could be perpetuated only through Torah, troped by the shawl. Without Torah, there is only darkness, like "the bad... black... wind... black [Nazi] body like a domino and a pair of black boots." (6,9) Without the shawl, Rosa can only go into the blackness.

However, even in the midst of darkness, Torah and its values are clearly discernible. The twin aspects of Jewish body and Jewish soul are made clear from the phrase: "asleep in her thin bones." The word "in" emphasizes the dual importance of Jewish soul and body. Stella, as the sum of her Jewish soul-essence, is greater and supersedes the relative meagerness of her finite and evanescent materiality. Rosa, in tearing the shawl free, reclaiming and unfurling it for all to see in the now-pathetic community of Jews lined up in the roll-call area of the death camp, reenacts God's giving of the Torah to the body of the Jewish people through Moses, their teacher and prophet.

However, what Rosa sees in the "arena" is the absolute Pan reverse, in its total negative manifestation. Just as Rosa the angel carried Magda, hidden separate, safe and sustained, under the shawl, so now does the camp's angel of Death—in the body of the Nazi black-booted soldier—carry Magda, in an absolute reversed scene of the Creator's creation of the world in total love. Similarly, Rosa has always heard voices coming from the electrified fence, itself also the negative image of the fence of the Law, whose separating function was always to remind her of her past and Jewish existence. Thus the electrified fence becomes converted into the trope for Jewish existence, but in a physical and completely inverted form:

> [Rosa] stood for an instant at the margin of the arena. Sometimes the electricity inside the fence would seem to hum; even Stella said it was only an imagining, but Rosa heard real sounds in the wire: grainy sad voices. The farther she was from the fence, the more clearly the voices crowded at her. The lamenting voices strummed so convincingly, so passionately, it was impossible to suspect them of being phantoms. The voices told her to hold up the shawl, high; the voices told her to shake it, to whip with it, to unfurl it like a flag: Rosa lifted, shook, whipped, unfurled. Far off, very far, Magda leaned across her air-fed belly, reaching out with rods of her arms. She was high up, elevated, riding someone's shoulder. But the shoulder that carried Magda was not coming toward Rosa and the shawl, it was drifting away, the speck of Magda was moving more and more into the smoky distance. Above the shoulder a helmet glinted. The light tapped the helmet and sparkled it into a goblet. Below the helmet a black body like a domino and a pair of black boots hurled themselves in the direction of the electrified fence. The electric voices began to chatter wildly. "Maamaa, maaa-maaa," they all hummed together. How far Magda was from Rosa now, across the whole square, past a dozen barracks, all the way on the other side! She was no bigger than a moth. (9)

This scene is similar to the moment when the "pagan rabbi" Isaac, as body, makes a reflexive decision to grab the prayer shawl from his Jewish soul and thereby hang himself in the public park. In the same way, Magda, losing the shawl, finds her (Jewish body's) end.

The fence, the tortured voices of their covenanted people, constantly call them back to the fence (of the Law) whenever they stray too far into the darkness of the Pan world. Voice here expresses authority, continuity and potency, but it takes the constructive and creative imagination to hear and believe in that voice. It is this Jewish, human voice of clarity and power which drives her on to retrieve the shawl as Torah, and proclaim its truth and voice. As Magda is propelled by the dark power of Pan, away from life and Torah, to "the far side", to the fence that kills Jewish bodies, the voice of the fence of the Law tells her to keep Torah in life and to flaunt it proudly.

By keeping Torah alive, there can be no real final death of Jewish existence—even in Pan's far "smoky distance" that has the amoral imagination only for death and destruction. Realizing that now Magda (as Jewish body) is dead, Rosa is faced with three choices: to do the bidding of what are now "the steel voices [that] went mad in their growling" which, "of course Rosa did not obey"; (10) to stand completely still, "because if she ran they would shoot" (10); to run and try "to pick up the sticks of Magda's body", in which case "they would [also] shoot". (10) Instead:

> She only stood because if she ran they would shoot, and if she tried to pick up the sticks of Magda's body they would shoot, and if she let the wolf's screech ascending now through the ladder of her skeleton break out, they would shoot; so she took Magda's shawl and filled her own mouth with it, stuffed it in and stuffed it in, until she was swallowing up the wolf's screech and tasting the cinnamon and almond depth of Magda's saliva; and Rosa drank Magda's shawl until it dried. (10)

Like Sheindel suppressing her "mouselike" ("Pagan" 19) laughter, fearing to wake her sleeping children, so Rosa brings, or rather could have brought, from her (human) voice the sound of the animal, which would have resulted in her (human) death. Human voice as the world of Moses can sometimes change into the animal sound of Pan. Separating through its symbolism, the two contrasting sides of the cosmos, the electric fence or the Law's fence, Pan or Moses, can be voiced either in steely, insane animal sounds, as "body" (reflected here in Rosa as "skeleton"); or in the grief-filled voice of Jewish existence which prevails through any catastrophe.

The only choice is the "taste" of the shawl's Jewish history, Torah, and the *havdalah*-like spices that represent and mark the division between God's holy sabbath day—and the holiness the Creator stands for—and the mundane or profane days of existence in a largely Pan world. The shawl, like the fence, marks the separation between destruction and salvation, protection, hope, the creative inspiration of a moral imagination that can bring healing and redemption.

Thus the story contains another set of code words and ideas representing and delineating the ubiquitous potentiality of art, specifically writing, as a creative act that gives rise to a process of mending and atonement. When Stella takes the shawl from Magda, "Magda flopped onward with her little pencil legs scribbling this way and that in search of the shawl; the pencils faltered at the barracks opening, where the light began." ("Shawl" 7) Ozick seems to provide here a most explicit statement on the connection between writing and redemption. Art, through writing, is the only way to usher in the messianic age and its concomitant consciousness. The search for, and meaning of, Torah and Jewish identity, is achieved through the writing process. An understanding of Divine enlightenment occurs only through the creative act of writing.

In the same scene, "Magda was wavering in the perilous sunlight of the arena, scribbling on such pitiful little bent shins... grieving for the loss of her shawl." (8) Through the process of writing, which itself could be interpreted as an inextricable combination of Pan and Moses, Stella, Rosa and Magda—dead or alive—can maintain their Jewish essence, even in the midst of the most extreme form of Pan. In this tale, Berger states, Ozick combines

> covenant Judaism and a mystical parapsychology.... Although women were freed from the so-called time-bound *mitzvot* (commandments), such as wearing a prayer shawl, Jewesses have donned this ritual object. The Talmud tells, for example, that Rabbi Judah the Prince, editor of the *Mishnah* (second century C.E.), affixed *tzitzit* (*tallit* fringes) to his wife's apron (*Menahot* 43a). Wrapping oneself in a prayer shawl is tantamount to being surrounded by the holiness and protection of the commandments; as well as conforming to the will of God. The wearer of the *tallit* is a member of the covenant community. Ozick's shawl/tallit is a talisman which protects both Rosa and Magda when they either wear or hold it. (Berger 53)

The shawl is like the *Shekinah* (the protective Divine cloud) that accompanied the Israelites in the wilderness. Torah is the communal voice from God's mouth, that gives form and historical continuity to the Jewish people. Also, Torah, as the story of the Israelites and humanity from the beginning of time, is reflected in Ozick's desire to use writing as a road to godliness. "Storytelling," as Victoria Aarons states, "serves as a means of establishing an ethical code, of providing guidelines for living in a community and for balancing personal morality with communal necessity." [148] It is the way to record and remember. The compulsion to relate the story, Aarons says, is as strong as the need to listen to it. (Aarons 12–13)

Thus in Ozick and other writers, voice and writing are the absolute necessities for maintaining and preserving Jewish identity and Jewish life. Through the shawl and Rosa's public actions with it, she ultimately asserts a desire for Jewish life to prevail, in spite of the greatest of losses. As with Rosa's "magic shawl", Jews must drink from Torah and continue to tell the story of the Book. Like Kornfeld, Edelshtein, Ostrover, Lucy and Jim, Rosa is enamored with language, literature and culture. By the end of "The Shawl", Rosa is a disconnected, displaced piece of junk which in its sequel will float up onto the shores of the American landscape (first in New York City, then Miami Beach, the American Jewish version of Israel), a shell of the Gentilized Jewish version of herself, maimed and disoriented by the Nazi killing-machine. She is, paradoxically, both a transcultural anomaly and a non-being culturally disconnected from any frame.

"Rosa"

The Holocaust, as the great "fence" of temporality separating the "before" from the "after", is the horrific event which emphasizes, as Joseph Lowin states, "the dual role—of culture and of cruelty—that Europe has played for Jewish heroes."[149] Lowin believes that the pair of short stories, "The Shawl" (1980) and "Rosa" (1983), which first appeared in *The New Yorker*, represent (at the time of the writing of Lowin's book) the apex of Ozick's writing career. (Lowin 106)

For Victor Strandberg, the "Kulture" that the Pre-Hitler German Jews had so active a part in creating and maintaining, ironically contrasted with Hitler's obsessively active need to eradicate them. As he says:

There is a special irony about Germany's being the center of the Holocaust. The five percent of Europe's Jews who lived there up to the Hitler years, comprising less than one percent of Germany's population, were the most privileged Jews on the continent—prosperous, fully emancipated and largely assimilated into German society. Conversely, the Jewish contribution to German culture and science was greater than in any other European country.... For Cynthia Ozick, the assimilationist character of pre-Hitler Germany is precisely the index by which to measure the evil of Holocaust betrayal. For her and many other Jews, Germany's pre-Hitler philo-Semitism implies a warning about what could happen in other friendly host countries, not excepting America.[150]

The German Jews' profound immersion into, and creation of, an ultimately Greek-inspired (Pan) Art and Culture was stopped, ironically, only through Hitler's identification of them as separate and "Jewish". Ozick's two related stories, "The Shawl" and "Rosa", describe the identical process from a cultural/social/artistic preeminence of Jews in Poland before Hitler, to their agonies and death in the Polish killing grounds of Auschwitz and other death-factories.

The stories are related in a number of ways. The first is that both describe and delineate the main character, Rosa, before, during and after Holocaust time. Secondly, the shawl, as the trope for the world of Moses—security, Jewish identity, historical continuity, Torah, the (Jewish) soul, and memory—is central to both stories. However, whereas in "The Shawl", the shawl was the Moses fence that contained, retained, and sustained Jewish memory and being (it gave warmth and helped keep Magda hidden and safe), in "Rosa" the shawl becomes the fence that ironically keeps death and sick fantasy alive, and most importantly, keeps Rosa separate from human companionship and a life-immersed Moses existence. The shawl is now the Nazi-Pan electric fence that dehumanizes, separates, isolates, then kills on contact.

From "The Pagan Rabbi" through "The Shawl" to "Rosa", the shawl as a fence invokes two sides of the same coin: the Moses enclosure that protects Jewish memory, Torah and Jewish life; and the Pan barrier that isolates and kills the spirit and body of Moses. The shawl that helped perpetuate Jewish life in "The Shawl" is the instrument that keeps death alive in its sequel, "Rosa". The shawl as image and trope, therefore, represents an inseparable complexity of Pan-Moses dialectic.

Also, as previously alluded to, throughout the three stories, the shawl image is related to another trope: voice and voicelessness, which serves to increase and intensify the intricacy of Pan-Moses entanglement.

Although the shawl protects, perpetuates and contains (Jewish) existence, one can still be rendered either mute or with voice, through the relative strength or weakness of the power of Pan. Thus in "The Pagan Rabbi" the narrator's father, for example, loses his voice not because the shawl of Torah, memory and Jewish existence is absent from his life, but because the shawl becomes a too inward-oriented, solipsistic barrier to human interaction. Moreover, the death-by-suicide with his own prayer shawl underscores not only the emotional gulf Rabbi Isaac Kornfeld's immersion into the world of Pan created, but also the cessation of all desire—even the ability—to communicate with or within the human community.

Similarly, but from a different (Pan) direction, the near-total silence in "The Shawl", specifically the final scene of Rosa's soundless scream, is both a result, and a manifestation of, the near-total process of dehumanization set into motion by the Third Reich. The only things with voice are the sounds of Pan: the natural world and the murderous techno-logical creations and objects. Lowin's statement that Ozick replaces human voice with "the double voice of nature and technology" (Lowin 108) is a valid one. However, his reason for stating this, it would seem, is not. He argues:

> Ozick's nature speaks in murmurs. "The sunheat [in the arena] murmured of another life, of butterflies in summer…. On the other side of the steel fence, far away, there were green meadows speckled with dandelions and deep-col-ored violets; beyond them even farther, innocent tiger lilies, tall, lifting their orange bonnets." This moment of lyricism provides relief in the tension-filled drama; it constitutes a delaying tactic at the precise moment of the greatest horror. (108)

As with any unwary reader lulled by Ozick's duplicity, Lowin is like the rabbi in Gertel's description of the public bath with a statue of Aphrodite; he is in the water with Pan. But unlike Gertel's rabbi, he doesn't know it. Lowin, like Rabbi Isaac Kornfeld, is overtaken by Ozick's description of the power of (Pan) nature's sensual beauty; he can't see, as the expression goes, the forest for the trees. Her scenic sketches in "The Shawl" are of the breathtaking beauty of those flowers that are both gorgeous and deadly. Nothing else could explain Ozick's descriptions of the "flowers", of "rain" in "the barracks"; or the "excre-ment, thick turd braids, and the slow stinking maroon waterfall that slunk down from the upper bunks"; or of Magda's final moment when she, "swimming through the air, looked like a butterfly touching a silver vine." ("Shawl" 8–9) Not only technology but also nature are Pan avenues for expression, and are the essential ingredients of horrific Nazi concoctions of creativity gone insane.

Rabbi Kornfeld also produced "creative" concoctions that ultimately could bring only a loss of everything positive, human and humane. In "The Pagan Rabbi", Ozick also mixes nature—beautiful or in ugly putrefaction—with Isaac's suicide: "The tree was almost alone in a long rough meadow, which sloped down to a bay filled with sickly clams and a bad smell…. I knew what the smell meant: that cold brown water covered half the city's turds." ("Pagan" 4) The reader leaves "The Shawl" and Rosa with her "wolf's scream" muffled by the shawl stuffed in her mouth and the taste of "the cinnamon and almond depth of Magda's saliva" on her tongue. ("Shawl" 10) Muteness is imagized in this final scene, in the form of a palpable silence in the pure-Pan Holocaust world of "The Shawl".

As well, the juxtaposition of the "wolf's scream" with "the cinnamon and almond depth of Magda's saliva" makes a riveting image of nature's Pan world contrasted with that of the Judaic one. Cinnamon and almond are two oft-used spices for the ritual ceremony, *Havdalah,* meaning "differentiation" marking the end of the holy Sabbath and the beginning of the mundane weekdays. In itself, *Havdalah* is a reminder that holiness and the terrestrial; the sacred and debasement; Moses and Pan exist in some sort of paradoxical and dynamic union. The *Havdalah* prayer enumerates the differences between "'holy and profane', between 'light and darkness', between 'Israel and the gentiles'" (*Religion* 309) In addition, "the wolf's scream" is swallowed up as if it is something originating from outside of her being. On the other hand, the symbols of Mosaic life and selfhood, in the deepest recesses of her being, are produced, created, emanated from within the depths of *her*. They are not external to her being. This saliva taste, in turn, comes from the Mosaic fence of the shawl which is the only border between Magda and the Pan world of Nazi bestiality. Once Magda loses her (Mosaic) shawl as fence, she is devoured by "the electrified fence" of the Pan Nazis.

As in Jerzy Kosinski's Holocaust-set book,[151] the natural world of Ozick appears to mutate into some grim nightmarish reflection of indescribable inhumanity and horror. Kosinski's six-year-old Jewish protagonist survives, after wandering from one Polish peasant village to another until the war's close, but survival comes at a very high price: not able to speak, he is himself a psychological mutation. As Sara R. Horowitz points out:

> In *The Painted Bird*, Jerzy Kosinski utilizes the perspective of a mute protago-
> nist to put words to something usually kept outside the boundaries of language:
> the experience of a self undone by atrocity, told from the perspective of the
> undone self. As an object of ongoing atrocity, the protagonist's narration comes
> from outside the linguistic system, outside of the self-defining and world-defin-
> ing power of words. (Horowitz 71)

Rosa's form of muteness, as in all fiction that has the Holocaust in the background or foreground, attests to the varieties of self-displacement that accompany the atrocities in the warp and weave of Hitler's killing-creation.

In "Rosa", with the addition of the shawl and Stella, as unseen but nevertheless powerfully present figural referents to Holocaust time, we find Rosa the main player now in this "after-the-time" story. She is here fully named as though in repossession of her own humanness: "Rosa Lublin [is] a madwoman and a scavenger [who] gave up her store—she smashed it up herself—and moved to Miami."[152] Rosa has not only become a ghost of the earliest self described later in the story; we are also witness to what, for Ozick, is the Pan process of Jewish emotional and psychic disfigurement and deformity, that began in pre-Holocaust Poland.

History, as both the larger picture of the Jewish nation and the personal and individual past of each member of that nation, represents the past from different perspectives. Later on, the reader learns that Rosa's shop was a "junkshop, [with] everything used, old, lacy with other people's history." ("Rosa" 15) Rosa's only response to the events played out in Holocaust-time is a lower-level mirroring of that wanton destruction. She wilfully destroys the post-transit-camp past she created in New York City:

> She knew about newspapers and their evil reports: a newspaper item herself.
> "WOMAN AXES OWN BIZ. Rosa Lublin, 59, owner of a secondhand furni-
> ture store on Utica Avenue, Brooklyn, yesterday afternoon deliberately
> demolished..." The *News* and the *Post*. A big photograph, Stella standing near
> with her mouth stretched and her arms wild. In the *Times*, six lines. (18)

The creation of another existence from destruction and displacement, however, can be highly problematic; and the description, the naming, the signifying of the fracturing during and after the Holocaust are difficult in another way. Edward Alexander says:

> It is to acknowledge that literary works [like the Holocaust-fractured characters described in them] that are characterized by uncertainty, paralysis, and ambivalence may provide a more adequate response to the Holocaust.... [This is what Lionel] Trilling called "the incommunicability of man's suffering" during the Holocaust.[153]

At the hands of the arch-Panists, Rosa is transformed by her victimization, becoming like her description of Magda: "one of their babies." Like Isaac Kornfeld, on the outer borders of everything considered human, Rosa too has lost her senses, direction and place in the world of human enterprise; that which Ozick associates with the world of Moses. She smashes her New York City life to bits with her own hands, just as her life was crushed at the hands of the Nazis, a Pan event that becomes re-reflected in her next life in Miami Beach. Although still in her mid-fifties,

> she lived among the elderly in a dark hole, a single room in a "hotel".... Over in a corner a round oak table brooded on its heavy pedestal.... There was a dumbwaiter on a shrieking pulley [that]... swallowed her meager bags of garbage. Squads of dying flies blackened the rope.... The streets [of Miami Beach] were a furnace, the sun an executioner....
> It seemed to Rosa Lublin that the whole peninsula of Florida was weighted down with regret. Everyone had left behind a real life. Here they had nothing. They were all scarecrows, blown about under the murdering sunball. ("Rosa" 13–14, 16)

In fact, even the geography of the state of Florida that contains this place, Miami Beach, is the very image of "regret" and powerlessness; with all its misplaced, displaced inhabitants, the whole of the place is a hagiography of empty lives. Ozick's description is a very common sociological phenomenon in American Jewish life. These Miami Beach inhabitants believe that by living in the Israel-of-America (Miami Beach), each has arrived in the promised land, but instead finds a killing place under a "killing" sun; nature's potential for beauty gone berserk. "Florida, why Florida?" Rosa asks herself. "Because here they were shells like herself, already fried from the sun.... [Like her] they were from the Bronx, from Brooklyn, lost neighborhoods, burned out." (15–16)

Ozick catalogues the shallowness of these displaced Floridian Jews. Each is a mere husk of a former self, which is, in turn, a shell of an earlier (Jewish) self. Like Rosa's family, they have replaced their forefathers' faith with a Pan religion of socialism: "Old ghosts, old socialists: idealists. The Human Race was all they cared for." (16) The words, "The Human Race" in capital letters, signifies the (Pan) universalism for which Ozick so harshly criticized George Steiner. These Jews think they are at the apex of Jewish identity, at the same time that they paradoxically lose themselves in universalist political-social causes, in "Kulture" or Art. They are all misguided Panists who lose their own precious Jewish particularity in a cosmos of "*isms*".

Rosa's contempt focuses on their American cultural primitivism, as opposed to (as she views it) her own greatly superior cosmopolitan European sophistication, since hers includes the eradication of even the slightest hint of ghetto (or any other identifying signs of) Jewishness. For Ozick, the ironic joke is that they are all in one stage or another of assimilation:

> Retired workers, they went to lectures, they frequented the damp and shadowy little branch library. She saw them walking with Tolstoy under their arms, with Dostoyevsky. They knew good material. Whatever you wore they would feel between their fingers and give a name to, faille, velour, crepe. She heard them speak of bias, grosgrain, the "season", the length. Yellow they called mustard. What was pink to everyone else, to them was sunset; orange was tangerine; red, hot tomato.... Once she met an ex-vegetable-store owner from Columbus Avenue.... Even in the perpetual garden of Florida, he reminisced about his flowery green heads of romaine lettuce, his glowing strawberries, his sleek avocados. (16)

Sprinkled throughout this quotation are Ozick's code-words for Pan: "vegetable", "garden", "flowery green heads of romaine lettuce". Not only is Florida itself a wonder of nature, but these Jewish residents translate everything into terms of nature.

Due to her European cultural origins, Rosa feels herself superior to the other females there. In the following quotation, the narrator expresses Rosa's point of view:

> In Florida the men were of higher quality than the women. They knew a little more of the world, they read newspapers, they lived for international affairs. Everything that happened in the Israeli Knesset they followed. But the women only recited meals they used to cook in their old lives.... Mainly the women

thought about their hair. They went to hairdressers and came out into the brilliant day with plantlike crowns the color of zinnias. Sea-green paint on the
eyelids. One could pity them: they were in love with rumors of their grandchildren, Katie at Bryn Mawr, Jess at Princeton. To the grandchildren Florida
was a slum, to Rosa it was a zoo. (17)

Ozick's highly ambiguous attitude towards art, culture and intellectual pursuits, and their relation to the male and female genders, is
apparent in this and the previous quotation. The code-words on the two
sides of Pan and Moses, and the various degrees of intermixing between,
are indicated through references to Israel, reading, politics *versus* domes-
tic activities, and the ludicrous self-beautification that turns the females
into objects of nature.

In one stroke and at the same time that Ozick takes on the dragons of
middle-class (assimilationist) upper mobility, emotional dislocation, loss
of the past, memory and a lack of essential humanness; she also venerates
the "higher quality" of intellectualism, art ("Dostoyevsky", "Tolstoy")
and international events. Again there is clear no line between what is Pan
and what is Moses. As Bonnie Lyons says in her essay:

Neither systematic nor totally self-consistent, Ozick sometimes contradicts
herself even on her most basic premises. While she insists on the uniqueness
of Judaism, attacking George Steiner's universalism and anti-nationalism and
denouncing Allen Ginsberg's perception of the essential sameness of all religious experience, in the same essay she calls the nineteenth-century novel...
"Judaized"... and adds that George Eliot, Dickens and Tolstoy, were ...
"touched by the Jewish covenant" ("Towards a New Yiddish" 164). That is,
sometimes she defines Judaism as a unique and distinct religious vision, at
other times she treats it as something like a synonym for moral seriousness.
Likewise, ...Ozick surprisingly observed that the term "Jewish writer" does
not describe a category but rather "a profundity".[154]

Rather than inconsistency, Ozick's work exhibits the dialectical Pan-
Moses web that can entice and ensnare the most conscientious Jews,
especially the intellectuals and artists among them. Idolatry takes many
forms and exhibits many faces. As Elaine M. Kauver states, of all its
manifestations, idolatry as a metaphor for "an unlived life" is nearly the
worst of biblical and Ozickian prohibitions:

Deed and redemption are, for Ozick, moored to the "metaphorical depths of
Commandment" (*A & A* 123). And the most uncompromising commandment

of all—the Second Commandment against idolatry—is the afflatus of Ozick's most pervasive and important theme, the "nimbus of meaning that envelopes" her stories (*A & A* 246). Serving no one, an idol stuns, transfixes and enslaves its worshippers with the mind-forged manacles that guarantee an unlived life. This perilous power is movingly explored in... "Rosa"... in which... Rosa Lublin... in late middle age, face[s] a shrinking and darkening future. In [her story]... Ozick dramatizes the tragic consequences of idolatry and provides a powerful answer to the question of how to live.[155]

To live an empty life is to be "one of their babies"; an assent to Pan-Moloch. After Rosa eliminates the source of her material sustenance, she becomes ironically dependent on the only relative she has left in the world, and on the person who helped precipitate Magda's death: Stella. Not having a telephone—a symbol of her continuing muteness and self-excommunication from the human community—she writes her niece many letters that are never mailed: "The room was littered with these letters. It was hard to get them mailed—"the post office was a block farther off than the laundromat, and the hotel lobby's stamp machine had been marked 'Out of Order' for years." ("Rosa" 14)

All means for humans to stay connected to each other are absent, lost, waylaid. Rosa, feeling "she was in hell", (14) is forced to stay in touch with a still coldhearted Stella, in order to continue to receive the support she needs to exist:

> "Golden and beautiful Stella," she wrote to her niece. "Where I put myself is in hell. Once I thought the worst was the worst, after that nothing could be the worst. But now I see, even after the worst there's still more." Or she wrote: "Stella, my angel, my dear one, a devil climbs into you and ties up your soul and you don't even know it." (14–15)

Stella still exhibits the Pan heartlessness—or it may be closer to the truth to say that her defect is a lack of artistic sensibility—that she had as a young teenager in the death camp. Rosa, however, is guilty of perhaps an even greater transgression *vis a vis* Ozick's twin hierarchies of Pan-Moses vices and virtues: wild imagination and the emotional severing of life within the society of humankind. As devilish as Stella may be, the "hell" Rosa alludes to is more a self-willed purgatory of the soul.

Stella, like the perfectly proportioned ideal human body of the Greek (Pan) statue, is as faultlessly formed as she is spiritually deadly:

You could not believe from all this beauty, these doll's eyes, these buttercup lips, these baby's cheeks, you could not believe in what harmless containers the bloodsucker comes....
Stella was cold. She had no heart. Stella, already nearly fifty years old, the Angel of Death. (15)

As Rosa observed Stella gazing "at Magda like a young cannibal", so does she have "cannibal dreams about Stella: she was boiling her tongue, her ears, her right hand, such a fat hand with plump fingers." (15) Nazi atrocities aside, the performance of cannibalism is itself the most extreme form of dehumanization—in a literal sense. From another point of view, Rosa's fractured image of human comportment mirrors a disjointed self-imaging. If, as Rosa describes, Stella is the very coldness of Death, then Rosa herself is the very image of a soul who chooses death. She lives a death, or a life of emotional dislocation, rather than finding a place within the human group. Like Joseph Brill in *The Cannibal Galaxy*, Rosa suffers from another kind of displacement: her prewar life of a sophisticated European culture and insight. This she finds, to some extent, only in the male population of Miami Beach, but all of them suffer from the commonness of a mercantile class of inhabitants who know vegetables, fruit, buttons and fabrics better than the ecstacies of a highly sensitive aesthetic life:

The Warsaw of her girlhood.... The house of her girlhood laden with a thousand books. Polish, German, French; her father's Latin books; the shelf of shy·literary periodicals... her mother's poetry.... Cultivation, old civilization, beauty, history!.... Whoever yearns for an aristocratic sensibility, let him switch on the great light of Warsaw. (20–21)

There is also one very special, even shocking (but highly likely) mix of Pan and Moses: the paternity of Magda. Ozick's phrase, "You could think that she was one of their babies", has more than one possible reference point. As Lowin states:

How do we know that Magda is the fruit of an illicit liaison with a non-Jewish, "Aryan" man? Not by her blue eyes, nor by the color of her hair which resembles the color of Rosa's star, but by the word *their* set off by italics." (Lowin 107–108)

Another supporting detail is contained in the letter that Rosa writes to Magda, wherein she would appear to protest too much about the nature of Madga's origins:

> Stella's accusations are all Stella's own excretion. Your father was not a German. I was forced by a German, it's true, and more than once, but I was too sick to conceive. Stella has a naturally pornographic mind, she can't resist dreaming up a dirty sire for you, an S.S. man? Stella was with me the whole time, she knows just what I know. They never put me in their brothel either. Never believe this, my lioness, my snowqueen. No lies come out of me to you. You are pure. A mother is the source of consciousness, of conscience, the ground of being, as philosophers say, I have no falsehoods for you. Otherwise I don't deny some few tricks: the necessary handful. To those who don't deserve the truth, don't give it. I tell Stella what it pleases her to hear. ("Rosa" 43–44)

Like the idol worship which Ozick, on some level, so often refers to, Magda is ambiguous: either an eerie, perverse "concocted" product of Rosa's impure Moses-Pan existence, or the mark of Pan that is forced on her by having been raped by a Nazi.

As with Rosa's seesawing state of cultural placement/displacement and *vice versa,* Ozick's description of her childhood life in Warsaw is a loosely woven fabric of contradictory directions and alliances: the America that does not satisfy one's aesthetic and cultural sense/sensibilities, and the height of European savvy plus high Kulture exquisitely embodied in the German spirit. The latter was like Stella (albeit to a lesser degree): beautiful on the surface, but so humanly perverse underneath.

Like another survivor, Joseph Brill, Rosa doesn't know where she belongs. She is without place or direction. One day she sees that the "sheets on her bed were... black.... The bed was black, as black as Stella's will. After a while Rosa had no choice, she took a bundle of laundry in a shopping cart and walked to the laundromat. Though it was only ten in morning, the sun was "killing". (13–15)

The direction that she takes, or that, by default, she is forced to take—like the direction in the death camp to the left or to the right, that meant death in the shower room or a living death in the death camp—determines whether she will continue to live in the hell of regret, cut off from humanity, or to begin a re-entry into human society. The act of going to wash out the blackness itself sets into motion her transformation from being one of *theirs* (Aryan, Pan, emotionally unconnected) to being one of *hers*: human, emotionally intact, of Moses, with a wholesome imagination that can envision a future of hope and love.

The "old man... Simon Persky, a third cousin to Shimon Peres, the Israeli politician", (22) whom she sees sitting in the laundromat reading a Yiddish newspaper, is the first sign in the process of redemption. Yiddish is an Ozickian trope for Jewish identity, memory and the Moses past, the perpetuation of which is a sign that Jewish memory is alive and well. It contrasts with Rosa's childhood Polish home: "her father, like her mother, mocked at Yiddish; there was not a particle of ghetto left in him, not a grain of rot." (21)

Persky's name is a complicated combination of cultural dialectic. The relative, Shimon Peres, is an Israeli statesman who is himself a true-life conversion of a Gentilized Jewish Eastern European in nomenclature and being (his real name, like Simon's, is Persky) into a true Hebrew— Shimon Peres. The Persky of Poland and Miami Beach and the Persky/ Peres of Poland and Israel are cultural dialectic crossovers.

Rosa, in fact, chooses to live (or avoid) life as a series of multiple pasts. There is the earliest past of the historical Jewish people, with which her family and she avoided identification. In a letter written to the imaginary Magda, Rosa states:

> Take my word for it, Magda, your father and I had the most ordinary lives— by "ordinary" I mean respectable, gentle, cultivated. Reliable people of refined reputation. His name was Andrzej. Our families had status. Your father was the son of my mother's closest friend. She was a converted Jew married to a Gentile; you can be a Jew if you like, or a Gentile, it's up to you. You have a legacy of choice, and they say choice is the only true freedom. (43)

Ozick's, and Rosa's, slippery sleight-of-hand brings in, from another direction, the whole question of Magda's paternity and again underscores the inextricably mixed web of Pan and Moses: Andrzej's mother, born Jewish but having converted, makes her a Moses-anti-Moses cultural mix of Catholic and Jewish. By Jewish law, she remains a Jew, having been born to a Jewish mother; but for the Church, she is a prized conversion of a Jew-turned-Christian.

Then there is the past of her childhood years, the "before". The Holocaust past, that preceded Madga's death, in effect took Rosa's past, what was at the time her present, and (it seemed also) any hope for another future. Magda was her future; the Magda who was the mixed product of Christian and Jewish, anti-Moses and Moses. In relation to this, there is much comic irony in Rosa's letter to Magda, her dead child—who was killed because she was Jewish—on the subject of choosing whether to be Jewish or not. There was also the past in the death camp after Magda's death; and finally, the latest past, in the transit camps after liberation.

Simon Persky tells Rosa a number of times: "You can't live in the past." (23) Stella also says: "Rosa, by now, believe me, it's time, you have to have a life." (32) The irony here is that Stella doesn't have a normal life either. This is to say that Rosa must stop living in the past and look to a redemptive future. It is also to say that, paradoxically, by regaining her Jewish past identity, she can make a leap into a future. From her earliest past, Rosa was on the way to a Pan future: the death of Jews through assimilation that occurred before the Holocaust, was eclipsed by their physical death during the Holocaust.

Simon Persky—a lonely, caring man with an insane wife whom he supports in a mental institution—frequents public places hoping to meet a woman. For Ozick, he has the right ingredients to be of the world of Moses: he reads Yiddish newspapers, is related to a famous Israeli political figure, does not want to live his life alone, and has great Jewish compassion for people underneath his typical European-derived, New York City, Jewish joke-cracking demeanor. He is, in truth, Rosa's Mosaic savior and redeemer sent by Heaven to tear her from the clutches of Pan. His game is to sit in the laundromat reading the Yiddish newspaper, commenting out loud to whatever woman is busy with her laundry, or who is waiting with boredom for her machine to stop, in order to engage her in conversation:

> "Excuse me, I notice you speak with an accent." Rosa flushed. "I was born somewhere else, not here."
> "I was also born somewhere else. You're a refugee? Berlin?"
> "Warsaw."
> "I'm also from Warsaw. 1920 I left. 1906 I was born."
> "Happy birthday," Rosa said. She began to pull her things out of the washing machine. They were twisted into each other like mixed-up snakes.
> "Allow me,".... He put down his paper and helped her untangle. (18)

Simon Persky thus begins the process of untangling Rosa's life. He, like the Yiddish-speaking niece, Hannah, in "Envy; or Yiddish in America" is "immune"; Persky unwittingly escaped the terrors of the Holocaust by leaving Poland in 1920, as Hannah did by being born in America. Rosa and Simon are from different worlds. Hers is an assimilated one. He came from a small town near Warsaw and, for whatever reason, has remained connectedly Jewish:

> "Two people from Warsaw meet in Miami, Florida. In 1910 I didn't dream of Miami, Florida."
> "My Warsaw isn't your Warsaw," Rosa said.
> "As long as your Miami, Florida, is my Miami, Florida." Two whole long rows of glinting dentures smiled at her; he was proud to be a flirt. Together they shoved the snarled load into the dryer....
> "You read Yiddish?" the old man said.
> "No."
> "You can speak a few words maybe?"
> "No. My Warsaw isn't your Warsaw...."
> "What," he said, "you're still afraid? Nazis we ain't got, even Ku Kluxers we ain't got. What kind of person are you, you're still afraid?"
> "The kind of person," Rosa said, "is what you see. Thirty-nine years ago I was somebody else."
> "Thirty-nine years ago I wasn't so bad myself. I lost my teeth without a single cavity," he bragged. "Everything perfect. Periodontal disease." (18–20)

Simon Persky has a lot of experience dealing with deranged females. His tactic is to deflect and humanize every remark that Rosa makes. Their past lives are starkly contrasted here: he has been left intact from his Warsaw, she has not. He lives in the present and looks ahead to a future. He is a "flirt" out of a deep zest for life. He begins to make order in her life. The word "together" signals the beginning of their human union. He jokes that he comes to the laundromat because he's "'devoted to Nature. I like the sound of a waterfall. Wherever it's cool it's a pleasure to sit and read my paper.'" (21) Rosa is not convinced, and neither should the reader be: Simon Persky, for Ozick, is not of Pan:

> "What a story!" Rosa snorted.
> "All right, so I go to have a visit with the ladies. Tell me, you like concerts?"
> "I like my own room, that's all."
> "A lady what wants to be a hermit!"

"I got my own troubles," Rosa said.
"Unload on me." (21–22)

The effects of Simon Persky's loving, caring and warm personality begin to stir in her.

Then the hotel desk clerk gives Rosa a box sent to her by Stella. Rosa is sure it contains Madga's shawl. She anticipates the great feeling and smell of it:

> She kept the package tight against her bosom and picked through the crowd, a sluggish bird on ragged toes, dragging the cart.
> In her room she breathed noisily, almost a gasp, almost a squeal…. Magda's shawl! Magda's swaddling cloth. Magda's shroud. The memory of Magda's smell, the holy fragrance of the lost babe. (30–31)

Before opening the box, she reads the two letters that the desk clerk also gave her. One is from Stella, the other from a Dr. Tree from the Department of Clinical Social Pathology. She first opens Stella's letter:

> "All right, I've done it. Been to the post office and mailed it. Your idol is on its way, separate cover. Go on your knees to it if you want. You make yourself crazy…. You're like those people in the Middle Ages who worshipped a piece of the True Cross." (31–32)

Ozick's comparison of Rosa's worship of the shawl with Christian worship of "a piece of the True Cross" underscores Ozick's attitude toward what she considers Christianity's idolatrous worship. After Rosa reads Stella's statement about living "your life!", Rosa's answer to Stella is:

> "Thieves took it," and [she] went scrupulously, meticulously as if possessed, to count the laundry in the cart.
> A pair of underpants was missing…. An old woman who couldn't even hang on to her own underwear….
> Then it came to her that Persky had her underpants in his pocket.
> Oh, degrading. The shame. Pain in the loins. Burning. Bending in the cafeteria to pick up her pants, all the while tinkering with his teeth. Why didn't he give them back? He was embarrassed. He had thought a handkerchief. How can a man hand a woman, a stranger, a piece of her own underwear? He could have shoved it right back into the cart, how would that look? A sensitive man, he wanted to spare her. (33–34)

In fact, Rosa has not lost her underpants, but is beginning to loosen her grip on her sick Pan life. She begins to feel exposed, a sense of intimacy, a nakedness opening up inside her. Walking together in the streets—a shadow harking back to the feeling of the forced marches in the Holocaust—she now feels forced by the compulsion of his fulsome benevolence. She plods "beside him dumbly; a led animal", (22) as if over so many years of lost selfhood, Rosa's movements have become Pan-like—either robotic or as an animal. Entering "a self-service cafeteria", Rosa followed "calflike." When she caught her reflection "in the window", she saw that "her bun was loose, strings dangling on either side of her neck. The reflection of a ragged old bird with worn feathers. Skinny, a stork." (23) The combination of animal and human imagery underscores, as in "The Pagan Rabbi" and "The Shawl", the Pan sense of dehumanization.

The topic of education is a touchy and precariously balanced one for Ozick. Like the whole subject of Art, it can go one way or another. Simon Persky, a basic simple heart, has no use for it: "Too much education makes fools." (25) Rabbi Isaac Kornfeld, if not a fool, was certainly fooled by the too creative, convoluted intricacies of intellectual erudition. In Warsaw, Rosa was in the Pan track of the world of Nature as well as assimilation:

> "*I* was a chemist almost. A physicist," Rosa said. "You think I wouldn't have been a scientist?" The thieves who took her life!.... [Once she was] a serious person of seventeen, ambitious, responsible, a future Marie Curie!.... And now she wrote and spoke English as helplessly as this old immigrant. From Warsaw! Born 1906! She imagined what bitter ancient alley, dense with stalls, cheap clothes strung on outdoor racks, signs in jargoned Yiddish. Anyhow they called her refugee. The Americans couldn't tell her apart from this fellow with his false teeth and dewlaps and his rakehell reddish toupee.... Warsaw! What did he know? In school she had read Tuwim: such delicacy, such loftiness, such *Polishness*. (20)

Like Joseph Brill's descriptions of himself as the budding astronomer, Rosa's interest in a scientific pursuit signals the decadence of Pan-Nature, an early warning sign of danger that any human being—Jew or Gentile—can fall prey to the intellectual excitement and beauty of/in the Pan world of nature. Simon Persky is the perfect Ozickian balance: human; a warm heart; anti-assimilationist; deeply related to (but not living in) Israel; Yiddish-speaking/reading; aware, world-connected, but not a Nature-worshipper; with an imagination that can envision a positive future, but with no "wild" imagination that broods on the past and fantasy like that of his institutionalized wife and Rosa, or who has fantastic illusions about the present. And he is in business: in the business of life. In the cafeteria Rosa worries that:

> "Maybe I didn't bring enough to pay."
> "Never mind, you got the company of a rich retired taxpayer. I'm a well-off man. When I get my Social Security, I spit on it."
> "What line of business?"
> "The same what I see you got one lost. At the waist. Buttons. A shame. That kind's hard to match...."
> "Buttons?" Rosa said.
> "Buttons, belts, notions, knickknacks, costume jewelry, a factory...."
> Rosa murmured, "I had a business, but I broke it up."
> "Bankruptcy?"
> "Part with a big hammer," she said meditatively, "part with a piece of construction metal I picked up from the gutter."
> "You don't look that strong. Skin and bones."
> "See," she said, "*now* you're sorry you started with me!"
> "I ain't sorry for nothing," Persky said. "If there's one thing I know to understand, it's mental episodes. I got it my whole life with my wife.... She's mixed up that she's somebody else." (25–27)

Simon Persky's wife, like Rosa, has too much imagination. Both women have not just forgotten who they really are, they have the added problem of the Jewish artist: being both too imaginatively creative and also Jewish. Mrs. Persky has become other people; Rosa, like the members of her family, lost her Jewish selfhood and soul early on, even before the Nazis threatened her Jewish physical self. Persky's wife thinks she's a famous actress; Rosa believes she's a writer of "letters". She wants to be alone so she can write "letters" to Stella and Magda, and to tell her stories to anyone else who will listen. Like Ozick, Rosa is of the world of "letters". After telling Rosa the story of his crazy wife, Persky says:

> "I unloaded on you, now you got to unload on me."
> "Whatever I would say, you would be deaf."
> "How come you smashed up your business?"
> "It was a store. I didn't like who came in it....
> Whoever came, they were like deaf people. Whatever you explained to them, they didn't understand." (27)

The people who came into Rosa's store weren't interested in her stories. Like Ozick in her past, Rosa had Jewish stories that the different ethnic types of people didn't want to listen to. Like Rosa, Persky also likes to tell and read stories, and admires readers and writers:

> Rosa read the sign [at the cafeteria]:
> KOLLIN'S KOSHER CAMEO:
> EVERYTHING ON YOUR PLATE AS PRETTY AS A PICTURE:
> REMEMBRANCES OF NEW YORK AND THE
> PARADISE OF YOUR MATERNAL KITCHEN:
> DELICIOUS DISHES OF AMBROSIA AND NOSTALGIA:
> AIR CONDITIONED THRU-OUT
> "I know the owner," Persky said. "He's a big reader." (23)

As in "The Pagan Rabbi", where voicelessness contrasts with voiced or written communication, the voiceless silence of "The Shawl" is contrasted in "Rosa" with the voiced communication of the letters Rosa writes. But the communication is either one-sided (as with a dead Magda), or parallel (as with Rosa's communication with Stella). Isaac Kornfeld likewise communicates with a childlike dryad, with his imagination, through fantastic stories, through his letters, or not at all.

When Rosa enters her hotel lobby she sees the "guests" who

> believed in the seamless continuity of the body. The men were more inward, running their lives in front of their eyes like secret movies....
> Rosa heard the tearing of envelopes, the wing-shudders of paper sheets. Letters from children, the guests laughed and wept, but without seriousness, without belief.... [She] pushed the cart through to where the black Cuban receptionist sat....
> "Mail for Lublin, Rosa," Rosa said.
> "Lublin, you lucky today. Two letters." (28–30)

One letter is Stella's; the other is from a university professor of Clinical Social Pathology engaged in a study of Holocaust survivors. The essential significance of these professors' studies of the effects of the Holocaust on survivors, and Rosa's outrage at them, underscores the other side of this horrific event: that there are many levels and types of cannibals and cannibalism. As the Nazis devoured their victims, so does academia dehumanizingly dissect and analyze the anatomy and effects of the victims' suffering. Similarly, there are writers, in the grip of a devouring imagination—the Isaac Kornfelds and Rosa Lublins of the world—who exploit humanity by way of detached observance or detachment from all things Mosaic in general, and lose themselves in a wilderness of fantasy, ill-guided imaginings and bizarre intellectual concoctions—all of which create disconnection from the human community. The Swiftian description of empirical data, and matter-of-factly stated horrific detail, underscore the clinical coldness of the tormentor and the agony of the tormented.

The letter is written by James W. Tree, Ph.D., whose work is "funded by the Minew Foundation of the Kansas-Iowa Institute for Humanitarian Context", and is chillingly signed, "Very sincerely yours". It describes Dr. Tree's (the name is a Pan sign post) amassing of "survivor data" and his investigation of "Repressed Animation". (36) The collection of this specific kind of detail has become his "speciality". He doesn't wish to go "into detail" now, but

> "it may be of some preliminary use to you to know that investigations so far reveal an astonishing generalized minimalization during any extended period of stress resulting from incarceration, exposure, and malnutrition. We have turned up a wide range of neurological residues (including, in some cases, acute cerebral damage, derangement, disorientation, premature senility, etc.), as well as hormonal changes, parasites, anemia, thready pulse, hyperventilation, etc.; in children especially, temperatures as high as 108 [degrees], ascitic fluid, retardation, bleeding sores on the skin and in the mouth, etc. What is remarkable is that these are all *current conditions* in survivors and their families." (36)

Dr. Tree's letter is a request to "receive" him during the time of his Association's annual meeting in Miami, because he believes that she is "ideally circumstanced" to contribute to his "Repressed Animation" study. Rosa's reaction to Dr. Tree's Pan-inspired enthusiasm is:

> Drop in a hole! Disease! It comes from Stella, everything! Stella saw what this letter was.... Dr. Stella!.... This is the cure for the taking of a life! Angel of Death!.... She threw the letter into the sink,... lit a match and enjoyed the thick fire. Burn Dr. Tree, burn up with your Repressed Animations! The world is full of Trees! The world is full of fire! (38–39)

Ironically, Dr. Tree's study of Repressed Animation does reflect Rosa's life, but for Ozick the objective study of people who have undergone the hell of a Death Camp could bear too great a similarity to the scientific experiments the Nazis performed on Death Camp inmates. Both lack the essential Moses quality of humane, sensitive and heartfelt caring of one for another.

Rosa's act of burning the letter mirrors a number of aspects: the incineration of Jewish bodies in the death camp crematoria; the helplessness of experiencing, as in "The Shawl", "the bad wind with pieces of black in it, that made Stella's and Rosa's eyes tear", ("Shawl" 6) but that, at this moment, was under Rosa's control. Lastly, the act signifies, after so many tortured years, the purification and healing of the past: "Big flakes of cinder lay in the sink: black foliage, Stella's black will. Rosa turned on the faucet and the cinders spiraled down and away." ("Rosa" 39) With that cleansing accomplished, Rosa could now sit down and write another letter:

> Then she went to the round oak table and wrote the first letter of the day to her daughter, her healthy daughter, her daughter who suffered neither from thready pulse nor from anemia, her daughter who was a professor of Greek philosophy at Columbia University in New York City. (39)

Another irony is revealed: Rosa wishes for her Magda to live a life steeped in all things "Greek", a life of Pan. Nevertheless, with Simon Persky now in the picture, the spirit of Pan is slowly but surely being replaced by the spirit of Moses. However, for Ozick, this healing process requires one more very important ingredient: the idea of writing as the ultimate road to total redemption. Up until now, Rosa's imagined concoctions of reality regarding the past have allowed her neither a present nor a future; but she also wants to tell the stories of the past in order to keep the memory of her people's history alive. In a letter to Magda she writes:

> When I had my store I used to "meet the public" and I wanted to tell everybody—not only our story, but other stories as well. Nobody knew anything. This amazed me, that nobody remembered what happened only a little while ago. They didn't remember because they didn't know. I'm referring to certain definite facts. The tramcar in the Ghetto, for instance. You know they took the worst section, a terrible slum, and they built a wall around it. It was a regular city neighborhood, with rotting old tenements. They pushed in half a million people, more than double the number there used to be in that place. Three families, including all their children and old folks, into one apartment. (66)

However, this Moses urge to tell the stories of the Jewish people (which is paradoxically linked with the Greek urge to tell stories for the sake of themselves, the love of Beauty) is paralleled by anti-Zionist, harshly anti-Mosaic statements. This is another reminder that everything positive can too easily pass over the line into Pan and idolatry. In her descriptions of the Ghetto, she also viciously describes those other Jews who "used up their energies with walking up and down, and bowing, and shaking and quaking over old rags of prayer books, and their children sat on the boxes and yelled prayers too." (67) The promised land of Israel, then Palestine, she also had contempt for:

> [Stella,] whom I plucked out of the claws of all those Societies that came to us with bread and chocolate after the liberation! Despite everything, they were selling sectarian ideas; collecting troops for their armies. If not for me they would have shipped Stella with a boatload of orphans to Palestine, to become God knows what, to live God knows how. A field worker jabbering Hebrew. It would serve her right. Americanized airs. My father was never a Zionist. He used to call himself a "Pole by right." The Jews, he said, didn't put a thousand years of brains and blood into Polish soil in order to have to prove themselves to anyone. (40)

In relation to her family, the Pan and Moses urges are impossible to separate. Rosa's family was not just assimilationist. Her father

> was the wrong sort of idealist, maybe, but he had the instincts of a natural nobleman,... not given over to any lightmindedness whatever. He had Zionist friends in his youth. Some left Poland early and lived. One is a bookseller in Tel Aviv. He specializes in foreign texts and periodicals. My poor little father. It's only history—an ad hoc instance of it, you might say—that made the Zionist answer. My father's answers were more logical. He was a Polish patriot on a temporary basis, he said, until the time when nation should lie down beside nation like the lily and the lotus. He was at bottom a prophetic creature. My mother, you know, published poetry. (40–41)

Rosa's parents, as Ozick once did, tried to find the way through Art only. It would be impossible for her parents to have kept the history and identity of their people alive through such assimilated forms of prophecy and art. Ozick contrasts them with Simon Persky: also having a close relative in Israel (Shimon Peres), but with greater Jewish substance. Persky's caring heart and reality-oriented balance cannot be swayed into taking any unstable course in life. His business is buttons, and he knows how to hold life together in a feeling, careful and steady way. He is a big reader, but without the obsessive, destructive, too-creative imagination of Rosa, her parents or his wife. He has, like Sheindel, the greater imagination to be able to envision a future of hope and redemption. Like Rosa before Magda's death, and Sheindel after Isaac's suicide, Simon's persistence will steal Rosa from the clutches of Pan futility and an overly-artful, destroying imagination. Although Sheindel is intellectually superior to Simon, both equally manifest Mosaic hope for the future.

The mirroring that occurs throughout "Rosa" interweaves Pan images and metaphors with those of Moses, as in the shop that Rosa smashed up which specialized "in both real and metaphorical mirrors. Every customer who enters... is offered not only things used, 'old... with other people's history,' as Lowin expresses it but also a story of Jewish suffering at the hands of the Nazis." (Lowin 110) The content of her stories and her storytelling artistry has no apparent effect on the customers who come to her store. She is a frustrated weaver of grim stories without any perspective of hope.

Ironically, her only "hope"—or so she believes—is focused on the shawl that Stella has been keeping in her possession in order to give Rosa time to gain emotional immunity over its effects on her; but Simon Persky is the hope-filled Angel of Mercy sent by fate to help her. After spending a number of hours reliving, and returning in her feelings and thoughts, to the scenes of the Holocaust, in her imagination roaming the streets and alleys of Miami Beach in search of her underpants, that is, her inner being, she returns empty-handed to the hotel, only to find Simon Persky

waiting for her. He sat in the torn brown plastic wing chair near the reception desk, one leg over the side, reading a newspaper.
He saw her come in and jumped up....
Rosa said, "How come you're here?"
"Where you been the whole night? I'm sitting hours...."
"What do you want?"
He flashed his teeth, "A date."
"You're a married man."
"A married man what ain't got a wife."
"You got one."
"In a manner of speaking. She's crazy."
Rosa said, "I'm crazy too."
"Who says so?"
"My niece."
"What does a stranger know?"
"A niece isn't a stranger."
"My own son is a stranger...."

"I'm a serious person," Rosa said. "It ain't my kind of life, to run around noplace."
"Who said noplace? I got a place in mind." ("Rosa" 53–54)

Simon Persky's touching persistence brings Rosa back into the human community. Thus, when the box finally arrives from Stella with Magda's shawl, Rosa (who, significantly, has also decided to connect her phone) opens it, sees the shawl and realizes that the long-awaited thrill of seeing it is completely missing. Setting fire to Tree's letter the day before was the emotional catharsis that Simon Persky's entry into Rosa's life had set into motion. It was

> as if yesterday's conflagration hadn't been Tree but really the box with Magda's shawl.
> She lifted the lid of the box and looked down at that shawl; she was indifferent. Persky too would have been indifferent. The colorless cloth lay like an old bandage; a discarded sling. For some reason it did not instantly restore Magda, as usually happened.... The shawl had a faint saliva smell but it was more nearly imagined than smelled.
> Under the bed the telephone vibrated....
> The Cuban's voice said: "Missis Lublin, you connected now." (62)

Rosa now gauges all of her reactions in terms of Simon. His Mosaic touch has dispelled her idolatrous Pan existence. Rosa has been reconnected into the human community by Simon Persky. Her sick imagination has been cured by Persky's lovingkindness. As Lowin states, Rosa "will not resist Persky's warm, humane, personal value-laden intervention in her life." (Lowin 111)

Wanting to connect with everything in her life now, she decides to call Stella. During the conversation with Stella, who is so connected to Rosa's past,

> Magda sprang to life.... The whole room was full of Magda: she was like a butterfly, in this corner and in that corner, all at once. Rosa waited to see what age Magda was going to be: how nice, a girl of sixteen;... they are always butterflies at sixteen. There was Magda, all in flower. She was wearing one of Rosa's dresses from high school. Rosa was glad: it was the sky-colored dress, a middling blue with black buttons seemingly made of round chips of coal, like the unlit shards of stars. Persky could never have been acquainted with buttons like that.... Madga's hair was still as yellow as buttercups.... And she was always a little suspicious of Magda because of the other strain, whatever it was, that ran in her.... The other strain was ghostly, even dangerous. It

was as if the peril hummed out from the filaments of Magda's hair, those narrow bright wires. ("Rosa" 64–65)

Magda, the very embodiment of Pan and Moses, is one synthesized
being of conflicting forces, sired from and a figment of, the imagination
which is itself of Moses or Pan—depending on the borders it stays within
or passes over. As when Magda was thrown against the electric fence and
Rosa imagined her as a butterfly flying through the air, she again appears
as one in Rosa's imagination. The difference now is that Persky's Mosaic
being and presence in her life is pulling her in the direction of life, and a
healthy creative imagination to envision hope. All of the codes for Pan—
"sky", "stars", "butterfly", "flower", "buttercups"—are foreign to Persky:
He "could never has been acquainted with… that…." Having "lost her
underpants", Rosa's unconscious is beginning to spill out its secrets. She
can now admit that she has never completely trusted this daughter sired
by "the other strain". Rosa's Jewish soul and consciousness is beginning
to open up. She can now see the world of Pan as "ghostly, even dangerous". Rosa's imagination begins to manifest the signs of Simon's positive
influence. It beings to turn from a Pan form of excessive and morbid hy-
peractivity to an imagination that can see a future of hope. Magda
disappears back into the black recesses of negativity and sick imagination. She dies a final death. Magda herself becomes the very "peril" of
the electric fence that finally killed her. Rosa can clearly identify what is
Pan and what is Moses.

Writing one last letter to Magda "to explain", she grows very "tired
from writing so much, even though this time she was not using her regular pen, she was writing inside a blazing flying… terrible beak of light
bleeding out of a kind of cuneiform on the underside of her brain." (69)

The writing that has fed her sick fantasy begins to fade, with the image of the Magda which Rosa imagines in front of her eyes:

And Magda! Already she was turning away. Away. The blue of her dress was
now only a speck in Rosa's eye. Magda did not even stay to claim her letter…. Magda collapsed at any stir, fearful as a phantom. She behaved at these
moments as if she was ashamed, and hid herself…. [The telephone rang.]
Rosa let it clamor once or twice and then heard the Cuban girl announce—oh,
"announce"! Mr. Persky: should he come up or would she come down?….
"He's used to crazy women, so let him come up," Rosa told the Cuban….
Magda was not there. Shy, she ran from Persky. (69–70)

Simon brings Rosa to a place, her place (?) in America in Miami Beach; to life; to a redeemed existence in a culturally dialectical Jewish-America, or an American Israel.

In the last work, *The Cannibal Galaxy*, the central character, Joseph Brill, like Rosa, Rabbi Kornfeld, Lucy, Jimmy, Edelshtein and Ostrover, is displaced or lost; converted, unconverted or unconvertible; a cultural anomaly; trapped, abandoned in time and space. As with the others, Joseph is the very essence of cultural dialectic; with cultures in conflicting modes; of imagination, the stuff of literary exploration, writers, readers, intellectuals. Joseph Brill is of multiple places, cultures—and also of none of them.

The Cannibal Galaxy

Ozick's rather coy inclusion of lines from both Emily Dickinson and Yehuda Amichai already begins to define the parameters of the complexly rich dialectic operating in this book. With a title that first sends an eerie chill down the spine—images of a world turned insane; humanity devouring humanity; the universe eating itself alive—the quotations would seem to belie the horror the appellation itself evokes.

Indeed there is a great degree of whistling-clean, Gentile, American innocence that pervades the three chosen Dickinsonian lines; intensified by the *gee-whiz* emphasis of a final exclamation mark and a curious patterning of capital letters: "The rest of Life to see!/ Past Midnight! Past the Morning Star!" Here we have a glimpse into a world that spins with great regularity: day becomes night and night, day. Nothing spells disaster. Such optimism of a chosen people in a new chosen place: America, the (new) promised land filled with the sense of unlimited hope; a God-blessed place. However, where is the place of this geographic entity, America, in *The Cannibal Galaxy*; and what, if any, is America's connection to it? Only the dialectic knows for sure the answer to this riddle.

As well, the Dickinson lines would seem to herald the hope that the artistic vision can cut through the ordinary; can make order and sense of existence; can somehow understand the inscrutable. In contrast, the quotation of Israeli writer Yehuda Amichai would appear to place the speaker outside the world of human endeavour and activity (the Western world perhaps), pondering his/her place in a very clear-cut, mundanely rotating universe of haters and lovers. Thus Dickinson and Amichai, in coherent but impenetrable partnership, hold the universe in balance. Amichai and Dickinson are the two halves: Gentile and Jewish; America and Israel, balancing all and each other even in their seemingly contradictory identities. Each is a dialectic of artistic savvy and the childlike innocence inherent in aesthetic wonder; the artist's pondering; the disassembly of experience/universe in the discovery of why and how; the dissection of life at all costs. As with the Dickinson lines, Ozick would seem to also be using Amichai to render a kind of manifesto of life which perhaps only the artistic enterprise can create, maintain, perpetuate, scrutinize. Nevertheless, the question must be repeated: what connection, if any, does not "a", but "the" Cannibal Galaxy have to artistic vision, humanity, life itself? This could be Ozick's riddle of the Ordinary.

In the column entitled "Aleinu" (meaning the moral responsibilities, if any, humanity has toward God's created world), Ozick discusses the duality with which the monotheistic Jews perceive, and are incumbent to perceive, the universe: "We all divide the world into the Ordinary and the Extraordinary." ("Riddle" 55) It is easy to recognize the Extraordinary, she says. In fact, the more intense the Extraordinary, the greater the ease in which it can be seen as such: "There is no one who does not know when something special is happening: the high, terrifying, tragic, and ecstatic moments are unmistakable in any life." We can't help but give the Extraordinary our complete attention. The Ordinary, on the other hand, is ironically much more difficult to recognize because it does not knock us over with its power:

> The Ordinary, simply by *being* so ordinary, tends to make us ignorant or neglectful; when something does not insist on being noticed, when we aren't grabbed by the collar or struck on the skull by a presence or an event, we take for granted the very things that most deserve our gratitude. (56)

This is the most important and most profound quality the Ordinary possesses: it wholly deserves the "gratitude" incumbent on us to manifest. "The Ordinary lets us live out our humanity." Awareness of the Ordinary brings the acknowledgment of the greatness of God's created world. However, more so, awareness of the Ordinary hones the "consciousness", makes us "sensitive" to the tiniest measure of time's passage; "for the sake of making life as superlatively polished as the most sublime work of art." (56–57) In short, being a good and moral Jew, a beneficent human being, makes one also an artist, grants one the benefit of being an aesthetic and highly perceptive individual: "What is Art? It is the first noticing, and then sanctifying, the Ordinary. It is making the Ordinary into the Extraordinary. It is the impairment of the distinction between the Ordinary and the Extraordinary." (57)

The commandment-fulfilling Jewish human being, she exclaims, is truly immersed in the artistic process. Nothing passes his/her ken; all is steeped in his/her awareness of every seemingly insignificant flutter of life; "nothing that passes before him is taken for granted, everything is exalted." (58)

In their somewhat paradoxical juxtaposition, Dickinson and Amichai are elements sifted through Ozick's awareness to form a symbolic union of human activity, consciousness; of the surprising shock of the Ordinary with the Extraordinary sifted through the artistic enterprise; this is also to say, the Jewish cosmology/Torah/peoplehood and its history, in concert with the process of making art.

This dialectic of human and extraordinary possibilities is fulsome, awesome, breathtaking, sobering and, most importantly, either in balance or in some aberration of human enterprise, within a moral, immoral or amoral universe. Anything and everything is possible. Cannibalism can take place next to an exquisitely rendered piece of art: the indescribable, heaven-sent chords of Mozart played at the death camps, executed by inmates playing for their lives. The Ordinary and Extraordinary thus are seen here in their full spectrum of hope and despair. This is the dialectic of indescribably intermixed intricacy, a perplexity.

Ozick's book *The Cannibal Galaxy* is balanced on a hair between all of these extremes and in-betweens. Joseph Brill, the book's central character, holds all of this within him; represents the contradictions inherent in existence; in a pre- and post-Holocaust existence of the Jew-as-artist or aesthete in a world of raw, often brutal, experience, the latter waiting to be tamed, perceived, ordered, aestheticized: "The Principal of the Edmund Fleg Primary School was originally (in a manner of speaking) a Frenchman, Paris-born—but whenever he quoted his long-dead father and mother, he quoted them in Yiddish."[156]

The school, itself named in honor of a man whose personal identity pointed in at least seemingly two contradictory directions, is set up and organized by Joseph Brill to have the dual curriculum of secular and Hebraic studies. Brill has at least two identities and educational directions. With parents "long dead", he is cut off from his past. The Holocaust keeps death in the perpetual foreground of his life and consciousness. It is, so to speak, his present. As he dies, or rather lives a living death in the present, even his "past" is his "present". Of course, a future barely exists for him. As in the Amichai lines, it is somehow out of reach, an ordinariness and innocence only for the Elect, the chosen. He was, like the other Jews of his European time, also chosen, selected; their fate was extinction. They were elected to live in a relentlessly devouring time which had cannibalized their past in a present, without hope for a future. Brill, everywhere but finally nowhere, "was a melancholic, a counter of losses." "Originally" in Europe, Brill (then in his present) was "in a manner of speaking" French, but in this "now": when he summons up the past from his memory, he quotes his "long-dead father and mother ...in Yiddish", the language of his past and his people's past.

Brill's joke-making, in his (one) identity of a clown/jester, tries to confuse, to obfuscate, to obscure any ability to bring anything into focus or clarify and erect boundaries that distinguish one thing from another. Is this the artistic pursuit? Is this the artist at his business? Everything is language. His jokes are multilingual snatches of creative plays of speech, verbal expression, literature; philological showmanship; legerdemain:

> Though he was Sorbonne-educated, his vowels strove to be American. Instead they palpitated with the insuppressible inflections of the *Rue des Rosiers*. Since there were no Frenchmen in the neighborhood to catch him out, those vowels might once have flourished, for all any of the parents knew, in Bourbon throats. (*Cannibal* 3)

In an intricate dialectic, Brill is Jewish, Yiddish, European, Parisian, Bourbon, and/or American—or not any/all of them; of a number of pasts, living in some pasts which are really his chronological present. Even his geographic location is indistinct, full of the "mappiness" of insignificance, unextraordinary Ordinariness. In "The Butterfly and the Traffic Light", Ozick explores the idea of "map". The more "mappiness" a place contains, the lighter its spiritual weight:

> Jerusalem, that phoenix city, is not known by its street names. Neither is Baghdad, Copenhagen, Rio de Janiero, Camelot, or Athens.... These fabled capitals rise up ready-spired, story-domed and filigreed; they come to us at

the end of a plain, behind hill or cloud, walled and moated by myths and an-
tique rumors.... There is no beauty in cross-section—we take our cities, like
our wishes, whole.[157]

The case is exactly the opposite, Ozick continues, for locations that
have no reputation, no historic or mythical dimension:

It is different especially in America. They tell us that Boston is our Jerusalem; but as anyone who has ever lived there knows, Boston owns only half a
history.... We hear of Beacon Hill and Back Bay, of Faneuil Market and State
Street: it is all cross-section, all map.... The whole, unlike Jerusalem, has not
transcended its material parts. Boston has a history of neighborhoods; Jerusalem has a history of histories. ("Butterfly" 209–210)

Ozick's use of "our" here is notable. Its meaning is nevertheless
inscrutable. In the same way, the geographic place of Brill's school,
firstly in America, is not even significant by America's standards: "The
school was on a large lake in the breast-pocket of the continent, pouched
and crouched in inwardness. It was as though it had a horror of coasts
and margins; of edges and extremes of any sort. The school was of the
middle and in the middle." (*Cannibal* 3)

The question is: where is Brill's location, his psychic and emotional
place? "He saw himself in the middle of an ashen America." (5) This is
the ashes of Europe revisited; the past as present, a futureless future. His
school is also middling, fringed by a lake, a place of Pan: "These waters
had a history of turbulence: they had knocked freighters to pieces in tidal
storms. Now and then the lake took human life." (4) The Pan world both
gives the living an existence and takes the life from the living. However,
this world of Pan consists not of a distinctly defined division or realm.
Pan wields its pitiless sword in the house of Moses, or *vice versa*. What
should be Moses becomes Pan. It is on the side of the school that borders
on the lake that Principal Brill

understood himself better. Shell shards and slimy rocks assaulted underfoot:
nature's sheddings and bones. The track to the water a junkyard, the beach a
trail of spotted junk. Here everything balanced; where he had come from,
where he had arrived. A lost shell. (4–5)

Brill is one of many lost shells of that unthinkable monstrosity of
aberrational nature, human invention concocted in hell, spat out of the
bowels of history. The Holocaust was nature, Pan, at its lowest level of

depravity. Joseph Brill is a sliver of broken pottery left over from another archaeological age, a splintered piece of disconnection, discontinuity, a piece of garbage. Even his present life was filled with bones of the past, of his own life and the people with whom he shared his love; this junk yard was like the graveyard of his European past. He finds in the beach on the fringes of his school a perverse sense of balance, symmetry, completion, discontinuous continuity. With its collection of death, there he feels at home, bereaved and lost.

However, on another level, Joseph Brill is guilty of his own Pan crimes. Firstly, at age fifty-eight he is still "a bachelor" and avoids life in the present. Secondly, as if to counter his sense of loss and insignificance, "he felt himself not so much a schoolmaster as a man of almost sacral power." (4) He long ago ceased to enjoy the Ordinary around him, and thus severed any possible ties to the world of humanity. The lines from *Talmud* which he knows by heart, "The world rests on the breath of the children in the schoolhouses," he turns to hypocritical farce. He stands totally blind, deaf and dumb to the profound sense of natural and inherent optimism referred to in the Talmudic lines: hope for the future, and continuity embodied in children educated in the Torah. In truth, he doesn't know who he is, or what his place is on the earth's landscape. His education and training in astronomy only serve to underscore the lack of connectedness he has to the earth; to everyday realities. As if to further complicate or confuse, Ozick alternates the chronological time frames of a number of European pasts with his American present.

In at least one fundamental way, Joseph Brill would seem to represent the darker side of the artistic force which focuses its light beam here, there and everywhere, in search of something to devour through the art process. In her essay,[158] Dinitia Smith explores the idea of the writer murdering, thieving and cannibalizing: "Some have argued that all writing is an act of betrayal or aggression. Indeed, writing often involves an invasion, a theft: an exposure of something private, and the issue of a writer's right to use the lives of real people in his work has always been debated." (Smith B9) Describing Cynthia Ozick, one of the panel speakers at the 1998 Authors Guild Symposium, Smith quotes Ozick, stating: "Writers feed that hunger [to write] by feeding on private lives. 'We are cannibals,' Cynthia Ozick admitted at the symposium. 'I think it's a terrible thing to be a friend of, an acquaintance of, a relative of, a writer.'" (B11)

Focused on the Ordinary, or even the Extraordinary, Brill neverthe-less constantly misses the point. His business, originally astronomy, was to bring into focus the stars of light-years past or present. Through a pro-cess of perception as an astronomer, Brill was taught to ponder, analyze and reassemble the cosmos. This was also the Heavens of prophecy, of the Creator of the universe. When he was hidden by nuns in the subcellar of a convent school, his benefactors "referred to him as *l'astronome*, and apologized to him for imprisoning him out of sight of the stars. He apologized for the pail of excrement they daily carried away." (*Canni-bal* 19) After the war, stargazing no longer satisfied him:

> He devoted himself to the study of the possibility of liquid nitrogen oceans on distant satellites; he puzzled over faraway fractures and vapors, he brooded about whether the rings of Saturn were electrically charged. He had reentered civilization: then why did he feel desiccated? Why, stretching toward the mar-gins of the remotest blue haze, did he judge himself to be middling? Through telescopes as huge as chimneys he looked toward the mathematical spheres. The radio emissions of orbs and powers and particles wheeled by in their shining dress. He was discovering himself not to be a discoverer—both too shabby and too cunning for the stars, so he abandoned his life to the chances and devisings of another continent. (34)

Joseph Brill measures and examines the cosmos through the eternal eye of the Holocaust. The grim, catastrophic message of the time of his life that began a living death frames everything in sight, the entire uni-verse from the biggest world to the littlest. In one enormous cosmic soup, a huge mix of images—innuendoes, strains, levels, worlds, places, people, events of history, the Holocaust, his various pasts, the Old and New worlds; Israel and America; Jewish and Gentile; Pan and Moses; far and near geographic location—becomes a psychic place, the palpable perception of all possibilities. Has Brill as artist/perceiver abandoned the visible or invisible stars for the richness of creative enterprise which he nevertheless lacks? Is Joseph Brill, artist-like, in search of all creative possibilities? Will he discover artistic inventiveness in America? The sense of a place that serves and facilitates artistic talent, the writing pro-cess, glares out in the words, "another continent".

Joseph Brill, displaced from his places (which were displaced as well), appears to be searching for something much less tangible than geographic reference points. He is, it would seem, like the story itself, the very essence of the writer-aesthete-Jew whose eternal homeland is the word/Word, the book/Book; which is to say language, that dialectic of dialectics. Like other Ozick stories, *The Cannibal Galaxy* is a dialectically unresolvable web of conflicting goals, wishes, dilemmas and worlds. This complexity of dialectic can be traced to the very language used to narrate it, or indeed, to language itself.

As well, in its paradoxically broader sense, language is the trope of Jewish existence that stands as the most global point of reference; the intersection at the pinnacle of all human enterprise: morality, immortality, language, art; the pagan-Gentile God Itself. This trope is the very essence of the human life-experience; its very site of origin. Thus as linguistic activity the Word/word and Book/book wait for the storyteller-as-prophet or messiah to redeem the Jewish people, and thereby also save the world. The written Word/Book of Torah, that is, God's Word given to the Jewish nation and eventually proclaimed to the world, becomes the type for the sacred truth entrusted to God's chosen (writers) who look after the holy writ of a hallowed artistic enterprise.

If Brill belonged to any one world, he would at least have a place, a name, by which to designate his life. So long has he been in a star-filled galactic whirl, he fails to recognize the "ordinary" realities staring him in the face; and he is too paradoxically ordinary to perceive the extraordinary, the thing whose essence means brilliance in the process of life. In an important sense, Brill and the life that bounds his being are reflecting and re-reflecting the being and life of one Edmund Fleg, re-mirrored in the now-dead priest whose library contained Fleg's books. These books Brill reads in the light of the lamp brought to him by the nuns while he is in hiding in the convent subcellar. This dead priest, who was perhaps a writer or at least a highly intelligent reader, had an avid interest in Fleg. The priest's library and the priest are re-counterpointed and counter-mirrored in the Brill family's friend and spiritual guide (also now dead), Rabbi Pult, martyred like most of the Brill family in the Holocaust. Both Pult's and the priest's taste were characterized by a dialectic mix of intellectual liberalism and orthodoxy. Fleg, formerly Flegenheimer, turned from Bohemian artist into "a Jew Panting for Jerusalem." (22) His intellectual "metaphysical travels, he [Brill] saw, led from agnosticism to Hebrew sympathies but via a Jewish Jesus." (22) As for the old priest, "it came clear to him [Joseph] that the old priest had loved thought more than Jesus." (21) While reading Fleg's books in hiding, Joseph comes across a strange book. He could not tell whether it was Jewish or Christian. The name of it was *Jesus, Raconte par le Juif Errant,* by one Edmund Fleg; out fell a fragile bit of paper, aging in the priest's old-fashioned stormy alphabet, with a quotation from Heinrich Heine: *The lizards on a certain hillside have reported that the stones expect God to manifest Himself among them in the form of a stone.* What mockery! And who was Edmund Fleg? (21)

Brill is thoroughly confused. What else had Fleg written? "Was he a Christian or a Jew? To which world did he belong?" (21) Only the dialectic knows for sure.

Other than Joseph Brill himself, and a book Rabbi Pult gives him before disappearing into the jaws of the great Holocaust cannibal galaxy, the only other survivors in Brill's circle of family and friends are his eldest sisters: "He did not know what had become of his three older sisters—the ABCs.... After the war he found the ABCs alive but no one else. His three older sisters had been scattered and starved; they had been caught and enslaved." (19, 34) With the book/Book, language and linguistic life preserved, Joseph can find some reason to go on. He himself "studied literature for a while—the nuances of Verlaine maddened him with idolatrous joy." (12) In America, it would seem, Joseph can create from a wilderness an identity to something from the blank void; a reality on which to create his own story; to make a fresh new start for a future to come in a new place.

Within the full range of its vast dialectic sweep, *The Cannibal Galaxy* is a story of many stories. On its most cosmic level, it surveys the past of history and memory, the present, and a redeeming future. Its sweep, however, is not just on a continuum of temporal horizontality. It is also vertical, for it dissects the universe into many dialectical halves: Torah and secularism, Jew and Gentile, Moses and Pan, thesis and antithesis. As a story of stories within stories, intersected by competing stories, *The Cannibal Galaxy* is ultimately about the process of telling stories.

Like Joseph's three sisters, "the ABCs", who were missing from their place but not irretrievable, *The Cannibal Galaxy* is also about the paradoxically missing story/book. The narrator of the story states that, like the linguistic ABCs, Joseph "himself (but it was a long story, and he did not often tell it) had been hidden for a long time in a storage room in a subcellar of a convent school." (19) In this "subcellar", where he learns to interpret—or could have learned to interpret—the signs and significance of things below their surfaces, he becomes a full-time reader/

interpreter; he believes he has found the secret of the two halves. Alternating in that subterranean dungeon between the *Ta'anit*, a Hebrew hermeneutical work, and, for example, Proust, the

> juxtaposition made him laugh. A joke, a joke! He had never before laughed down here.... Rav and Proust, the half-Jew (on his mother's side; hence, according to Jewish code, as much a Jew as Rav himself); both measured the world, one by passion for the ideal, the other by passion for the sardonic detail. How different they were! *And neither told a lie.* This was a marvel, that two souls, two such separated tonalities, so to speak, could between them describe the true map of life. (28)

Dialectic makes paradox of reality. This is Amichai's perfect matching of opposites—instantaneous moments of perfect harmony through contrast. All is real, and also somehow fake. The Truth/truths fall between the gaps, the cracks of language. Life is the charting of oppositions in collision, uniting for a moment's peace, then dissolving in their essential conflict, into infinity. By reading stories, it would seem Joseph has become a perfect map-reader of truths on the road of life.

There are other storytellers in Ozick's tale: Renée le Févre née Levin. Born of a Jewish mother, she nevertheless calls herself

> "a Catholic,"... "the third generation in our family. My grandfather on my father's side was the first. The sisters say I'm a blood relative of Our Lord." "But you're a Jew." "I don't care. I'm not afraid.".... "Renée," he said, "you shouldn't spy like this. Don't come back." "I'm not normal. They gave me a psychological test." He wanted to send her away, but he was afraid; every strange sentence she spoke frightened him more. (29–30)

Joseph, now fearful that someone knows he is in hiding, tells the nun that Renée le Févre has wandered into

> his hiding place. The nun kept up her unremitting smile: "She is our privilege. It is a privilege to invite you, Monsieur Brill, and also to invite this child." "Is she a Jew?".... "She is already beautiful in the faith. She wishes to be as we are.... She is known to be a storyteller, Monsieur Brill,.... They say she fabricates. And what if a child fantasizes a very little bit?" (30–31)

Renée, the crossover: is she Jewish or Catholic? When Joseph asks, he receives an ambiguous answer. But it would appear that the nuns have "invited" Joseph to hide out there in order to save his soul. Joseph is confused. He doesn't know what "truth" to uphold, what is real. However, the nuns, themselves remaking reality, still have a real sense of danger. Downplaying Renée, the nun says that all is "'safe on the tongue of a liar.' But the next day all four of the nuns came to him. This was nothing ordinary." (31) Joseph's life is in danger. The story (of his life) is taking another nasty turn. The nuns whisk Joseph away to safe hiding on the farm of a gnarled old childless couple, where Joseph "spent the rest of the war in a hayloft." (32) Where is Joseph's "place"? Where does he belong? Who is he? What is he?

> He flitted like a barn wraith, beginning to believe himself invisible. The sub-cellar, with its cot, its lamp, its cave of books, its meal-carriers and water-carriers—all of that struck him now as paradise lost. He defecated side by side with oxen. (32)

Joseph has become the "other half". He has descended into the world of Pan; the world of nature. "He was part ghost, part beast, part shard. He never once meditated on the intellectual union of Paris and Jerusalem." (33–34) The three nuns become some kind of tropic counterpart of his three sisters, the ABCs. They smuggle him out of a hellish Paris in a plush car:

> Through a chink in the curtains he saw Paris fly away: buntings, swastikas, but also the airy life of the streets as always. Sunlight! *Delicieux.* He envied the living and the free. He envied the dead and the free. In his long skirts and his flowing headgear he was feverishly afraid. They warned him to lie back, to keep his face from the window, to pretend to be sick and asleep, to cover himself with his veil. Somewhere in the suburbs they were stopped, checked, passed; then they turned into a leafy road and drove all day and into the night. He fell asleep in earnest and heard, repeatedly, a single sentence: *These are holy women.* The sentence seemed to refer not to the nuns, but to his sisters, the ABCs. (31–32)

The nuns, among themselves known as "sisters", are the mirror image of Joseph's "real" sisters, the ABCs, the last remnants of his Jewish family and also of the hope-filled basis of language itself. In like fashion, the nuns save not only Joseph's life, but the dead priest's highly controversial, even life-threatening, would-be library. In truth, who are the nuns, and why do they save Joseph, Renée and the Books? What world are they part of? They whisk him out of the convent school hiding place when Renée appears to be on the verge of discovering his real story. From his life in a damp subterranean hideout, he is moved to the heights of a hayloft. In America, he jogs on the flat "middleness" of the American Midwestern landscape. From the sense of powerlessness, lowliness and drift of his European existence and physical place/s, Joseph now in his present life can construct/create a future from nothing except the ABCs—the only remnants of the past, his past. Luck brings a rich Jewish benefactress into his life. With her money, her faith in him and his motivation, he implements his dream of a dual curriculum.

Resounding with the image of the young Joseph safely hiding in a schoolhouse sub-room, he can perpetually recreate his own salvation through/by language and the Book/book. He constantly brings to mind the Talmudic quotation linking the very redemption of humanity to the truisms he has read in books. Joseph, still missing from his place, is re-created on American soil. Lost from a locus point, he nevertheless now feels in control of his future, his destiny and the destiny of a school full of children. The redemption of all rests in the mysterious waters, the sacred font, the union of the splendidly paradoxical ordinariness of language, and the equivocally intricate suppleness of the imagination, the dialectic of dialectics:

> He said to himself: *The Made and the Yet-to-be-Made are equally eloquent when expressed in their source-language, the divine locution of the equation; then who is to declare which is more comely, which superior? What we deem to be Reality is only Partial Possibility coarsely ground into the mere dumb Matter, a physicists's model framed on the crude armature of gravity and chemicals.*
> Gravity and chemicals! Atoms and forces! Crudity of systems. The galaxies might easily be rough alternatives to some other Principle yet untried in Matter. And the Principal himself—was he too a rough alternative to some other man who might have been standing there instead, on the cold sand? (5)

Through linguistic enterprise and fancy, all things can be invented and created, reinvented and re-created, mirrored, inversed, reversed into a divinely inspired egalitarianism of imagination that is part and parcel of the caverns and heights, imbedded in the twists and turns, the gaps, spaces, silences of the "word", the letter itself. However, like Edelshtein, no matter what he did and does, Joseph Brill is and remains the "flawed incarnation" of a "principle embodied in a Principal", a "comfortless comical theory." Moreover, although "Principal Brill scared and awed" people, Joseph ultimately "believed in the prevalence of ash", (5) the old story of his life interpreted by a mind overrun with memories. He "feared for himself, because he was of the elect, the fearful elect who are swallowed up by a look at immortality. The look flashed in him often and often. He saw how he had not died in the middle of the time of dying." (45)

Joseph, as the dreaded, revered and feared Principal Brill, the pretended arch-reader of everyone else's life story, fools this Midwestern, American-Jewish community into believing himself to be the very principle of cultured and educated being, that which by American-Jewish standards is synonymous with the European image of a Sorbonne-educated Parisian Jew. The (American-Jewish) parents of Brill's schoolchildren are like the school's teachers:

> like children themselves.... They taught "respect for books" but they wrote childish memos (even their handwriting was childish) and, though they had by heart the causes of the War of 1812, they were ignorant. They all had a certain childish liveliness. (47)

They were all, in short, immune to the physical and psychological devastation of the Holocaust.

One day, into the flat middling life of the Midwestern American-Jewish community comes one who is even a better reader than Brill of the human map and its geography, and who is able "to catch him out," to pin him to the wall, to "place" him. She is Hester Lilt, a kind of Jewish counterpart of Hawthorne's shadowy and mysterious Hester Prynne from *The Scarlet Letter*. Like Hawthorne's character, Hester is a splendor, a wonder of brilliant creative enterprise, a splendor of the inventive spirit. Hawthorne's Hester creates hand-decorated works, including the letter "A" she designs and wears which gives the story its name. What the letter "A" represents is anyone's guess. The linguistic sign/symbol/code Hawthorne's Hester chooses to wear is the very essence of ambiguity, irony and/or dialectic on which ambiguity (as this study views it) is based. In a similar way, Ozick's Hester "was an imagistic linguistic logician, a phrase foreign to Brill. He had no idea of its purport. But he had seen her interviewed on a television program, and that was what they had called her then: an imagistic linguistic logician. A mouthful." (47)

Hester Lilt is a highly creative linguist, but much more. Her work is fully synonymous with the writer's clearest, most fecund and awesome capacity for turning the letters of the alphabet into verbal manna from Heaven. Regarding this image, *Exodus* 16:4–35 describes the miraculous food God provided the Israelites in their forty-year wilderness wandering. Its actual physical properties remain a mystery. (*Religion* 440–441)

Brill is able to remember the name and contents of her most acclaimed work, *The World as Appearance*. The book, whose title is taken from Kant, is never read by Brill. In fact, he has never read any of Lilt's four other works: *Mind; Ancient and Modern; Metaphor as Exegesis, Divining Meaning;* and *Interpretation as an End in Itself*. Reading from the last page of one, he sees the sentence: "'The eternal concurrence of language is the shadow of language by which we intend its effects; language without consequence, i.e., the "purity" of babble, is inconceivable in the vale of interpretation.' It made him feel weak." (*Cannibal* 47–48)

Hester Lilt's child, Beulah, apparently fatherless (or at least fraught with great mystery as to her origins, her past), is a candidate for Brill's school. The child has already been diagnosed by school psychologist Dr. Glypost as "tense", "anxious", "constricted", unspontaneous, "withdrawn", rigid, unsmiling, "slow", a "non-achiever; not recommended for Dual Curriculum." (46) Brill nevertheless doesn't want her luminous mother to "'slip through my fingers' —even if the child is dull." (46) Brill sees this child's mother as a star; "A luminary. She'll do us good." (47) Beulah, like the real Cynthia Ozick as a child, is branded and read as a dullard. Any creative potential she might have is invisible to them.

Interviewing Hester Lilt for the application procedure of her child, Brill is struck by Hester's alienness. Something in her seems very familiar: "She did not volunteer whether she was divorced or widowed. Her accent, in which Brill heard unknown segments of Europe, mystified him. So did her age. Was she forty-five, fifty?" (48) Brill cannot read her exactly. Looking into her face, Brill sees that

> her foreignness—it was not excessive—gave her away. It suggested her surrender at least; they were, after all, he and she, in the middle of America, connected by that other Middle, the true and horrific Middle, the Middle of their time, of which the intact and impregnable Americans understood nothing. He apprehended what it was that lay in her: a brokenness. She could never fool him. (49)

Her response to his query as to her origins is a simple:

> "No. I'm not what you are!"

"What am I!" he asked. He knew what he was. It was not a proper inquiry for
an interview. In thirty years he had never put such a question to anyone.
"An American."
Slippery. Out of the blue. In two sentences she had backed him away and exposed him. He disliked irony. He disliked it that she withheld homage,
solidarity, even plain comfort. He expected her to recognize him as he had
recognized her. He saw that they were unfailingly alike, members of the same
broken band, behind whose dumb show certain knowings pace and pitch. (49)

In an inscrutable dialectic of both conflict and identity, their ostensible disagreement is about Beulah; but the roots go much deeper, for
Brill is mediocre and unable to fathom creative brilliance. He is a reader,
not a writer, of texts and stories. He can only absorb, copy, spit out what
has already been fabricated from the splendor of someone else's intellect.
Ultimately he cannot recognize creative genius—since he has none of his
own. Through the creative enterprise, and even the paradoxical absence
of language as a kind of voicelessness, Hester, like her daughter Beulah,
has a handle on the dialectic. Her ABCs are intact, retrieved, perhaps
were never lost; alive, responsive, responding. Outside of something
familiar in her accent, and the horrible familiarity of their common European experiences, Joseph hasn't a clue as to what Hester is saying or
what her books are really about. Neither has he any ideas as to the creative talents imbedded in Beulah's future adult life.

Brill also has many "infatuations". They "were terrible. They were
also secret—trancelike, heavy." (59) He has an infatuation with the wife
of a Unitarian minister, whom he meets with her husband in a New
England hotel. They correspond by mail for several years:

"My dearest Mrs. Carstairs," he wrote in his last letter, growing breathless to
match her, "it would be my joy to instruct you in the Holy Tongue. I would
put each stroke and shape of the Hebrew alphabet into the palm of your hand
like a most fragrant and rosy-colored pomegranate, a *rimon*." (60)

Language and its production have an ecstatic, erotic dimension. The
Hebrew language appears to be the source of all sexual and productive
enterprises. Beyond that, the production of language as writing would
seem to border on the excessive, the world of Pan: the Hebrew language,
the Holy Tongue of God Himself, becomes equated with the world of
nature. Language, therefore, is a two-edged sword: it can both reinforce
and undermine the sacred. It is the tool, nay the very essence, of the dialectic in its proclivity for irony and ambiguity.

Brill allows rumors to spread at school that his heart has been broken by a love killed in the war. The school mothers constantly search for eligible women for him. His fantasies, however, take other twists and turns. He also fantasizes about a mahogany-fleshed woman he follows into the African jungles:

> All these insubstantial mismatchings—woven of cloud and chimera—he attributed to the strangeness, the duality, of his own heart. Two worlds split him. A school that teaches Chumash and Rashi and Gemara [Biblical studies] is called a yeshiva; its head is called the Rosh Yeshiva. Whereas he, in his mock-Sorbonne, was a Principal and ran a Dual Curriculum. It could be done and it could not be done. Rather, it could be done only in imagination: in reality, it was all America, the children America, the teachers America, the very walls of the chair factory America. Egalitarianism—the lowest in the lead. And therefore all things lost to any hope of the patrician, himself the betrayer of Edmund Fleg. (61)

Brill sees himself as a failure. Hester Lilt reads only failure in him. After "reading" Hester Lilt, Joseph realizes that she is impossible for him to fathom. She makes him feel ashamed. In a self-generated phone conversation, Joseph hears himself telling her that he "disappointed my sisters." (63) That is to say, it could be understood that he abandoned—or was abandoned by—the creative expression of language. This is his fantasy, or a possibility of truth: what Anne, Bertha, Claire might have been without the devastation of Europe. They are rather like tropes for the force of creative enterprise, the potential that can never be annihilated, the messiah of redemption and hope of humanity, the very crux of the deep irony and ambiguity inherent in dialectic.

To Hester, Joseph is a straggler. "She was ambitious in a way he had never before encountered, or, if he had, he had forgotten. Her ambition was the same as desire, and her desire was unlike his; it had long ago put away dream." (63) Inviting him to her lecture on what she calls "the hoax of pedagogy", he realizes that she is fearfully learned. "What awed him most were the strange links she wove between vivid, hard circumstance and things that were only imagined." (67) Hers is a Jewish dialectic of *pilpul*. His is a scientific, empirical, European-based dialectic that posits a strife-torn world of diametrically opposed opposites endlessly fighting for dominance. His life and vision are the embodiment of a duality: observational apprehension, versus that which he finds difficult now to access in himself—the aesthetic appreciation of the most sensitive and intangible things of life.

Like Talmudic scholars well-versed in the Jewish dialectic of *pilpul*, Hester balances truth and fiction, the imperceptible grey zone where all possibilities implode into a dialectic of perpetual promise. *Midrashic* stories add a coy charm to her intellectual lacework. To him these little stories are only that: little stories made up to color a moral lesson; and when she begins with, "There ran the little fox," he knows at once which *midrash* it will be, and cannot, for himself, see the connection with her subject.

Hester Lilt also describes what she calls "the cannibal galaxy", connecting "the devouring galaxy" to her interpretation of the pedagogue's misreading of "every sign": mistaking "aggressiveness for intelligence, and thoughtfulness for stupidity, and diffidence for dimness, and arrogance for popularity, and freamers for blackheads, and brazenness for the mark of a lively personality." (68) He is thoroughly stung by her daring, brilliance and bitter condemnation of his educational philosophy, which in turn has condemned her daughter Beulah to intellectual death. Hester describes

> the cannibal galaxies, those megalosaurian colonies of primordial gases that devour smaller brother-galaxies—and when the meal is made, the victim continues to rotate like a Jonah-dervish inside the cannibal, while the sated, ogre-galaxy, its gaseous belly stretched, soporific, never spins at all—motionless as digesting Death. (69)

Fully unmasked by Hester, Joseph decides to abandon Europe and his past horrors and begin anew; a life with a future that points forward rather than back:

> It was clear he would get no more from her just then.... Between them there ought to have been the bond of the ravished. Europe the cannibal galaxy. Edmund Fleg's Parisian Jerusalem a smoky ruin. He saw how France was Egypt. But she was finished.... He relinquished the philosopher's daughter.... Beulah was not the first dim pupil in his school. She would not be the last. His school was not the children's Sorbonne, it was only, despite Dual Curriculum, mediocre America. America the vulgar. Its children had not language. (82–83, 85)

Nevertheless, he has nowhere else, no other place. He is nearly dead from changelessness. America will be his place, like it or not, fitting or not. He decides to get married and to abandon the weight of memory; he wants normalcy; to create a future of his own. He decides to marry "Iris", a spontaneous, impertinently bold young woman with a six-year-old son of average intelligence named Albert. He likes Iris and Albert for their healthy optimism and animal forthrightness. Iris, unlike Hester, is uncomplicated, American-born: "They were normal. Brill analyzed it; his infatuation was with normality. He wanted to be normal, at last, at last. Not to negate." (105) Brill is attracted to her Pan effusiveness, her uncomplicated intellectuality. Iris' simple American type of intellect is the very antithesis of Hester's Hebraic complexity. For Joseph, Iris seems "rosier and shinier" day by day. (105)

Planning their marriage and how they will live, Iris decides that the "hayloft", his school-apartment quarters as it is called, has to be redesigned, changed. Iris wants to banish Joseph's past to its rightful chronological place: the time before the present which precedes and presupposes a future. From the astronomical heights and distances of the Sorbonne telescope that viewed the heavens; to the subcellar of a more recent past; to the hayloft of another closer past where he was taken by the nuns and hid out of ken of the Nazi cannibals, Joseph is found now in another soon-to-be past: the hayloft of his present. Iris will redeem, redesign, redo his present, which is to say, give him a future; a dialectic of time and memory. Joseph decides to call Hester again and tell her of his plans to marry. He wants, he tells her, a simple woman, not someone "too clever... too acute." Hester's retort is:

> "It's not a wife you want. It's not a child you want. It's yourself," she contradicted. "Yourself continued. Yourself redeemed. You put yourself at the center. You've been looking into the grave. You want immortality.... You are a coward," she flung out.... "You want to know how to manage fate, only because once upon a time fate managed you. You think because they saved you in the convent, you've earned salvation forever. After that no more sullying! The end of stain. No more sorrow. You want to know how to manage"—she spread out a length of her own laughter with so much wide distrust that he was able to perceive how it differed in every grain from Iris's busy gurgle— "anguish. Anguish, that's your word for it!" (112)

Between Hester and Iris is the European past and the American present: a dialectic of old and new pointing to a future of redemption from sorrow, guilt and remembrance. Iris is young, a new world for his old European body to explore. Hester's is ravished by time; like ashes of the past. After marrying Iris, whose name underscores a non-Mosaic significance, they quickly become expectant parents. Joseph no longer needs memory; memory need no longer plague his waning and unconscious thoughts. He now has a future life that points him in a new direction.

He, along with Iris and her son Albert, travel to Paris to visit the ABCs. No road travelled can avoid the matrix of language which binds all life experience. Only the ABCs, and the intellectual (albeit second-class) *literati* like Joseph, survived the European conflagration. They too have a future in him and his new family. The source of life, language, is (re)united with a neoteric promise, America. Brill has left Europe and Hester behind. The ABCs are very satisfied with Joseph's life choices now. They, as well, want only the future. They do not want to speak of the past.

Joseph, after ostensibly leading his life out of enslavement to history, the pain of the past, the Egypt of his memory, becomes like Moses before his death: close enough to his promised land but unable to enter it. Ultimately, he may still be unable to find a home in America. His memory is too weighted. However, on a day when he is left alone to wander in Paris, through the streets and places of his past, he discovers that his home is no longer in the past either:

> He thought he was headed for the sisters' flat, and he might have been; but he caught the brilliant crinkle of the Seine, the telltale leafiness that was the Tuileries, the honey-colored endless walls of the Louvre. It was still only early afternoon—impulsive as any other visitor, he jumped out and wandered among ancient dark paintings in baroque gilt frames. He understood how he was no longer a native of this place; he was no different from all the dozens of strangers, Germans, Spaniards, Danes, Italians; he sat on a bench and watched them come and go. Purposeless, he got up again, gravitating toward opening after opening, toiled up a vast stairway past bronzes and sarcophagi, and was startled, at the top, by the Winged Victory, mounted on a height of rubble. (130–131)

This is not his place. He looks at room after room of European, which is to say, Christian-based, art of gladiators, Apollos, and Spartan horsemen. "It was as if there had never been a Hebrew people, no Abraham or Joseph or Moses. Not a trace of holy Israel." (131)

Joseph aimlessly wanders back to his sisters' home. Just one of the ABCs, Anne, is there. He tells her that he visited the Louvre, and immediately feels that he will be admonished for having wasted his time on foolish art-related pursuits. Anne, in a chronically weakened state, is sitting in bed. They sip tea and talk. Anne remarks that life has turned out well for Joseph. His reply is that he has always been accused of "drifting". Anne relates to Joseph the conversation she had with Iris about the renovated hayloft. "'She says you have the most up-to-date kitchen and bathroom. America's good at plumbing.' This made her laugh, and laughing made her cough." (132)

Joseph, misplaced in Europe, nevertheless does not appreciate or find value in the superficiality of American life. Europe has culture, but it also has eradicated him and his Israelites from its memory—as if there had never been such a people and a history. Anne and the other ABCs, in one way or another too infirm to leave their past completely, want only to look ahead, not behind them:

> It was all at once as plain as air that [Anne] would not let [Joseph] speak of long ago; she would not let him speak of loss. It struck him that he had returned to Egypt only to count his losses. Whereas his sisters counted blessings: the wisdom of old women. The ABCs were optimists and hedonists. They resisted memory. It was plumbing they meant to think about; they were like Iris. (132–133)

Joseph, between words and time frames, still adrift in memory, still counting his losses, gives birth through Iris to a future. He has a son, Naphtali. The name is a Biblical reference to Jacob's son, born to Rachel's servant Bilhah. Rachel names this son to reflect her conflict with her sister Leah, who was also one of Jacob's wives. In Hebrew, the name refers to the wrestling of God and Rachel's fate; and the "wrestling" with her sister over whom Rachel triumphed. (*Religion* 493)

Joseph, at long last, feels "normal. It made time go differently. He wheeled the baby up to the road, and showed him the rabbits and the blades of grass in the wind." (*Cannibal* 137) His old meditations

> no longer scared him. All his old torments were dim.... The old cold cosmic knowledge of recurrence and perpetuity abandoned him; all the while he was thinking of Naphtali. Everything about Naphtali sailed on in a forward line— he always progressed, and he was always singular. You could not duplicate him—he was very bright. He chattered, his eyes sparked like Iris's; but he could learn anything, and in a flash. (137)

Like Joseph's own early introduction to the world of Pan, he begins to do the same for his infant son Naphtali. The father now has a future. Naphtali is the perfect dialectical synthesis of the Jewishness of a European past and Gentilism of a new America; America and Israel; old and new; the past and the hint of a redemptive future.

Conclusion

The six Ozick texts chosen here: "Rosa", "Envy; or Yiddish in America", "The Pagan Rabbi", "The Shawl", *The Cannibal Galaxy*, and "Levitation", underscore this perplexity, contradiction, ambiguity of signification and presence; dilemma of being and existence engendered by such a complexity of cultural dialectic in a matrix of linguistic enterprise. Rosa Lublin, the assimilating Polish Jewish culture hound, falls into the tragic snare of the Nazi German Killing Machine but somehow picks up the threads of her farthest past, her Jewish past, in America's (Jewish) Promised Land, Miami Beach. Hershel Edelshtein, the epitome of displacement, desperately wants to translate the European Yiddish culture of his past into some kind of an American form of it. Both he and Rosa dream of the language of their pasts but can find no way of bridging that past with an American present. Rabbi Isaac Kornfeld, born in America, but with the culturally bridging existence of his Holocaust-survivor wife, like Rosa, has too much imagination. He is too much the writer. His prayer shawl, which is the protective fence in "The Shawl", becomes (like in "Rosa") the border that tragically is not heeded: it becomes the very instrument that brings about his physical extinction. Joseph Brill, also bewitched by Western civilization and aesthetic endeavors, tries to forge a seamless harmony between Judaism's moral prescriptions and his all-devouring desire for that great maze of intellectual, philosophical and aesthetic interests that both a Judaic and Gentile perspective represent for him. Hershel Edelshtein, Rosa Lublin, Rabbi Isaac Kornfeld, Joseph Brill weave stories; stories about their lives, existence and being from *pilpul*, the finely-meshed dynamic lacework of the very nature and process of Jewish thinking itself. Lucy Feingold is ultimately a stranger to *pilpul* and storytelling: a mediocre writer condemned to remain a non-Jew, but who is also not able to be the Gentile her father wants her to be. Her husband is condemned to remain the Jew he truly is. To whatever degree, Rosa Lublin, Rabbi Isaac Kornfeld, Joseph Brill, Hershel Edelshtein, Lucy and Jimmy Feingold combine those elements of Jewish, Gentile,

American, European, Yiddish, English, the past and present, which in
their totality signify dislocation: the situation where language, self, place,
country, culture, time, and ultimately hope, are missing from their place;
a place without place, where the ever-looming Holocaust blackness
frames all into one great trope of cultural dialectic.

Notes

95   Letter from Cynthia Ozick to the present writer, August 19, 1999.

96   Cynthia Ozick, "Esau and Jacob", *Art & Ardor* (New York: Alfred A Knopf, 1983) 130–131.

97   This essay was first published as "America: Toward Yavneh", *Judaism* 19/3 (Summer 1970). Later reprinted as "Towards a New Yiddish", *Art & Ardor* 163.

98   Cynthia Ozick, "Literature as Idol: Harold Bloom", *Art & Ardor* 188.

99   Harold Bloom, *Kabbalah and Criticism* (New York: Continuum, 1984).

100 Cynthia Ozick, *"Bloodshed" and Three Novellas* (New York: Alfred A. Knopf, 1976) 4.

101 Cynthia Ozick, "Innovation and Redemption: What Literature Means", *Art & Ardor* 247.

102 Cynthia Ozick, "Mrs. Virginia Woolf: a Madwoman and Her Nurse", *Art & Ardor* 31. Reprinted in *What Henry James Knew and Other Essays on Writers* (London: Vintage 1994).

103 Cynthia Ozick, "Morgan and Maurice: A Fairy Tale", *Art & Ardor* 70.

104 Cynthia Ozick, "Literary Black and Jews", *Art & Ardor* 102.

105 Cynthia Ozick, "Bech, Passing", *Art & Ardor* 121.

106 As stated by Ozick in an interview. Diane Cole, "I Want to Do Jewish Dreaming", *Present Tense* (Summer 1982) 56.

107 Cynthia Ozick, "Untitled", *Response Magazine* (Fall 1972) 8.

108 Cynthia Ozick, "The Biological Premises of Our Sad Earth-Speck", *Art & Ardor* 236–237.

109 Cynthia Ozick, "The Lesson of the Master", *Art & Ardor* 293. See also *The New York Review of Books*, August 12, 1982.

110 Elaine Kauver, "An Interview with Cynthia Ozick", *Contemporary Literature* 4 (Spring 1985) 384–385.

111 Joseph Lowin, *Cynthia Ozick* (Boston: G. K. Hall, 1988) 2.

112 Leo Baeck, *Judaism and Christianity* (New York: The Jewish Publication Society of America, 1958).

113 Cynthia Ozick, "Remembering Maurice Samuel", *Art & Ardor* 214.

114 Cynthia Ozick, "The Riddle of the Ordinary", *Moment* 1 (July–August 1975) 56.

115 Baeck's citations are from *Matthew* 1:1–21, *Luke* 2:21; 3:23–38.

116 Cynthia Ozick, *The Messiah of Stockholm* (New York: Alfred A. Knopf, 1987).

117 Cynthia Ozick, *The Puttermesser Papers* (New York: Alfred A. Knopf, 1997).

118 Cynthia Ozick, "Letter to the Editor", *Commentary* (May 1983) 12, 13.

119   This story is recorded in David A. Cooper, *God Is a Verb: Kabbalah and the Practice of Mystical Judaism* (New York: Penguin Putnam, 1997) 99–100.

120   Cynthia Ozick, "George Steiner's Either/Or: A Response", *Salmagundi* 50–51 (Fall–Winter 1980–81) 93. Reprinted in Cynthia Ozick, *Portrait of the Artist as a Bad Character* (London: Pimlico, 1996).

121   Cynthia Ozick, "The Moral Necessity of Metaphor", *Harper's Magazine* (May 1986) 63. Reprinted as "Metaphor and Memory," *Portrait of the Artist as a Bad Character*.

122   Irving Howe, *World of Our Fathers* (New York: Simon and Schuster, 1976) 411.

123   Cynthia Ozick, "Hadrian and Hebrew", *Moment* 1 (September 1975) 77.

124   Cynthia Ozick, "Four Questions of the Rabbis", *Reconstructionist* 18 (February 1972) 20.

Chapter Four
Conclusion

Perhaps the most valid and definitive conclusion that can be drawn about the life and work of Ludwig Lewisohn and Cynthia Ozick is that there is a difficult-to-frame ubiquitous sense of ambiguity that pervades the totality of their lived experiences and art. Each represents a jumble of contradictions. As essayists and spokespersons for certain oft-stated political agendas that intersect/ed their lives as Americans and Jews, female or male, German, or, more remotely, Ozick as a descendant of Jews of the Russian Pale, Lewisohn and Ozick in many ways are subverted by their writing, an art which declares allegiance to no one, no place, nothing; or multi allegiances, even temporarily, to more than one people, place, to everything that their aesthetic appetites fix on to devour. Their art, therefore, is characterized by obfuscation, confusion, contrariness, ambiguity which frustrates any effort to pinpoint any political point of view or agenda in their respective work.

In the "Forewarning" to *Metaphor and Memory* and elsewhere, Ozick warns the reader to not expect her essays to speak for her fiction. The Ludwig Lewisohn as polemicist or propagandist is undermined also by the counter-evidence of Lewisohn as fiction writer. Furthermore, both writers exasperatingly insist that their fiction is truer than the supposed factuality of their essays. As Ozick puts it:

> All these notions are, I am afraid, plain foolishness. They [readers] imagine that there is a commanding difference between essays and stories, and that the difference is pure: essays are "honest" and stories are made up. The reality is otherwise; all good stories are honest and most good essays are not. [159]

Lewisohn similarly prevaricates. "The metaphysical truth," he asserts, "is irrefutable, but a margin of freedom and responsibility is a fact of human consciousness and human experience." (*Island* 6)

Ozick insists that stories and essays in equal measure are hypotheses, tryouts. When an essay, in the same way as a story, is completed, "the mind moves on." (*Metaphor* x.) Essays, like stories, are experiments, not credos. Ozick would most likely disagree with Vera Emuna Kielsky's conclusion that the former's ideological convictions induce "her to carry over from her essays to her fiction her gracefully expressed but frequently combative views on morals, politics and literature."[160] Like Victor Strandberg, Kielsky, in positing a duality of mind and body, experience and reason, conceptuality and emotionality, can't help but discover a metaphysical duality or conflict-plagued writer in Cynthia Ozick. Ozick, Kielsky insists, "appeals to reason rather than to emotion. Her inventions seem to spring not so much from experience as from the brain." (Kielsky 204) However, Kielsky, Strandberg and the majority of other Ozick readers, like those in the nascent renaissance of rediscovering Lewisohn and his work, praise her and him for the Jewish, even religious and ethnic orthodoxy of their essays and fiction. In truth, these readers' admiration of that writing, on three accounts, ironically serves to merely minimize the appreciation of them as both a part and parcel of the mainstream American literary tradition, but also for the paradoxical universalism that their membership in the Hebrew tribe confers on them. This Hebraicism makes them not only a special type of native-born American (referring to the Hebrew Scriptural base of American culture), but their Jewishness also becomes a prototype for humankind in the same way that the Jewishness of the Gospel Jesus brought an essentially Hebraic message to the world.

Lewisohn also is conscious of the "flat" contradictions in everything that he otherwise insists is consistent with the truth. This, he says, is the nature of "human thought". Everything is contradiction, but not necessarily mutually exclusive. (*Island* 7) Cultural dialectic has at its base, therefore, a contrariness which is not dualistic but of complementary contrasts; an ultimate baselessness, a paradox. The only thing that is true but nevertheless inscrutable is the process of the consciousness which creates, weaves, fabricates and spins out language, words, text on the once-empty page. Thus Ozick's and Lewisohn's language is both the height of (aesthetic) precision but also the depth of ambiguous meaning. In this sense, as artists born into and from a Hebraic genetic, ethnic and cultural pool, their writing has the unmistakable stamp of the rabbinical hermeneutical process; of the open (non) signification of textuality; of a Derridean textless text without focus or center. Ozick as writer and person is her own Rabbi Isaac Kornfeld, both within and without the fence; playing the dangerous game of art in writing. Like Magda she is both "one of them" and one of us, in danger of death from the fence but also safely hidden under the shawl of her Judaism. Lewisohn as person and writer is his Reb Moshe Hacohen who preserves the history of his people through/with the text. He is also his Dr. Arthur Levy who both is entrusted with "the documents" which are a factual account and proof of his Jewish identity, but which at the same time help create the ambiguity of cultural dialectic in forward time by fathering his progeny, a son John, who is and isn't Jewish; is and isn't an American; is and isn't a Gentile grandson of a Protestant minister. Lewisohn's own real life took this identical turn. The mother of his only son, James, by Jewish law, was not Jewish since only her father was a Jew. In reverse direction, James first had a strong Jewish identity, then flip-flopped to become a zealous Catholic which he is to this day.[161]

In the same way, the events of Ozick's life do not offer a uniform picture of what might be called a devout or religiously Orthodox Jew. This does not in any way signify that Ozick is not a sincere and loyal member of her tribe and well within the historical continuity of her Israelite nation as that history began at Mt. Sinai. After her marriage to Bernard Hallote in 1952, Ozick, waylaid by her religion of art at the altar of the Master, Henry James, spent the rest of that decade and part of the next monkishly at work on a novel, *Mercy, Pity, Peace and Love.* This was abandoned after about seven years but she had cut her writer's teeth; then *Trust* was begun in 1959 and published in 1966. So devoted was she to the Master and the sense of the perfectly rendered word that she "became Henry James", as described in "The Lesson of the Master". She put off child-bearing and a life with the living, much like some of the characters in her stories: Joseph Brill, Rosa, Rabbi Kornfeld. All of this is totally contrary to Jewish custom and biblical commandments. As Joseph Lowin explains: "During the first thirteen years of marriage, Ozick devoted herself exclusively to what she called 'High Art'." (Lowin 6) Ozick, Lowin asserts, became a writer in large part because of the strong influence of her maternal uncle, Abraham Regelson, who was a Hebrew poet. As Lowin describes: "She feels that, somehow, he paved the way for her to embark on such a 'strange' career. Because of him, she says, 'it seemed quite natural to belong to the secular world of literature.'" (4)[162] As Lewisohn did at age forty, Ozick then went through, beginning at age twenty-five, what Lowin calls a "cultural transformation", absorbing and gaining mastery over "the Jewish textual tradition." (7)

Cultural dialectic exists at every turn, each juncture of the weave of their art and life, in a kind of continuous discontinuity that frames their being and art; the totality of who they are and it is. On this account the respective works of Ozick and Lewisohn deserve more aesthetic and literary respect more for the complexities and subtleties they generate rather than for the significances they are believed to contain.

In truth, both Ozick's and Lewisohn's style and language, as with the nature of language itself, inherently confounds, confuses obfuscates, delays, deters meaning. Within the twists and turns of language, its gaps, openness and ambiguity, an absolute or static understanding is deferred and frustrated. How, for example, are we to understand the ethnic origin of Ozick's Magda, Rosa's daughter: is she Jew, Gentile or some cultural mix of both? To which world do we fit Lewisohn's Dr. Arthur Levy or his son John? Is *Trumpet of Jubilee* with its final line, "Bear us the Christ again!", Jewish, Gentile, an interbraiding of both or even of other cultural affiliations? No one can know for sure. Both write in scrupulously clear prose; unadorned, understated, simple, matter-of-fact; the prose of speech; dissecting subject after subject, description after description like the surgeon with scalpel in hand laying open the body of the text. Their writing and its language is the very lacework of their consciousness, aestheticism and imagination. In this way, their ostensible themes become nearly covers for an overriding one: writing and the creative process itself. There is no other apparent way to explain the previously discussed descriptions of Magda in Ozick's "The Shawl", flopping "onward with her little pencil legs scribbling this way and that"; or as "pencils" faltering at the barracks' opening, where the light began." ("Shawl" 7); and for a third time describing Magda's "pencil legs". (10) In a story not just in Holocaust time, but set in a Death Camp, writing as art becomes a trope for Jewishness, for life in juxtaposition to the unthinkable grotesqueness of an art turned macabre; turned against humanity, life, the living; without pity; a killing art. The Black pure-Pan satanic Nazi art of death and killing is shown not so much as the opposite of art, but as a stark contrast to the art of life, of the creative spirit, that the living Magda represents. Under the cover of the shawl, the fence of Torah, Magda's (or Ozick's) art is safe. However, without the shawl Magda becomes one of theirs; they claim paternity through her death. One slides too easily into the other. Thus the art of the Nazis and the art of the creative spirit of the living are somehow a contrast in degree, not in kind. Jew or Gentile can become either or some combination of both, through cultural dialectic. Ozick characterizes Stella in "The Shawl" as, for example: "Stella, cold,

cold, the coldness of hell." There are, as well, the descriptions of her as "a young cannibal"; "Stella gave nothing", and "Rosa saw that Stella's heart was cold". (7)

Similarly with Lewisohn, Peter Lang and Jehuda Brenner in *Trumpet of Jubilee* are combinations of the true Christian and Jew, which is to say that they are more alike than they are different, held in union even in their contrasting essences through the complex paradoxical lacework of the cultural dialectic.

For all their essayistic pronouncements about assimilation (of Jews into Gentile belief systems), Ozick's and Lewisohn's ultimate goal is to assimilate the world—Jews and Gentiles alike—into an art that is creative and not destructive; an art that can pity while it dissects. In this way it becomes a fundamentally Jewish (read as "language") art wherein their text/story reflects the Text/Story; where their identities as Jews serve the mission of art.

The specific works of Ozick and Lewisohn were selected not because they are examples of Jewish writing. Nor were they chosen, especially in Lewisohn's case, because they represent some linear progression from some absolute Gentilism to a simply signified Jewishness. Moreover, they were not chosen to identify the warring dualities of a Jewish writer set in dead conflict with a Gentile perspective. Neither were these works chosen to isolate or describe (as some of the earliest Lewisohn scholarship of the pre and post World War I and II periods did) some supposed mental imbalance or sociopathic behavior in the author; or to reveal the anti-Semitic attitudes couched in academic or literary terminology and style manifested by so many of these early Lewisohn readers and analysts. Ozick ascended to the literary stage in the entirely different world of 1960s America, when cultural revolution was sweeping through nearly every sphere of American life. That part of the literary and academic world that could be considered Gentile seized on the Jewish ambience and thematic material of her work with respect and admiration, at a time when a newer generation, a genre of Jewish writers, seemed to be emerging from the American literary landscape. On the other side, the Jews of the literary and academic establishment seized on what they viewed as a flag of Judaism, the chauvinistic and polemically prescriptive style of her essays by which they read her stories. In this study, the works discussed have been chosen for the complex ambiguity of language and language-as-writing in the matrix of cultural dialectic.

Five works by Lewisohn have been analyzed: *Up Stream* (1922); *Holy Land* (1926); *The Case of Mr. Crump* (1926); *The Island Within* (1928); *Trumpet of Jubilee* (1937). The reasons for choosing these works vary somewhat from story to story, but the most important reason is for their focus on writing, the writer, the art process and language as the blood supply of an inherent mesh of cultural dialectic. *Up Stream* has been described as the autobiographical work that fleshes out the anatomy of Lewisohn's return from a Gentile to a Jewish world and being. More complex, however, than a linear progression from Gentile to Jewish, this study describes a complicated lacework of interrelated complementary and contrasting realms that form a rich picture of Lewisohn's life and work which is often difficult to penetrate. In *Holy Land*, a so-called fictional work, Lewisohn is perhaps freer to express himself in a Jewish persona. Nevertheless, neither the final scene of this short story set in the Holy Land nor the narrator's voice makes anything completely clear. Neither the narrator nor the writer ever reveals on which side of the complex cultural divides they themselves sit. *The Case of Mr. Crump* contains some well-disguised Jewish innuendos, such as the reference to a skull cap worn by Herbert's father, which Ludwig's father also wore in an identical scene described elsewhere as a real life scene. In spite of the volume of biographical detail about Anne/Mary (?) and Herbert/Ludwig (?), there is the distinct impression that something somehow is being obfuscated, disguised and left unrevealed. *The Island Within* comes closest perhaps to what can be described as a Jewish novel, but it too is riddled with ambiguity. At the end of the book, Reb Moshe warns Arthur about overzealousness in either hating or loving Judaism and its history. He says, "'Avoid both errors.'" (*Island* 350) As well, the narrator claims that "the earth which his foot trod was his natural habitation and his home." (350) Is Arthur's place in Gentile America? Nothing but ambiguity can be read in this last sentence. Finally, *Trumpet of Jubilee*, published after the rise of Hitler and the height of anti-Semitic sentiment, would seem to end on a totally Christian note, even though its major players are Gina, Gabriel and Kurt, Jewish members of a German-Jewish family whose return to Judaism (minus a live Kurt) is anatomized in this book.

In every one of Ozick's fictional works, the writer and/or the creative process is prominent. This is the very matrix and soul of cultural dialectic at play in her writing. Certainly in the six works chosen for this study— "The Pagan Rabbi" (1966), "Envy; or Yiddish in America" (1969),

"Levitation" (1979), "The Shawl" (1980), "Rosa" (1983) and *The Canni-bal Galaxy* (1983)—the major characters (and minor ones as well) are caught precariously poised in the process of exploring language, art, writing and the creative process, in grave danger of crossing the line, or the fence. Ozick's most recent work, a collection of essays, published in the fall of this year, appeared too late for inclusion in this study.[163]

In "The Pagan Rabbi", the pious Rabbi Isaac Kornfeld possesses brilliant intellectual capabilities. This is to say he is a profoundly subtle reader and highly creative synthesizer of Tannaic and Talmudic language with their many commentaries. However, the imagination that allows him to imagine God is also the conduit that leads to other excessive qualities: too much imagination and cerebral curiosity. Isaac, as his narrator-friend states, "read everything." ("Pagan" 9) Isaac also tells a lot of stories and, of course, kept a notebook of his writing. In "Envy; or Yiddish in America", writing itself is the stream that cultural dialectic floats on. It is the organ of intercultural address and access, the key to the door of redemption which opens onto a messianic future. "Levitation" clearly undermines the expectation that doing art in the form of writing can somehow turn a (Hebrew) Gentile into a Jewish Jew. Lucy Feingold simply lacks the real imagination necessary to imagine a God without a physical presence, and therefore lacks the potential to produce "high art". In cultural dialectical fashion, she is not Gentile enough to be the Christian her father was, and not Jewish enough to be the Jew her husband Jimmy is. Rosa of "Rosa" and "The Shawl", born Jewish, seeks to escape from what she perceives as the primitive narrowness of (her) Jewish history, into the maze of cultural dialectic. Her progeny, Magda, is of doubtful paternity; a cultural dialectical mix which is finally claimed by "them" and Death. Rosa respects "high culture" and education. She is a reader but also a writer with an excessive imagination. Joseph Brill is in the grip both of "high culture" and Jewish history, Gentile and Hebraic culture. He tries to form a cohesion between the competing realities of cultural dialectic through his dual curriculum. He is ultimately, however, too ordinary; too "middling", without imagination, therefore incapable of being a profound reader and writer like Hester Lilt. His own ordinariness cannot perceive the artistic brilliance of Hester's daughter, Beulah. Where Hester artfully balances and synthesizes all the threads of cultural dialectic through her brilliant linguistic and logical intellectuality, Joseph muddles along, enamored by her brilliance but utterly confounded by it.

Very little has been written about Lewisohn and Ozick as American writers, as opposed to generic, Jewish or even marginal writers within mainstream American literary history. Vera Kielsky, for example, can state: "For Cynthia Ozick's fiction is deeply rooted in contemporary American life, endeavoring to find out 'what it means to remain—culturally and, above all, religiously—Jewish in a world that for the most part is hostile.'" (Kielsky 209)[164]

Kielsky's assertion that Ozick is "deeply" connected to American culture is a valid one, but not for the reason she states. In truth, from the mid 1960s to the more recent publication of *The Messiah of Stockholm* in 1987, this so-called cultural or religious Jewishness is not set in a denial of Jewishness or of Jewish subject matter. If not a wrong assertion, it is a highly simplistic one in which the reader falls victim to the magic of Ozick's prose, which beautifully says much but reveals nothing as to the ultimate significances on which her work can be understood to stand. Rather, her fiction is culturally Hebraic, for the same reasons that American fiction can be said to be culturally Hebraic; the former is simply, if you will, a Jewish version of a Biblically-based American cultural literary voice, or even a more authentic version.

Ozick herself views Lewisohn as a marginal writer, which is to say a too outspokenly Jewish writer, and resists or even resents any comparisons between their works.[165] Ironically, as earlier noted, Ozick's charges against Lewisohn manifest the same type (although not the same degree) of hostility that condemned him to the kind of literary death that Ozick fears for her own work. To be viewed as a Jewish writer, she believes, is to be sentenced to artistic marginality and extinction.

Neither Ozick nor a revived Lewisohn need fear such a charge or threat. Lewisohn's writing has never been explored in and of itself, that is, apart from the type of myth which has been gaining ground on the American literary and cultural landscape, and which views him as the mantle-bearer of a born-again Judaism. Both Lewisohn's and Ozick's writings have never been examined for the complex, open-ended, meaning-deferring, subtle, coy—in a word, Midrashic, which is to say Hebraically American—creations that they are.

Somehow mixing Lewisohn's Gentile background with the evolving Jewish one he had from birth, one polemic in the dialectical mix of identities and affinities could never be put to rest or compromised: his outrage over what he perceived as the raw "injustice he endured from an

[American] environment against which he was constantly in rebellion."
(Melnick I: 449) Lewisohn, perhaps quixotically, wished in Arnoldian
style to end the barbarous and superficial American philistinism, which
desired to eradicate the constitutionally legitimized freedoms to be, think,
voice opinions, and act in conformity only to one's conscience.

Melnick's assessment of Lewisohn is also applicable to Ozick:

> I would guess that he would be a transculturalist. He was an eclectic person.
> This was one of the appealing things about him. He was so involved in non-
> Jewish Western culture. He was against full assimilation of any kind. He
> remained attracted to all the things he had loved: German literature, all litera-
> ture, ideas, art.[166]

Lewisohn, Melnick continues, "was first and foremost a German Jew
whose writing and thought were more in the nineteenth than the twentieth
century. For him that was a big difference from his own home."

Both Ozick and Lewisohn could be described as having been Jewish
in their hearts and personal lives, but also fully part of the greater Gentile
world outside.

Notes

159   Cynthia Ozick, *Metaphor and Memory: Essays by Cynthia Ozick* (New York: Alfred A. Knopf, 1989) x.

160   Vera Emuna Kielsky, *Inevitable Exiles: Cynthia Ozick's View of the Precariousness of Jewish Existence in a Gentile Society* (New York: Peter Lang, 1989) 204.

161   As James Lewisohn stated in a conversation with the present writer on December 16, 1998.

162   Quoting from a transcript of Bill Moyers' "Heritage Conversations", WNET-TV (New York, 3 April 1986) 32.

163   Cynthia Ozick, *Quarrel and Quandary* (New York: Alfred A. Knopf, 2000).

164   Kielsky here is quoting from Eve Ottenberg, "The Rich Vision of Cynthia Ozick", *The New York Times Magazine* (April 10, 1983) 46–47, 62–66.

165   Ralph Melnick, in a conversation with the present writer on September 23, 1999, related that Ozick greatly fears being labelled a Jewish writer, rather than an American writer who is (undeniably) Jewish. In his opinion, she would be vexed by being grouped with Lewisohn.

166   Melnick in a conversation with the present writer, May 5, 2000.

Bibliography

Aarons, Victoria. *A Measure of Memory: Storytelling and Identity in American Jewish Fiction*. Athens: The University of Georgia Press, 1966.

Alexander, Edward. *The Resonance of Dust: Essays on Holocaust Literature and Jewish Fate*. Columbus: Ohio State University Press, 1969.

Angus, S. *The Mystery Religions: A Study of the Religious Background of Early Christianity*. New York: Dover Press, 1975.

Arnold, Matthew. *Culture and Anarchy*. Ed. J. Dover Wilson. Cambridge: Cambridge University Press, 1960.

Baeck, Leo. *Judaism and Christianity*. New York: Leo Baeck Institute, 1958.

Bercovitch, Sacvan, ed. *Reconstructing American Literary History*. Cambridge: Harvard University Press, 1986.

———. *The American Jeremiad*. Madison: University of Wisconsin Press, 1978.

———. *The Puritan Origins of the American Self*. New Haven: Yale University Press, 1975.

———. Typology in Early American Literature. Boston: The University of Massachusetts Press, 1972.

Berger, Alan L. *Crisis and Covenant: The Holocaust in American Jewish Fiction*. New York: State University of New York Press, 1985.

Bloom, Harold, ed. *Cynthia Ozick*. New Haven: Chelsea House, 1986.

———. *Kabbalah and Criticism*. New York: Continuum, 1984.

Buber, Martin. *Between Man and Man*. Trans. Ronald Gregar Smith. Boston: Beacon Press, 1955.

———. *Jewish Mysticism and the Legends of Baal Shem*. Trans. Lucy Cohen. New York: Bloch, 1931.

————. *The Knowledge of Man*. Ed. Maurice Friedman. Trans. Maurice Friedman and Ronald Gregar Smith. London: George Allen and Unwin, 1965.

Cohen, Jeremy. *The Friars and the Jews: The Evolution of Anti-Judaism*. Cornell: Cornell University Press, 1982.

Cooper, David A. *God Is a Verb: Kabbalah and the Practice of Mystical Judaism*. New York: Penguin Putnam Press, 1997.

Culler, Jonathan. *The Pursuit of Signs: Semiotics, Literature, Deconstruction*. Ithaca: Cornell University Press, 1981.

Davis, Robert Con and Schleifer, Ronald, eds. *Contemporary Criticism*. New York: Longman, 1989.

Friedman, Lawrence S. *Understanding Cynthia Ozick*. Columbia: University of South Carolina Press, 1991.

Gertel, Elliot B. "Visions of the American Jewish Messiah". *Judaism* 31/122 (1982): 153–165.

Gillis, Adolph. *Ludwig Lewisohn: The Artist and His Message*. New York: Duffield and Green, 1933.

Girgus, Sam. *The New Covenant: Jewish Writers and the American Idea*. Chapel Hill: The University of North Carolina Press, 1984.

Grayzel, Solomon. *A History of the Jews*. New York: Mentor, 1968.

Hartman, Geoffrey H. and Budick, Sanford, eds. *Midrash and Literature*. New Haven: Yale University Press, 1986.

Hegel, G. W. F. *The Phenomenology of Mind*. Trans. J. B. Baillie. London: Allen and Unwin, 1949.

Hirshfeld, Georg. *The Mothers*. Trans. and Introduction Ludwig Lewisohn. Garden City: Doubleday, 1916.

Horowitz, Sara R.. *Voicing the Void: Muteness and Memory in Holocaust Fiction*. Albany: The State University of New York Press, 1997.

Howe, Irving. *World of Our Fathers*. New York: Simon and Schuster, 1976.

Jones, W. T. *The History of Western Philosophy*. New York: Harcourt Brace and Jovanovich, 1980.

Kant, Emanuel. *Critique of Pure Reason*. Trans. N. Kemp. London: Smith Macmillan, 1924.

Katz, Steven. *Jewish Ideas and Concepts*. Schocken Books: New York, 1977.

Kauvar, Elaine M. "An Interview with Cynthia Ozick". *Contemporary Literature* 4 (Spring 1985): 384–385.

———. "The Dread of Moloch: Idolatry as Metaphor in Cynthia Ozick's Fiction". *Studies in American Jewish Literature* 6 (1987): 111–128.

Kielsky, Vera Emuna. *Inevitable Exiles: Cynthia Ozick's View of the Precariousness of Jewish Existence in a Gentile Society*. New York: Peter Lang, 1989.

Konvitz, Milton. *Judaism and the American Idea*. Ithaca: Cornell University Press, 1978.

Korshin, Paul. *Typologies in England: 1650–1820*. Princeton: Princeton University Press, 1982.

Kosinski, Jerzy. *The Painted Bird*. New York: Scientia-Factum Press, 1967.

Lainoff, Seymour. *Ludwig Lewisohn*. Boston: Twayne Publishers, 1982.

Lelyveld, Arthur J. "Ludwig Lewisohn: In Memoriam". *American Jewish Archives* xvii/2 (1965): 109–113.

Lewisohn, James. "My Father, Ludwig Lewisohn: A Personal Reminiscence". *Midstream* xii/9 (1966): 48–50.

Lewisohn, Ludwig, ed. *A Modern Book of Criticism*. New York: The Modern Library Press, 1919.

———. "A Study of Matthew Arnold", *Sewanee Review* ix/4 (October 1901): 442–446 (Part I, "His Poetry"); x/2 (April 1902): 143–159 (Part II, "Formative Influences: The Influence of Goethe"); x/3 (July 1902): 302–319 (Part III, "Arnold's Critical Method").

———. *Cities and Men*. New York: Harper & Brothers, 1927.

———. *Gegen Den Strom: Eione Amerikanishe Chronik*. Frankfurt: Frankfurter Societats-Druckerei GMBH Abteilung Buchverlog, 1924.

———. "Holy Land". *Harper's Magazine* (October 1925): 523–527.

———. *Holy Land*. New York: Harper & Brothers, 1926.

———. *Mid-Channel*. New York: Farrar, Straus and Giroux, 1929. Reprint: New York: Arno Press, 1975.

———. *The Answer; The Jew In the World: Past, Present and Future*. New York: Liveright Press, 1939.

————. *The Case of Mr. Crump*. New York: Farrar, Straus & Giroux, 1965.

————. *The Golden Vase*. Hamburg: The Albatross Press, 1932.

————. *The Island Within*. New York: Harper & Brothers, 1928.

————. "The Return to Jerusalem", *The Nation* 119/3104 (December 31, 1924): 724–725.

————. *Trumpet of Jubilee*. New York: Harper & Brothers, 1937.

————. *Up Stream: An American Chronicle*. New York: Boni and Liveright Publishers, 1922.

————. *What Is This Jewish Heritage?* New York: Binai Brith Hillel Foundation Press, 1954.

————. "Workers in Palestine", *The Nation* 123 (September 16, 1925): 301–302.

Lipsker, Rabbi Avraham. Lecture, The Rabbinical College of America, Morristown, New Jersey, U. S. A., July 4, 1977.

Lowin, Joseph. *Cynthia Ozick*. Boston: G. K. Hall Press, 1988.

Lyons, Bonnie. "Ozick as a Jewish Writer". *Studies in American Jewish Literature* 6 (1987): 13–23.

Melnick, Ralph. *The Life and Work of Ludwig Lewisohn*, Vol. I, II. Detroit: Wayne State University Press, 1998.

Merowitz, M. "Ludwig Lewisohn's Zionism". *The American Zionist* LXI/2 (October 1970): 37–38.

Miller, Perry. *Errand in the Wilderness*. Cambridge: The Belknap Press of Harvard University, 1956.

————. *The New England Mind: New Colony to Province*. Boston: Beacon Press, 1956.

Miller, Perry and Johnson, Thomas H. eds. *The Puritans: A Sourcebook of Their Writings*. New York: Harper and Row, 1938.

Muller, John P. and Richardson, William J., eds. *The Purloined Poe: Lacan, Derrida and Psychoanalytic Reading*. Baltimore: Johns Hopkins University Press, 1988.

Ozick, Cynthia. "America: Toward Yavneh". *Judaism* 19/3 (1970): 264–282.

————. *Art & Ardor*. New York: Alfred A. Knopf, 1983.

————. *Bloodshed and Three Novellas*. New York: Alfred A. Knopf, 1976.

————. "Four Questions of the Rabbis". *Reconstructionist* 18 (February 1972): 20–23.

————. "George Steiner's Either/Or. A Response". *Salmagundi* 50–51 (Fall–Winter 1980–1981): 90–95.

————. "Hadrian and Hebrew". *Moment* 1 (September 1975): 77.

————. *Levitation: Five Fictions*. New York: Alfred A. Knopf, 1982.

————. Letter to Jane Statlander, August 19, 1999.

————. Letter to the Editor, *Commentary* (May 1983): 12–13.

————. *Metaphor and Memory*. New York: Alfred A. Knopf, 1980.

————. *The Cannibal Galaxy*. New York: E. P. Dutton Press, 1983.

————. *The Messiah of Stockholm*. New York: Alfred A. Knopf, 1987.

————. "The Moral Necessity of Metaphor". *Harper's Magazine* (May 1986): 62–68.

————. *The Pagan Rabbi and Other Stories*. New York: E. P. Dutton Press, 1983.

————. *The Puttermesser Papers*. New York: Alfred A. Knopf, 1997.

————. "The Riddle of the Ordinary", *Moment* 1 (July–August 1975): 55–59.

————. *The Shawl: A Story and Novella*. New York: Alfred A. Knopf, 1980.

————. "Untitled". *Response Magazine* (Fall 1972): 8.

Ragussis, Michael. *Figures of Conversion: 'The Jewish Question' and English Narrational Identity*. London: Duke University Press, 1995.

————. "Representation, Conversion and Literary Form: Harrington and the Novel of Jewish Identity", *Critical Inquiry* 16/1 (Autumn 1989).

Sherman, Stuart Pratt. *Americans*. New York: Charles Scribner's, 1922.

Silver, Jeremy and Martin, Bernard. *A History of Judaism*. New York: Basic Books, 1974.

Smith, Dinitia. "Writers as Plunderers". *The New York Times* (October 24, 1998): B9, B11.

Sollars, Werner. "Region, Ethnic Group and American Writers: From 'Non-Southern' and 'Non-Ethnic' to Ludwig Lewisohn; or the Ethics of Wholesome Provincialism". *Prospects* 9 (1984): 441–462.

Strandberg, Victor. *Greek Mind/Jewish Soul: The Conflicted Art of Cynthia Ozick.* Madison: The University of Wisconsin Press, 1994.

Sutton, Walter. *Modern American Criticism.* Englewood Cliffs: Prentice Hall, 1963.

The Oxford Dictionary of the Jewish Religion. Eds. R. J. Werblowsky and Geoffrey Wigoder. New York: Oxford University Press, 1997.

Third Millennium Bible, Authorized Version. Gary, South Dakota: Third Millennium Press, 1998.

Torah, Nevi'im, Ketuvim. Hebrew Masoretic Text.

White, Hayden. *The Content of Form: Narrative Discourse and Historical Representation.* Baltimore: Johns Hopkins University Press, 1987.

———. *The Tropics of Discourse: Essays on Cultural Criticism.* Baltimore: The Johns Hopkins University Press, 1978.

Whitehead, A. N. *The Adventure of Ideas.* New York: Mentor, 1964.

Williams, Raymond. *Keywords A Vocabulary of Culture and Society.* Glasgow: William Collins, 1976.

———. *The Sociology of Culture.* Chicago: University of Chicago Press, 1981.

Twentieth-Century American Jewish Writers

The **Twentieth-Century American Jewish Writers** series will present the very best, up-to-date, imaginative scholarship. Studies on novelists, writers, poets, essayists, and critics are needed and will be carefully read. New interpretations will be especially welcomed.

All manuscripts should be sent to:

Dr. Daniel Walden, Editor
Twentieth-Century American Jewish Writers Series
English Department
Penn State University
University Park, PA 16802

To order other books in this series, please contact our Customer Service Department:

(800) 770-LANG (within the U.S.)
(212) 647-7706 (outside the U.S.)
(212) 647-7707 FAX

Or, browse online by series:

www.peterlang.com